Evolution or Revolution?

Evolution or Revolution?

Rethinking Macroeconomic Policy after the Great Recession

edited by Olivier Blanchard and Lawrence H. Summers

PIIE PETERSON INSTITUTE FOR
INTERNATIONAL ECONOMICS

The MIT Press
Cambridge, Massachusetts
London, England

This book was set in Sabon by Toppan Best-set Premedia Limited. Printed and bound in the United States of America.

Library of Congress Cataloging-in-Publication Data

Names: Blanchard, Olivier (Olivier J.), editor. | Summers, Lawrence H., editor.
Title: Evolution or revolution? : rethinking macroeconomic policy after the Great Recession / edited by Olivier Blanchard and Lawrence H. Summers.
Description: Cambridge, MA : MIT Press, [2019] | Conference proceedings. | Includes bibliographical references and index.
Identifiers: LCCN 2018020783 | ISBN 9780262039369 (hardcover : alk. paper)
Subjects: LCSH: Macroeconomics. | Fiscal policy. | Economic policy.
Classification: LCC HB172.5 .E946 2019 | DDC 339--dc23 LC record available at https://lccn.loc.gov/2018020783

10   9   8   7   6   5   4   3   2   1

Contents

Responses:

Responses:

Preface

The 2008 financial crisis and Great Recession are no longer front and center as a policy challenge. The issue of how and when to apply restraint is now more dominant than the issue of how to increase demand. Worries about excessive exuberance in financial markets exceed those about insufficient confidence. After a period of great ferment in financial regulation, attention has shifted to questions of implementation and to concerns about areas where the pendulum may have swung too far.

In all these ways a sense of normalcy has returned to the global economy and to economic policy debates. While the change is welcome, it is slightly unsettling when one remembers that periods of complacency historically have a way of being rudely interrupted by adverse developments.

We therefore felt it worthwhile to continue the conferences titled "Rethinking Macroeconomic Policy," a biennial series started in 2011 when Olivier Blanchard was the IMF's Chief Economist. And we were delighted when the Peterson Institute for International Economics offered to support and host the conference.

The three preceding conferences sought to bring cutting-edge thinking to bear on the new challenges thrown up by the financial crisis. The objective was to bring policymakers and scholars into closer proximity. Policymakers could benefit from new ideas coming from research, while researchers were encouraged to address policymakers' most pressing issues.

Given the return of a sense of normalcy, we felt that this was an appropriate moment to distill lessons from the crisis and to explore critical issues. How should the experience of the crisis alter macroeconomic thinking and macroeconomic policy? Are policymakers prepared for the next crisis? Can more be done to prevent future crises? Should the experience of the crisis affect the way policy is carried out in normal times?

We also felt the recent events pointed up the importance of political economy issues for macroeconomics, particularly those associated with inequality and the current functioning of the international monetary and financial system.

The volume comprises the proceedings of the fourth "Rethinking Macroeconomic Policy" conference. After the introduction, which presents the issue of evolution versus revolution in macroeconomics after the crisis, there are five substantive sections. Each section begins with a background paper, followed by wide-ranging discussions by distinguished researchers and major policymakers. We cover five topics: monetary policy, fiscal policy, financial policy, inequality and political economy, and the international monetary and financial system.

The results are for the reader to judge. We came away from the conference with the perhaps predictable conclusion that while much had been learned, there was still much we needed to understand better. Certainly, the kind of complacency that preceded the recent crisis is unlikely to recur at least for many years. And the kind of blind faith in the self-restorative properties of economies that some expressed in the early phase of the crisis is now widely rejected. But issues such as how best to operate in a world where traditional monetary policy is unlikely to have its usual room for response when a downturn comes remain substantially unresolved.

Perhaps the only thing we can be certain of is that, owing to the pace of change in the structure of the global economy, rethinking macroeconomics will be an ongoing preoccupation in the years ahead. We hope this volume contributes to the effort.

Introduction: Rethinking Stabilization Policy: Evolution or Revolution?

Olivier Blanchard and Lawrence H. Summers

Nearly ten years after the onset of the Great Financial Crisis, both researchers and policymakers are still assessing the policy implications of the crisis and its aftermath. Previous major crises, from the Great Depression to the stagflation of the 1970s, profoundly changed both macroeconomic thinking and macroeconomic policy. The question is whether this crisis should and will have similar effects.

We believe it should, although we are less sure it will. Rather obviously, the crisis has forced macroeconomists to (re)discover the role and the complexity of the financial sector and the importance of financial developments, including financial crises, in affecting economic activity. But the lessons should go well beyond these observations and force us to question a number of cherished beliefs. Among other things, the events of the past ten years have put into question the presumption that economies are self-stabilizing and have raised again the issue of whether temporary shocks can have permanent effects.

These issues call for a reappraisal of macroeconomic thinking and macroeconomic policy. As the chapters look in more detail at the implications of specific policies, we make no attempt to be encyclopedic here and feel free to pick and choose the issues we see as most salient.[1]

In the first section of this introduction, we review the response to two major previous crises, the Great Depression of the 1930s and the stagflation of the 1970s. The first led to the Keynesian revolution, a worry about

The work presented in this volume was prepared for the "Rethinking Macroeconomic Policy IV" conference at the Peterson Institute for International Economics, Washington, D.C., October 2017. The original papers presented at the conference and podcasts of the presentations are available at https://piie.com/events/rethinking-macroeconomic-policy.

destabilizing processes, a focus on aggregate demand and the crucial role of stabilization policies, and tighter constraints on the financial system. The second led instead to a partial rejection of the Keynesian model, a more benign view of economic fluctuations and the self-stabilizing properties of the economy, a focus on simple policy rules, and a more relaxed attitude with respect to the financial system. The question is then what the crisis we have just emerged from should and will do.

In the second section, we focus on what we see as the three main lessons of the last ten years. The first lesson, not surprisingly, has to do with the crucial role of the financial sector and the costs of financial crises. The second lesson is the complex nature of fluctuations, from the role of nonlinearities in leading to potentially exploding or imploding paths, to the limits of policy, to the persistent effects of shocks. The third lesson is that we are now and may be for the foreseeable future in an environment of low nominal and real interest rates, an environment that interacts with the first two factors and forces a rethinking not only of monetary policy but also of fiscal and financial policies.

We then focus on the joint implications of these changes for monetary, fiscal, and financial policies.

In the third section, we consider the implications for monetary policy. In an environment of low neutral rates and higher perceived risks, we see the main challenge facing monetary policy as being how to deal with the liquidity trap, both ex ante and ex post. Should the inflation target be increased? Should central banks adopt a price level or a nominal GDP target? Can the scope for negative nominal interest rates be widened? We believe the issue must be tackled now even in countries where the constraint is not currently binding.

We also take up two other issues. First, we explore whether and how monetary policy should concern itself with financial stability; we conclude that monetary policy can be of little help, and that financial stability should be left to financial policies, as imperfect as they might be. Second, we consider how central banks should deal with the large balance sheets they have accumulated as a result of the crisis; we conclude there is no convincing reason why central banks should keep those large balance sheets. To the extent that there are reasons to affect spreads, this is better handled through debt management and fiscal policy.

In the fourth section, we focus on the implications for fiscal policy. In an environment of limits to monetary policy and neutral interest rates below growth rates, we argue, fiscal policy should play a much more active role in stabilization. Automatic stabilizers should be improved, and the scope for a discretionary response to adverse shocks should be revisited. And, in an environment in which the interest rate is likely to remain below the growth rate for some time to come, the usual discussion of debt sustainability must be reexamined. At a minimum, debt consolidation should take place more slowly, and there is a strong case for debt-financed increased public investment.

In the fifth section we focus on financial policies, from financial regulation to macroprudential and microprudential policies. While many measures have already been adopted, how best to address financial risks, both ex ante and ex post, remains uncertain. We take up two issues. The first issue is whether simple tools, such as capital ratios and stress tests, can be relied on to do most of the work. The evidence makes us skeptical that they can. The second issue is what the right mix of financial regulation and macroprudential policy might be. We conclude that it may be better to rely primarily on financial regulation. For example, it might be better to have higher and constant capital ratios rather than lower and varying ones.

We state our conclusions in the sixth section. Ten years ago, few would have predicted the events that were to unfold, from runs on the largest world financial institutions, to interest rates at liquidity trap levels for close to a decade, to inflation still below target today, to output gaps still large and negative in many advanced economies. We observe a temptation to go back to the precrisis ways, a return to inflation targeting and to a Taylor-like rule, with no use of fiscal policy for stabilization purposes and a pushback against financial regulation and macroprudential measures. This temptation should be resisted. In what we now understand to be a world in which financial instability, binding lower bounds on interest rates, and the protracted effects of cyclical downturns are ever-present threats, strong stabilization policies are key. At a minimum, monetary policy must reestablish its margin of maneuver. Fiscal policy must be reintroduced as a major stabilization tool. And financial policies must continue to be adjusted and reinforced. We can call this evolution. If, however, neutral rates remain extremely low, perhaps even negative, or if financial regulation falls short, more dramatic changes may be needed, from reliance on fiscal deficits, to active policy efforts to promote private spending, to higher inflation to achieve lower real rates, to much tighter constraints on the financial sector. We can call this revolution. Time will tell.

1   Crises and Macropolicy Changes of the Past

In the wake of the Great Depression, macroeconomists—at least in the Anglo-American world—converged on a common set of ideas that came out of Keynes's general theory. Rather than being seen as inevitable, natural, and mostly unproblematic, like seasonal fluctuations, business cycles and recessions in particular came to be seen as highly problematic manifestations of shortfalls in aggregate demand. Maintaining adequate demand through the tools of fiscal and monetary policy became the primary concern of macroeconomic policy. And, in the light of the financial crisis at the origin of the Great Depression, governments took a much heavier hand in managing financial systems, regulating rates on bank liabilities, regulating the composition of bank assets, and, in some cases, limiting competition between financial intermediaries.

The very strong performance of the American and British economies during World War II was seen as a demonstration of the power of fiscal policy. The subsequent strong performance of advanced economies led to great confidence in stabilization policy. One of us remembers being told as a child in the 1960s of how the U.S. Department of Commerce publication *Business Cycle Digest* had been renamed *Business Conditions Digest* to preserve the initials BCD while also reflecting the fact that business cycles were no longer inevitable. Confidence in policy was based on the conviction that deep understanding, reflected in large econometric models, had been achieved. There was, to be sure, a concern that increased economic activity would lead to increased inflation as reflected in the Phillips curve. But the idea was that prudent policymakers would choose an optimal point on the curve that would balance the benefits of higher output and less unemployment against the costs of higher inflation.

A combination of intellectual developments and real-world events led to a dramatic reconceptualization of macroeconomics between the late 1960s and the early 1980s. Phelps (1968) and Friedman (1968) pointed out that, on theoretical grounds, one would not expect to see a stable trade-off between inflation and unemployment as postulated by the simple Phillips curve. At the same time, by the late 1970s, and in apparent contrast to the Keynesian view, stagflation emerged as a major problem throughout advanced economies as inflation and unemployment both increased in unison.

The result was again a dramatic change in macroeconomic thinking. By the mid-1980s the mainstream view was that there was no long-run trade-off between inflation and unemployment. Fluctuations in output associated with changes in nominal demand were, in the freshwater view, an illusion, or, in the saltwater view, the temporary consequence of wage and price stickiness. Demand management policy could aspire to containing inflation and reducing the volatility of economic fluctuations but not to raising the average level of output over time. Reducing discretion in monetary policy through a combination of political insulation of central banks and the adoption of explicit targets and policy rules would contribute to improved economic performance with less inflation, no loss of output over time, and damped economic fluctuations. In parallel, financial regulation was relaxed and restrictions on commercial banks were gradually lifted.[2]

As a consequence of this change in thinking, all major central banks were granted substantial independence and set inflation targets as the principal guidepost for policy. It came to be accepted that one major stabilization policy tool was enough, and interest in fiscal policy diminished greatly. Events such as the 1993 Deficit Reduction Program in the United States, in which deficit reduction led to lower interest rates at all maturities and an increase of growth, encouraged the view that fiscal policy decisions should be made on long-run grounds with little attention to issues of demand management.

The period from roughly the mid-1980s to the mid-2000s saw a steady decrease in the variance of inflation, unemployment, and output. Christened the "Great Moderation," it was widely seen as proof of the success of the new approach to policy, and in particular to monetary policy. To be sure, there were dramatic developments in financial markets over this period, notably the 1987 stock market crash, the bursting of the Japanese bubble in the early 1990s, the emerging markets dramas in Latin America and Asia during the 1990s, and the bursting of the tech bubble in 2000.

But these events were seen as a series of epiphenomena that could be dealt with on an ad hoc basis and that did not, with the exception of the bursting of the Japanese bubble, lead to major changes in advanced economies' macroperformance. Even Japan's "lost decade" was interpreted as the result of a succession of policy failures rather than a challenge to the prevailing paradigm.

Indeed, confidence that the business cycle had been tamed and that central banks had learned they needed to respond rapidly to financial crises combined to enable then Fed governor Ben Bernanke (2002) to apologize on behalf of the Fed for the Great Depression and make clear that such an event could not happen again, owing to the understanding that had been achieved. While Bernanke's own aggressive actions in 2008 made his earlier statement prophetic, as a replay of the Great Depression was indeed avoided, it is probably fair to assume that Bernanke's listeners in 2003 did not expect anything like the Great Financial Crisis to materialize. Yet, just as mounting confidence in the existing paradigm and policy approach was followed by disaster in the 1970s, the same thing happened again with the Great Financial Crisis. As figure I.1 illustrates, output per person of working age in the United States likely will have increased no more over the twelve years since 2007 than it did during the twelve years after 1929.[3] The outcome is even worse in other parts of the advanced world.

Be it in monetary, fiscal, or financial policies, many measures were taken in the heat of the crisis. Ten years after the start of the crisis, however, it is not clear to what extent these extraordinary measures will be seen as one-off ad hoc crisis responses and to what extent they will lead to a rethinking of both macroeconomics and macroeconomic policy, similar to what we saw in the 1930s or in the 1970s. If so, in what ways should policy evolve? This is what we explore in the rest of this introductory chapter.

2   Three Main Lessons

We focus on what we see as three main lessons from the last decade, namely, the centrality of finance, the more complex and problematic nature of fluctuations, and the implications of very low neutral interest rates.

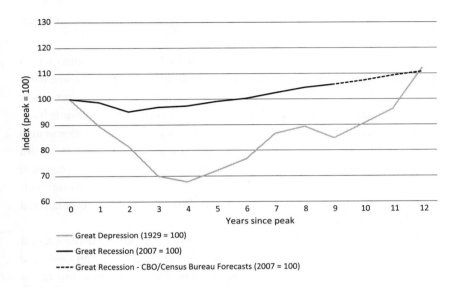

Figure I.1

U.S. Real GDP per 18- to 64-Year-Old: Great Recession versus Great Depression. *Source:* Department of Commerce, Bureau of Economic Analysis, National Income and Product Accounts.

The Centrality of Finance

Hyman Minsky (1992) had warned for decades about the consequences of buildups in financial risk. The NBER (Hubbard 1991) and others had held conferences on financial crisis risk. Financial crises were endemic in emerging market countries. And, in advanced countries, the poor performance of Japan after the bursting of the bubble was there for all to see. Yet prevailing macroeconomic paradigms largely ignored the possibility of financial developments as drivers of economic performance. Neither financial euphoria as a source of booms nor financial crisis as a cause of busts played a prominent role in the macroeconomic thinking of academics or policymakers. In macroeconomic models, the role of the financial system was often reduced to the determination of a yield curve and stock prices, based mostly on the expectations hypothesis with fixed term premia.

The recent crisis has obviously changed that. It has triggered a very large amount of research on the entrails and the behavior of the financial system.[4] But many questions remain unanswered, and there is not yet a canonical model of a financial crisis. Let us give two examples of issues crucial for policy that remain unresolved.

First, granting that asset price or credit bursts and their interaction with excessive leverage are crucial in understanding financial crises, what is the relative importance of different mechanisms? One mechanism is that financial intermediaries lose capital and respond by cutting back lending, thereby choking off economic activity. This aspect dominates the accounts of the 2008 crisis by Paulson (2010), Bernanke (2015), and Geithner (2014). Another is instead that excessive indebtedness, coupled with declining asset values, leads consumers and businesses to retrench and cut back on consumption and investment, a mechanism emphasized by Koo (2011) and Mian and Sufi (2014).

Which channel dominates is a central issue for policy. If the second channel is the most important, measures that write off existing debts are crucial to the resolution of a financial crisis. This is the position taken by those who, like Geanakoplos (2010), believe that the failure to write off mortgage debt on a large scale was a grave error in how the United States handled the financial crisis. If, on the other hand, the key issue is impairment of intermediaries, then such debt write-downs may be highly counterproductive by substantially reducing the regulatory capital of intermediaries and leading them to scale back lending. Indeed, for an institution that is constrained in its lending by an 8 percent regulatory capital requirement, each dollar of imposed capital losses may reduce lending by up to $12. It may be that both aspects are central but at different stages of the crisis: addressing the first may be essential early on to avoid the economy going into free fall, while reducing debt overhangs may be crucial later in making rapid recovery possible. On which side to intervene and when are still very much open issues.[5]

Second, the age-old issue of the relative roles of solvency versus liquidity in precipitating a crisis is still not settled. Official sector accounts of the crisis in the United States suggest that the problems at the major institutions were primarily problems of liquidity rather than solvency—a judgment supported by the finding of the April 2009 stress tests that very little capital was required by the major financial institutions and by the observation that the vast majority of the TARP funds were paid back quite quickly. On the other hand, critics like Bulow and Klemperer (2013) have noted that there were substantial reasons to doubt the solvency of some of the largest banks as early as the summer of 2008 and point out that the stress tests represented a kind of implicit liability guarantee for the banks, which was like the government providing capital without charging for it. In that view, the success of TARP may have been accidental, the result of a gamble for resurrection that turned out right. While Diamond and Dybvig's (1983) celebrated paper on bank runs provides a framework for thinking about liquidity crises, the question of how to deal, in the middle of a generalized crisis, with institutions that are suddenly recognized to be in trouble remains open.

In short, our understanding of the financial system has improved, but it remains limited. When to this is added that the financial system is substantially more complex than it was in the past, that it is highly reactive to regulation, and that it is very good at regulatory arbitrage, the challenge facing financial policies appears considerable. This has a straightforward implication: financial crises will probably happen again.

The Nature of Fluctuations

Over the three decades before the crisis, macroeconomics had largely converged on a "shock and propagation mechanism" view of economic fluctuations in advanced economies. The economy was constantly hit by many shocks, some to components of demand and some to components of supply, most of them small, each of them with its own propagation mechanism. And one could think of these propagation mechanisms as largely linear, with the economy ultimately returning to potential after any given shock.

The technical machinery of modern macroeconomics was largely based on that view. In a world of shocks and linear mechanisms, one could think of vector autoregressions (VARs) as capturing the reduced form of these dynamics. Dynamic stochastic general equilibrium (DSGE) models could be constructed to fit and interpret the reduced form and to give a deeper structural interpretation to the observed dynamics.

Not only did this view become the basic paradigm of much of macroeconomic research, but it shaped the design of macroeconomic policy. In a world of regular fluctuations, optimal policy takes the form of stable feedback rules. In the years before the crisis, the focus had been nearly exclusively on monetary policy, and much of the rather Talmudic discussion was about the precise form of the "interest rate rule," that is, the best reaction function of the interest rate to inflation and to the output gap. Fiscal policy was ignored as a stabilization tool, although, inconsistently, policymakers were still happy to let existing automatic stabilizers function, no matter how accidental and unadapted they were. And macroprudential policies were simply not the subject of mainstream discussions.

The financial crisis does not fit this image of fluctuations, in a number of dimensions:

First, financial crises challenge how we should think of shocks. The notion of random shocks always raised nearly metaphysical issues: presumably behind a shock to consumption or to wages is some deeper explanation, some underlying shock, which itself should be explained, and so on. But for a macroeconomist, it is reasonable to just take some unexplained movements as given, call them shocks, and not try to further explain them (Romer [2016] has made fun of such an approach, referring to such shocks as phlogistons). One can indeed think of shocks to components of aggregate demand that affect output over time, with the effects building up and then disappearing over time. But this seems singularly unadapted to the description of financial crises. Such crises appear to build up slowly, in the form of either asset price bubbles or credit booms, until perceptions change, prices crash, and the financial system is impaired. The relevant image is much more of plate tectonics and eventual earthquakes than of regular random shocks.

Second, financial crises are characterized by essential nonlinearities and positive feedback whereby shocks are strongly amplified rather than damped as they propagate. The quintessential example is bank runs, in which a small shock, or even no shock at all, leads creditors or depositors to run and makes their fears self-fulfilling. This is where the earlier discussion of liquidity versus solvency is important: liquidity is intrinsically associated with multiple equilibria, or at least with large effects of small shocks.

Third, financial crises are followed by long periods of depressed output, and the Great Financial Crisis has been no exception. One of the most dramatic facts of the crisis is shown in figure I.2, which plots the evolution of log GDP in the United States and the EU since 2000. In both cases the crisis led to a step decrease in output relative to the precrisis trend (estimated over 2000–2008). In neither case does output appear to be returning to the old trend. This low growth has come largely as a

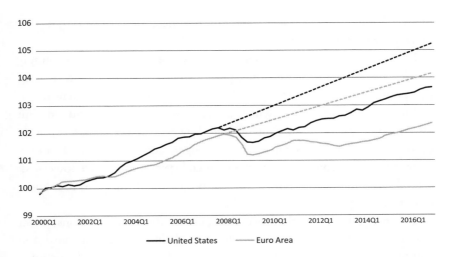

Figure I.2

Advanced Economies, Log Real GDP and Extrapolated Trend (Index 2000 = 100).
Source: Blanchard (2018).

surprise. For example, Fed forecasts of GDP have been too optimistic in all of the last six years.

These evolutions have led to a revival of the hysteresis discussion, that is, whether temporary shocks have persistent or even permanent effects on potential output. By itself, the evidence in figure I.2 is not dispositive:

It could be that these economies are still some distance from potential. Sharp limits on the scope of policies to sustain aggregate demand may have led to output remaining below potential even today. Indeed, this is probably the case in much of the EU. In the United States, however, the low rate of unemployment suggests that output is now close to potential, and that what we are seeing is indeed lower potential output relative to the precrisis trend.

It could be the coincidence of two independent evolutions—on the one hand, the sharp initial drop in output due to the crisis and, on the other, an underlying decrease in trend productivity growth, and thus lower trend growth of potential output, largely unrelated to the crisis. There is indeed some evidence that, at least in the United States, the decline in measured productivity growth started before the crisis, and thus may be due in part to other factors (see, e.g., Fernald et al. 2017). The evolutions shown in figure I.2 might, under this interpretation, reflect a return of output to a more slowly growing potential output trend.

It may be instead that financial crises are like permanent supply shocks, leading to a long-lasting, perhaps even permanent, decrease in potential output relative to trend. They may lead to a less efficient financial intermediation system, which affects not only the demand side but also the supply side. In the United States, however, private debt levels have decreased, and the financial system no longer seems impaired. Or it may be that tighter regulation leads the financial system to finance lower-risk (but also, by implication, lower-return) projects and thus lead to a lower if more stable potential output path.

Or finally, it may be that recessions, especially deep recessions, affect potential output, that there is hysteresis (Phelps 1972; Blanchard and Summers 1986), through either higher unemployment, lower labor force participation, or lower productivity (Blanchard 2018). There is indeed some evidence that in the United States, the high unemployment associated with the financial crisis has contributed to the decline in labor force participation.

Implications for policy depend on which of the mechanisms described above is most relevant. The first points to the need for ways of using demand policies more aggressively. The second and third point to the difficulties of assessing potential output. The fourth, on which we put some weight, has more dramatic implications, as it suggests that the effects of adverse shocks and thus the role of policy may be much larger than in a world in which potential output is unaffected by cyclical fluctuations.

Some of the issues we just discussed are specific to financial crises. But some apply to all fluctuations. The crisis has brought into focus a number of first-order nonlinearities, which are relevant more generally, even more so in the current low-growth, low-inflation, low-interest-rate environment. The most obvious one is the lower bound on nominal interest rates, which, when it binds, leads the economy to have dramatically different responses to shocks and policies. Another, which has been binding in some southern European countries, is the zero lower bound on nominal wage changes. As for nominal interest rates, this zero lower bound is not absolute, and some nominal wages have declined, but it has strongly limited the usual process of wage and price adjustment to high unemployment. Yet another nonlinearity has come from the interaction between public debt and the banking system, a mechanism known as "doom loops," which played a central role early in the euro crisis: higher public debt leads to worries about public debt restructuring, decreasing the value of the bonds held by financial institutions, which leads in turn to a decrease in financial institutions' capital, worries about their health, and the expectation that the state may have to bail them out and be itself in trouble as a result.

In contrast to the standard precrisis view, these nonlinearities have the potential to amplify initial shocks, potentially leading to implosive paths, leading again to strong policy challenges.

Low Interest Rates

Low interest rates are a major feature of the current macroeconomic environment. Figure I.3 shows the evolution of the ten-year real rate on indexed bonds for the G-7, based on the updating of Rachel and Smith (2015). It shows how the real rate started decreasing long before the crisis,

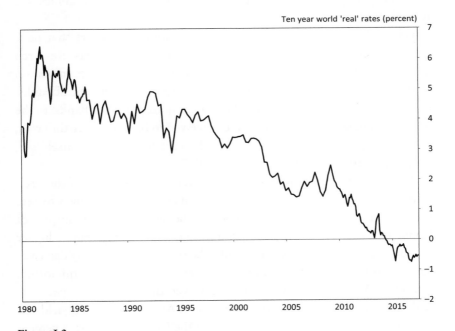

Ten year world 'real' rates (percent)

Figure I.3

Ten-Year Real Rate on Indexed Bonds (G-7 not including Italy).
Source: Rachel and Smith (2015).

but the crisis lowered it further. As of this writing, it is still in negative territory.[6] In reference to Hansen (1939), one of the authors has referred to this evolution as "secular stagnation."

What factors are behind this steady decrease are not well identified. Explanations fall into two groups. The first is that the rate of return on capital has decreased, leading to a decrease in all rates, risky or safe. The second is that the safety premium has increased, leading to a lower safe rate for a given rate of return on capital.

Under the first explanation, one is looking for factors that have increased saving or decreased investment. Given the large degree of financial integration and the largely similar decrease in interest rates across countries, one must look for factors of potentially global importance. Research has identified a large number of potential culprits, from the "global savings glut" emphasized by Bernanke (2005), to the interaction between taxes and inflation, to the decrease in the relative price of capital goods, to the impact of lower growth on investment, to the effect of rising inequality and profit shares in raising saving, to demographics (see Rachel and Smith 2015).

Under the second explanation, one is looking for factors that have increased the demand for or reduced the supply of safe assets. Research has also identified a number of potential culprits, from the accumulation of reserves in the form of safe assets by emerging market central banks, to financial regulation and higher liquidity requirements for banks, to the decrease in the set of assets that were perceived to be safe before the crisis, to the perception of higher risk as a result of the financial crisis itself (see, e.g., Caballero, Fahri, and Gourinchas 2017).

The abundance of potential factors, without a clear sense of their relative importance, makes it difficult to predict what will happen to safe rates. For example, the sharp decrease in the current account surplus of China and, even more so, of oil-producing countries may lead to higher rates. Or, as memories of the crisis fade, the equity premium may decrease, as it did after the Great Depression, leading to an increase in equilibrium safe rates. Market pricing indicates, however, that investors expect low real rates to prevail for a long time to come. As of this writing, yields on ten-year indexed bonds are 0.4 percent in the United States, −1.1 percent in Germany, and −0.4 percent in Japan.

Low interest rates, especially interest rates lower than growth rates, have essential implications, not only for monetary policy but also for fiscal and financial policies.

So far the focus has been primarily on the implications for monetary policy and the effective lower bound. While central banks have explored and used other tools, there is little question that the binding lower bound on short-term nominal interest rates (zero or slightly negative) limited the scope of monetary policy to sustain demand during the recovery.

Indeed, this has raised an old but fundamental issue of whether market economies naturally return to potential (as we saw earlier, a potential that might itself be moving, but this is a different issue). One of the first formal discussions was given by Patinkin (1948): in response to low output, the price level would decrease, leading to an increase in the real value of money and an increase in demand. The standard story, as captured in the aggregate demand/aggregate supply model of textbook fame, is the following: lower output would lead to a lower price level, which would lead to a higher real money stock, which in turn would lead to a lower interest rate, which, finally, would increase aggregate demand and output. This never felt like a very convincing stabilizing mechanism, especially in a world where central banks increasingly ignored the money supply and focused instead on the interest rate. When central banks adopted inflation targeting and interest rate rules, stability was shown not to be automatic but to depend on a sufficiently aggressive feedback rule from output and inflation to the policy rate. The effective lower bound, which prevents this feedback from operating, puts into question whether the economy will indeed return to potential after a bad shock. Even away from the lower bound, a positive probability that the constraint will bind raises the same fundamental issue. The observation that ten-year breakeven inflation as inferred from indexed bond yields is 1.8 percent in the United States, 1.2 percent in Germany, and 0.5 percent in Japan—all below 2 percent inflation targets—suggests that investors are not convinced about the ability of central banks to return and maintain economies at potential in the future.

The limits of monetary policy imply, other things equal, a larger role for other policies, in particular fiscal policy. And low interest rates raise many questions about the design of fiscal policy in such a context. If the interest rate is below the growth rate, could this be a signal that the economy is dynamically inefficient, in which case larger public debt is actually not only feasible but also desirable? If the economy is dynamically efficient but the safe rate is below the growth rate, can the state still issue debt without ever paying it back, and if it can, should it do so?

Finally, low interest rates also have implications for financial regulation and macroprudential policy, although these are less obvious. The main issue is the relation between low interest rates and risk taking. It has been argued that a combination of human nature, leading to reach for yield, and of agency issues leads to more risk taking when interest rates are low. Also, by inflating asset values and reducing debt service costs, low rates may also lead to high leverage. Some channels suggest the relevance of low real rates, others the relevance of low nominal rates, such as the "break the buck" constraint perceived to be binding by money market funds. In either case, there is again an important role for financial regulation and macroprudential policy to play.

Having described the landscape, we turn to the implications for monetary, fiscal, and financial policies.

3   Monetary Policy

The crisis forced central banks to drastically change the way they conduct monetary policy. Most of the changes and the new instruments were introduced in the heat of the crisis. The question is, looking forward, how many of these instruments should remain, and how should monetary policy be reconstructed? We focus on three issues: how to deal with the effective lower bound on interest rates, whether and how monetary policy should address financial stability concerns, and whether central banks should return to smaller balance sheets.[7]

The United States has experienced six recession episodes in the last fifty years. The reductions in policy interest rates have averaged five percentage points, ranging from 2.1 to 10.5 percentage points, as policymakers responded to these downturns. Insofar as the Fed now believes the long-run normal federal funds rate is only 2.75 percent and that markets do not expect rates to rise to this level for a decade or more, it is clear there will be less scope for interest rate reduction as a response to economic downturn in the relevant future than in the past. This raises the risk that future downturns will be more serious, and that if this comes to be anticipated, investment will be reduced even in advance of downturns.

What can be done to mitigate this risk? As we have learned, and as Yellen (2016) recently emphasized, even when interest rates are at the lower bound, central banks have a range of tools at their disposal. These include the much-discussed various forms of quantitative easing (QE), forward guidance, and more ambitious strategies of committing to higher inflation when full employment is restored. We are skeptical that these tools will be sufficient. Were a recession to start in the United States, Europe, or Japan, we would expect long rates to fall to very low levels without any help from forward guidance or QE. This would leave little room for QE policies to decrease them further.

A natural solution, as argued by Rogoff (2017), would be to eliminate cash so as to eliminate the effective lower bound altogether. If people only had access to electronic demand deposits, those deposits could pay negative nominal rates without the risk of people moving into cash. It is indeed conceptually the most appealing solution. Like the other solutions discussed below, it has potential shortcomings: to the extent that banks are reluctant to pass on negative rates to depositors, negative rates may reduce bank profits, and reduce lending. For large enough negative rates, the effect of reduced lending may dominate and lead to lower rather than higher demand (Brunnermeier and Koby 2017).[8] And, while many economies are increasingly moving from cash to electronic money, it will take some time before cash is no longer an empirically relevant alternative. To the extent that there remains an effective lower bound and nominal rates cannot go too negative, other solutions must be found.

An alternative solution is to generate expectations of higher inflation when they are needed, namely, when policy rates have hit the effective lower bound. Price-level targeting, if credible, does achieve that. If the economy is in a recession and inflation is low, the commitment to return to the price-level path implies a commitment by the central bank to generate higher inflation later. Price-level targeting, however, has a major shortcoming. It is symmetric: if the economy is operating at potential but inflation has been too high in the recent past, the central bank must be willing to return to the price-level path, and thus must be willing to tighten monetary policy and risk a recession for no good reason beyond the previous commitment. This may be politically difficult and, by implication, not fully credible. Other solutions have been offered—for example, the proposal by Bernanke (see chapter 1) to commit to undo the shortfall of inflation during the time monetary policy is constrained by the effective lower bound through higher inflation later. Yet another alternative, suggested in Summers (2018), would be a shift to a nominal GDP target calibrated to ensure nominal interest rates in normal times in the 4 percent range.

All these proposals rely on the credibility of commitments to achieve higher inflation in the future and on the ability of the central bank to move inflation expectations when and as needed. Japan's difficulty over the past four years in moving inflation expectations and achieving its inflation target, despite the strong commitment of both the fiscal authority and the central bank, reinforces our sense of the difficulty of moving expectations in this way. If such commitments are de facto incredible, then this leads one to consider permanent increases in target inflation, say, from 2 percent to 4 percent (Blanchard, Dell'Ariccia, and Mauro 2010).

Whichever approach is chosen, we believe that the question of creating the capacity to respond to downturns is a critical one facing monetary policy today.

Turning to the role of monetary policy vis-à-vis financial stability, it is clear that financial regulation and macroprudential policies should be the first lines of defense. One cannot expect, however, that they will be fully successful. The question is then whether monetary policy—that is, the use of the policy rate—should be the second line of defense. This discussion is known as "leaning against cleaning" (i.e., increasing the interest rate in the face of a credit boom or an asset bubble versus taking measures in response to the later decrease). We are skeptical that monetary policy, in the form of preventive movements in the policy rate, can play a very useful role, for three reasons.

First—and this is common to monetary policy and time-varying regulatory policies—it is in the nature of asset bubbles or unhealthy credit booms to be difficult to assess in real time. Alan Greenspan's famous "irrational exuberance" observation was made in December 1996 when the Dow was at 6300. In light of subsequent history, it is pretty clear that the stock market was not at that moment overvalued. More generally, Goetzmann (2015) has shown that even when markets double over short intervals, they are more likely to double again than to fall by half, an observation pointing up the difficulty of pricking bubbles without responding to upward movements in asset prices that in fact reflect fundamentals. In the same way, unhealthy credit booms are often unhealthy only in retrospect.

Second, lags in the effects of monetary policy make it even harder to act in a way that is stabilizing. Monetary policy acts with a significant lag. A tightening of policy just before a bubble bursts is likely to exacerbate the subsequent contraction. The ability to use monetary policy to promote financial stability therefore depends on the ability not just to identify bubbles but to be sufficiently confident to act in response to them well before they would burst of their own accord.

Third, the interest rate is a very poor instrument to decrease risk. Higher interest rates may slow down credit growth and lead to less risk taking. At the same time, however, higher rates worsen the position of existing debtors, both directly and through their adverse effect on activity, increasing debtors' risk of bankruptcy. They also weaken the position of financial intermediaries that have borrowed short and lent long.

For all these reasons, we believe, along the lines of Svensson (2017) and against the arguments of Borio and Lowe (2002) and Kashyap, Gourio, and Sim (2016), that interest rates should not be used to fight asset bubbles or credit booms, and that, even when their limits are taken into account, financial regulation and macroprudential policies should bear responsibility for financial stability ex ante.

If a crisis materializes, however, we have little doubt that central banks should generously provide liquidity against good collateral, and in doing so limit the cost of cleaning. For reasons we develop later when discussing financial policies, we are skeptical of the moral hazard argument in this context. Liquidity provision is not the same as a bailout, is unlikely to have strong incentive effects, and can make the difference between a recession and a depression.

Turning finally to balance sheets: between 2007 and 2016, the liabilities of the Bank of Japan increased from 21 percent to 89 percent of GDP, those of the Fed from 6 percent to 24 percent, and those of the European Central Bank from 16 percent to 34 percent. The increase in liabilities has mostly taken the form of interest-paying money, that is, reserves held by banks at the central bank. Assets are a mixture of government bonds and private securities, with the composition varying across central banks.

Looking forward, as central banks increase interest rates, should they keep such large balance sheets, or should they go back closer to the pre-crisis balance sheets?

It is important to recognize at the outset that in the institutional environment now prevailing in all major economies, where central banks pay interest on bank reserves, "money" is now the equivalent of floating rate government debt. The monetary transmission mechanism stressed by both Friedman and Tobin, which relied on money paying zero interest rate, with the result that changes in the quantity of money changed all other interest rates and prices, is no longer a feature of modern economies. Rather, what we call monetary policy is really interest rate policy, as central banks set policy interest rates directly, and changes in "money" represent changes in the maturity and perhaps the credit structure of the debt the public has to absorb. In this world, the size of central bank balance sheets is not per se a measure of inflationary pressure, even in the long run.[9]

As Greenwood and co-authors (2014) stress, any judgment about central bank balance sheets must reflect two quite different sets of considerations. The first set has to do with an assessment of the optimal maturity structure of the debt that the consolidated government—that is, the Treasury and the central bank—makes available to the public. Once this judgment has been made, the second set of considerations relates to the optimal division of labor between the Treasury and the central bank.

Perhaps the best argument in favor of large balance sheets focuses on the liability side of the balance sheet and has been made by Greenwood and co-authors (2016). They stress that some investors have a preference for very short-maturity, very liquid assets, and that the government is in a unique position to offer such assets. And the larger public provision of very liquid assets reduces the risk that the private sector manufactures its own through securitization, tranching, and other means, an activity that proved dangerous and costly during the crisis. These assets can also be provided by the Treasury, for example, in the form of long-maturity floating rate debt, or, as is now the case, by the central bank in the form of interest-paying reserves. One may argue that the central bank is in a better position to assess fluctuations in demand for these very liquid assets, allowing the Treasury to focus on more traditional debt management. If the central bank does it, however, it should do so in such a way as to allow access not just by banks but also by those institutions that have the most need for such liquid assets.

A different line of argument holds that the risk premia associated with longer-maturity bonds and with private-sector instruments, including equities, are excessive for reasons related either to capital market constraints or to behavioral factors affecting investors. In this case, the public sector can reduce its financing costs by borrowing short-term and holding longer-term assets. In the language of traders, it can advantageously engage in carry trades and even collect the risk premium. At a minimum, it can avoid being on the other side of the carry trade. Even if there are no such distortions, decreasing term premia loosen the zero lower bound constraint: other things equal, if and when the short nominal rate reaches zero, longer maturity rates will be lower, thus helping aggregate demand.

Whatever the case is for shortening the maturity structure of the government debt that the public must absorb, we see, however, little argument for the current approach in the United States and most other countries, where both the Treasury and the central bank act largely independently to affect the maturity structure of the debt and, as in the United States during the QE period, can even do it at cross purposes. We believe that for the most part, debt management decisions should be made by the Treasury, or through actions coordinated between the central bank and the Treasury. This leaves little role for large central bank balance sheets at times when the zero lower bound is not binding. Overall, we find the case for maintaining large balance sheets in normal times to be weak.[10]

In short, we are skeptical that monetary policy proper can be used to decrease the risk of a financial crisis. We also do not believe that the central bank needs to keep a large balance sheet in normal times. The central bank can increase its balance sheet quickly if and when needed. We see the priority for monetary policy to reacquire enough margin of maneuver to fight the next recession, wherever it comes from.

4   Fiscal Policy

Out of necessity, fiscal policy was rediscovered as a stabilization tool during the crisis, although, in the face of deficits, large increases in debt, and worries about debt sustainability, fiscal expansion quickly turned to fiscal austerity and debt stabilization. Today, fiscal policy faces a highly unusual environment. On the one hand, and largely because of the financial crisis, debt levels relative to GDP are high by historical standards. On the other hand, interest rates on government debt are low, and in many countries, they are expected to remain lower than growth rates for some time to come. As a consequence, levels of government debt service relative to GDP are low by historical standards.

These evolutions raise two main issues:[11]

The first is how fiscal policy can be used as a stabilization tool. Given how short-handed governments were in reacting to the fall in demand in 2008–2009, one might have expected both academic work and policy progress on the scope for discretionary policy, for example, on whether it is feasible to have a set of truly "shovel-ready" projects for public investment, or on improving or designing new automatic stabilizers. There has been surprisingly little academic work (for an exception, see McKay and Reis 2016) and no policy progress that we know on this front. Work on the use of fiscal policy as a stabilization tool must actually go beyond just stabilizers. Another lesson from the crisis and the renewed interest in fiscal policy is the complexity of "multipliers," that is, the effects of fiscal policy on demand and output, of their dependence on the specific type of fiscal adjustment and the economic environment. Despite a large amount of research since the crisis, we still have a poor understanding, for example, of the effects of spending cuts versus tax increases, and on the supply-side effects of alternative fiscal policies.

The second is how fiscal policy should be conducted in an environment of high initial debt but low rates on government bonds—indeed, lower than the growth rates.

If the safe rate were to remain smaller than the growth rate forever, this would have fairly dramatic implications. The government could issue debt, distribute the proceeds in the form of reduced taxes or increased spending, and never raise taxes or repay the debt: the debt-to-GDP ratio would not explode but would instead converge to a finite value, no matter how large the deficit. There would be no future tax burden associated with debt.

Because of our limited understanding of the relative role of the factors that lie behind the low safe rate, however, one cannot be sure that the inequality will not reverse at some point in the future. If so, if and when it happens, the government would need to raise taxes or decrease spending in order to stabilize debt. From the government's point of view, it may still be an attractive debt gamble (to use the expression coined by Ball, Elmendorf, and Mankiw [1998]): the lower the probability that the inequality is to reverse, the smaller the expected tax burden associated with any initial debt issuance. Furthermore, the concern that the safe rate may eventually exceed the growth rate is substantially mitigated if governments can actually lock in this low rate for a long time through the issuance of long-term indexed debt. The real interest rate on thirty-year inflation indexed debt is 0.9 percent in the United States today and negative in Germany, Japan, and the UK, rates that seem very low relative to even pessimistic views about long-term growth.

If governments can indeed issue debt at little or no cost in terms of future taxes, does this mean that they should do it? Even if the likely tax burden of higher debt is small, it is still the case that, at least if the economy is operating at potential, higher debt will lead to lower capital accumulation, and thus lower output.[12] Will it lead however to lower consumption and thus lower welfare? One has been trained to think of the issue in terms of dynamic efficiency or inefficiency, and thus to compare the rate of return to capital to the growth rate. And the evidence is that the average rate of return to capital is, at least in the United States, substantially higher than the average growth rate, suggesting an adverse effect of public debt not only on output but also on consumption and thus on welfare.[13]

Looking at the rate of return to capital, however, may not be the right way to think about the issue. What consumers care about is not the average rate of return to capital but the risk-adjusted rate of return. And, absent distortions in financial markets, this risk-adjusted rate is, to the extent that government bonds are indeed considered safe, the rate on government bonds. If this rate is below the growth rate, it may well be that the adverse effects of debt on welfare are limited or, indeed, nonexistent.[14]

How do these theoretical considerations translate into practical policy advice?

Let's take stabilization first. To the extent that low safe rates imply sharper limits on monetary policy, this implies an increased need for the use of fiscal policy for stabilization purposes. At the same time, the same low safe rates imply more space to use fiscal policy for such purposes.

Both go in the same direction, an increased use of fiscal policy relative to monetary policy.

Turning to debt policy, this suggests, at a minimum, a more relaxed attitude to debt and to debt reduction. High debt may have limited costs in terms of both the future additional tax burden, and future lower consumption. Just as low safe nominal rates suggest the need to reexamine the inflation target, lower safe real rates imply the need to reexamine the acceptable levels of debt.

The case for reexamination is even stronger if debt is used to finance public investment. Public investment is worth doing if its risk-adjusted social rate of return equals or exceeds the risk-adjusted rate of return on private investment, which again might be closely proxied by the rate on government bonds. We believe that, partly because of the cuts coming from fiscal austerity and partly because of insufficient public investment even before the crisis, the social rate of return to public capital is high. Hysteresis, which we discussed earlier, is also directly relevant here. Even if the interest rate exceeds the growth rate, and to the extent that higher actual output leads to higher potential output, it may be that public spending pays for itself, leading to a decrease in the debt-to-GDP ratio even in the long run (DeLong and Summers 2012). The case becomes even stronger when the interest rate is below the growth rate.

5   Financial Policies

Based on recent experience, a large fraction of whatever consequential instability takes place in advanced economies over the next decades is likely to be associated with financial instability. Note that, in addition to the experience of the Great Recession, the other recent economic downturns in the United States had some roots in financial factors—whether the credit problems associated with real estate and the consequent credit crunch in the late 1980s or the stock market bubble and its collapse in 2000.

This raises the issues of both crisis prevention and crisis resolution.[15]

Let's take crisis resolution first. Some believe that one lesson of the crisis is that policymakers need stronger tools for responding to financial strains, so that, for example, next time there would be clear legal authority to bail out an institution like Lehman Brothers in 2008. Others believe instead that the moral hazard associated with the excessive availability of bailout funds was an important contributor to the excessive risk taking that led to the crisis.

We are skeptical of the moral hazard fundamentalism that has taken hold in many quarters and concerned that both legal changes and the painful political lessons of the past crisis may make the provision of emergency liquidity more difficult the next time a crisis comes along. Serious concerns have been expressed by Geithner (2017) and others that legal restrictions contained in the Dodd-Frank legislation on the provision of support to individual institutions could make an appropriate response to the next crisis more difficult. To a substantial extent, crises have their roots not in conscious risk taking by financial institutions but in "black swan" events that they do not anticipate—something that cannot be changed by altering incentives. Moreover, the provision of liquidity that contains runs arguably does not represent a moral hazard cost because it need not be socially costly. Indeed, as we mentioned earlier, the U.S. government turned a profit on the TARP program of support for financial institutions. Because major crises occur only every half century or so, we are skeptical that actions in one crisis are important as precedents for the next.

Crisis prevention has been a major preoccupation since the onset of financial crisis in 2008, leading to the passage of Dodd-Frank in the United States and the myriad of internationally coordinated activities under the auspices of the Financial Stability Board. Capital ratios have been substantially increased. Systemic banks are subject to tighter constraints. Stress tests have steadily improved. Liquidity ratios have been introduced to limit the risk and the consequences of runs.

Yet, by necessity, regulatory practice has run somewhat ahead of theory. There is a multitude of unresolved questions ranging from how central the adequacy of capital is relative to the desirability of using multiple capital ratio requirements, to how regulation should vary with cyclical and financial conditions, to whether and how best to regulate the "shadow financial system," to how to avoid liquidity breakdowns and major disruptions in asset markets.[16] Here we focus on just two—the efficacy of capital regulation and stress tests and the desirability of time-varying regulatory policies to promote stability.

It is tempting to suppose that, with sufficiently high capital requirements, the stability of major institutions and hence of the financial system can be assured. High levels of capital can be assured in a static sense through direct capital regulation and in a dynamic sense through stress tests that ensure that capital levels will be adequate even in an adverse scenario (leaving aside issues of liquidity, which indeed require an additional instrument).

Bulow and Klemperer (2013) and Sarin and Summers (2016) discuss a number of issues raised by current approaches to capital regulation. Most of the institutions that failed in 2008 and 2009 were reported by their regulators to have had high capital ratios up to the moment when they failed. As a particularly egregious example, Bear Stearns was reported by its regulator to have a tier 1 capital ratio of 11.6 percent the week before it failed. But it is not an isolated example: Wachovia, Washington Mutual, and Lehman Brothers all were judged to have high capital ratios on the eve of their failures. Haldane and Madouros (2012), looking at the universe of large global banks, report there was no correlation between prior capital ratios and the chance of surviving through the crisis. Bulow and Klemperer (2013) note that banks that are resolved by the FDIC typically have liabilities 15 percent or more in excess of assets, suggesting large flaws in regulatory capital as a measure of economic capital.

While the official line is that the banking sector is far better capitalized than it was prior to the crisis, Sarin and Summers (2016) note that ratios of the market value of equity to bank assets, measures of equity volatility, and returns on preferred stock all suggest otherwise. Stress tests suggest an extraordinary robustness of the banking system at least in the United States today, but we suspect that claims that the system would weather a storm far worse than 2008 without any large institution needing to raise capital say more about stress test methodologies than they do about banking system robustness.

This has direct policy relevance. A major policy error made in association with the 2008 crisis was the failure of regulatory authorities in the United States to force the raising of capital or at least the reduction of dividend payments and stock repurchases in the spring and summer of 2008, even as markets were signaling serious concerns about the health of the financial system. It can be debated whether this reflected failure of the authorities to perceive the extent of the risk or their lack of legal authority. How to avoid similar delays in the future, and how to design approaches using market information as an input to regulatory policy, seem to us a priority.

While we believe that regulatory policies that are more responsive to changes in firms' economic capital are desirable, we are more skeptical of time-varying capital requirements or leverage limits. In part this is for the reasons discussed earlier with respect to the use of monetary policies to promote financial stability. It is very difficult to identify bubbles or excessive credit booms ex ante and even more difficult to confidently identify them enough ahead of their bursting to make countercyclical policy worthwhile. We need only contrast the difficulty of noticing and acting on capital depletion of banks in 2008, at which the authorities failed despite clear market signals, with the difficulty of gauging early incipient bubbles and acting on them. Political economy issues further complicate the task: increasing required down payments on mortgages in the face of an increase in housing prices, which is likely to primarily affect young buyers, may be extremely unpopular and, as a result, applied too little or too late. Indeed, there is a clear risk that time-varying macroprudential measures respond to recent experience and end up pro- rather than countercyclical.

This suggests adopting, for example, higher and constant capital ratios rather than lower and cyclically sensitive ones. The cost of doing so may be small. Indeed, one of the most interesting findings of the research since the crisis is that, leaving aside the risk that some activity shifts to the shadow banking sector (which thus needs to be regulated as well), higher capital ratios have limited effects on either the cost of funds for banks or on bank lending, leading to the conclusion that higher capital ratios than the current regulatory ratios may well be appropriate (Goldstein 2017).

In short, while much more attention is now paid to financial regulation and macroprudential policies, the task is far from finished. The very complexity of the financial system, our limited understanding of its workings, and the ability of financial players to adjust and engage in regulatory arbitrage are formidable obstacles. We are likely to face more financial crises in the future.

6 Conclusions

As the crisis fades in the rear-view mirror, we perceive a risk that macroeconomic policy returns to business as usual, that central banks return to the inflation targeting of the past, that little progress is made on the use of fiscal policy, and that there is a successful pushback on the part of financial institutions against what they argue are excessive capital and liquidity requirements.

This would clearly be wrong. Ten years ago, few would have predicted the events that were to unfold, from runs on the largest world financial institutions, to interest rates at liquidity trap levels for close to a decade, to inflation still below target today, to output gaps being still large and negative in many advanced economies. We view the basic lessons from the great financial crisis to be largely similar to those drawn by the Keynesian revolution in response to the Great Depression: economies can be affected by strong shocks and cannot be expected to automatically self-stabilize. We have no doubt that, absent the strong monetary and fiscal policy responses we have observed, the financial crisis would have led to an outcome as bad or worse than the Great Depression. Thus, strong stabilization policies are simply of the essence.

Should we think of the required changes as evolution or revolution?[17]

The case for evolution goes as follows. True, on the research front, our models have been more models of regular tides than models of potential tsunamis. But we can incorporate in our models many of the nonlinearities that the crisis has revealed (e.g., Gertler, Kiyotaki, and Prestipino 2017). On the policy front, macroeconomic policy must rely on all three legs—monetary, fiscal, and financial. Monetary policy has to recreate a sufficient margin of maneuver to respond to adverse shocks in demand, something it can achieve in a number of ways. Fiscal policy has to play a larger stabilization role, through the development of better stabilizers, and debt consolidation can happen at a slower pace. Better financial regulation has already substantially decreased the risk and the consequences of financial crises but needs to be further adjusted. If these steps are taken, we should be able to handle future shocks in a better way.

The case for revolution goes as follows. Suppose that secular stagnation turns out to require large negative interest rates or unsustainable asset price increases and credit expansions to maintain demand and keep output at potential. To recover its margin of maneuver, monetary policy must then consider more dramatic measures, such as a much higher inflation target, or the purchase of private assets on a large scale. Large sustained fiscal deficits may be needed to sustain demand without excessive private sector leverage and risk taking. In light of the limits of financial regulation and the increased risk taking triggered by negative safe rates, more dramatic measures may have to be taken to redefine the scope and the size of the financial system.

The case for revolution may seem far-fetched, but the experience of Japan over the last twenty years must serve as a warning. As is well known, the potential growth rate of Japan is low, around 1 percent, reflecting limited productivity growth and adverse demographics. Think of what Japanese macroeconomic policy has had to resort to in order to sustain demand and maintain 1 percent annual growth over the last twenty years: interest rates, both short and long, close to zero, large fiscal deficits leading to a very large increase in public debt, massive central bank purchases, and recourse to external demand in the form of a current account surplus. Put another way, in the face of very weak internal private demand, Japanese macroeconomic policy has had to rely on extreme macroeconomic policies, including recourse to foreign demand, an option that would not be available to other countries if the same weakness were to affect all of them. Were Japan to be a template of things to come for the rest of advanced economies, what would be needed would indeed be a macroeconomic policy revolution.

Could this realistically be the case? As we write, the cyclical outlook in the United States and Europe looks good, with strong growth. This growth is sustained on the demand side by strong growth in asset prices, especially corporate stock prices, a growth we should not expect to continue at the same rate in the future. History teaches that recessions are almost never forecast even a year in advance. If the United States or Europe were to go into recession in the next couple of years, in all likelihood their situation would look much like that of Japan, with zero rates, large fiscal deficits, below-target inflation, and inadequate growth. We may be one cyclical downturn away from a need for revolution. Time will tell whether it comes.

Notes

The authors thank Vivek Arora, Ben Bernanke, Bill Cline, Giovanni dell'Ariccia, Stanley Fischer, Morris Goldstein, Greg Ip, Colombe Ladreit, Thomas Pellet,
Lukasz Rachel, Martin Sandbu, Andrei Shleifer, Robert Solow, Anna Stansbury,
Nicolas Veron, and David Vines for comments, and Andrew Sacher for research
assistance.

1. We also limit our focus to stabilization issues, referring the reader in particular
to the presentations at the conference on open economy issues (see chapter 19),
and on the relation between macroeconomic policy and inequality (see chapter
16).

2. This paragraph does not do justice to the factors behind the change in policy. Many forces were at work. The failure of the Keynesian approach was more
apparent than real, owing more to a failure to anticipate supply shocks, a failure
that could be and was repaired ex post. This apparent failure was used, however,
to promote an alternative approach to macroeconomics, more tightly based on
micro foundations, more confidence in market outcomes, and less confidence in
activist policy.

3. This reflects in part the very strong growth in 1940 and 1941, owing to the
mobilization for war.

4. Anybody who questions the ability of the economics profession to respond to
events should look, for example, at the long list and the content of NBER working
papers dealing with the financial system since 2008.

5. Another way of asking the question is to ask where debt should be relocated
during and after the crisis to allow the strongest recovery: with borrowers, with
lenders, or with the state? Work by Ganong and Noel (2017) suggests that providing relief on debt service might be more cost-efficient than writing off debt
altogether.

6. Since the crisis, long rates reflect in part the effects of QE, and thus the decrease in the term premium. The short real rate shows, however, the same general
evolution.

7. In this and the following sections, we also refer the reader to specific presentations at the conference on monetary, fiscal, and financial policies. See Ben Bernanke's contribution in chapter 1 on monetary policy.

8. Brunnermeier and Koby (2017) refer to the rate at which the effect on demand
changes sign as the "reversal rate."

9. To be more explicit, when money pays interest, monetary aggregates become
irrelevant to the determination of the price level, and so do velocity measures.

10. This raises another set of issues related to the optimal transition from the
current balance sheets to smaller ones and the joint use of the interest rate and
balance sheet adjustment along the way. In general, as a result of the larger uncertainty associated with the effects of balance sheet changes relative to policy
rate changes, so long as output is not at potential and inflation is below target,

the interest rate should remain the primary instrument of adjustment. We do not discuss the issue further here.

11. For a wider discussion of fiscal policy, we refer the reader to the work of Auerbach in chapter 6, this volume.

12. We assume, reasonably, that Ricardian equivalence does not hold, and that public debt is partly perceived as net wealth by consumers.

13. One caveat here: Rates of return to capital may reflect in part markups over marginal costs, and thus may include a rent component. Recent work by De Loecker and Eeckout (2017) suggests that markups have substantially increased over the past forty years, implying lower marginal products of capital for given rates of return to capital.

14. The tentative tone of this paragraph reflects the fact that the authors are currently doing research on this topic and do not yet have a set of established conclusions.

15. For a wider discussion of financial policies, we refer the reader to the analysis of Aikman and co-authors in chapter 11, this volume.

16. For an assessment of bank regulation, see Goldstein (2017).

17. The authors have different views on this question. Blanchard is inclined to see the need for evolution, Summers is more inclined to see the need for revolution.

References

Ball, Laurence, Douglas Elmendorf, and N. Gregory Mankiw. 1998. "The Deficit Gamble." *Journal of Money, Credit and Banking* 30 (4): 699–720.

Bernanke, Ben. 2002. "On Milton Friedman's Ninetieth Birthday." Remarks at the Conference to Honor Milton Friedman, University of Chicago, 2002.

Bernanke, Ben. 2005. "The Global Saving Glut and the U.S. Current Account Deficit." Sandridge Lecture, Virginia Association of Economics, Richmond. March.

Bernanke, Ben. 2015. *The Courage to Act: A Memoir of a Crisis and Its Aftermath*. New York: Norton.

Blanchard, Olivier. 2018. "Should We Reject the Natural Rate Hypothesis?" *Journal of Economic Perspectives* 32 (1): 97–120.

Blanchard, Olivier, Giovanni Dell'Ariccia, and Paolo Mauro. 2010. "Rethinking Macroeconomic Policy." IMF Staff Position Note 10/03. Washington, DC: International Monetary Fund.

Blanchard, Olivier, and Lawrence Summers. 1986. "Hysteresis and the European Unemployment Problem." *NBER Macroeconomics Annual 1986*, vol. 1, 15–90. Cambridge, MA: National Bureau of Economic Research.

Borio, Claudio, and Phillip Lowe. 2002. "Asset Prices, Financial and Monetary Stability: Exploring the Nexus." BIS Working Paper 114. Basel: Bank for International Settlements.

Brunnermeier, Markus, and Yann Koby. 2017. "The 'Reversal Interest Rate': An Effective Lower Bound on Monetary Policy." Working paper, Department of Economics, Princeton University, May.

Bulow, Jeremy, and Paul Klemperer. 2013. "Market-Based Bank Capital Regulation." Economics Working Paper 2013–W12, Nuffield College, Oxford University.

Caballero, Ricardo, Emmanuel Farhi, and Pierre Olivier Gourinchas. 2017. "The Safe Assets Shortage Conundrum." *Journal of Economic Perspectives* 31 (3): 29–46.

De Loecker, Jan, and Jan Eeckhout. 2017. "The Rise of Market Power and the Macroeconomic Implications." NBER Working Paper 23687. Cambridge, MA: National Bureau of Economic Research, August.

DeLong, J. Bradford, and Lawrence H. Summers. 2012. "Fiscal Policy in a Depressed Economy." *Brookings Papers on Economic Activity* 2.

Diamond, Douglas, and Philip Dybvig. 1983. "Bank Runs, Deposit Insurance, and Liquidity." *Journal of Political Economy* 91 (3): 401–419.

Fernald, John, Robert Hall, James Stock, and Mark Watson. 2017. "The Disappointing Recovery of Output after 2009." *Brookings Papers on Economic Activity*, BPEA Conference Draft, March 23–24.

Friedman, Milton. 1968. "The Role of Monetary Policy." *American Economic Review* 1968:1–17.

Ganong, Peter, and Pascal Noel. 2017. "The Effect of Debt on Default and Consumption: Evidence from Housing Policy in the Great Recession." Working paper, Harvard University, January.

Geanakoplos, John. 2010. "Solving the Present Crisis and Managing the Leverage Cycle." *Economic Policy Review* 16:101.

Geithner, Timothy. 2014. *Stress Test: Reflections on Financial Crises*. New York: Crown.

Geithner, Timothy. 2017. "Are We Safe Yet? How to Manage Financial Crises." *Foreign Affairs* (January/February).

Gertler, Mark, Nobuhiro Kiyotaki, and Andrea Prestipino. 2017. "A Macroeconomic Model with Financial Panics." NBER Working Paper 24126. Cambridge, MA: National Bureau of Economic Research.

Goetzmann, William. 2015. "Bubble Investing: Learning from History." NBER Working Paper 21693. Cambridge, MA: National Bureau of Economic Research.

Goldstein, Morris. 2017. *Banking's Final Exam: Stress Testing and Bank-Capital Reform*. Washington, DC: Peterson Institute for International Economics.

Greenwood, Robin, Samuel Hanson, Joshua Rudolph, and Lawrence Summers. 2014. "Government Debt Management at the Zero Lower Bound." Hutchins Center Working Paper 5. Washington, DC: Hutchins Center on Fiscal and Monetary Policy at the Brookings Institution.

Greenwood, Robin, Samuel Hanson, and Jeremy Stein. 2016. "The Federal Reserve's Balance Sheet as a Financial-Stability Tool." Paper presented at Federal Reserve Board of Kansas City Economic Policy Symposium.

Haldane, Andrew, and Vasileios Madouros. 2012. "The Dog and the Frisbee." In *Proceedings: Economic Policy Symposium, Jackson Hole*, 109–159. Kansas City: Federal Reserve Bank.

Hansen, Alvin. 1939. "Economic Progress and Declining Population Growth." *American Economic Review* 29 (1): 1–13.

Hubbard, Glenn. 1991. *Financial Markets and Financial Crises*. Chicago: NBER and University of Chicago Press.

Kashyap, Anil, Francois Gourio, and Jae Sim. 2016. "The Tradeoffs in Leaning against the Wind." NBER Working Paper 23658. Cambridge, MA: National Bureau of Economic Research.

Koo, Richard C. 2011. "The World in Balance Sheet Recession: Causes, Cure, and Politics. *Real-World Economics Review* 58.

McKay, Alisdair, and Ricardo Reis. 2016. "Optimal Automatic Stabilizers." CEPR Discussion Paper 11337. London: Centre for Economic Policy Research.

Mian, Atif, and Amir Sufi. 2014. *House of Debt*. Chicago: University of Chicago Press.

Minsky, Hyman. 1992. "The Financial Instability Hypothesis." Jerome Levy Economics Institute Working Paper 74. Annandale-on-Hudson, NY: Jerome Levy Economics Institute of Bard College.

Patinkin, Don. 1948. "Relative Prices, Say's Law, and the Demand for Money." *Econometrica* 16 (2): 135–154.

Paulson, M. Henry. 2010. *On the Brink: Inside the Race to Stop the Collapse of the Global Financial System*. New York: Business Plus.

Phelps, Edmund. 1968. "Phillips Curves, Expectations of Inflation and Optimal Unemployment over Time." *Economica*, n.s., 34 (135): 254–281.

Phelps, Edmund. 1972. *Inflation Policy and Unemployment Theory*. New York: Norton.

Rachel, Lukasz, and Thomas Smith. 2015. "Are Low Real Interest Rates Here to Stay?" Bank of England Staff Working Paper 571. London: Bank of England.

Rogoff, Ken. 2017. *The Curse of Cash: How Large-Denomination Bills Aid Crime and Tax Evasion and Constrain Monetary Policy*. Princeton, NJ: Princeton University Press.

Romer, Paul. 2016. "The Trouble with Macroeconomics." Commons Memorial Lecture of the Omicron Delta Epsilon Society. *American Economist*, forthcoming.

Sarin, Natasha, and Lawrence H. Summers. 2016. "The Bank Capital Volatility Puzzle." *Brookings Papers on Economic Activity*.

Summers, Lawrence H. 2018. "Secular Stagnation and Macroeconomic Policy." *IMF Economic Review* 66 (2) (June): 226–250.

Svensson, Lars. 2017. "Cost-Benefit Analysis of Leaning against the Wind." *Journal of Monetary Economics* 90 (October): 193–213.

Yellen, Janet. 2016. "The Federal Reserve's Monetary Policy Toolkit: Past, Present and Future." Paper presented at "Designing Resilient Monetary Policy Frameworks for the Future," a symposium sponsored by the Federal Reserve Bank of Kansas City, Jackson Hole, WY.

I

Monetary Policy

1

Monetary Policy in a New Era

Ben S. Bernanke

In 2017, the flagship research conferences of the European Central Bank and the Federal Reserve—held in Sintra, Portugal, and Jackson Hole, Wyoming, respectively—had something in common: Both had official themes unrelated to monetary policy, or even central banking. The ECB conference (theme: Investment and Growth in Advanced Economies) did include an opening speech by President Mario Draghi on monetary policy and the outlook before turning to such issues as the prospective effects of technological advances on employment. However, the Fed's meeting (theme: Fostering a Dynamic Global Economy), which included papers on topics ranging from fiscal policy to trade to income distribution, made almost no mention of monetary policy. Whether intended or not, the signal, I think, was clear. After ten years of concerted effort first to restore financial stability, then to achieve economic recovery through dramatic monetary interventions, central bankers in Europe and the United States believe they see the light at the end of the tunnel. They are looking forward to an era of relative financial and economic stability in which the pressing economic issues will relate to growth, globalization, and distribution— issues that are the responsibility of other policymakers and *not* primarily the province of central bankers.

Would that it were so simple! Although central bankers may hope that the next ten years will be less dramatic and demanding than the past ten, there will certainly be important new challenges to be met. In this chapter, I focus selectively on two such challenges: the implications of the secular decline in nominal interest rates for the tools and framework of monetary policy and the status of central banks within the government, in particular the questions of whether central banks should and will retain their current independence in making monetary policy. These two challenges are related in that the low-inflation, low-interest-rate environment in which we now live calls into question some of the traditional rationales for central bank independence.

The long-term decline in nominal interest rates is well known and has been extensively studied (Rachel and Smith 2015). The decline appears to be the product of many causes, including lower inflation rates, aging populations in advanced economies (Gagnon, Johannsen, and López-Salido 2016), slower productivity growth and "secular stagnation" (Summers 2015), global patterns of saving and investment (Bernanke 2005), and increased demand for "safe" assets (Del Negro et al. 2017; Caballero, Farhi, and Gourinchas 2017). Some of these factors may reverse in the medium term—for example, recent historically low rates of productivity growth could revert to more normal levels (Byrne and Sichel 2017), and there is some evidence that the global savings glut may be moderating (Chinn 2017)—which could lead to somewhat higher rates in the future. For now, though, the combination of low nominal rates and the difficulty of reducing short-term interest rates (much) below zero implies that monetary policymakers may have limited scope to address deep economic slowdowns through the traditional means of cutting short-term interest rates. Recent research by Kiley and Roberts (2017) illustrates the problem. Based on simulations of econometric models, including the Fed's main model for forecasting and policy analysis, these authors show that the use of conventional, precrisis policy approaches could lead to policy rates being constrained by the zero lower bound (ZLB) as much as one-third of the time, with adverse effects on the Fed's ability to hit its 2 percent inflation target or to keep output near potential.[1]

How should central banks respond? Beyond making a stronger case for proactive fiscal policies, there are two broad possibilities (interrelated and not mutually exclusive). First, rather than relying on the management of short-term interest rates alone, as assumed by Kiley and Roberts, monetary policymakers could make greater use of new tools developed in recent years. In the first part of the discussion in this chapter, I review some of these tools. I argue that both forward guidance and quantitative easing are potentially effective supplements to conventional rate cuts, and that concerns about adverse side effects (particularly in the case of quantitative easing) are overstated. These two tools can thus serve to ease the ZLB constraint in the future, as argued by Yellen (2016). Two other tools—negative interest rates and yield curve control—are less likely to play important roles, at least in the United States. European and Japanese policymakers have successfully employed negative rates, but overall they appear to have relatively modest benefits (because the option to hold cash limits how far negative rates can go), as well as some offsetting costs. Yield curve control, or the direct management of longer-term interest rates, has been adopted by the Bank of Japan and makes sense in the current Japanese context. However, as I will discuss, the depth and liquidity of the markets for U.S. government securities would make it difficult for the Fed to peg rates beyond a horizon of two years or so.

Although unconventional tools can increase the potency of monetary policy, the ZLB is still likely to be a binding constraint on the monetary response to a downturn that is more serious or that occurs when rates remain (as they are today) below neutral levels. A second broad response to the problem is to modify the overall policy framework, with the goal of enhancing monetary policymakers' ability to deal with such situations (Williams 2017). Focusing on the case of the Federal Reserve, in the second part of the discussion I briefly consider two proposed alternatives: (1) raising the Fed's inflation target from its current level of 2 percent and (2) introducing a price-level target. I argue that a higher inflation target has a number of important drawbacks. It would, obviously, lead to higher average inflation (possibly inconsistent with the Fed's mandate for price stability), and, more subtly, it implies a Fed reaction function that theoretical analyses suggest is quite far from the optimal response. A price-level target performs better on both counts, as (1) it is fully consistent with the goal of price stability and (2) it implies a "lower-for-longer" response to periods when rates are at their ZLB, which approximates what theory tells us is the optimal approach. However, a price-level target can be problematic in the face of supply shocks, and the switch to a price-level target from the current inflation-targeting approach would be a significant communications challenge. In the last part of the chapter, I propose and discuss a third possible alternative, a "temporary price-level target" that kicks in only during periods in which rates are constrained by the ZLB. I argue that the adoption of a temporary price-level target would be likely to improve economic performance, relative to that achieved in the current framework. Notably, it would do that while both maintaining price stability and requiring only a relatively modest shift in the Fed's framework and communication policies. However, this proposal is a tentative one at this stage, and more analysis would be needed before taking it further.

Beyond the problems arising from low nominal interest rates, monetary policymakers also face challenges to central bank independence (CBI). The challenge to CBI has been heightened by the political blowback that followed the financial crisis. But, as already noted, questions about CBI are also related to the change in the macroeconomic and interest rate environment, linking this issue to the themes explored in the first part of the chapter. In the United States, the doctrine of CBI emerged in part from the inflationary experience of the 1960s and 1970s, which was blamed in part on undue political influence on monetary policymakers. Following these events, both formal models and informal conventional wisdom held that, to avoid pressures to overheat the economy and allow higher inflation, the Fed needed greater independence from politics. However, the inflation-centric rationale for CBI looks a bit outdated in a world in which inflation and nominal interest rates are too low rather than too high and in which politicians have criticized central banks for being too expansionary rather than not expansionary enough. Indeed, the same logic that holds that CBI is necessary to avoid excess inflation can be turned on its head, to imply that CBI is a barrier to the fiscal-monetary coordination needed to combat deflation (Eggertsson 2013).

The last principal section of the chapter briefly takes up these issues. I argue that the case for CBI has always been broader than the anti-inflationist argument and that CBI should remain in place in the new economic environment. At the same time, I contend that the case for CBI is instrumental, that it depends on costs and benefits rather than on philosophical principles, so that the limits of independence appropriately depend on the sphere of activity under consideration and on economic conditions. The general principle of CBI thus does not preclude coordination of central bank policies with other parts of the government in certain situations.

Defeating the ZLB: Unconventional Policy Tools

Central bankers in 2008 faced extraordinarily difficult challenges, in particular the combination of a deep recession—which made a sharp easing of monetary conditions desirable—and the proximity of short-term interest rates to zero, which made easing difficult. In response, monetary policymakers employed a number of unconventional policy measures. Which ones will become part of the standard toolbox? In what order or combination might the various tools of monetary policy be used in the future? In this section, I comment on these issues. I take as given that management of a short-term policy rate (e.g., the federal funds rate in the United States) will remain the primary tool, so long as the ZLB is not binding. I discuss, sequentially, forward guidance, quantitative easing, negative rates, and yield curve control (the management of longer-term yields).

Forward Guidance

The nonstandard tool on which central bankers are most likely to rely in the next easing cycle is forward guidance, or communication about the expected or intended future path of the policy rate. The Fed used variants of forward guidance in the Greenspan era, for example, in references to keeping rates low for "a considerable period" (Federal Open Market Committee [FOMC] 2003). Even earlier, a number of central banks experimented with forward-looking policy commitments, a notable case being the Bank of Japan's zero interest rate policy (ZIRP), in which the BOJ said that it would not lift rates from zero until certain conditions had been met (Bank of Japan 1999). The prices of longer-term financial assets (including those most closely tied to economic activity, such as corporate bonds, mortgages, and stocks) depend not only on the current setting of the policy rate but on its entire expected future path. Consequently, central bank "open-mouth operations" that influence market expectations of future policies can affect financial conditions today, even if the short-term policy rate is close to its effective lower bound (Guthrie and Wright, 2000).

Forward guidance comes in a number of forms. A useful distinction is between *Delphic* and *Odyssean* forward guidance (Campbell et al. 2012). Delphic guidance is a simple statement of how monetary policymakers see the economy and interest rates as likely to evolve. Delphic guidance is advisory only and makes no promises about future policy. In contrast, Odyssean guidance—the phrase is motivated by Odysseus's decision to tie himself to the mast to be able to resist the calls of the Sirens—is intended to pre-commit the central bank to some (possibly contingent) set of future policies.

The goals of Delphic and Odyssean guidance are different. Delphic guidance—as seen, for example, in the Fed's famous "dot plot," which shows the interest rate forecasts of individual FOMC participants—is designed primarily to help the public and market participants understand the committee's outlook, reaction function, and policy plans. More informally, central bankers' public remarks about the likely course of the economy and policy are usually Delphic in intent. Increasingly, central banks are incorporating Delphic guidance into their communication strategy during normal times; this development primarily reflects trends to increased transparency by central banks rather than the emergence of the ZLB as an important policy constraint. By improving the clarity of central bank communications, Delphic guidance is intended to increase the predictability of monetary policy and make it more effective.

Odyssean guidance, in contrast, is most likely to be relevant when the policy rate is at or close to the ZLB, so that the scope for short-term rate cuts is limited. Typically, monetary policymakers use Odyssean guidance to communicate a promise to keep rates lower for longer than implied by their "normal" reaction function. If the promise is credible, then market participants should bid down longer-term yields and bid up asset prices today, effectively adding stimulus despite the ZLB constraint. The key word here is "commitment." If prior commitment were impossible, for the reasons explored in the time-consistency literature (Kydland and Prescott 1977), then Odyssean forward guidance could not materially change market expectations and would consequently be useless. In practice, central bank guidance does appear to have significant effects on asset prices (Campbell et al. 2012; Swanson 2017) and thus, presumably, on the economy. Central bankers' concerns for their own reputations and those of their institutions, as well as the tendency of market participants to look for focal points around which expectations can coalesce, appear in practice to provide monetary policymakers some ability to commit to future policy actions.

The Federal Open Market Committee (FOMC), the Fed's policymaking body, provided regular forward guidance during the recovery from the crisis. Some controversy has arisen about the FOMC's approach. Michael Woodford (2009) and others have argued that the FOMC inappropriately used Delphic rather than Odyssean formulations in its guidance, limiting its benefit. For example, at the same meeting at which the policy rate was cut effectively to zero, the December 2008 FOMC statement indicated, "The Committee anticipates that weak economic conditions are likely to warrant exceptionally low levels of the federal funds rate for some time" (FOMC 2008). By speaking of "anticipating" or "expecting" rates to remain low, rather than using the stronger language of commitment or intention, Woodford argues, the FOMC created less stimulus than it might have. Indeed, by signaling pessimism about the outlook, the FOMC's guidance (in Woodford's view) might have been counterproductive.

Woodford is right in principle, and all else equal, a policy committee whose intent is to provide Odyssean guidance should try to make its commitments as clear and as nearly ironclad as possible. A real-world complication is that policy committees are not typically unitary actors but may include participants of diverse views, trying to reach compromise in an uncertain environment. Some hedging or ambiguity in the committee's official statements may therefore be difficult to avoid. In practice, however, the FOMC's guidance after the crisis—as mediated by the public comments of policymakers—did seem to have Odyssean effects. Notably, the Fed's introduction of forward guidance was typically followed by changes in longer-term interest rates, exchange rates, and equity prices consistent with substantial increases in monetary accommodation (Femia, Friedman, and Sack 2013; Swanson 2017) and by reduced sensitivity of near-term rate expectations to economic news (Williams 2014). The increases in equity prices in particular suggested that markets were focused on the FOMC's signal of greater policy patience (the Odyssean aspect) rather than on an indication of greater pessimism. Moreover, professional forecasters reacted to FOMC guidance by repeatedly marking down the unemployment rate they expected to prevail at the time that the Committee began to lift the funds rate away from zero, implying a perceived shift in the Fed's expected reaction function (Bernanke 2012; Femia, Friedman, and Sack 2013). The apparent success of the FOMC's guidance, developed on the fly, is promising for the future use of verbal interventions. As both central bankers and market participants gain experience with forward guidance, the tool should become increasingly effective.

Another important distinction is between *qualitative* guidance ("considerable period") and *quantitative* guidance, for example, describing specific economic conditions that would lead to a change in policy. Over the years, Fed guidance has evolved from qualitative toward quantitative, reflecting the desire to enhance transparency as well as the imperative of adding substantial accommodation during the ZLB period. Economic logic suggests that quantitative guidance will be more effective because it is both more precise and more verifiable ex post (and thus easier to support by reputational concerns). However, again, a policy committee may not always be able to agree on quantitative guidance. It may also be the case that uncertainty about the economic situation favors the relative ambiguity of a qualitative formulation, at least initially. Experience suggest, though, that qualitative guidance, if maintained for a while, often morphs into quantitative guidance, as market participants, legislative committees, and other stakeholders press policymakers to clarify the meaning of key phrases.

Yet another dimension of forward guidance is *time dependency* versus *state dependency*. The FOMC used both types after the crisis, indicating first that it expected to hold rates low through a certain date, then tying rate increases to thresholds based on the prevailing unemployment and inflation rates.[2] In principle, policy settings should depend on the state of the economy, and so state-dependent guidance should be the default in the future (Feroli et al. 2016).[3] As pointed out by Williams (2016), however, date-based guidance may at times be more effective, perhaps because it is more definitive and more credible to market participants.

I've been discussing forward guidance about rates, but guidance can be provided about aspects of policy other than rates, notably, about plans for asset purchases. Such guidance is a natural extension of rate guidance and can be Delphic or Odyssean in intent. The main point here is that guidance about the components of policy needs to be carefully coordinated so that the planned sequencing of policy changes is clear. For example, the famous 2013 "taper tantrum" followed Fed guidance that it anticipated reducing the pace of its asset purchases, conditional on economic developments. However, the tantrum reflected not so much the expectation of reduced asset purchases per se but rather the inference in some quarters of the market (as could be seen in futures quotes) that increases in short-term rates would quickly follow the slowing of asset purchases. (See below for more on the "signaling" aspects of quantitative easing.) Fed policymakers had communicated their intention to keep rates low for a long time after the end of asset purchases, but evidently those promises had not sunk in, and coordinated reiterations of the point had to be made before market expectations readjusted and market conditions calmed.

A final observation on forward guidance: In this section I have been treating guidance, particularly of the Odyssean variety, as an ad hoc intervention, a supplement to management of the short-term rate. Alternatively, or in addition, the central bank could adopt an overarching framework that implies systematic Odyssean responses to ZLB episodes. I'll explore this possibility below in the section on policy frameworks.

Quantitative Easing

Probably the most controversial form of unconventional policy adopted in recent years was what the Federal Reserve called large-scale asset purchases (LSAPs) but most of the rest of the world persisted in calling "quantitative easing" or QE.[4] The Federal Reserve engaged in three rounds of QE, during which its balance sheet expanded from less than a trillion dollars to $4.5 trillion. The Bank of England, the European Central Bank, the Swedish Riksbank, and the Bank of Japan (which had pioneered asset purchases as a form of monetary policy well before the crisis) have also undertaken QE.

Quantitative easing involves central bank purchases of securities in the open market, financed by the creation of bank reserves held at the central bank. By law, the Fed was able to purchase only Treasury securities and mortgage-related securities issued by government-sponsored enterprises. Other central banks, in contrast, have been able to buy a range of private securities, including corporate bonds and equities. The limits on the Fed did not seem to prevent its version of QE from being effective, although it was perhaps fortunate that, following a crisis centered on housing finance, the law did permit Fed purchases of mortgage-related securities.

Research suggests that QE works through two principal channels: the signaling channel and the portfolio balance channel. The signaling channel arises to the extent that asset purchases serve to demonstrate the central bank's commitment to monetary easing, and in particular to keeping short-term rates lower for longer (Bauer and Rudebusch, 2013). As discussed above, the so-called taper tantrum in 2013 demonstrated the practical relevance of the signaling channel of QE. As noted, because of the importance of the signaling channel, it is essential that asset purchases and interest rate policy be closely integrated, and that in particular the central bank be clear about its planned sequencing of the introduction and withdrawal of its various tools.

The portfolio balance channel depends on the premise that securities are imperfect substitutes in investors' portfolios, reflecting differences in liquidity, transactions costs, information, regulatory restrictions, and the like. Imperfect substitutability implies that changes in the net supply of a security affect asset prices and yields, as investors must be induced to rebalance their portfolios (Bonis, Ihrig, and Wei 2017). In principle, the two channels of QE can be distinguished by the fact that the signaling channel operates by affecting expectations of future policy rates while the portfolio balance channel works by changing term premiums.

There have been many studies of the effectiveness of QE, mostly through event studies of the impact of QE announcements on interest rates and asset prices; for surveys, see, for example, Gagnon (2016), Bhattarai and Neely (2016), and Williams (2014). There is not a large sample of QE programs to study, and econometric identification of the unexpected (and thus not fully discounted) components of QE announcements is difficult. Consequently, disagreements remain among researchers about the magnitude and persistence of QE effects and about the relative importance of the two primary channels of effect. Nevertheless, the strong view that QE is ineffective has been pretty decisively rejected. There appears instead to be a broad consensus that QE has proven a useful tool, with demonstrable effects on financial conditions.[5] QE has been found to have significant effects on both rate expectations and term premiums, suggesting that both the signaling and portfolio balance channels are operative (Bauer and Rudebusch 2013; Huther, Ihrig, and Klee 2017). And, although showing direct links to macroeconomic outcomes is not straightforward, the experiences of the U.S., U.K., Japan, and Europe all suggest that the use of large-scale QE has been followed, over the subsequent couple of years, by strengthening aggregate demand and improved economic performance (Engen, Laubach, and Reifschneider 2015).[6]

Controversies about QE have focused less on whether the medicine works and more on the possible side effects. Many dark warnings accompanied the introduction of QE programs by major central banks after the financial crisis. In a memorable example, the Republican leadership of the U.S. Congress wrote to the Fed in November 2010 to express concerns about further asset purchases. Their letter argued that "such a measure introduces significant uncertainty regarding the future strength of the dollar and could result both in hard-to-control long-term inflation and potentially generate artificial [sic] asset bubbles that could cause further economic disruptions" (Herszenhorn 2010). The congressional leaders also were worried about foreign criticism of the Fed's actions, noting that "any action … that impairs U.S. trade relations at a time when we should be fighting global trade protection measures will only further harm the global economy and could delay recovery in the United States." As the legislators noted, there was indeed foreign criticism of Fed plans for more QE, including from Brazilian finance minister Guido Mantega, who argued that the Fed's actions presaged a "currency war," and German finance minister Wolfgang Schäuble, who reportedly called the policy "clueless" (Atkins 2010; Garnham and Wheatley 2010). A subsequent letter from conservative economists and market participants echoed the themes of the congressional letter, warning against "currency debasement and inflation" and adding that QE could "distort financial markets and greatly complicate future Fed efforts to normalize monetary policy" (*Wall Street Journal* 2010). Less well remembered is that in September 2011 the Republican Congressional leadership wrote a similar, follow-up letter, adding the concern that QE could "promote borrowing by overleveraged consumers" (*Wall Street Journal* 2011). Of course, these themes were staples of *Wall Street Journal* and *Financial Times* op-eds throughout the period.[7]

I think it's fair to say that these warnings, and many more like them, have not proved prescient. Certainly, there has been no massive upsurge in inflation—quite the opposite, of course—or a collapse in the dollar, as predicted by proponents of crude monetarism (of a type, certainly, that Milton Friedman would never have endorsed). Without a sustained decline in the dollar and with a stronger U.S. economy providing increased demand for imports, Mantega's concern about a currency war also proved baseless. Household leverage has not risen as the second congressional letter predicted; indeed, household debt and interest burdens have fallen significantly since the crisis.

Concerns about asset bubbles have been especially persistent (although these would appear to relate more to accommodative monetary policies in general than to QE in particular). To be clear, there is no doubt that monetary policy affects the prices of stocks and other assets; indeed, those effects are an important vehicle of monetary transmission. The intended effects of monetary easing on asset prices work through fundamentals, including the reduced discounting of future returns implied by lower interest rates, expectations of stronger economic performance, and moderate increases in risk-bearing capacity. Asset price increases due to those fundamental causes are desirable and pose no significant risks to economic or financial stability. Concern about bubbles is therefore properly focused on asset price increases that significantly exceed what can be justified by fundamentals. Claims that QE has generated asset bubbles in this relevant sense are difficult or impossible to disprove; and, of course, at some point there will inevitably be a downward correction in asset prices, as has happened periodically in the past. However, it's been seven years since the first congressional letter, and the Fed stopped purchasing securities three years ago (although other central banks have continued it), so if QE has generated bubble dynamics, we can at least conclude that some pretty long lags are involved.

What about other critiques? The claim that QE "distorts" financial markets, raised in the letter from economists and market participants, is heard fairly often. It's not clear exactly what that means. The goal of QE, and of monetary policy generally, is to set financial conditions consistent with full employment and stable prices, which can be thought of as trying to undo the economic distortions arising from price and wage stickiness, monopolistic competition, credit market frictions, and the like. In this respect, appropriate monetary policy is "un-distorting"; in particular, allocations under active monetary policy should be closer rather than further from the competitive, free-market, flexible-price ideal.

A possible rationalization of the "distortion" claim is that QE works, at least in part, by affecting term premiums (and through them, the whole gamut of asset prices). From a market participant's point of view, when QE is active it feels as if government (central bank) decisions, rather than private sector fundamentals, are setting asset prices. Moreover, in such situations it may appear that the highest returns go to the best Fed-watchers rather than to those whose expertise is in evaluating economic fundamentals. Some frustration with this state of affairs on the part of professional investors is understandable. Note, though, that QE affects term premiums largely by affecting the net maturity distribution of government debt held by the private sector. In this respect, a QE program—which amounts to a replacement of longer-term government obligations in private hands with shorter-term obligations (bank reserves, in the case of QE)—is not fundamentally different from a change in the maturity structure of debt issued by the Treasury. That government decisions about the maturity structure of its debt would affect term premiums seems natural, and, since the government has to choose *some* maturity distribution, it's not clear what it would mean for government policy to be "neutral" with respect to the term premium (Greenwood et al. 2014). In short, there is no such thing as an "undistorted" value of the term premium, not so long as the mix of outstanding government liabilities is relevant to asset pricing.

A possible response to this point is that at least Treasury maturity decisions are largely nonresponsive to short-term economic conditions, with issuance policies generally being smooth and set well in advance. In contrast, Fed QE programs are typically large in size and less predictable, responding to economic developments and (importantly) to how monetary policymakers choose to interpret those developments. To the extent that Fed decisions are hard to forecast, even conditional on the outlook, they add noise to asset prices. But of course, that is true for any form of monetary policy. I think it comes down to whether Fed policy, inclusive of policy errors and misjudgments, is economically stabilizing on net, or not. If it is stabilizing, then though the unpredictable components of Fed policy and communication may be a nuisance for market participants, overall monetary policy (including QE) reduces rather than increases the overall level of distortions in the economy.[8]

Another common critique of QE is that it purportedly promotes increased inequality, primarily because of its effects on the prices of stocks and other assets. This claim is questionable on its face (Bernanke 2015; Bivens 2015). Empirically, it is far from obvious that QE (or easy money generally) worsens inequality in any meaningful way, once all the diverse effects of policy are taken into account. It is of course true that, all else equal, higher stock prices mean greater inequality of wealth—although the effect on *income* inequality is mitigated by the fact that easy money also lowers the rate of return on assets, so that income from capital rises by less than the rise in asset values.[9] However, QE also yields gains in income and wealth that are more broadly based, including (1) positive effects on house prices, the principal asset of the middle class; (2) the benefits of lower interest rates and higher prices for debtors, including homeowners able to refinance to lower payments; (3) the savings for taxpayers of lower government borrowing costs and (possibly) increased seigniorage; and (4) most important, the effects of monetary accommodation on jobs, wages, and incomes (Bivens 2015; Engen, Laubach, and Reifschneider 2015). It's revealing that in public debates, advocates for workers—like the group Fed Up, which met with FOMC members at Jackson Hole in 2016—have tended to favor the continuation of easy money, while the typical op-ed about the adverse effects of easy money on the distribution of income and wealth is written by a hedge fund manager, banker, or right-wing politician—people who have otherwise not traditionally exhibited much concern about inequality (Fleming 2016). That political alignment—workers' groups in support of easy money, financiers in favor of higher interest rates—is of course the historical pattern in the United States, going back to William Jennings Bryan and beyond.

In any case, whatever effects monetary policy has on inequality are likely to be transient, in contrast to the secular forces of technology and globalization that have contributed to the multidecade rise in inequality in the United States and some other advanced economies. If the monetary effects on inequality are modest (indeed, of indeterminate sign) and mostly temporary, as seems most likely, then it makes sense for monetary policymakers to ignore distributional effects and to focus on their legal mandate to promote price stability and full employment, leaving distributional concerns to be addressed by other policies, including fiscal policy. If, on the other hand, the effects of monetary policy on inequality are *not* transient, then presumably the reason is what economists have called hysteresis, the idea that a "hot" economy promotes higher long-term growth by promoting labor force participation, higher skills, and higher wages. However, the presence of significant hysteresis effects would likely imply that easy money during periods of economic weakness *reduces* inequality, rather than the reverse.

A final criticism of QE is that it exposes the central bank to capital losses, in the event that longer-term interest rates rise unexpectedly quickly. Although central banks don't have to mark to market and they can operate perfectly well with negative capital, losses on their asset holdings would ultimately be reflected in reduced seigniorage payments to the Treasury. Central banks naturally see this outcome as a political risk to their independence and institutional reputations, which, all else equal, may make them more hesitant to use QE. However, political risk to the central bank is not equivalent to a loss in social welfare. From the perspective of society as a whole, the fiscal risks of QE have to be balanced against the substantial benefits of a tool that gives monetary policymakers additional scope to respond to a serious economic downturn or to unwanted disinflation.

Moreover, the fiscal risks of QE are not one-sided. QE programs can be quite profitable for the central bank and the Treasury because on average, the yields on the longer-term assets the central bank acquires are higher than those on its short-term liabilities, and because declining yields create capital gains on the central bank's existing bond holdings. Since 2009, the Federal Reserve has remitted more than $650 billion in profits to the U.S. Treasury (Federal Reserve Board of Governors 2017), a much higher rate of remittances than usual before the crisis. On the other hand, if fiscal losses do occur as the result of a QE program, it will likely be because the economy recovered more quickly and strongly than expected, resulting in higher interest rates; since losses are most likely to occur at times when the economy is unexpectedly strong, they are hedged, from a social perspective. Finally, and importantly, the beneficial fiscal effects of an effective QE program go well beyond seigniorage, as the government's budget also benefits from low borrowing rates, avoidance of deflation or very low inflation, and the higher revenues that result from increased economic activity.

All that said, the fiscal argument seems to me to be more balanced than some of the other criticisms of QE. There are difficult governance issues and competing values in play here, and people could reasonably come to different conclusions. One approach, similar to that taken by the United Kingdom, is for the central bank to consult with the Treasury on QE plans. I don't advocate that approach because of the implied reduction in central bank independence, but I appreciate that it may reduce the political risks associated with the use of QE.

Negative Interest Rates and Yield Curve Control
I will comment briefly on two monetary tools in use outside the United States but that I don't expect to be used by the Fed in the foreseeable

future: negative (nominal) interest rates and pegging longer-term interest rates (so-called yield curve control).

Negative interest rates have been recently employed in Japan and a number of European countries (Bernanke 2016c). To enforce negative rates, central banks generally charge a fee on the reserve holdings of commercial banks. Arbitrage ensures that the negative return to reserves translates into negative returns to other short-term liquid assets. Negative short rates need not imply negative rates on longer-term assets, particularly those that are less liquid or involve credit risk. Rather, negative short-term rates give the central bank a new tool for bringing down the longer-term rates, like mortgage rates, that matter most for economic activity. The evidence suggests that negative rates have helped to ease overall financial conditions in the countries in which they have been used, thereby promoting economic recovery (Dell'Ariccia, Haksar, and Mancini-Griffoli 2017).

For economists, who are used to thinking about negative real interest rates, moderately negative nominal rates are not a big deal. There is very little practical difference between a 0.1 percent return and a return of negative 0.1 percent, for example. However, many noneconomists find the idea of negative nominal rates disorienting, a reaction that has contributed to political resistance and on the margin has probably made central bankers more hesitant to use this tool. Putting aside the politics, and excluding limitations on the use of currency (Rogoff 2016) as beyond the scope of this chapter, negative interest rates appear to provide relatively modest benefits and have modest costs. So while the tool may well be appropriate and useful in some contexts, it does not merit the overheated public attention it has received.

Under current institutional arrangements, the potential benefit of negative rates are relatively modest because attempts to push rates too far below zero will induce substitution into cash. The most negative rate yet imposed is minus 75 basis points, by Denmark (Danmarks Nationalbank 2015). To date, negative rates have so far not triggered much movement into cash, as best as we can tell, but it is likely that more such adjustment would occur if rates were to go much further below zero, or if negative-rate policies were perceived to be recurring or persistent.

The costs of negative rates mostly arise from their interaction with certain institutional features of financial markets. For example, in the United

States, money market mutual funds (MMMFs) generally guarantee a nominal return of no less than zero, and failure to meet that standard (called "breaking the buck") led to a run on MMMFs in 2008, after the Lehman Brothers failure. Concerns about possible destabilization of MMMFs were an important reason that the Fed did not use negative rates during the postcrisis period (Burke et al. 2010). Recent reforms have reduced this risk, by forcing many money market funds that invest in private assets to shift to a system of floating net asset values (which allows for a negative nominal return) and by inducing a shift toward lower-risk government funds (U.S. Securities and Exchange Commission 2014; Chen et al. 2017).

A more frequently heard concern is that negative rates could decapitalize the banking system because banks are supposedly unable to pass negative rates on to depositors. There is little evidence from the European or Japanese experiences that modestly negative rates have hurt bank profits or bank lending. Retail deposits are only a portion of bank funding; presumably, banks can pass on negative yields to wholesale funders or institutional depositors. Moreover, central banks can implement negative rates in ways that mitigate the effects on bank profits; for example, the Bank of Japan exempts a significant portion of bank reserves from its fees, which are applied only on the margin. Overall, there are few costs of negative rates that could not be managed over time through institutional reform or alternative approaches to enforcing negative rates by central banks. Whether undertaking such changes is worthwhile, insofar as political resistance to negative rates appears disproportionate to their generally modest benefits, is an open question. At the Fed, there was little support for negative rates during the postcrisis period, a situation that does not appear to have changed.[10]

Yield curve control, recently introduced by the Bank of Japan, is the targeting of yields on longer-term bonds. Yield curve control is "dual" to conventional QE: instead of setting targets for securities purchases and letting the market determine yields, as in ordinary QE, under yield curve control the central bank targets the yield on one or more securities and adjusts its purchases as necessary to hit the targets (Bernanke 2002; Chaurushiya and Kuttner 2003; Bernanke 2016d).

Yield curve control has some potential advantages: because yields directly affect borrowing and investment decisions, a rate-targeting strategy affords greater precision in estimating the amount of financial accommodation delivered than does ordinary QE. A credible yield target may also be enforceable with reduced quantities of purchases by the central bank because deviations from the target will be arbitraged away by market participants. Yield curve control can also be an efficient strategy when the securities available for purchase are potentially limited in quantity and supplied with less-than-perfect elasticity, as is the case with the Japanese government bonds that make up the bulk of the BOJ's purchase program. In particular, the adoption of yield curve control by the BOJ has allowed the Japanese authorities to maintain substantial stimulus, even as the supply of bonds available for purchase by the Bank of Japan has shrunk (Bernanke 2016a).

On the other hand, in jurisdictions with deep and liquid securities markets, like those for U.S. government bonds, a rate-targeting central bank might have to buy up most of the market if the target it set were not fully credible. A rate target for a security whose maturity exceeded the expected duration of the targeting program would be particularly hard to enforce, as incoming news would affect investors' views of the time of exit from the targeting regime and of the post-regime yield. For that reason, Fed staff considering rate-targeting strategies concluded that only relatively short-term yields—perhaps up to a couple of years—could be fixed, potentially limiting the utility of the program (Bowman, Erceg, and Leahy 2010; Bernanke 2016d). An intriguing possibility, however, is that a relatively short-horizon peg could be used to complement forward guidance about future short rates.[11]

Policy Sequencing

What policy tools will be used, and in what sequence, when the next recession hits? Yellen (2016) has described the Fed's prospective toolbox. In the face of an economic slowdown, the FOMC would respond first with conventional rate cuts. The current thinking is that, when the ZLB looms, rate cuts should be aggressive (no "saving ammunition"); see Reifschneider and Williams (2000). However, in practice, uncertainty about the state of the economy might lead the Fed to put off decisive action until the situation became clearer.

Forward guidance, of the Odyssean variety, would come next (substantial Delphic guidance is already in place). Relative to earlier experience,

I would expect a much earlier adoption of state-contingent, quantitative commitments to hold rates low.

What about QE? Fed policymakers have been clear that QE is now part of the toolkit and that it would be used if necessary (U.S. Congressional House Committee on Financial Services and Senate Committee on Banking, Housing, and Urban Affairs 2017; FOMC 2017). I am sure that's true, but I would not be surprised if there were a period of hesitation before the FOMC started up new rounds of asset purchases. The effects of QE on financial markets and the economy are less well understood and less precisely estimated than those of more conventional policies. QE's effects likely vary over time, depending, for example, on whether financial markets are stressed or operating normally. Moreover, because some significant part of its power comes through signaling effects, QE is also a difficult tool to use in a continuous, gradated manner. I expect that QE will be used only occasionally in the future, during more severe downturns, and then typically in large discrete chunks.

Speaking positively rather than normatively, I don't see much likelihood that negative rates or yield curve control will be employed in the United States in the foreseeable future, unless circumstances become dire. With current institutional arrangements, negative rates have only modest benefits and may create problems for some financial institutions. Targeting longer-term interest rates, at least at maturities out beyond a couple of years, could be a hazardous undertaking owing to the deep and liquid markets for U.S. government obligations. However, there is the possibility that such targeting could be used to reinforce forward guidance.

Defeating the ZLB: The Policy Framework

As discussed in the previous section, the Fed and other central banks retain a number of effective monetary tools, even if the current low level of neutral rates persists. We should also not ignore the countercyclical potential of fiscal policy. Political and ideological constraints, as well as constraints on fiscal space in some jurisdictions, limit the flexibility and timeliness of fiscal tools; that's why monetary policy has normally been the first line of defense against short-term economic instability. But recent experience suggests that fiscal policy can provide some backstop in the most severe slowdowns, as in the United States in 2008 and 2009 (Matthews 2011; Auerbach and Gorodnichenko 2017).

All that said, I am less sanguine than Yellen (2016) that the current monetary toolbox would prove sufficient to address a sharp downturn. In particular, there is no guarantee that the next recessionary shock will occur only when policy rates are at or above neutral levels. If the Fed had to react to a new slowdown today, it would have only 100 basis points or so of room to cut short rates, and other major central banks, including the European Central Bank and the Bank of Japan, would have virtually no room to cut, even at the long end of the curve. I am consequently sympathetic to the view of Williams (2017) and others that we should be thinking now about what can be done to enhance the potency of monetary policy. In this section I discuss some recent proposals to improve the effectiveness of monetary policy by changing the policy target or framework. I'll focus here on two leading options: raising the inflation target and switching to a price-level target.[12] After discussing some pros and cons of these two leading options, I'll suggest a compromise approach.

As noted, one proposal for modifying the policy framework is to keep the current inflation targeting framework of the Fed and other major central banks but raise the level of the target—from 2 percent or so to 3 or even 4 percent. Presumably, after a period of transition, an increase in the inflation target would result in a comparable increase in nominal interest rates, giving more room for cuts.[13] Most recently, a group of economists signed a letter to the Fed arguing for a higher inflation target, and the aforementioned Fed Up group held a seminar at this year's Jackson Hole conference endorsing the idea (Baker et al. 2017; Leubsdorf 2017).

As a measure to increase the potency of monetary policy, raising the inflation target has some advantages: it's a straightforward step, one that should be easy to communicate and explain, and it would allow the Fed and other major central banks to stay within their established policy frameworks. These are important benefits. At the same time, I see some problems with this proposal.

First, proponents may be underestimating the costs, uncertainties, and delays associated with the transition to a higher target. We have seen, most recently in Japan, that managing inflation expectations through central bank announcements can be tricky. Insofar as inflation expectations in advanced economies seem well anchored at 2 percent or below, trying to raise expectations and to re-anchor them at a higher level could well be a protracted and uncertain process, with side effects including financial volatility and increases in risk premiums. (Inflation uncertainty would be particularly challenging for bond markets, where investors would be simultaneously skeptical of the central bank's statements and fearful of capital losses.) If inflation expectations were to remain sticky near current levels, then the Fed would have to demonstrate its commitment to the higher target by intentionally overheating the economy for an extended period. It's possible that sustained overheating could have beneficial effects—through hysteresis channels, for example—but it might also prove to be destabilizing and difficult to manage, particularly if inflation expectations became volatile.

Second, to be fully effective in raising longer-term nominal yields, the increase in the inflation target must be perceived as permanent, or at least a very long-term commitment. However, that perception would be undermined by the apparent willingness of the Fed to raise its target for what might appear to be tactical reasons. Looking forward, it is likely that the determinants of the "optimal" inflation target—such as the prevailing equilibrium real interest rate, the costs of inflation, and aspects of the monetary transmission mechanism—will change over time. If the Fed raised its inflation target today based primarily on the low level of real interest rates, would it change the target again in response to future changes in fundamentals? That would be important to clarify when making the first change to the target, but it is not an easy matter on which to commit, since the membership of the policy committee and the state of knowledge about monetary policy and the economy both change over time.

Third, although quantifying the economic costs of inflation has proved difficult, we know that inflation is very unpopular with the public. This unpopularity may be due to reasons that economists find unpersuasive— various forms of money illusion, for example. Or perhaps the public perceives costs of inflation—the greater difficulty of planning and calculation when inflation is high, for example—that economic models don't well capture. In any case, it's not a coincidence that the promotion of "price stability" is a key part of the mandate of the Fed and most other central banks. Certainly, a substantial increase in targeted inflation would invite a backlash, perhaps even a legal challenge. Proponents have suggested convening a national commission to approve the increase in the inflation target, to increase its legitimacy and durability. Those proponents should be careful what they wish for. In the United States, rather than validating a higher inflation target to afford scope for discretionary monetary policy, I suspect that the political process would be more likely instead to reaffirm the centrality of "price stability" and possibly even eliminate the "maximum employment" component of the Fed's dual mandate. Even if the political process supported the higher target in the first instance, market participants would put some weight on a future reversal, undermining the target's credibility.

Fourth, and importantly, we know from a great deal of insightful theoretical work that an increase in the inflation target is an inferior response to the problems created by the ZLB (Krugman 1998; Eggertsson and Woodford 2003; Werning 2011). Rather, the theoretically preferred response is for the central bank to promise to follow a "makeup" policy (or, in Woodford's term, for policy to be "history-dependent"). Specifically, suppose the ZLB binds for a period, keeping monetary policy tighter than it otherwise would have been. Then (speaking very loosely) the optimal policy involves the central bank promising to keep rates lower for longer than it otherwise would have, where the length of the "makeup" period increases with the severity of the episode and the cumulative shortfall in monetary ease. If the public understands and believes this promise, then the expectation of easier policy and more rapid growth in the future should act to mitigate declines in output and inflation during the period in which the ZLB is binding. Note, by the way, the close analogy to Odyssean forward guidance, discussed earlier. The difference is that, rather than being implemented by ad hoc forward guidance, the optimal policy is conceptualized as part of the central bank's permanent policy framework, about which the public is supposed to learn over time.

In comparison to this theoretically optimal policy, an increase in the inflation target is inefficient in at least two respects. First, as Woodford (2009) has pointed out, it forces society to bear the costs of higher inflation at all times, whereas under the optimal policy, inflation should rise only temporarily, following ZLB episodes. Second, a one-time increase in the inflation target does not optimally calibrate the vigor of the policy response to a given ZLB episode to the duration or severity of the episode.

A somewhat better option than raising the inflation target is to adopt a price-level target, an approach advocated by a number of economists and policymakers (Svensson 1999; Gaspar, Smets, and Vestin 2007; Williams 2017). Effectively, a price-level targeting central bank tries to keep the long-run average inflation rate close to a targeted value, say, 2 percent. The principal difference between price-level targeting and conventional inflation targeting is the treatment of "bygones." An inflation-targeting central bank aims to keep inflation stationary around its target, an approach that allows policymakers to "look through" a temporary change in the inflation rate, so long as inflation returns to target after a time. A price-level targeter, by contrast, commits to reversing temporary deviations of inflation from target, for example, by following a temporary surge in inflation with a corresponding period of inflation below target. Of note, both inflation targeters and price-level targeters can be "flexible." That is, they can take output and employment considerations into account, in that the speed at which they return to target can depend (and in formal models, usually optimally depends) on the state of the real economy.[14] In this section, I consider only "flexible" variants of policy rules.

Switching to a price-level target has at least two principal advantages over raising the inflation target. The first is that price-level targeting is consistent with low average inflation (say, 2 percent) over time and thus with the price stability mandate. Indeed, price-level targeting arguably promotes price stability better than does inflation targeting because its commitment to stabilizing long-run average inflation should lead to considerably less uncertainty about the level of prices far in the future. The second advantage is that price-level targeting has the desirable "makeup" feature of the theoretically optimal monetary policy. In particular, under price-level targeting, periods of below-target inflation (as is likely to happen when interest rates are stuck at their ZLB) are followed by periods in which the central bank shoots for inflation above target, leading to "lower-for-longer" rate setting.

Adopting a price-level target seems preferable to raising the inflation target, but this strategy too is not without its drawbacks. It would amount to a significant change in the central bank's policy framework and reaction function, and it is hard to judge how difficult it would be to get the public and markets to understand and accept the new approach. In particular, switching from the inflation concept to the price-level concept might require considerable education and explanation by policymakers. How quickly, for example, would markets and the public adjust to the implication of price-level targeting that a burst of inflation today should lead them rationally to expect *lower* than normal inflation in the future?

Another possible concern about price-level targeting is that the "bygones are not bygones" aspect of this approach is a two-edged sword. Under price-level targeting, the central bank cannot "look through" supply shocks that temporarily drive up inflation but must commit to tightening policy to reverse the effects of the shock on the price level. This reversal could be gradual and responsive to real-side conditions, but it would nevertheless imply a possibly painful tightening even as the supply shock depresses employment and output. Although a once-and-for-all commitment to such an approach is theoretically optimal (under full credibility), in practice, the commitment to reverse the effect of supply shocks by engineering a period of below-target inflation might not be credible; if it is not, efforts to offset positive inflation shocks would likely be costly.

Is there a compromise approach? One possibility, which I will describe briefly here, is to apply a price-level target and the associated "makeup" principle only to periods around ZLB episodes, retaining the inflation-targeting framework and the current 2 percent target at other times. (Evans [2010] was an early proponent of a similar approach.) As I will develop, the central bank can explain this combined policy in familiar inflation-targeting terms, which I take to be an advantage.

So, to be concrete, at some moment when the economy is away from the ZLB, suppose the Fed were to make an announcement something like the following:

1. The FOMC has determined that it will retain its inflation-targeting framework, with a symmetric inflation target of 2 percent. The FOMC will continue to pursue its balanced approach to price stability and maximum employment, meaning, in particular, that the speed at which the FOMC aims to return inflation to target will depend on the state of the labor market and the outlook for the real economy.

2. However, the FOMC recognizes that, at times, the ZLB on the federal funds rate may prevent it from reaching its inflation and employment goals, even with the use of unconventional monetary tools. The committee agrees that, in future situations in which the funds rate is at or

near zero, a *necessary* condition for raising the funds rate will be that average inflation *since the date at which the funds rate first hit zero* be at least 2 percent. Beyond this necessary condition, in deciding whether to raise the funds rate from zero, the committee will also consider the outlook for the labor market and whether the return of inflation to target appears sustainable.

The figures below illustrate the necessary condition above as it might have been applied to the recent ZLB episode. To be clear, *nothing in this illustration should be taken as a commentary on current Fed policy.* I am considering instead a counterfactual world in which the announcement above had been made, and internalized by markets, prior to 2008. In that counterfactual world, it would be important for the Fed to follow through on that commitment. However, in reality, no such commitment was made, of course, and actual policy today is not constrained by earlier promises.

Figure 1.1 shows the behavior of (core PCE) inflation since 2008 Q4, the quarter in which the federal funds rate first reached zero, or effectively zero.[15] As the figure shows, since 2008, inflation has been below the 2 percent target most of the time. Figure 1.2 shows the cumulative, annualized inflation rate—roughly, the average inflation rate—from 2008 Q4 to the present. Consistent with figure 1.1, the average inflation rate since 2008 Q4 is also below 2 percent, by about half a percent. As average inflation *since the beginning of the ZLB period* is below the 2 percent target, by the criterion in paragraph 2 above, the FOMC would not yet have lifted the federal funds rate from zero. Again, I am using the recent episode to illustrate my suggested rule, not to make a recommendation about what the FOMC should do now. Note, though, that if this policy rule had been in place prior to 2008, and if it had been understood and anticipated by markets, then longer-term yields would likely have been lower and the effective degree of policy accommodation during the past decade might have been significantly greater. In that counterfactual world, inflation might have been higher and the average inflation criterion might have already been met.

The average inflation criterion, in paragraph 2 above, is couched in the language of inflation targeting, which I take to be an advantage from a communications perspective. My readers will recognize, though, that the

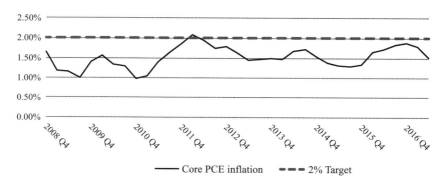

Figure 1.1

Inflation since 2008 Q4 (Annual Rates).
Note: Inflation is the year-over-year percent change.
Source: Federal Reserve Economic Data database.

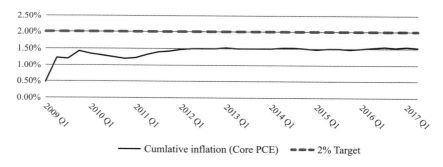

Figure 1.2

Cumulative Inflation (Annualized) since 2008 Q4.
Note: Figure shows the cumulative annualized inflation rate of the core PCE price index since 2008 Q4.
Sources: Federal Reserve Economic Data database; author's calculations.

average inflation criterion is equivalent to a *temporary price-level target,*
which applies only during the ZLB episode. Expressing this in terms of
the price level rather than inflation, figure 1.3 shows recent values of
the (core PCE) price level, relative to a 2 percent trend starting in 2008
Q4. (Again, 2008 Q4 is the base quarter because that's when the federal
funds rate first reached the ZLB.) The necessary condition, that average
inflation over the ZLB period be at least 2 percent, is equivalent to the
price level (solid line) returning to its trend (dashed line). As figure 1.3

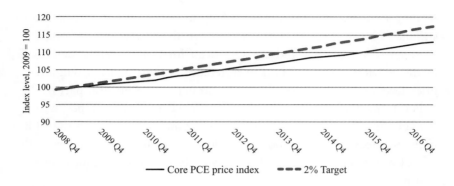

Figure 1.3

Price Level since 2008 Q4 vs. 2 percent Target.
Note: Figure shows the core PCE price level against the target core PCE price level, assumed to rise at a 2 percent annual rate since 2008 Q4. Equivalently, the target price level is the level implied by a 2 percent cumulative (annualized) inflation target during the ZLB period. Data are seasonally adjusted.
Source: Federal Reserve Economic Data database.

suggests, a period of inflation exceeding 2 percent would be necessary to satisfy that criterion.

I should emphasize that, in my proposal and as stated in paragraph 2, meeting the average inflation criterion is a necessary but not a sufficient condition to raise rates from the ZLB. There are at least two additional considerations. First, monetary policymakers would want to be sure that the average inflation condition is being met on a sustainable basis and not as the result of a transitory shock or measurement error. Second, consistent with the concept of "flexible" targeting, policymakers would also want to factor in real economic conditions in deciding whether it was time to raise rates. Specifically, even if the average inflation criterion is met, the FOMC might delay liftoff until labor market conditions are, or are expected soon to be, healthy. For example, the FOMC might stipulate the additional necessary condition that the unemployment rate be at or below estimates of the natural or sustainable rate.

What I have called a temporary price-level target shares several advantages with an ordinary, permanent price-level targeting regime. As already noted, it has the critical makeup feature that it delays the exit from the ZLB relative to the prescriptions of conventional policy rules, like the Taylor (1993) rule. Moreover, the makeup period will generally be longer following more severe ZLB episodes, thereby delivering more stimulus when it is most needed. It's also worth reiterating the distinction between this approach and the Odyssean forward guidance described in the previous section. The key difference is that, under a temporary price-level target, the lower-for-longer strategy is an integral part of the policy framework and thus can be explained (and, one hopes, antici-pated by market participants) *in advance* of an encounter with the ZLB. If this strategy is understood, it should serve to make encounters with the ZLB not only shorter and less severe but also less frequent in the first place.

The temporary price-level target also shares with the ordinary price level target the benefit of preserving price stability, in contrast to the strategy of simply raising the inflation target. In particular, under this approach, inflation during both ZLB and non-ZLB periods should aver-age about 2 percent.

My proposal has two potential advantages over an ordinary price-level target, however. First, it does not require a major shift in existing policy frameworks since (1) inflation targeting would continue to define policy away from the ZLB and (2) the temporary price-level target could be rein-terpreted as part of an inflation-targeting regime in that, as we have seen, it amounts to targeting the average inflation rate over the ZLB period. Second, like inflation targeting, it avoids the need to tighten policy in the face of temporary inflation shocks away from the ZLB.

As Lael Brainard points out in chapter 2, a drawback of my proposal is a possible discontinuity at the moment when policy switches from pur-suing the temporary price-level target (during which short rates are at the ZLB) to the "normal" inflation-targeting regime with positive inter-est rates. That discontinuity could be reduced through several means, for example, by using a policy approach that penalizes sharp movements in interest rates. This issue requires further research.

To summarize this section, a temporary price-level target, invoked only during ZLB episodes, appears to have many of the benefits of ordinary price-level targeting, including the preservation of price stability and the implication that ZLB episodes are followed by "makeup" periods of low rates. Among its additional advantages are that it could be folded into existing inflation-targeting regimes in a straightforward way, minimiz-ing the need to make changes in long-standing policy frameworks and communications practices, and that it would not require the reversal of inflation shocks that occur away from the ZLB.

Central Bank Independence and Institutional Reform

Of course, monetary policy decisions are not made in a vacuum, and any changes, particularly to the framework, need to be discussed in a political and institutional context. The future of monetary policy depends in part on the structures and powers of central banks themselves. The political blowback from the financial crisis and the ensuing recession raises the possibility that legislatures will impose institutional change, including additional constraints on central bank independence. In this last section, I revisit the case for central bank independence in a world of low inflation and interest rates.

The term "central bank independence" is sometimes used loosely, so it's worth spelling out what it means in a contemporary context. In particular, in a modern pluralist democracy, CBI does *not* mean full autonomy or lack of accountability for monetary policymakers, nor does it mean that political actors have no role in influencing policy, at least over the longer term. Although institutional details differ quite a bit across countries and jurisdictions, I associate contemporary CBI with four elements:

First, democratically elected representatives establish the central bank's institutional structure, including its authorities and powers; set its broad objectives; and appoint its leadership. For example, the Federal Reserve's congressional mandate is to promote maximum employment and price stability. The Fed has an idiosyncratic structure, which includes regional Reserve Banks with private sector boards, but it is ultimately accountable to the president and to Congress, who determine the Fed's authorities and the membership of the Federal Reserve Board. The Fed's monetary and lending authorities, established by Congress, are generally narrower than other advanced-economy central banks—for example, under normal circumstances and unlike other central banks, the Fed cannot buy private sector assets such as corporate bonds or stocks, or lend outside the banking system—but it has some emergency powers that can be called on.

Second, elected representatives regularly review the central bank's monetary policy decisions and progress toward mandated goals. To facilitate effective review, the central bank provides extensive information about its plans and policies, and in general is as transparent as possible consistent with the effective implementation of policy. It is not a coincidence that the global trend toward greater central bank transparency has occurred at the same time that monetary policy has assumed a more prominent role in managing the economy. In particular, a critical motivation for the rise of inflation targeting and similar frameworks is the communication enhancements they bring, including the regular release of forecasts and policy projections, as well as the accountability that is facilitated by explicit objectives. The Fed's steps toward increased transparency in recent years include adopting an explicit inflation target; releasing the forecasts, including interest rate forecasts, of FOMC participants; and instituting a quarterly press conference by the chair. The FOMC also releases the minutes of its meetings after three weeks and full transcripts with a five-year lag.

Third, subject to the system of mandated objectives and regular review and oversight, the central bank is allowed to manage the instruments of monetary policy without overt political interference. So, for example, the Fed manages its policy interest rate without congressional or executive branch intervention, so long as its policy decisions can reasonably be seen to be in pursuit of its mandated objectives. (In economists' parlance, the Fed has instrument independence but not goal independence.) This operational independence is enforced in large part by norms (in the United States, presidential acceptance of the norm of Fed independence has been particularly important) but also by speed bumps to intervention that are part of the institutional design. In the Fed's case, these speed bumps include the long, overlapping terms of Fed governors; the fact that governors can be discharged before the ends of their terms only for inappropriate behavior, not for policy reasons; the Fed's budgetary independence; the long terms and nonpolitical appointment of Reserve Bank presidents; the political influence of the Reserve Banks' private sector directors; and other factors. Notably, though, the protections of the Fed's independence are mostly indirect or implicit and are not explicitly guarded by statute or treaty, as is the case in some other jurisdictions, including Japan, the United Kingdom, and the euro area.

A standard description of the terms of central bank independence might end here; but I think we should recognize that, at least in the medium term, democratically elected officials must be able to respond to institutional deficiencies of or poor execution by the central bank.

Fourth, in the medium term, elected representatives may react to inadequate central bank performance by changing leadership or, as necessary, through institutional reform. A viable principal-agent relationship requires the possibility of rewards or punishments for realized outcomes, and for the possibility that the agent's contract itself must change in light of changing circumstances. Thus I don't consider periodic changes to the structure or powers of the central bank to be necessarily inconsistent with CBI unless the reform either directly constrains policy decisions (e.g., by giving the legislature a veto of interest rate changes) or eliminates bulwarks of CBI (e.g., by allowing governors to be dismissed for political reasons).[16]

This description of CBI captures, in general terms, the current institutional and political equilibrium in most advanced economies, and it remains an influential principle constraining the relationship between politicians and central bank governors in many countries. Several questions arise: (1) What is the rationale for CBI in the current environment? (2) Should CBI apply equally to all central bank activities? (3) Will CBI continue to be a key principle of monetary policymaking in the future?

On the first question, the most prominent argument of the research literature is that CBI helps to solve time consistency problems of monetary policy (Kydland and Prescott 1977; Barro and Gordon 1983). The basic story, with some simplification, posits that promises of low inflation may be difficult to make credible if decision makers are too focused on the short term. In particular, if the public expects low inflation, then policymakers may be tempted to achieve a short-run increase in output by engineering a near-term inflation "surprise." But the public will come to expect such surprises, with the result in equilibrium being that inflation and inflation expectations are higher than desired, with no ultimate benefit in terms of higher output. CBI addresses the inflation credibility problem, in this traditional view, because independent central bankers—perhaps because they are selected for their hawkish tendencies, or because of professional or institutional incentives—will be seen by the public as less inclined than politicians to push for short-term output gains at the expense of higher inflation. The canonical example of "credibility through delegation" is Jimmy Carter's appointment of Paul Volcker to the Fed (Rogoff 1985). Indeed, it's very plausible that CBI has contributed to the global reduction in inflation of the past couple of decades. Essentially, in this view, an independent central bank is a commitment device by which politicians control their own inflationary biases.

The general thesis that independent central bankers have longer horizons and thus are better able than short-term-oriented politicians to take into account the longer-term interests of the economy rings true, as I'll discuss. However, the specific argument that CBI reduces inflation bias is looking shaky these days. In recent years, the problem faced by central banks has been too little rather than too much inflation. Moreover, some of the strongest political opposition to the strong monetary measures of the Fed and other major central banks has come not from those who wanted the monetary authorities to do more but from those who wanted them to do less. I have already mentioned the 2010 letter from congressional leaders to the FOMC warning against embarking on a new round of QE. Similar objections to monetary easing have been raised in Europe—especially in Germany, where QE and low interest rates have provoked popular protest and court cases—and elsewhere. The phenomenon of intense political opposition to easy money has diverse causes, including the political power of creditors (savers and financial institutions), but in any case it is difficult to reconcile with the traditional time consistency story.

One might be tempted to conclude that, in a low-inflation world, CBI is no longer desirable, and that central banks should coordinate directly with governments when needed to get higher inflation (Eggertsson 2013). I'll return to the issue of central bank-government coordination below. But the point I want to make here is that the time-consistency argument for CBI was never the complete rationale, and that there are other good reasons to delegate monetary policy to an independent central bank:

First, monetary policymaking can be highly technical. Congress hires the Fed to manage monetary policy in part for the same reasons that I hire a professional to solve my plumbing problems—and while I hold the plumber accountable for fixing the problem, I don't second-guess the specific actions that he takes, because I recognize that my kibitzing would only worsen the outcomes.

Second, monetary policy is also often time-sensitive. It needs to be managed by a body that can respond quickly and accurately to changing economic and financial conditions.

Third, effective monetary policy requires consistent, coherent, and timely communication with financial markets. Legislatures are not equipped to do this, and even ex post interference with central bank decisions or communication will create uncertainty in markets and reduce the effectiveness of monetary policy.

If monetary policy's technical aspects, need for timeliness, and market sensitivity were the only reasons for delegating this responsibility, then it might be sufficient to have monetary policy run out of the finance ministry or Treasury rather than by an independent central bank. Indeed, there have been significant examples of monetary policy oversight by developed economy finance ministries, as recently as the 1990s in the United Kingdom and Japan, for example. An argument for delegating monetary policy to the Treasury is precisely that it might be more democratically responsive, at least in the short run. Moreover, as noted earlier, monetary policy (including QE) can have fiscal implications, including for seigniorage revenue, debt management, and the functioning of government debt markets, providing some additional rationale for leaving monetary policy to finance ministers.

However, these points notwithstanding, the long-standing global trend toward entrusting monetary policy to independent central banks rather than finance ministries seems justified by the weight of experience. First, monetary policy operates with substantial lags, and campaigns of policy easing and tightening can play out over a number of years. So, even if inflation bias is itself not a problem, it is important that *monetary policymakers keep a longer-term perspective and ensure policy continuity and coherence over time.* Finance ministers (who in most jurisdictions are elected politicians) may turn over quickly—as Fed chair I worked with four Treasury secretaries (two Republicans and two Democrats), and Alan Greenspan worked with seven—and changes in government shorten time horizons as well. For similar reasons, independent central banks are better placed to develop long-run institutional credibility—to anchor inflation expectations, establish a reputation for carrying through on forward guidance, establish a predictable reaction function, and avoid policy lurches. Second, even beyond their effects on time horizons, *political considerations would create other problems for a Treasury-led monetary policy*. For example, there would be suspicions of (and temptations toward) "spin" around economic forecasts and the timing of key policy actions or announcements. Would a finance ministry be tempted to cut interest rates to distract from an unrelated political setback? Even if not, would the markets suspect that might happen? Fiscal considerations, mentioned above as an argument for keeping monetary policy in the Treasury, might cut the other way in a short-run political context. Would there be concerns, for example, that the Treasury is setting interest rates to influence the size of the government's current deficit?

In sum, the avoidance of inflation bias is far from the only rationale for delegating monetary policy to an independent central bank. Other reasons include the technical, time-sensitive, and market-sensitive aspects of monetary policymaking; the benefits of the longer-term perspective on the economy that apolitical central bankers bring; the development over time of institutional credibility and predictability; and the avoidance of incentives to react to short-term political developments. The delegation of monetary policy to central banks may also be in the interest of politicians, as well as in the public interest, which helps explain why it's sustainable. For example, delegation provides distance, allowing politicians to enjoy the benefits of a good economy while having someone else to blame if things go wrong (Binder and Spindel 2017). Less cynically, politicians may recognize that delegation, by putting policy in the hands of specialists and eliminating their own incentives to over-react to short-term political pressures, is good for the economy and their constituents as well as for themselves (Eggertsson and Le Borgne 2007).

These arguments for CBI pertain primarily to monetary policy. What about other central bank activities? Should they be carried out with the same presumption of independence as monetary policy?

CBI is an instrumental principle, not an ideological or philosophical proposition: it makes sense when it leads to better policy outcomes (on average) and not otherwise. Thus, the applicability of CBI may vary according to policy function or to economic circumstances. In its supervisory functions, for example, the central bank should not make special claims to independence over and above that afforded to other regulators. Independence seems well justified in some aspects of supervision; for example, allowing political interference in the determination of (say) the capital adequacy of a particular bank would involve obvious risks and potential conflicts of interest. But legislators may appropriately weigh in on regulatory and supervisory policies applied to the banking system broadly. In the response to a systemic crisis, the case for CBI is that it may allow the central bank to fulfill its vital lender-of-last-resort function rapidly and effectively, making use of supervisory and other confidential information. However, in a financial crisis, coordination of the central bank with the executive (including other agencies) and the legislature may be essential for achieving stability. In the 2007–2009 crisis, the Fed and other central banks worked closely with finance ministers without compromising their independence in monetary policy or as lenders of last resort.

A special case of interest arises when an economy faces significant deflation risk, and when monetary policy is unable to contain the problem on its own. As Eggertsson (2013) has pointed out, that situation turns the traditional "inflation bias" argument for independence on its head. If the purpose of CBI is to avoid inflation bias in normal times, then it would seem to follow that CBI should deliberately be sacrificed when more rather than less inflation is desired. Historically, of course, inflation has often been associated with the subjugation of the central bank to the fiscal authorities.

The perspective of this chapter offers a somewhat different take on this issue. CBI does not depend only on the inflation bias argument, I have argued; there are other reasons to delegate monetary policy to an independent, technocratic institution. Accordingly, the absence of inflation is not in itself a reason to abandon CBI. However, in my view, CBI does not necessarily preclude coordination of monetary policymakers with the fiscal authorities, if two conditions are satisfied:

First, the goals of the coordination should be both consistent with the central bank's mandate and not achievable in the absence of coordination. So, if fiscal-monetary coordination is essential for meeting the central bank's inflation goal or to preserve financial stability, then it's better to coordinate than to fail to meet the mandated objectives. In contrast, the central bank should not coordinate if the result is inconsistent with or outside its mandates, or if its mandated objectives can be achieved without coordination. Second, the central bank must continuously evaluate whether the first condition is satisfied, retaining the power to stop coordinating at any point if it is not. These two criteria seem to me to protect CBI, which has long-run value for the economy, while not ruling out temporary periods of monetary-fiscal coordination that may be essential for achieving key policy goals.

As a positive matter, will CBI survive? There are certainly worrying signs. In the United States, the Fed remains unpopular in many quarters, and hostility between some members of Congress and Fed leadership has been frequently evident. The Fed also has fewer institutional protections than most other advanced economy central banks; in particular, as noted, its policy independence is not explicitly protected by law or treaty (except indirectly, through the speed bumps mentioned earlier).

However, there are also reasons to be guardedly optimistic. First, recent economic performance—at least the dimensions of it amenable to monetary policy—has been good, with the Fed near its inflation and unemployment objectives. At the same time, postcrisis reforms have addressed many aspects of the crisis response, including the most unpopular interventions. The objective case for major institutional change at this point thus seems rather weak. Second, as is normal in a democracy, the winners of recent elections are in the process of appointing new leadership to the central bank, with the result that the Fed's current political opponents will now find themselves with a stake in the institution's success. Since CBI is important for that success, the new political leadership may increasingly appreciate the value of preserving that norm.

Continued vigilance is essential, of course. The greatest danger is short memories. The financial crisis and the ensuing recession were fought with financial and monetary policies that, while ultimately successful, engendered political backlash. After the crisis, necessary reforms helped strengthen the system and rationalize crisis-fighting authorities. The risk is that politicians may be tempted to constrain or eliminate some of the powers, including monetary powers, that proved essential in the past decade. Such changes might have little immediate effect, but unless carefully thought through they could expose the American and world economies to severe financial and economic risks in the future.

Conclusions

Even as central banks emerge from the shadow of the global financial crisis and the ensuing recession, they face new challenges. Among the most important of these are the constraints on conventional monetary policy posed by low inflation and low nominal interest rates. In this chapter, I have argued that unconventional tools, especially forward guidance and QE, can provide significant additional scope for monetary policy.

However, even with additional tools and absent reliable fiscal support, existing monetary frameworks may prove insufficient to offset a severe economic slowdown. That leads to the question of whether alternative monetary frameworks could increase the potency of monetary policy. One leading suggestion, to keep the current inflation-targeting regime but to raise the inflation target to 3 or 4 percent, raises a number of concerns. Targeting the price level is a better approach, but it also has drawbacks, including the communications challenge of making such a large change in the policy framework and the requirement that central banks reverse (rather than "look through") temporary inflation shocks. In this chapter I have proposed for consideration a "temporary price-level targeting" approach, which would apply only at times when policy rates were at or very close to zero; at other times, standard inflation targeting would prevail. Under this approach, monetary policymakers would commit in advance not to raise rates from zero at least until (1) average inflation over the entire ZLB period is at target and (2) unemployment has returned to normal ranges. This approach involves only modest changes to the current framework, and it is consistent with the Fed's current mandates for maximum employment and price stability.

The low-inflation, low-rate environment also raises questions about central bank independence, which the economics literature has rationalized as a bulwark against high inflation. I agree with Eggertsson (2013) that fiscal-monetary coordination, rather than independent monetary policy, may at times be necessary to fight persistent deflation or low inflation. However, I argue that the case for CBI goes well beyond the avoidance of inflation bias and is based on factors that include technical competence, institutional credibility, and the need for a longer-term perspective. I am guardedly optimistic that CBI will survive in the United States and other advanced economies, but memories are short, and thus vigilance in defense of CBI will be important.

Notes

Work was originally presented at the conference "Rethinking Macroeconomic Policy," held at the Peterson Institute for International Economics, Washington, D.C., October 12–13, 2017. I thank Olivier Blanchard, Donald Kohn, and David Wessel for comments and Michael Ng for excellent research assistance.

1. As some major central banks have employed modestly negative rates, conventional usage now often refers to the "effective lower bound" (ELB) on interest rates rather than the ZLB. The Federal Reserve has not used negative rates, however. Since I am focusing on the Fed here, for simplicity, I'll stick with the ZLB initialism.

2. The FOMC experimented with three variations of qualitative forward guidance in December 2008 (FOMC 2008), March 2009 (FOMC 2009a), and November 2009 (FOMC 2009b). In August 2011 (FOMC 2011), January 2012 (FOMC 2012a), and September 2012 (FOMC 2012b), the FOMC used different versions of calendar-based forward guidance in which they set a date for keeping rates "exceptionally low." In December 2012 (FOMC 2012c), the FOMC switched to a state-dependent form of forward guidance in which it committed to keeping interest rates "exceptionally low" at least as long as the unemployment rate was above 6.5 percent, inflation was below 2.5 percent based on one- to two-year ahead forecasts, and inflation expectations remained anchored.

3. In principle, optimal policy depends not only on the current state of the economy but on its history as well. I discuss this point further below.

4. I also tried, without success, to name the program "credit easing," to distinguish it from the Bank of Japan's earlier foray into asset purchases (Bernanke 2009). I argued that "credit easing" focused on removing duration from bond markets, in contrast to BOJ-style QE, which had the primary goal and metric of increasing the high-powered money stock.

5. For example, Gagnon (2016), table 1, reports eighteen estimates from sixteen studies of the effects of QE bond purchases on bond yields. For U.S. data, the median effect of a hypothetical program sized at 10 percent of GDP on ten-year yields is 82 basis points. Using the conventional rule of thumb that a 10 basis point reduction in the ten-year yield is about equivalent to a 25 basis point cut in the federal funds, that's roughly equal to 200 basis points of funds rate reductions for a program of that size. (The Fed's program was considerably larger than 10 percent of GDP.) According to Gagnon's survey, the median effect of purchases programs on the term premium component of ten-year yields only is 44 basis points, suggesting that both signaling effects and portfolio balance effects operate.

6. It is true that QE has not been sufficient in a number of those cases to return inflation to target. However, the weak link in the causal chain appears to be in

the influence of declining slack on inflation, not the effect of monetary policy (including QE) on aggregate demand. The apparent flatness (or downward shift) of the Phillips curve is a problem for any macroeconomic policy aimed at raising inflation.

7. See, for example, Taylor and Ryan (2010).

8. As James Tobin (1977) once said, "It takes a heap of Harberger triangles to fill an Okun gap." Translated from economist, this aphorism suggests that distortions at the microeconomic level are hardly of consequence when the economy as a whole is operating far from its potential. The goal of monetary policy is to close Okun gaps.

9. Hence the apparently contradictory claims that QE both helps wealth-holders and hurts savers; see Bernanke (2015) for a discussion.

10. John Williams, the president of the New York Fed, said in 2016 that negative interest rates "are at the bottom of the stack in terms of net effectiveness" (Mui 2016). However, interestingly, former Fed chair Yellen has indicated that she believes the Fed has the legal authority to impose negative interest rates should it choose to do so (U.S. Senate Committee on Banking, Housing, and Urban Affairs 2016).

11. For example, a promise to keep rates low for two years would be reinforced by a commitment to peg yields out to a date two years from the announcement. This strategy would be difficult to implement for state-dependent (as opposed to time-dependent) guidance, however.

12. An option that deserves further study, but that I don't have space to discuss here, is nominal GDP targeting. A practical issue with this approach is that measurements of nominal GDP are not as timely as those of inflation and unemployment, and are more subject to revision.

13. Should the increase be to 3 percent or 4 percent? The literature offers limited guidance (Diercks 2017). An increase to 4 percent provides more room for future rate cuts, but it might be difficult to defend 4 percent inflation as being consistent with central bank mandates for price stability. An increase to 3 percent adds only modest scope for rate cuts; if that is the increase contemplated, it would be desirable to compare the costs and benefits of that increase with the adoption of negative rates, which add similar amounts of policy space (Bernanke 2016b).

14. Erceg, Kiley, and López-Salido (2011) show that strict price-level targeting, which ignores fluctuations in output and employment, does not perform well.

15. I assume for this illustration that the FOMC relies on the core inflation measure, excluding food and energy prices, to better capture the underlying inflation trend.

16. Binder and Spindel (2017) provide evidence for a political cycle in which Congress largely ignores the Fed during good times but acts to reform the institution after episodes of poor economic or financial performance.

References

Atkins, Ralph. 2010. "Germany Attacks US Economic Policy." *Financial Times*, November 7. http://www.ft.com/intl/cms/s/0/c0dca084-ea6c-11df-b28d-00144 feab49a.html#axzz3c6g2tFNf.

Auerbach, Alan J., and Yuriy Gorodnichenko. 2017. "Fiscal Stimulus and Fiscal Sustainability." Paper presented at the Jackson Hole Economic Symposium, Jackson Hole, WY, August 29.

Baker, Dean, Laurence Ball, Jared Bernstein, Heather Boushey, Josh Bivens, and David Blanchflower. J. Bradford DeLong, …, Justin Wolfers. 2017. "To Federal Reserve Chair Janet Yellen and the Board of Governors," The Center for Popular Democracy, June 8. http://populardemocracy.org/sites/default/files/Rethink%202 %25%20letter.pdf.

Bank of Japan. 1999. "Announcements of the Monetary Policy Meeting Decision (Feb. 12)." Tokyo, February 12, https://www.boj.or.jp/en/announcements/ release_1999/k990212c.htm/.

Barro, Robert J., and David B. Gordon. 1983. "Rules, Discretion and Reputation in a Model of Monetary Policy." NBER Working Paper 1079. Cambridge, MA: National Bureau of Economic Research, February.

Bauer, Michael D., and Glenn D. Rudebusch. 2013. "The Signaling Channel for Federal Reserve Bond Purchases." Federal Reserve Bank of San Francisco Working Paper 2011–21. Federal Reserve Bank of San Francisco, April.

Bernanke, Ben S. 2002. "Deflation: Making Sure 'It' Doesn't Happen Here." Remarks at the National Economists Club, Washington, DC, November 21.

Bernanke, Ben S. 2005. "The Global Savings Glut and the U.S. Current Account Deficit." Sandridge Lecture, Virginia Association of Economists, Richmond, March 10.

Bernanke, Ben S. 2009. "The Crisis and the Policy Response." Stamp Lecture, London School of Economics, January 13.

Bernanke, Ben S. 2012. "Monetary Policy since the Onset of the Crisis." Paper presented at the Jackson Hole Economic Symposium, Jackson Hole, WY, August 31.

Bernanke, Ben S. 2015. "Monetary Policy and Inequality." *Ben Bernanke's Blog*, Brookings Institution, June 1. https://www.brookings.edu/blog/ ben-bernanke/2015/06/01/monetary-policy-and-inequality.

Bernanke, Ben S. 2016a. "The Latest from the Bank of Japan." *Ben Bernanke's Blog*, Brookings Institution, September 21 https://www.brookings.edu/blog/ ben-bernanke/2016/09/21/the-latest-from-the-bank-of-japan.

Bernanke, Ben S. 2016b. "Modifying the Fed's Policy Framework: Does a Higher Inflation Target Beat Negative Interest Rates?" *Ben Bernanke's Blog*, Brookings Institution, September 13. https://www.brookings.edu/blog/ ben-bernanke/2016/09/13/modifying-the-feds-policy-framework-does-a-higher -inflation-target-beat-negative-interest-rates.

Bernanke, Ben S. 2016c. "What Tools Does the Fed Have Left? Part 1: Negative Interest Rates." *Ben Bernanke's Blog*, Brookings Institution, March 18. https:// www.brookings.edu/blog/ben-bernanke/2016/03/18/what-tools-does-the-fed-have -left-part-1-negative-interest-rates.

Bernanke, Ben S. 2016d. "What Tools Does the Fed Have Left? Part 2: Targeting Longer-Term Interest Rates." *Ben Bernanke's Blog*, Brookings Institution, March 24. https://www.brookings.edu/blog/ben-bernanke/2016/03/24/what-tools-does -the-fed-have-left-part-2-targeting-longer-term-interest-rates.

Bhattarai, Saroj, and Christopher Neely. 2016. "A Survey of the Empirical Literature on U.S. Unconventional Monetary Policy." Federal Reserve Bank of Saint Louis Working Paper 2016–021A. Federal Reserve Bank of St. Louis, October 28. https://dx.doi.org/10.20955/wp.2016.021.

Binder, Sarah, and Mark Spindel. 2017. *The Myth of Independence: How Congress Governs the Federal Reserve*. Princeton, NJ: Princeton University Press.

Bivens, Josh. 2015. "Gauging the Impact of the Fed on Inequality during the Great Recession." Hutchins Center Working Paper 12. Hutchins Center on Fiscal and Monetary Policy at the Brookings Institution, Washington, DC, June 1.

Bonis, Brian, Jane Ihrig, and Min Wei. 2017. "The Effect of the Federal Reserve's Securities Holdings on Longer-term Interest Rates." *FEDS Notes*, April 20. https:// doi.org/10.17016/2380-7172.1977.

Bowman, David, Christopher Erceg, and Mike Leahy. 2010. "Strategies for Targeting Interest Rates Out the Yield Curve." Memorandum to the Federal Open Market Committee. Washington, DC, October 13. Released by the FOMC secretariat on January 29, 2016.

Burke, Chris, Spence Hilton, Ruth Judson, Kurt Lewis, and David Skeie. 2010. "Reducing the IOER Rate: An Analysis of Options." Memorandum to the Federal Open Market Committee. Washington, DC, August 5. Released by the FOMC secretariat on January 29, 2016.

Byrne, David, and Dan Sichel. 2017. "The Productivity Slowdown Is Even More Puzzling Than You Think." *Vox Policy Portal* (blog), Center for Economic Policy Research, August 22. http://voxeu.org/article/productivity-slowdown-even-mor e-puzzling-you-think.

Caballero, Ricardo J., Emmanuel Farhi, and Pierre-Olivier Gourinchas. 2017. "The Safe Assets Shortage Conundrum." *Journal of Economic Perspectives* 31 (3): 29–46.

Campbell, Jeffrey R., Charles L. Evans, Jonas D. M. Fisher, and Alejandro Justiniano. 2012. "Macroeconomic Effects of Federal Reserve Forward Guidance." *Brookings Papers on Economic Activity* (Spring): 1–80.

Chaurushiya, Radha, and Ken Kuttner. 2003. "Targeting the Yield Curve: The Experience of the Federal Reserve, 1942–51." Memorandum to the Federal Open Market Committee. Washington, DC, June 18. Released by the FOMC secretariat on January 29, 2016.

Chen, Catherine, Macro Cipriani, Gabriele La Spada, Philip Mulder, and Neha Shah. 2017. "Money Market Funds and the New SEC Regulation," *Liberty*

Street Economics (blog). Federal Reserve Bank of New York, March 20. http://libertystreeteconomics.newyorkfed.org/2017/03/money-market-funds-and-the-new-sec-regulation.html.

Chinn, Menzie D. 2017. "The Once and Future Global Imbalances? Interpreting the Post-Crisis Record." Paper presented at the Jackson Hole Economic Symposium, Jackson Hole, WY, August 26.

Danmarks Nationalbank. 2015."Interest Rate Reduction." Press release, Denmark National Bank, February 5. http://www.nationalbanken.dk/en/pressroom/Pages/2015/02/DNN201521789.aspx.

Dell'Ariccia, Giovanni, Vikram Haksar, and Tommaso Mancini-Griffoli. 2017. "Negative Interest Rate Policies-Initial Experiences and Assessments." IMF Policy Paper. Washington, DC: International Monetary Fund, August 3.

Del Negro, Marco, Marc P. Giannoni, Domenico Giannone, and Andrea Tambalotti. 2017. "Safety, Liquidity, and the Natural Rate of Interest." *Brookings Papers on Economic Activity* (Spring): 235–294.

Diercks, Anthony M. 2017. "The Reader's Guide to Optimal Monetary Policy." Social Science Research Network, June 18. https://ssrn.com/abstract=2989237.

Eggertsson, Gauti. 2013. Fiscal Multipliers and Policy Coordination. In *Fiscal Policy and Macroeconomic Performance*, ed. Luis Felipe Cespedes and Jordi Gali, 175–234. Santiago: Central Bank of Chile; http://si2.bcentral.cl/public/pdf/banca-central/pdf/v17/Vol17_175_234.pdf.

Eggertsson, Gauti, and Eric Le Borgne. 2007. "Dynamic Incentives and the Optimal Delegation of Political Power." IMF Working Paper. Washington, DC: International Monetary Fund, April.

Eggertsson, Gauti, and Michael Woodford. 2003. "The Zero Bound on Interest Rates and Optimal Monetary Policy." *Brookings Papers on Economic Activity* (Spring): 139–233.

Engen, Eric M., Thomas Laubach, and David Reifschneider. 2015. "The Macroeconomic Effects of the Federal Reserve's Unconventional Monetary Policies." Finance and Economics Discussion Series 2015–005. Washington, DC: Board of Governors of the Federal Reserve System, January 14.

Erceg, Christopher, Michael Kiley, and David López-Salido. 2011. "Alternative Monetary Policy Frameworks." Memorandum to the Federal Open Market Committee. Washington, DC, October 6. Released by the FOMC secretariat on February 15, 2017.

Evans, Charles. 2010. "Monetary Policy in a Low-Inflation Environment: Developing a State-Contingent Price-Level Target." Remarks at the Federal Reserve Bank of Boston, October 16. https://www.chicagofed.org/publications/speeches/2010/10-16-boston-speech.

Federal Open Market Committee. 2003. Press release. Washington, DC, August 12. https://www.federalreserve.gov/boarddocs/press/monetary/2003/20030812/default.htm.

Federal Open Market Committee. 2008. "FOMC Statement." Washington, DC, December 16. https://www.federalreserve.gov/newsevents/pressreleases/monetary 20081216b.htm.

Federal Open Market Committee. 2009a. "FOMC Statement." Washington, DC, March 18. https://www.federalreserve.gov/newsevents/pressreleases/mone tary20090318a.htm.

Federal Open Market Committee. 2009b. "FOMC Statement," Washington, DC, November 4. https://www.federalreserve.gov/newsevents/pressreleases/monetary 20091104a.htm.

Federal Open Market Committee. 2011. "FOMC Statement." Washington, DC, August 9. https://www.federalreserve.gov/newsevents/pressreleases/monetary 20110809a.htm.

Federal Open Market Committee. 2012a. "Federal Reserve Issues FOMC Statement." Washington, DC, January 25. https://www.federalreserve.gov/newsevents/ pressreleases/monetary20120125a.htm.

Federal Open Market Committee. 2012b. "Federal Reserve Issues FOMC Statement." Washington, DC, September 13. https://www.federalreserve.gov/ newsevents/pressreleases/monetary20120913a.htm.

Federal Open Market Committee. 2012c. "Federal Reserve Issues FOMC Statement." Washington, DC, December 12. https://www.federalreserve.gov/ newsevents/pressreleases/monetary20121212a.htm.

Federal Open Market Committee. 2017. "FOMC Issues Addendum to the Policy Normalization Principles and Plans." Washington, DC, June 14. https:// www.federalreserve.gov/newsevents/pressreleases/monetary20170614c.htm.

Federal Reserve Board of Governors. 2017. "Federal Reserve Board Announces Reserve Bank Income and Expense Data and Transfers to the Treasury for 2016." Press Release, January 10. https://www.federalreserve.gov/newsevents/ pressreleases/other20170110a.htm.

Femia, Katherine, Steven Friedman, and Brian Sack. 2013. "The Effects of Policy Guidance on Perceptions of the Fed's Reaction Function." Federal Reserve Bank of New York Staff Report 652. Federal Reserve Bank of New York, November.

Feroli, Michael, David Greenlaw, Peter Hooper, Frederic S. Mishkin, and Amir Sufi. 2016. "Language after Liftoff: Fed Communication away from the Zero Lower Bound." Prepared for the 2016 U.S. Monetary Policy Forum, New York, February 26.

Fleming, Sam. 2016. "Fed Faces Its Critics at Jackson Hole." *Financial Times*, August 27. https://www.ft.com/content/193b2db8-6b27-11e6-a0b1-d87a9fea0 34f.

Gagnon, Etienne, Benjamin K. Johannsen, and David López-Salido. 2016. "Understanding the New Normal: The Role of Demographics." Finance and Economics Discussion Series 2016–080. Washington, DC: Board of Governors of the Federal Reserve System, October. http://dx.doi.org/ 10.17016/FEDS.2016.080.

Gagnon, Joseph E. 2016. "Quantitative Easing: An Underappreciated Success." Policy Brief Number PB16–4. Washington, DC: Peterson Institute for International Economics, April.

Garnham, Peter, and Jonathan Wheatley. 2010. "Brazil in 'Currency War' Alert." *Financial Times*, September 28. https://www.ft.com/content/33ff9624-ca48-11df -a860-00144feab49a.

Gaspar, Vítor, Frank Smets, and David Vestin. 2007. "Is Time Ripe for Price Level Path Stability?" European Central Bank Working Paper Series 818. European Central Bank, October.

Greenwood, Robin, Samuel G. Hanson, Joshua S. Rudolph, and Lawrence H. Summers. 2014. "Government Debt Management at the Zero Lower Bound." Hutchins Center Working Paper 5. Washington, DC: Hutchins Center on Fiscal and Monetary Policy at the Brookings Institution, September 30.

Guthrie, Graeme, and Julian Wright. 2000. "Open Mouth Operations." *Journal of Monetary Economics* 46 (2): 489–516. http://www.sciencedirect.com/science/ article/pii/S0304393200000350.

Herszenhorn, David M. 2010. "Dear Mr. Bernanke: No Pressure, But … ." *The Caucus* (blog), *New York Times*, November 17, 2010. https://thecaucus .blogs.nytimes.com/2010/11/17/dear-mr-bernanke-no-pressure-but/?mcubz =0.

Huther, Jeffrey, Jane Ihrig, and Elizabeth Klee. 2017. "The Federal Reserve's Portfolio and Its Effect on Interest Rates." Finance and Economics Discussion Series 2017–075. Washington, DC: Board of Governors of the Federal Reserve System, June. https://doi.org/10.17016/FEDS.2017.075.

Kiley, Michael T., and John M. Roberts. 2017. "Monetary Policy in a Low Interest Rate World." *Brookings Papers on Economic Activity* (Spring): 317–396.

Krugman, Paul. 1998. "It's Baaack: Japan's Slump and the Return of the Liquidity Trap." *Brookings Papers on Economic Activity* (Fall): 137–205.

Kydland, Finn E., and Edward C. Prescott. 1977. "Rules Rather Than Discretion: The Inconsistency of Optimal Plans." *Journal of Political Economy* 85 (3): 473–492.

Leubsdorf, Ben. 2017. "Activists in Jackson Hole Pressure Fed on Inflation, Endorse Yellen." *Wall Street Journal*, August 24. https://www.wsj.com/articles/ activists-in-jackson-hole-pressure-fed-on-inflation-endorse-yellen-1503621341.

Matthews, Dylan. 2011. "Did the Stimulus Work? A Review of the Nine Best Studies on the Subject." *Washington Post*, August 24. https://www.washingtonpost.com/ blogs/ezra-klein/post/did-the-stimulus-work-a-review-of-the-nine-best-studies-on -the-subject/2011/08/16/gIQAThbibJ_blog.html?utm_term=.5a6527454988.

Mui, Ylan Q. 2016. "Why This Top Official Thinks the Federal Reserve Should Raise Interest Rates This Year." *Wonkblog, Washington Post*, August 11. https:// www.washingtonpost.com/news/wonk/wp/2016/08/11/why-this-top-official -thinks-the-federal-reserve-should-raise-interest-rates-this-year/?utm_term=.33fb 6184fc76.

Rachel, Lukasz, and Thomas D. Smith. 2015. "Secular Drivers of the Global Real Interest Rate." Bank of England Staff Working Paper 571. London: Bank of England, December.

Reifschneider, David, and John C. Williams. 2000. "Three Lessons for Monetary Policy in a Low-Inflation Era." *Journal of Money, Credit and Banking* 32 (4): 936–966.

Rogoff, Kenneth S. 1985. "The Optimal Degree of Commitment to an Intermediate Monetary Target." *Quarterly Journal of Economics* 100 (November): 1169–1189.

Rogoff, Kenneth S. 2016. *The Curse of Cash: How Large-Denomination Bills Aid Crime and Tax Evasion and Constrain Monetary Policy*. Princeton, NJ: Princeton University Press.

Summers, Lawrence H. 2015. "Have We Entered an Age of Secular Stagnation?" IMF Fourteenth Annual Research Conference in Honor of Stanley Fischer. *IMF Economic Review* 63 (1): 277–280. http://dx.doi.org/10.1057/imfer.2015.6.

Svensson, Lars E. O. 1999. "Price-Level Targeting versus Inflation Targeting: A Free Lunch?" *Journal of Money, Credit and Banking* 31 (3, pt. 1): 277–295.

Swanson, Eric T. 2017. "Measuring the Effects of Federal Reserve Forward Guidance and Asset Purchases on Financial Markets." NBER Working Paper 23311. Cambridge, MA: National Bureau of Economic Research, MA, June.

Taylor, John B. 1993. "Discretion versus Policy Rules in Practice." *Carnegie-Rochester Conference Series on Public Policy* 39: 195–214.

Taylor, John B., and Paul D. Ryan. 2010. "Refocus the Fed on Price Stability Instead of Bailing Out Fiscal Policy." Op-ed. *Investor's Business Daily*, December 1. http://media.hoover.org/sites/default/files/documents/Refocus-Fed-on-Price-Stability-Instead-of-Bailing-Out-Fiscal-Policy.pdf.

Tobin, James. 1977. "How Dead Is Keynes?" Cowles Foundation Discussion Paper 458. New Haven, CT: Cowles Foundation for Research in Economics at Yale University, June.

U.S. Congress House Committee on Financial Services and Senate Committee on Banking, Housing, and Urban Affairs. 2017. "Semiannual Monetary Policy Report to Congress." 115th Cong. 1st sess. Washington, DC: Federal Reserve Board (statement of Janet L. Yellen, Chair, Federal Board), July 12, 13.

U.S. Securities and Exchange Commission. 2014. "SEC Adopts Money Market Fund Reform Rules." Washington, DC, July 23. https://www.sec.gov/news/press-release/2014-143.

U.S. Senate Committee on Banking, Housing, and Urban Affairs. 2016. "Federal Reserve's First Monetary Policy Report to Congress for 2016." 114th Cong. 1st sess. Washington, DC: Federal Reserve Board (statement of Janet L. Yellen, Chair, Federal Board), February 11.

Wall Street Journal. 2010. "Open Letter to Ben Bernanke." *Real Time Economics* (blog), November 15. https://blogs.wsj.com/economics/2010/11/15/open-letter-to-ben-bernanke.

Wall Street Journal. 2011. "Full Text: Republicans' Letter to Bernanke Questioning More Fed Action." *Real Time Economics* (blog), September 20. https://blogs.wsj.com/economics/2011/09/20/full-text-republicans-letter-to-bernanke-questioning-more-fed-action.

Werning, Ivan. 2011. "Managing a Liquidity Trap: Monetary and Fiscal Policy." NBER Working Paper 17344. Cambridge, MA: National Bureau of Economic Research, August.

Williams, John C. 2014. "Monetary Policy at the Zero Lower Bound: Putting Theory into Practice." Hutchins Center Working Paper 3. Washington, DC: Hutchins Center on Fiscal and Monetary Policy at the Brookings Institution, January 16.

Williams, John C. 2016. "Discussion of Language after Liftoff: Fed Communication Away from the Zero Lower Bound." Paper presented at the US. Monetary Policy Forum, New York, February 26.

Williams, John C. 2017. "Preparing for the Next Storm: Reassessing Frameworks and Strategies in a Low *R*-Star World." Paper presented at the Shadow Open Market Committee, New York, May 5.

Woodford, Michael, 2009. "Comment on 'Heeding Daedalus: Optimal Inflation and the Zero Lower Bound.'" *Brookings Papers on Economic Activity* (Spring): 38–45.

Yellen, Janet L. 2016. "The Federal Reserve's Monetary Policy Toolkit: Past, Present and Future." Paper presented at the Jackson Hole Economic Symposium, Jackson Hole, WY, August 26.

2

Rethinking Monetary Policy in a New Normal

Lael Brainard

Ben Bernanke in chapter 1 presents a compelling diagnosis of the issues facing policymakers and proposes an approach to policy that is elegant and straightforward to communicate. Here I focus on those elements I find particularly relevant for the challenges faced by policymakers and suggest some implications and complications. My comments are not intended to address current policy.

The New Normal

Policymakers in advanced economies are confronting a different constellation of challenges today than those that dominated the canon of U.S. monetary policymaking over the previous half century. I refer to today's set of challenges as the "new normal."[1] A key feature of the new normal is that the neutral interest rate—the level of the federal funds rate that is consistent with the economy growing close to its potential rate, full employment, and stable inflation—appears to be much lower than it was in the decades prior to the crisis. In the Federal Open Market Committee's (FOMC's) most recent Summary of Economic Projections (SEP), the median FOMC participant expected a longer-run real federal funds rate, after subtracting inflation, of ¾ percent, down sharply from the value the first time the policy projection was published in the January 2012 SEP of 2¼ percent—and the average value in the decades prior to the financial crisis of 2½ percent.[2]

The low level of the neutral rate limits the amount of space available for cutting the federal funds rate to offset adverse developments and thereby can be expected to increase the frequency and duration of periods when the policy rate is constrained by the effective lower bound, unemployment is elevated, and inflation is below target. In this environment, frequent or extended periods of low inflation run the risk of pulling down private sector inflation expectations, which could amplify the degree and persistence of shortfalls of inflation, thereby making future lower bound episodes even more challenging in terms of output and employment losses. To the extent it is weighing on longer-run inflation expectations, the persistently low level of the neutral federal funds rate may be a factor contributing to the persistent shortfall of U.S. inflation from the FOMC's target.[3]

Further complicating the ability of central banks to achieve their inflation objectives in today's new normal is the very flat Phillips curve observed in the United States and many other advanced economies, which makes the relationship between labor market conditions and price inflation more tenuous. For instance, inflation has remained stubbornly below the FOMC's 2 percent target for the past five years even as unemployment has fallen from 8.2 percent to 4.2 percent, a level that most experts believe is in the vicinity of full employment.[4]

In chapter 1, Bernanke provides an excellent review of the Federal Reserve's efforts to operate in this new environment and makes some interesting new proposals. Reflecting on the Fed's available "policy toolbox," Bernanke concludes that the available tools are not likely to be sufficient and proposes a framework that relies on forward guidance with commitment to help central banks achieve their inflation and employment objectives.

The Makeup Principle

The academic literature on monetary policy suggests a variety of prescriptions for preventing a lower neutral rate of interest from eroding longer-run inflation expectations. Bernanke argues convincingly that many of these proposals present practical difficulties that would create a very high bar for their adoption. For instance, raising the inflation target sufficiently to provide meaningfully greater policy space could engender public discomfort or, at the other extreme, could risk unmooring inflation expectations. The transition to a notably higher target is likely to be challenging and could heighten uncertainty.

As I have noted previously, the persistence of the shortfall in inflation from our objective is an important consideration for monetary policy.[5]

The makeup principle, in which policy would make up for past misses of the inflation target, is not reflected in most standard monetary policy frameworks, though it is an important precept in theory.[6] Some of the proposals that have been advanced to implement this principle present some difficulties. For example, while price-level targeting would be helpful in the aftermath of a recession that puts the economy at the effective lower bound, it could require tightening into a negative supply shock, which is a very unattractive feature, as Bernanke points out in chapter 1.[7]

Bernanke proposes a framework that avoids this undesirable possibility by implementing a temporary price-level targeting framework only in periods when conventional policy is constrained by the lower bound. Bernanke's proposal thus has the advantage of maintaining standard practice in normal times while proposing a makeup policy in periods when the policy rate is limited by the lower bound and inflation is below target. His proposed temporary price-level target would delay the liftoff of the policy rate from the lower bound until the average inflation over the entire lower bound episode had reached 2 percent and full employment was achieved. This type of policy, which would result in temporary overshooting of the inflation target to make up for the previous period of undershooting, is designed to, in Bernanke's words, "calibrate the vigor of the policy response to ... the severity of the episode."

The Normalization Bias

The proposed temporary price-level targeting policy is designed to address what I see as one of the key challenges facing policymakers. Following deep recessions of the type we experienced in 2008–2009, there appears to be an important premium on "normalization." This was apparent in 2010, for instance, when there was substantial pressure among G-20 officials to commit to timelines and targets for reducing fiscal support and to articulate exit principles for monetary policy.[8] This inclination proved premature, as was evident from the subsequent intensification of the euro-area crisis.

Moreover, the benchmark for "normal" tends to be defined in terms of precrisis standards that involved policy settings well away from the lower bound, at least initially, because it may take some time to learn about important changes in underlying financial and economic relationships.

For example, the factors underlying what we now understand to be the new normal of persistently low interest rates were in many cases initially viewed as temporary headwinds. In such circumstances, a standard policy framework calibrated around the precrisis or "old" normal may be biased to underachieving the inflation target in a low neutral rate environment. The kind of policy framework that Bernanke proposes, which precommits to implementing the makeup principle based on the actual observed performance of inflation during a lower bound episode, could guard against premature liftoff and help prevent the erosion of longer-term inflation expectations.

Monetary policymakers operate in an environment of considerable uncertainty and therefore must weigh the risks of tightening too little or too late against those of tightening too much or too soon. While past experience has conditioned U.S. policymakers to be highly attentive to the risks associated with a breakout of inflation to the upside, as happened in the 1970s, policymakers balance these risks against those associated with undershooting the inflation target persistently, as happened in Japan in the late 1990s and the 2000s.

In weighing these risks, the standard approach is typically designed to achieve "convergence from below," in which inflation gradually rises to its target. Owing to lags in the effects of monetary policy, convergence from below would necessitate raising interest rates preemptively, well in advance of inflation reaching its target. Moreover, particularly in the early stage of a recovery, this kind of preemptive approach tends of necessity to rely on economic relationships derived from precrisis observations, when policy rates were comfortably above the lower bound.

During a period when the policy rate is limited by the lower bound, Bernanke's proposal would represent a substantial departure from the standard approach. While a standard policy framework would tend to prescribe that tightening should start preemptively, well before inflation reaches target, Bernanke's temporary price-level target proposal would imply maintaining the policy rate at the lower bound well past the point at which inflation has risen above target. In principle, policymakers would have to be willing to accept elevated rates of above-target inflation for a period following a lengthy period of undershooting.

Just as policymakers could run a risk of low inflation becoming entrenched in the standard preemptive framework, so too there are risks in the temporary price-level target framework. One risk is that the public, seeing elevated rates of inflation, may start to doubt that the central bank is still serious about its inflation target. It is worth noting that the policy is motivated by the opposite concern—that convergence from below, following an extended lower bound episode, may lead to an unanchoring of inflation expectations to the downside. Still, a conscious policy of overshooting may be difficult to calibrate, especially since the large confidence intervals around inflation forecasts suggest that the risks of an undesired overshooting are nontrivial. A related risk is that the central bank would lose its nerve: maintaining the interest rate at zero in the face of a strong economy and inflation notably above its target would place a central bank in uncomfortable territory.

One additional challenge of the proposed framework is specifying a path for the policy rate immediately following liftoff that smoothly and gradually eases inflation back down to target and facilitates a gradual adjustment of the labor market. In the proposed framework, once the cumulative average rate of inflation during the lower-bound period reaches the target of 2 percent, policy would revert to a standard policy rule.[9] This implies that a standard policy rule would kick in at a point when inflation is above target and the economy is at or beyond full employment. Even with a smoothing (inertial) property, a standard policy rule could result in a relatively sharp path of tightening, and the anticipation of the steep post-liftoff rate path itself could undo some of the benefits associated with the framework. Thus there would likely need to be a transitional framework to guide policy initially post-liftoff that might make both communications and policy somewhat more complicated.

Integrating the Policy Rate and the Balance Sheet

The temporary price-level targeting framework proposed by Bernanke is appealing on a conceptual level because it proposes a simple and clear mechanism to help policymakers deal with the challenges posed by the lower bound on the policy rate in an environment of uncertainty. The reality is more complicated, however, especially if, as the paper suggests, many central banks in advanced economies are likely to operate with an additional tool when the policy rate is constrained. Bernanke cites former Fed chair Yellen's 2016 Jackson Hole speech, which suggests that in a recession, the FOMC could be expected to turn to large-scale asset purchases as well as forward guidance after the federal funds rate is lowered to zero.[10]

Today, when many central banks in advanced economies are operating with two distinct tools, policymakers consider the effects of the balance sheet as well as the policy rate in their assessment of the extent of accommodation provided by monetary policy. In the United States, from the time tapering was first discussed to the September 2017 meeting, when the path for balance sheet runoff was adopted, FOMC minutes and statements suggest that participants considered the degree of accommodation provided by both policy tools in their discussions of the sequencing and timing of changes to policy settings. Discussions about the sequencing of "normalization" and the delay of balance sheet runoff "until normalization of the level of the federal funds rate is well under way" effectively consider the extent to which maintaining the balance sheet may continue to provide makeup support for the economy while enabling the policy rate to escape the lower bound earlier than otherwise in a low neutral rate environment.

As Bernanke acknowledges, now that many central banks have developed playbooks specifying the operational modalities associated with asset purchases, and there is some familiarity with their effects on asset prices and financial conditions, there is a greater likelihood that asset purchases would become a part of the policy reaction function, along with forward guidance, during lower-bound episodes. Yet, as I have noted previously in the international context, asset purchases can complicate policy frameworks and communications because their deployment and withdrawal has tended to be discontinuous and discrete and thus may be associated with greater uncertainty about the policy reaction function.[11] It appears the public closely follows statements about both the policy rate and asset purchases to glean possible information about the future overall stance of monetary policy. This suggests there may be benefits to communications and predictability of a unified policy framework across the tools that is more predictable and continuous. Relatedly, one helpful elaboration of the framework Bernanke proposes might be to incorporate a unified measure, or shadow rate, that would capture the degree of policy accommodation provided through the combined settings of both asset purchases and the policy rate.[12]

Greater Cross-Border Spillovers

Moving away from the policy proposal in chapter 1, there are two other aspects of a low neutral rate world that I want to touch on briefly: cross-border spillovers and financial imbalances. The new normal appears to be characterized by low neutral rates and a weak relationship between overall inflation and unemployment not only in the United States but also in many other advanced economies, with lower-bound episodes likely to be more prevalent. The current environment appears also to evidence intensified cross-border feedback into financial conditions.[13] In this kind of environment, it is conceivable that the kind of committed forward guidance associated with the temporary price-level targeting framework proposed by Bernanke, by helping rule out anticipation of a standard preemptive tightening, could help avoid unwarranted premature tightening through the exchange rate.

With available data, it is difficult to disentangle whether the heightened cross-border feedback effects are attributable to the low level of neutral rates, particular features of today's lower-bound episodes, or the interaction of the policies adopted by many central banks. In any case, recent Federal Reserve staff analysis suggests that cross-border spillovers have increased notably since the crisis and are quite large. For instance, European Central Bank policy news that leads to a 10 basis point decrease in the German ten-year term premium is associated with a roughly 5 basis point decrease in the U.S. ten-year term premium; by contrast, these spillovers were smaller in the years leading up to the crisis.[14]

Moreover, news about policy rates and term premiums appears to have quite different effects on exchange rates, such that the ordering of policy normalization can have important implications for exchange rates and associated financial conditions, as I discussed earlier this year.[15] Recent staff estimates suggest that news about expected changes in the policy rate tends to have a large spillover through the exchange rate, whereas news about changes in term premiums tends to lead to corresponding cross-border changes in term premiums, as discussed previously, with much smaller effects on the exchange rate. Moreover, the exchange rate effect of changes in short-term rates is much greater than it was before the crisis. For instance, policy news that leads to a 25 basis point increase in the expected interest rate portion of the ten-year Treasury yield is associated with a roughly three percentage point appreciation in the dollar, which is three times greater than the precrisis response. By contrast, policy news surrounding a change in U.S. term premiums has had a muted effect on the exchange rate both now and precrisis.

Financial Imbalances

Finally, a low neutral rate environment may also be associated with a heightened risk of asset price bubbles, which could exacerbate the trade-off for monetary policy between achieving the traditional dual-mandate goals and preventing the kinds of imbalances that could contribute to financial instability. Standard asset valuation models suggest that a persistently low neutral rate, depending on the factors driving it, could lead to higher ratios of asset prices to underlying income flows—for example, higher ratios of prices to earnings for stocks or higher prices of buildings relative to rents. If asset markets were highly efficient and participants had excellent foresight, this would not necessarily lead to imbalances. However, to the extent that financial markets extrapolate price movements, markets may not transition smoothly to asset valuations that reflect underlying fundamentals but may instead evidence periods of overshooting.[16] Such forces may have played a role in both the stock market boom that ended in the bust of 2001 and the house price bubble that burst in 2007–2009.

The risks of such financial imbalances may be greater in the context of the kind of explicit inflation target overshooting policies proposed in the paper. Again, if market participants were perfectly rational, overshooting policies would not likely pose financial stability risks. But the combination of low interest rates and low unemployment that would prevail during the inflation overshooting period could well spark capital markets to overextend, leading to financial imbalances.

Macroprudential tools are the preferred first line of defense to address such financial imbalances, which should in principle enable monetary policy to focus on price stability and macroeconomic stabilization. But the development and deployment of macroprudential tools is still relatively untested in the U.S. context, and the toolkit is limited. Although important research suggests that the situations under which monetary policy should take financial imbalances into account are likely to be very rare, some recent research has pointed out that the case in favor of taking financial imbalances into account is strengthened when the consequences of financial crises are longlasting.[17] In this case, another complication of a persistently low neutral rate may be a sharper trade-off between achieving the traditional dual-mandate objectives and avoiding financial stability risks, which may make it even more difficult to achieve our price stability objective.

Notes

I am grateful to John Roberts for his assistance in preparing the text of this chapter. The remarks herein represent my own views, which are not necessarily those of the Federal Reserve Board or the Federal Open Market Committee.

1. See Brainard (2015, 2016a).

2. The well-known Laubach-Williams model currently suggests an estimate of the longer-run neutral federal funds rate that is close to zero. The latest estimates are available on the Federal Reserve Bank of San Francisco's website at http://www.frbsf.org/economic-research/files/Laubach_Williams_updated_estimates.xlsx. Over the 1960–2007 period, the real federal funds rate—measured as the nominal federal funds rate less trailing four-quarter core PCE (personal consumption expenditures) inflation—averaged 2½ percent.

3. See, for example, Nakata and Schmidt (2016), Brainard (2017b), and Kiley and Roberts (2017).

4. The inflation information refers to core PCE inflation measured on a twelve-month average basis.

5. See Brainard (2017b).

6. See, for example, Reifschneider and Williams (2000) or Eggertsson and Woodford (2003).

7. As Bernanke notes, one way to avoid this feature is to adopt "flexible price-level targeting," in which policy takes into account resource utilization as well as the deviation of the price level from its target. Kiley and Roberts (2017) examine a form of flexible price-level targeting—which they refer to as a "shadow rate rule"—and find that it performs well.

8. The 2010 G-20 Toronto communiqué indicated that advanced economies "committed to fiscal plans that will at least halve deficits by 2013 and stabilize or reduce government debt-to-GDP ratios by 2016." The document is available on the U.S. Treasury Department's website at https://www.treasury.gov/resource-center/international/Documents/The%20G-20%20Toronto%20Summit%20Declaration.pdf.

9. In the paper, this rule is specified as an inertial Taylor rule.

10. See Yellen (2016).

11. See Brainard (2015).

12. See, for instance, Krippner (2016) and Wu and Xia (2016).

13. See Brainard (2016a, 2016b).

14. See Curcuru et al. (2018).

15. See Brainard (2017a).

16. See, for example, Case, Shiller, and Thompson (2012) and Greenwood and Shleifer (2014).

17. See, for example, Svensson (2016). See Gourio, Kashyap, and Sim (2016) and Gerdrup and others (2017).

References

Brainard, Lael. 2015. "Normalizing Monetary Policy When the Neutral Interest Rate Is Low." Speech delivered at the Stanford Institute for Economic Policy Research, Stanford, CA, December 1.

Brainard, Lael. 2016a. "The 'New Normal' and What It Means for Monetary Policy." Speech delivered at the Chicago Council on Foreign Affairs, Chicago, September 12.

Brainard, Lael. 2016b. "What Happened to the Great Divergence?" Speech delivered at the 2016 U.S. Monetary Policy Forum, New York, February 26.

Brainard, Lael. 2017a. "Cross-Border Spillovers of Balance Sheet Normalization." Speech delivered at the National Bureau of Economic Research's Monetary Economics Summer Institute, Cambridge, MA, July 13.

Brainard, Lael. 2017b. "Understanding the Disconnect between Employment and Inflation with a Low Neutral Rate." Speech delivered at the Economic Club of New York, New York, September 5.

Case, Karl E., Robert J. Shiller, and Anne K. Thompson. 2012. "What Have They Been Thinking? Homebuyer Behavior in Hot and Cold Markets." *Brookings Papers on Economic Activity* (Fall): 265–298.

Curcuru, Stephanie E., Steven B. Kamin, Canlin Li, and Marius D. Rodriguez. 2018. "International Spillovers of Monetary Policy: Conventional Policy vs. Quantitative Easing." International Finance Discussion Papers. Washington, DC: Board of Governors of the Federal Reserve System.

Eggertsson, Gauti B., and Michael Woodford. 2003. "The Zero Bound on Interest Rates and Optimal Monetary Policy." *Brookings Papers on Economic Activity* (Spring): 139–233.

Gerdrup, Karsten R., Frank Hansen, Tord Krogh, and Junior Maib. 2017. "Leaning against the Wind When Credit Bites Back." *International Journal of Central Banking* (September).

Gourio, Francois, Anil K. Kashyap, and Jae Sim. 2016. "The Tradeoffs in Leaning against the Wind." Paper presented at the 17th Jacques Polak Annual Research Conference, Washington, DC, November 3.

Greenwood, Robin, and Andrei Shleifer. 2014. Expectations of Returns and Expected Returns. *Review of Financial Studies* 27 (March): 714–746.

Kiley, Michael T., and John M. Roberts. 2017. "Monetary Policy in a Low Interest Rate World." Finance and Economics Discussion Series 2017–080. Washington, DC: Board of Governors of the Federal Reserve System, August.

Krippner, Leo. 2016. "Documentation for Measures of Monetary Policy." Reserve Bank of New Zealand Working Paper. Wellington: Reserve Bank of New Zealand, July.

Nakata, Taisuke, and Sebastian Schmidt. 2016. "The Risk-Adjusted Monetary Policy Rule." Finance and Economics Discussion Series 2016–061. Washington, DC: Board of Governors of the Federal Reserve System, July.

Reifschneider, David, and John C. Williams. 2000. "Three Lessons for Monetary Policy in a Low-Inflation Era." *Journal of Money, Credit and Banking* 32 (November): 936–966.

Svensson, Lars E. 2016. "Cost-Benefit Analysis of Leaning against the Wind." NBER Working Paper 21902. Cambridge, MA: National Bureau of Economic Research, January.

Wu, Jing Cynthia, and Fan Dora Xia. 2016. "Measuring the Macroeconomic Impact of Monetary Policy at the Zero Lower Bound." *Journal of Money, Credit and Banking* 48 (March–April): 253–291.

Yellen, Janet L. 2016. "The Federal Reserve's Monetary Policy Toolkit: Past, Present, and Future." Remarks at "Designing Resilient Monetary Policy Frameworks for the Future," a symposium sponsored by the Federal Reserve Bank of Kansas City, Jackson Hole, WY, August 26.

3

Postcrisis Monetary Policy from the Perspective of Small Open Economies

Philipp Hildebrand

Whenever I talk about central banking during the 2008–2009 crisis, I refer to Ben Bernanke as something like the chief architect of policy at the time. We all had to design our own plans to suit our own problems and our own legal, political, and economic circumstances, but there is no doubt that the master plan came from Bernanke and shaped our thinking and our actions.

Of course, the ultimate jury on our extensive unconventional policies is still out. Nonetheless, I would say it worked out rather well, especially when we consider the alternatives.

My sense is that the alleged problems around unwinding the measures undertaken are probably overstated, with one caveat, however.

I'd like to look at the issues raised in chapters 1 and 2 through the lens of a small open economy (SOE) and highlight a couple of notable differences from what larger economies faced.

QE and Price-Level Targeting for Small Open Economies

Unfortunately, for some SOEs with limited sovereign bond markets, balance sheet expansion can mean foreign exchange (FX) market intervention, which adds some complications. Most important, it introduces significant FX risk to the central bank balance sheet, which is not the case for the major central banks that Ben Bernanke focuses on in chapter 1.

That means, of course, that unwinding the balance sheet will be far more challenging insofar as one cannot rely simply on a well-timed rolling off of maturing bonds. Unlike in the case of the Fed, ultimately—presumably a long time from now—unwinding the balance sheet will require outright selling of securities.

It should be noted that not all SOEs resorted to FX interventions. My own country, Switzerland, was a special case because of the enormous safe haven effects on its currency relative to the euro. This led to completely distorted monetary conditions that could only be addressed by a forceful central bank response.

There is no question that in the case of an SOE in which FX interventions were a necessary feature of the balance sheet expansion, the policy choice of expanding the balance sheet entailed considerable risks, which the Swiss National Bank pointed to explicitly at the time of the introduction of the minimum rate.

Therefore, Bernanke's reflections about a policy option that makes resorting to quantitative easing less likely is certainly important for SOEs to consider, and at least in theory, going forward, price-level targeting is such a potential regime.

I remember fondly a very good conference Mark Carney and Jean Boivin organized at the Bank of Canada on price-level targeting some years ago. Conceptually, price-level targeting was appealing then and perhaps even more so now in the context of what looks like a persistent low-rate environment: in the event of a significant renewed downturn, there is a high likelihood of the effective lower bound quickly becoming binding again.

By the way, I completely agree with Ben that while negative rates have played a useful role, not least in Switzerland, as part of the monetary arsenal, any sense of using them more forcefully is highly unlikely as long as we remain in a world where cash is used on a large scale.

Now, if we think about the practical applicability of price-level targeting in the specific case of SOEs, its feasibility looks doubtful to me.

The problems begin with the fact that SOEs are more susceptible to FX swings than the major economies, which are much more closed. In Sweden, for example, the estimated exchange rate pass-through to consumer prices is more than twice that of the United States.

Price-level targeting would therefore require small central banks to lean quite forcefully against these FX shocks, which could presumably induce more volatility in output. I am not sure this would be a worthwhile trade-off.

Moreover—and this is generally applicable—price-level targeting would require that central banks have the credibility to shape inflation expectations at all times, and presumably over a relatively short time horizon. Can we really assume this to hold? Even now, in an environment of extensive monetary expansion and a synchronized global recovery, central banks appear to be struggling in a number of places to return inflation to target and keep long-run expectations from falling. Blanchard and Summers refer to the case of Japan in the introduction to this book. We can all think of other cases as well.

For an SOE, surely the problem would be even more pronounced. A small central bank would hardly be able to go it alone on price-level targeting; some kind of global coordination would presumably be required. Based on my experience during the crisis, this seems a difficult proposition. Indirectly, this is one of the reasons why the Swiss National Bank has always shied away from any attempts to define precisely what the time horizon is over which price stability must be ensured.

Central Bank Independence

With respect to Ben Bernanke's valuable discussion of central bank independence in chapter 1, a key takeaway is that we need to make it very clear that coordination should in no way be seen as equivalent to the end of independence of central banks.

Like Bernanke, I remain convinced that the case for central bank independence remains extremely robust, in theory and in practice. However, this does not mean there should be no coordination between the central bank and the fiscal authorities or, at the very least, attempts to align broadly the aims of fiscal policy and monetary policy. Such coordination or alignment is particularly important during times of crisis. Indeed, inflation targets are easier to achieve in difficult times if both fiscal and monetary policy are more or less aligned toward this end.

Recent history suggests that without coordination, fiscal policy can make the central bank's task of returning inflation to target more difficult. The recent European experience is a good example. One of the reasons the policy burden on the European Central Bank has been so significant is that during the initial period of the euro-zone crisis, fiscal policy pointed in the opposite direction. There is, of course, some good news in this, as there is now more fiscal space in Europe in the event of a renewed downturn.

Coordination is even more important for resolving issues affecting financial stability. Without coordination, fiscal authorities may be unwilling to enact prudential measures, and that reticence might force the central bank to enact monetary policy measures that are inappropriately tight for the macroeconomy. As an example, the rescue and stabilization of UBS and our banking system in 2008 almost certainly would not have worked without close coordination between the government and the central bank.

So, for very good reasons, I have come to think of the central bank as an organ of the state, with wide-ranging policy autonomy. But to conclude from that there must be no sense of coordination with fiscal authorities strikes me as deeply flawed, in theory and certainly in practice.

4

Monetary Policy in the Wake of the Crisis

Adam S. Posen

I admire the achievements during the global economic crisis of the distinguished central bank leaders from the Federal Reserve, the European Central Bank, the Swiss National Bank, and other institutions who have offered their thoughts on rethinking macroeconomic policy. We owe them a great debt, along with my former colleagues at the Bank of England, for the policies they devised and executed in real time starting a decade ago that saved the world economy.

But on reflection, and even with benefit of Ben Bernanke's excellent analysis in chapter 1, it seems they have not rethought monetary policy sufficiently. It is incumbent on us to take very seriously the failures, both real and perceived, of both monetary policy and theory over the past ten years.

I would like to make two points regarding the rules-based policy approach and the particular proposal that Ben has put forward.[1] The first is that, as I have been arguing for some time, the constant referral to unconventional tools for monetary policy is ahistorical and misleading. We must recognize that most central banks, right up through the 1970s, engaged in asset purchases and other forms of administrative guidance. These tools were perhaps suboptimal, but they also did not lead to enormous distortions or cause the temple walls to fall, as Mario Draghi has pointed out with respect to recent quantitative easing (QE). We cannot in honesty just say, "Oh, those were the emergency tools, and now we're getting away from them." As policymakers we should not act as though we were ashamed of this fact but make best use of these tools going forward.

Furthermore, I do think that as we rightly force central banks to take responsibility for some of the financial stability issues, there will be no way for central banks to avoid getting their hands messy. If anything, central bankers will have to intervene more in markets other than government securities in times to come, if they wish to deliver the results that their democracies want them to deliver. And in a sense, that is already the message for most central banks. If you are a small open economy like Israel, Singapore, or Switzerland, let alone an emerging market, your central bank has no choice but to do that. As Stan Fisher once said with respect to his being someone some Americans would call a currency manipulator, he had no choice but to do so when he was governor of the Bank of Israel.

The second point I would make is that while we toss about the idea of "rules" in theory, we must remember that rules are a politically charged concept, particularly in the U.S. discussion of monetary policy. It is not a neutral statement. "Rules" is a code word that is associated with an extreme literal belief in the time-inconsistency view as the source of inflation and instability. The concept of rules as invoked usually takes too seriously the idea that there has to be an asymmetric bias by monetary policymakers against inflation. The concept militates toward the idea that the main problem of economies blowing up relates to central bank caused uncertainty. This view is, at best, vastly exaggerated. I believe it is largely false. And as we shed the mistaken generalization of the experience of the 1970s, or at least, as Larry Summers put it, if we look realistically at the likely low-inflation, low-return environment expected over the next twenty years, we should discard some of this belief.

So price-level targeting as an operational idea I am fully willing to consider. But let us not appeal to it because it can be cloaked as a rule. Just as when we wrote about inflation targeting twenty years ago,[2] I still consider inflation targeting as disciplined discretion as an alternative to rules. So, when we are facing excessively persistent near zero subtarget inflation, there is no need to go down the rules path. That is a place where we should start laying the intellectual groundwork for the new Federal Open Market Committee membership.

Let me turn to two other points. The first point is, again, we need to think more about what the performance of our recent policies implies for our understanding of the economy. I take very seriously what has been argued by Ben Bernanke, by Mario Draghi, and by many of us (including my PIIE colleague Joseph Gagnon) through the years, that QE and certain other inventions generally were effective and generally did not have the negative effects they were predicted to have by many. They may or may not have been as effective as rate cuts in a normal environment, but we are not in that kind of normality.

I would argue that the inability to raise inflation quickly, despite QE observably working through the channels of monetary transmission, is a strong challenge to the old-fashioned time-inconsistency macroeconomics. It is very difficult to reconcile this outcome with the idea that the Phillips curve is vertical in all but the very short run and that forward-looking expectations are the main driver of actual inflation in the medium term, let alone with the fact that none of the feared side effects have happened. This is a genuine challenge to macroeconomics overall. It should not be seen as a challenge just to notions of operational macroeconomic policy.

Whether you believe that the Phillips curve is a cloud, or you believe that it is flat, or you believe that it is kinked, over the ten-year span of very persistent low inflation, it matters that we have had enormous expansions of central bank balance sheets and have not seen the inflation that so many neoclassical critics predicted and expected. We have had the central bank in Japan, for example, effectively give up much of what was considered independence and done everything else forward-looking to commit to higher inflation, and the anchoring of inflation expectations has not eroded. In light of all this, it is unreasonable to keep harking back to the idea that you have to treat the Phillips curve in the short term as rapidly vertical and inflation expectations as subject to easy dislocation or upward rises.

That doesn't mean there is no long-term limit to the inflation/output trade-off. It does not mean one could not at some point go back to the 1970s in terms of overly aggressive monetary expansion causing inflation spirals. But recent developments in practice also must inform theory, or at least be taken seriously, instead of the old consensus being accepted as still valid. This is why, for example, Olivier Blanchard and I argued for trying to engineer a wage-price spiral in Japan.[3] A wage push would be a key transmission mechanism for inflation, and would be critical both politically and economically for establishing a symmetric central bank mandate. It turns out that sticking to the widely held extreme vertical Philips curve and forward-looking expectations views as the sole source of inflation does not work. I want to commend President Draghi and Governor Brainard for taking up the issue of wage inflation in their contributions to this book and Governor Kuroda for saying so in Japan. I think that is where the focus, rightly, is going.

Moreover, I want to pick up and reinforce, again in my own words, Olivier Blanchard's call for a higher inflation target. Ben Bernanke said, seemingly quite reasonably, as have others, that raising the inflation target would be pretty awful in its political impact. That political impression is why some say we would not necessarily want to go from 2 percent to 4 percent. I would push back against this assumption, both with respect to the costs of remaining where we are and with respect to the potential problems if we do increase the inflation target. When we wrote the book on inflation targeting, one of the things we assumed was that the people overseeing the central banks, the elected officials, could change their inflation targets, perhaps not often, but as needed. Looking back, and speaking just for myself, that is one of the things I most regret having contributed to in that book. Because in practice, almost all central banks treated inflation targets like exchange rate targets—that is, once fixed, never adjusted.

Once a central bank got to 2 percent, or below the publicly announced target, officials were afraid of appearing "soft" by raising the target, no matter what happened in the real economy, no matter the current situation. Again, this was partly the misleading intellectual overhang of the 1970s and of time-inconsistency models taken too literally, that officials were worried about eroding credibility because of an asymmetry, not from being inflexible. They also worried politically about opening a Pandora's box if elected officials were reminded that the target could be reset.

Nonetheless, if we take seriously the simulations that many people at the Federal Reserve Board, the Bank of England, the Federal Reserve Bank of San Francisco, the European Central Bank, and others have done with respect to the dangers of the zero lower bound (ZLB) and the inability to target inflation very precisely, this reluctance to change the target seems penny-wise and pound-foolish. The trade-off for not creating a bigger space between us and the ZLB seems to be quite steep.[4] And the political risks of creating hysteresis in unemployment and inducing secular stagnation seems quite large compared to those of adjusting upward the inflation target.

I have two practical suggestions to make as a result of these recognitions of reality. First, we must think seriously about a coordinated effort, not between fiscal policy and monetary policy but internationally, across G-7 or some G-20 subset of central banks, to raise inflation targets simultaneously. There is a collective action problem that unless you are a very small, open economy and quite desperate, you do not want to be the only one in the central banker club who suddenly is labeled as devaluing your credibility. It also is harder to believe that the central bank will stick with the higher target consistently, and achieve the target sustainably, if raising the target is done by one economy on its own. Therefore, I think it is reasonable for those governments to coordinate and raise inflation targets across the major central banks in a coordinated fashion, since the inflation targets are set by elected governments for the most part. That would be the most credible, simple, lasting, and obvious way to make up for the price-level undershoots of the past. It would also make it clear that central banks are accountable to their electorates and that inflation targets like 2 percent are not written in stone.

Second, with respect to central bank independence, the actual justification for it has to be, frankly, a proximate and pragmatic one that must be re-won over and over by central banks[5]—it cannot be deemed a settled question based on Barro-Gordon and Rogoff models. This is an area of policy like the military or the judiciary, or like certain aspects of health care, where you set the goals and you evaluate the competence of the people pursuing the goals, but you do not mess in day-to-day operations. This is the famous Debelle and Fischer definition of operational versus goal independence.

But I would go one step further on these issues of policy coordination for independent central banks. There is a technocratic argument being made, for good reason, that we want to have better, easier coordination between fiscal and monetary policy when near or at the ZLB. But I think this ignores the actual area where this need for coordination is required. Throughout the crisis, the problem was not so much that we could not get central banks and fiscal policy to coordinate so they could do more fiscal policy. The problem was recurrent threats lodged against central banks by fiscal authorities saying "We are not going to renew your capital" or "We are not going to indemnify you against the losses that you incur doing QE."

And you can see a marked difference in the political environment in, say, the UK, where I had the privilege to serve, where successive chancellors of both parties publicly gave an indemnity to the Bank of England, saying "You don't have to come back to us for money if you lose money doing your necessary monetary policy operations," from what the Federal Reserve or, during an earlier stage, the ECB or the Bank of Japan had to face. In those monetary zones, the central bankers would often express the idea that "I cannot undertake an asset purchase policy, despite macroeconomic needs, because then I might run out of central bank capital. We know central bank capital doesn't really mean anything, but then we have to go back to the politicians." So, I think arguing for and protecting operational independence must be defended on that front, assuring room to execute policy as well.

Notes

The views expressed in this chapter are solely the author's and do not necessarily represent the views of the Peterson Institute for International Economics or any other members of its staff or of its board of directors.

1. As noted, that proposal follows on the earlier good work of Jean Boivin when at the Bank of Canada, Michael Kiley and others at the Federal Reserve, and Charles Evans of the Federal Reserve Bank of Chicago.

2. Ben Bernanke, Thomas Laubach, Frederic Mishkin, and Adam Posen, *Inflation Targeting: Lessons from the International Experience* (Princeton, NJ: Princeton University Press, 1999).

3. Olivier Jean Blanchard and Adam S. Posen, "Getting Serious about Wage inflation in Japan," *Nikkei Asian Review*, December 15, 2015, https://asia.nikkei.com/ Viewpoints-archive/Viewpoints/Getting-serious-about-wage-inflation-in-Japan.

4. We, of course, also want to look to our colleagues at the Reserve Bank of India to see how their demonetization shock went. That is a shock to a flow rather than a permanent regime change, but obviously it is also interesting in terms of attacking the monetarist views and the fears of the ZLB. Also, if the low-inflation world is where we will be for the next ten or twenty years, it will be interesting to see whether China is less constrained by the ZLB. There is indeed clear evidence that cash is disappearing in China in favor of mobile payments on a very large scale, suggesting the possibility of negative interest rates could be open to the People's Bank.

5. Adam S. Posen, "Independence 20 Years On," presentation at the Bank of England conference, London, September 29, 2017, https://piie.com/newsroom/ short-videos/posen-bank-englands-independence-20-years-conference.

5

Historical Lessons from the Euro Area Crisis for Monetary Policy

Mario Draghi

Ben Bernanke's chapter 1 offers an excellent overview of the main issues involved in unconventional monetary policy, and there are many areas where the European experience has been similar to the U.S. experience. We have both substantially reduced policy rates and have injected additional stimulus by resorting to asset purchases and other tools to expand the policy stance.

But rather than reiterating these points of similarity, I would like to highlight some areas where our experience has been different, and the lessons we can draw from those differences for the future. To my mind, there are two areas in particular.

The first is the very different history of the crisis in the euro area, which has led us to adopt a unique set of unconventional measures designed to combat financial fragmentation. The second difference is how we have adapted our measures to our specific institutional and financial structure, especially when faced with the lower bound on policy rates.

The History of the Crisis in the Euro Area and Its Implications for Monetary Policy

The crisis in the euro area evolved in four main stages. The first, which followed the Lehman Brothers shock, was broadly similar in both the United States and the euro area. Banks exposed to toxic U.S. assets ran into difficulties, and some had to be bailed out by their governments. These banks were mostly located in Germany, France, and the Netherlands.

While U.S. authorities reacted by implementing the Troubled Asset Relief Program (TARP) and purchases of mortgage-backed securities (MBS) by the Fed, in the EU, bank bailouts took place at the national level on a staggering scale. The public sector aid provided in 2008 was around 5 percent of EU GDP and around 9 percent in 2009[1]—mostly in the aforementioned countries. But bailouts were carried out in a relatively tranquil fashion and did not much affect sovereign borrowing costs. This was made possible by the fairly strong fiscal positions of the governments implementing the bailouts.

In the second stage, the crisis spread to banks in Spain and Ireland that were overexposed to the collapsing domestic real estate market. Another wave of bailouts followed, pushing up public debt levels rapidly in these previously low-debt countries.

The third stage began when the Greek crisis shattered the impression that public debt was risk-free, triggering a rapid repricing of sovereign risk. This affected all countries now perceived as vulnerable by financial markets. But it touched most of all those that shared three features: (1) a weak fiscal position with high debt levels, (2) a banking sector that had not so far been bailed out, since it did not have relevant exposures to either U.S. subprime assets or to domestic real estate, and before the crisis had capital levels broadly in line with the European average, but where (3) domestic banks were heavily exposed to domestic government bonds.

The crisis was propagated by a pernicious feedback loop between banks and sovereigns as government bond prices deteriorated. Between January 2010 and July 2012, the aggregate economic losses on sovereign bonds of vulnerable countries[2] for banks in Greece, Italy, and Portugal amounted to €38.1 billion, €19.8 billion, and €6.4 billion, respectively, equivalent to 161 percent, 22 percent, and 36 percent of their core tier 1 capital.[3]

Regardless of whether these losses directly affected regulatory capital,[4] they had a dramatic effect on perceptions of solvency in those national banking systems. Banks became cut off from cross-border funding and financial markets fragmented along national lines, producing a renewed credit crunch. From January 2010 to July 2012, credit flows to firms[5] contracted from 2.9 percent to −6.2 percent in Greece and from 2 percent to −6 percent in Portugal, while remaining negative in Italy (−1.9 percent to −1.3 percent).

In light of the central role played by banks in financial intermediation in the euro area, this credit crunch aggravated the ongoing recession, in turn increasing loan losses and further depleting bank capital. Sovereigns' borrowing costs then rose in a vicious circle.

These dynamics produced the fourth stage: the credibility crisis of the euro. Redenomination risk was increasingly priced into sovereign debt, reflecting fears of a catastrophic breakup of the euro area. The transmission of monetary policy across countries became fundamentally impaired.

Interest rates faced by firms and households became increasingly divorced from short-term central bank rates. In fact, vulnerable countries faced asymmetrically restrictive credit conditions, with bank lending rates tightening in the places where stimulus was most required. As those economies represented a third of euro-area GDP, this posed a profound threat to price stability.

This context explains why the unconventional measures the ECB adopted in this period had a different focus from those adopted by the United States. Our measures were initially aimed not so much at overcoming the lower bound as at tackling this fragmentation and reviving the transmission of our policy through banks.

Different policies were targeted at different types of fragmentation. Our Outright Monetary Transactions in 2012 were aimed at reducing redenomination risk premia caused by breakup fears. This was hugely effective in bringing down sovereign spreads. The simple dispelling of redenomination risk meant that from July 2012 to mid-2014, when the ECB began its credit easing, spreads fell by 3.2 percentage points in Italy, 3.9 in Spain, 7.1 in Portugal, and by 19.1 percentage points in Greece.

Likewise, with cross-border credit markets malfunctioning, our long-term refinancing operations were designed to provide banks with stable term funding and to reverse the cycle of falling credit supply, weak economic growth, and rising loan losses triggered by the sovereign debt crisis.

Most notable here was our Targeted Long-term Refinancing Operations, particularly their second vintage, launched in March 2016, where we allowed banks to borrow at an interest rate as low as the (negative) interest rate applied on our deposit facility, but only on condition that they demonstrated strong performance in loan origination. We have plenty of evidence that this helped unblock the bank lending channel and restore the normal transmission of policy.[6]

Overcoming the Lower Bound in the Euro Area's Institutional and Financial Structure

Alongside addressing fragmentation, we have also—like other central banks—used unconventional policies as a way to inject additional stimulus as policy interest rates approached zero. But in the euro area we have delivered this accommodation in a distinct way—and this is the second difference compared to the United States.

Most obviously, the tools we have deployed, though having the same broad aim, have been tailored to our own institutional and financial structure. Hence we have implemented an asset purchase program that encompasses a wide range of public sector securities as well as an array of private sector assets: asset-backed securities, covered bonds, and corporate bonds.

With multiple different sovereign bond markets, purchasing a basket of public sector bonds split across eligible jurisdictions has been essential to achieve an even easing effect across the euro area. And we have purchased private sector assets to complement our measures aimed at banks. In a weakened banking sector, such purchases allowed us to inject liquidity into the system outside the banks, especially as the share of nonbank financing in the euro area was rising during the crisis.

This contrasts somewhat with the experience of the Fed, whose purchases of MBS were found to have empowered bank lending. The first and third rounds of quantitative easing, in which MBS were included, led to a lowering of lending standards and increased risk-taking by those banks that had relatively more MBS on their books.[7]

Another tool that has been necessary in our environment is a negative interest rate policy. By opening up the lower bound—and so removing the expectation that when rates reach zero, they can only go up, not down—we have been able to drive overnight rates well into negative territory and strongly anchor the short- to medium-term segment of the yield curve in particular.

Indeed, since we paired negative rates with asset purchases beginning in mid-2014, the short- to medium-term segment of the overnight index swap forward rate curve, which arguably reflects investors' rate expectations most accurately, has clearly shifted down and become flatter. During the period in which the Fed carried out its large-scale asset purchases, there was no comparable pattern.[8] Because of the structure of the euro area financial system, this is especially stimulative since shorter-term rates are key benchmarks that banks use for pricing loans, in particular to firms.

It is important that we have not seen the types of distortions from negative rates that many people expected. As Ben Bernanke highlights, the Fed eschewed negative rates in part out of concern about their effects on the money market funds industry, which is a key intermediary in the U.S. financial system.

But this is less relevant in the euro area, since in our economy the money market funds industry plays a much smaller role.[9] In addition, certain idiosyncratic characteristics of the U.S. money market funds industry posed higher challenges, in particular the persistent prominence of "constant net asset value funds," which face more difficulties in offering negative nominal returns.

Euro-area money market funds have actually seen inflows in recent years, reflecting factors such as the implementation of the liquidity coverage ratio by banks, relative value considerations among investors, and the flexibility of variable net asset value funds to extend duration to seek additional returns.

The positive effects of negative rates are also not neutralized by harmful effects on bank profits, as is sometimes claimed. New analysis by ECB staff finds that, though low-for-long short-term rates reduce interest rate margins, substantial adverse effects materialize only after a relatively long period. Moreover, the main components of profitability largely offset each other, with the positive impact on loan-loss provisions largely canceling out the negative effect on net interest income.[10]

What is also distinct from other jurisdictions is how we have constructed our forward guidance, which is interlinked between our different policy tools. The first leg of this guidance applies to the asset purchase program, which is both time- and state-based. Namely, it will run at its current pace "until the end of December 2017, or beyond, if necessary, and in any case until the Governing Council sees a sustained adjustment in the path of inflation consistent with its inflation aim."[11]

This is then tied to our guidance on interest rates, which will stay "at their present levels for an extended period of time, and well past the horizon of our net asset purchases." In this way, our rate guidance also has both time- and state-based dimensions, since rates cannot rise until we see an improvement in the inflation outlook sufficient to end net asset purchases.

This chained and sequenced forward guidance reflects the fact that, as noted by Ben Bernanke in chapter 1, expectations about interest rate policy and asset purchases are complementary.

Policy commitments vis-à-vis asset purchases not only compress the term premium but also reinforce the signal that the central bank will keep rates low well into the future. And expectations that rates will remain low—at least until net asset purchases are completed—support those purchases by preventing that the stimulus introduced by them through compressing the term premium is offset by expectations of an early rate hike.

This is why the ECB has repeatedly reaffirmed the sequencing of policy measures as laid out in our forward guidance. Our experience is that this has succeeded in preventing short-term interest rate expectations from creeping up while asset purchases are still ongoing.

Lessons for the Future

What lessons can we draw from our experience for future monetary policy—and in particular for responding to future recessions?

A first lesson is that there is an interdependence between institutional and financial structures and the tools deployed during a crisis.

As the comparison with the U.S. experience shows, the specific measures we deployed were determined crucially by the context we encountered. While several central banks faced transmission problems, the euro area was confronted with financial fragmentation along national lines that did not have a parallel elsewhere. This reflected our incomplete institutional framework that became visible as a result of the crisis.

The implication is that institutional reform in the euro area could affect not only the efficacy of the single monetary policy but also the set of unconventional monetary policies applied in a crisis.

The second lesson I would draw is that, when conventional policy is not enough to secure price stability, we have no shortage of tools to steer the economy back toward our inflation aim.

The combination of negative rates and asset purchases, coupled with our targeted lending operations, has proved powerful in easing financial conditions and stimulating aggregate demand—much more so than most observers expected when we launched our program. We have also shown that we can respond flexibly to adverse circumstances as they arise, whether by adopting new measures or recalibrating the various parameters of our policy.

Indeed, rather than highlighting the limits of central banks, our experience with unconventional policies has, if anything, strengthened our confidence in the effectiveness of monetary policy.

Notes

1. This includes recapitalization measures, asset relief interventions, liquidity measures, and guarantees. For 2009, the numbers as a percentage of GDP are around 12 percent for the Netherlands, 8 percent for Germany, 5.4 percent for Spain, and 5 percent for France.

2. The calculation assumes all exposures had been subject to fair valuation and applies to bonds of Cyprus, Greece, Ireland, Italy, Portugal, Slovenia, and Spain.

3. Based on end-2010 core tier capital.

4. A significant share of government bonds was held by banks at amortized cost.

5. Annual growth rate of loans to nonfinancial corporations (annual percentage changes).

6. See ECB (2017), box 5, pp. 42–46.

7. Kurtzman, Luck, and Zimmermann (2017).

8. See Praet (2017).

9. In August 2017, the euro-area money market industry managed a total amount of €1.2 trillion, compared with $2.7 trillion in the United States.

10. See Altavilla, Boucinha, and Peydró (2017).

11. This reflects the forward guidance as it stood at the time of the conference. On October 26, 2017, the ECB Governing Council decided, "From January 2018 our net asset purchases are intended to continue at a monthly pace of €30 billion until the end of September 2018, or beyond, if necessary, and in any case until the Governing Council sees a sustained adjustment in the path of inflation consistent with its inflation aim."

References

Altavilla, C., M. Boucinha, and J.-L. Peydró. 2017. "Monetary Policy and Bank Profitability in a Low Interest Rate Environment." ECB Working Paper 2105. European Central Bank, October.

European Central Bank (ECB). 2017. "The Targeted Longer-Term Refinancing Operations: An Overview of the Take-up and Their Impact on Bank Intermediation." *Economic Bulletin* 3.

Kurtzman, R., S. Luck, and T. Zimmermann. 2017. "Did QE Lead Banks to Relax Their Lending Standards? Evidence from the Federal Reserve's LSAPs." Finance and Economics Discussion Series 2017–093. Washington, DC: Board of Governors of the Federal Reserve System.

Praet, Peter. 2017. "Unconventional Monetary Policy and Fixed Income Markets." Remarks at the Fixed Income Market Colloquium, Rome, July 4.

II

Fiscal Policy

6

Fiscal Policy

Alan J. Auerbach

Fiscal policy is back, largely as a consequence of the very severe, prolonged Great Recession/global financial crisis that led into the challenges facing monetary policy as it was forced to confront the limitations presented by the zero lower bound (ZLB). But the practice of fiscal policy remains subject to some controversy, related to long-standing issues as well as ones of relatively recent vintage. In this chapter, I address several challenges that currently confront the United States and other developed countries in seeking the appropriate fiscal policy path.

Below, I discuss the following four issues:

1. The role that fiscal rules should play in limiting fiscal policy actions;
2. The potential for stabilization policy to limit the severity of economic fluctuations;
3. The practice of fiscal policy in a low-interest-rate environment; and
4. Coordination and distinction between monetary and fiscal policies.

A brief conclusion follows this discussion.

Role of Fiscal Rules

The debate between following rules and practicing discretion may have originated in the monetary policy sphere, but it has become central to fiscal policy as well. Fiscal rules are everywhere, yet so is discretionary fiscal policy.

There is little doubt that some fiscal rules make more sense than others. For example, it is hard to see much value in having the national debt limit that has caused so much political distress in recent years in the United States: since Congress decides on spending and taxes, why require it to decide separately on the difference between the two, insofar as it lacks the power to violate an identity? (And, in addition, why base the limit, as the U.S. rule does, on a gross measure that includes debt held by government agencies?) Limits on certain classes of expenditures invite substitution by spending in other categories, and overall expenditure limits can be circumvented through the use of tax expenditures (i.e., expenditure programs carried out through the tax code). But even logical and well-written fiscal rules require justification, because constraining a government's ability to practice fiscal policy has obvious disadvantages as well.

The standard arguments favoring rules for monetary policy, such as avoiding destabilizing actions or dynamic inconsistency on the part of government, also apply here, but there are others as well, owing to the many dimensions of choice and effect that fiscal policy can have. Most notably, fiscal policies can have important distributional effects within and across generations, and fiscal sustainability and the avoidance of fiscal crises are paramount concerns. Yet there are also significant arguments *against* fiscal rules that haven't been central in the monetary policy context, including the difficulty of measuring fiscal policy's stance, an issue discussed below.

Another key difference between fiscal and monetary rules is that fiscal rules can and often do apply at subnational levels of government. Nearly all U.S. states have some version of a simple, easily described balanced-budget rule, which typically specifies an adjustment process for dealing (possibly immediately) with general fund deficits and permits borrowing on a regular basis only for smoothing very short-run (e.g., seasonal) revenue fluctuations or funding capital spending. At the other extreme, perhaps the most elaborate fiscal rules in existence are those that apply to member countries of the EU, the culmination of a process dating to the original Stability and Growth Pact in the 1990s and now enshrined in a 224-page volume (European Commission 2017) specifying the rules and the enforcement process in great detail. This framework has undergone substantial revision over the years, with new features added as the actions of member countries were seen to reveal weaknesses in the existing structure. But rule complexity does not guarantee success, as it invites subjective interpretation and reduces transparency. The problems are particularly severe when the underlying objectives are unclear.

In a single jurisdiction, such as at the U.S. federal level, a potential objective for fiscal rules may be to counteract the myopia that is built into the political process by the short tenure of officeholders, which encourages excessive transfers of resources from future generations to current ones or from future governments with different objectives than the current one. Clearly, the limits on spending or deficits that the United States has attempted over the years were at least partly motivated by such concerns. Also, while not a major issue for the United States, more practical concerns might play a role, motivating governments that seek to maintain access to capital markets to use self-imposed restrictions to establish a more credible commitment to fiscal sustainability.

In a federal system, such as the EU, other possible reasons for fiscal rules arise, including limiting the transmission of fiscal shocks among member countries and avoiding pressure for bailouts, either through direct fiscal assistance or through support from the central bank. The fact that the EU fiscal rules are centrally imposed suggests motivations of this kind, although one might also justify centralized imposition of budget rules as providing help to the governments of individual countries in resisting political pressure from local interest groups, in much the way that international trade agreements can. While it is hard to judge the design of fiscal rules without knowing their motivation, the EU rules make little sense with regard to some of these possible objectives.

For example, the cross-border linkages within the EU are far weaker than those among states within the United States (for which the fiscal rules are not centrally imposed but rather were adopted voluntarily for reasons relating to capital market access), and limiting the transmission of shocks could well require fiscal policy *action* rather than inaction.[1] As for other objectives, the successive failure at getting countries to abide by deficit targets, culminating in the ongoing Greek bailout, has resulted in a series of refinements, especially in 2005 and 2011, aimed at making the rules more effective. But modification has not proved very helpful, in the EU or in the United States, where a succession of budget rules, from the Gramm-Rudman-Hollings legislation of the 1980s to the Budget Enforcement Act of the 1990s, seems to have had little lasting impact.

Indeed, a very basic question is whether fiscal rules can have any effect at all, good or bad, given these experiences. Empirical analysis is quite difficult in the EU or U.S. context because there are no clear natural experiments that would allow us to separate the effects of rules from those of other factors, such as a change in a government's commitment to budget discipline; one cannot treat budget rule adoption or modification as a random event if it results from a change in the policy environment.[2] Perhaps the clearest evidence comes from analyses of U.S. states, for which budget rule characteristics typically date to the nineteenth century. This variation is arguably unrelated to current unobservable differences among states. The evidence finds that budget rule stringency does affect the speed and nature of fiscal responses (Poterba 1994), with the consequence that state-level economic fluctuations are more severe where rules are more stringent (Clemens and Miran 2012).

These findings provide support for greater rule flexibility, especially during recessions. The case is made stronger (as discussed below) by recent fiscal consolidation outcomes following the Great Recession of 2008–2009. But the very existence of stringent fiscal rules is a reminder of the challenge of providing such flexibility without compromising the rules' enforceability, in light of the disagreements that arise in real time about the severity of economic conditions and the need for countercyclical policy.

As rules become more complex and lose transparency, they may effectively become guidelines, especially in a setting where, as in Europe, there is no credible enforcement mechanism; it is implausible that cash-strapped countries will actually be hit with large fines or expulsion because it is not in the interest of the organization to take such actions, even if they are threatened ex ante. This is unlike in the context of U.S. states, where states can be held to account because of a strong central government that performs important fiscal functions, including stabilization policy, and provides most of the safety net for the residents of individual states, and because of the ease with which state residents can "vote with their feet" by moving elsewhere. Though many have argued for an EU fiscal union, for this and other reasons, that outcome seems quite unlikely at this point.

One of the most challenging issues for budget rules to deal with involves control and monitoring of long-term commitments, particularly for age-based programs like public pensions and health care.[3] Unfunded commitments for future expenditures represent a rapidly growing implicit liability for virtually all developed countries because of rising health care costs and old-age dependency ratios. They swamp explicit government liabilities, in present value.

For example, as of the beginning of 2017, the official government-estimated (infinite-horizon) unfunded liability of the U.S. Social Security old-age pension and disability system was $34.2 trillion (Board of Trustees, OASDI Trust Funds 2017, table VI.F2) and that of the Medicare old-age health care system was $56.4 trillion (Board of Trustees, HI and SMI Trust Funds 2017, tables V.G2, V.G4, and V.G6).[4] By comparison, national debt held by the public at that time was $14.4 trillion.[5] Controlling what amounts to less than one-seventh of total liabilities seems like a bad start for a fiscal rule, and particularly ill-suited to a setting in which entitlement reform is an important policy issue. Indeed, this omission is currently a major fiscal problem for the U.S. states, for which balanced-budget rules exclude the large public employee pension obligations that have been incurred over the years and left many states with unfunded liabilities that are quite large in comparison to their explicit debt (Novy-Marx and Rauh 2011).

But for several reasons, simply adding implicit and explicit liabilities together to form some overall measure of indebtedness is not a solution either. First, such liabilities do not have the same legal status as explicit debt, even though they may be difficult to reduce politically. Second, the corresponding claims are not marketable and so are essentially an internal component of a country's national debt, denominated in the country's own currency. Third, also because these claims are not tradable, their market value can only be estimated, and estimates typically vary considerably depending on assumptions about economic growth, future interest rates, and demographic factors, making them more subject to political pressure and also more volatile from year to year, as forecasting assumptions are updated based on new information.

Recognizing the importance of addressing implicit liabilities, the current EU budget rules now include a specific "pension reform clause" (European Commission 2017, 41) that is intended to provide flexibility by ignoring additions to a country's deficit and debt that would be produced by a pension reform that substitutes explicit debt for implicit debt. Such increases in measured debt would result, for example, if a country substituted individual retirement accounts, funded with current workers' pension contributions, for these workers' future public pension benefits, while using public borrowing during transition to cover the legacy costs of the existing public system no longer financed by the ongoing pension contributions. Current workers would have assets in place of claims against the government, the government would have more debt outstanding but would be liable for smaller future pension claims, and current retirees would be unaffected.[6]

While, perhaps, a step in the right direction, the pension reform clause clearly increases the complexity and subjectivity of the budget rules. Yet at the same time, it deals only partially with the implicit liability problem. First, pension reform can reduce implicit liabilities without having any consequences for explicit debt. An example would be a permanent, equal-sized reduction in a public pension program's annual benefits and dedicated taxes, starting from a position of annual cash-flow balance.[7] Second, the provision applies only to pension reform, even though, for many countries, old-age health commitments may be a bigger fiscal problem. Third, while old-age spending may account for the most important "off-budget" component of a government's balance sheet, a country's tax structure matters as well.

An example to illustrate this last point is the taxation of private pensions, which, even if no tax is applied to the inside buildup during the middle, accumulation phase, can occur either at the initial, contribution stage (by taxing pension contributions along with other employee compensation, following the so-called T(axed)E(xempt)E(xempt) approach) or at the final, withdrawal stage (by allowing tax-free pension contributions but taxing all withdrawals, following the EET approach).

Under certain assumptions,[8] the two approaches yield the same economic outcomes for individuals and government, in terms of incentives for saving and the present value of tax revenues. If these assumptions do not hold, there may be policy reasons to prefer one approach to the other, or to wish to utilize some combination of the two. But unrelated to these policy reasons is the fact that, in relation to the TEE approach, the EET approach provides lower short-term tax revenues and offsets these with a deferred tax asset associated with future withdrawals. Budget rules that ignore this relationship provide governments with a simple way of dealing with deficit limits, by replacing deferred taxes with current ones.[9] Rather than this being a unique or unusual case, the issue is quite pervasive within tax systems[10] and can distort tax policy in favor of measures that accelerate the government's receipt of tax revenues.

Finally, achievement of a sustainable fiscal policy does not guarantee that the policy is equitable on a generational basis. Two policies can have the same trajectory of revenues and spending and impose quite different patterns of fiscal burden on different generations. This is the primary rationale for the development of generational accounting (Auerbach, Gokhale, and Kotlikoff 1991), which goes beyond the assessment of sustainability by allocating components of the government's intertemporal budget constraint among current and future age cohorts.

Though some advocates have suggested incorporating generational accounts within budget rules, this has not occurred. Such a step would be even more challenging than a comprehensive inclusion of implicit assets and liabilities because of the necessary breakdown among cohorts, which in turn would require much more detailed projections, as well as a series of tax incidence assumptions. Generational accounts have been constructed not only by individual academic researchers but also by many governments over the years. Their main use has been and is likely to remain to provide information about existing generational burdens and how prospective policies could influence them. In this practice, one may see the provision of information as an alternative to budget rules. But the same alternative is available more generally, even in cases where the budget rules are far less ambitious and more easily specified.

In light of the conflict between flexibility and credibility, a logical step to consider seriously is whether to jettison the rule-based approach altogether and to strive to achieve some of the same ends through the provision of information, to make markets, voters, and indeed governments themselves aware of the possible pitfalls and benefits of policies being proposed or undertaken. In a sense, this is already the approach being taken through the detailed information provided by such documents as the EU's triennial *Aging Report*, which projects the pension payments of member countries and highlights the successes that several have achieved in recent years in reducing their long-term liabilities through pension reform.[11] Yet this approach can be strengthened by ensuring that evaluations of this kind are independent of government pressure, and can go further by incorporating assessments of the likelihood that enacted policy reforms will succeed, rather than simply taking current policy as given, and by evaluating policy changes in other dimensions, for example, with regard to distributional consequences.

Regarding this objective, there has been an important trend toward the creation of independent entities for fiscal evaluation, dating at least to the creation of the U.S. Congressional Budget Office (CBO) in 1974, and more recently including entities with greater autonomy and ability to evaluate government proposals, including the Swedish Fiscal Policy Council, established in 2008, and the UK's Office of Budget Responsibility, established in 2010. Such entities can confront complicated situations in a way that fiscal rules simply cannot. As is the case in the United Kingdom, the fiscal entity can also be given the power to lay out the economic and fiscal projections on which the government's policy evaluations must be based. Although there are many potentially relevant characteristics of such councils, there is some preliminary evidence that having a fiscal council that is legally independent and with a broad responsibility for monitoring fiscal policy may enhance economic performance as well as the quality of fiscal forecasts (Debrun and Kinda 2014).

Fiscal councils should be viewed as having the potential to serve an important auditing role, rather than to directly constrain or determine fiscal policy in the manner intended for fiscal rules. Because of the political determination of fiscal policy, no such delegation of the kind now provided to independent monetary authorities is really conceivable for these fiscal entities. But this is not really a limitation, relative to the power of budget rules, given what budget rules actually can do. Further, more than simple budget rules, independent fiscal bodies can expose gaps in logic and provide additional support and pressure for needed changes in fiscal policy that may require implementation over a period of years.

Although the fiscal council is still a relatively new and evolving mechanism, it may well play a much more important role than explicit fiscal rules in helping countries undertake large and long-term fiscal adjustments. For the future, coming up with the right combination of independence, scope, and authority for such entities probably deserves more attention than the continuing refinement of formal budget rules. This is especially so in light of two factors, the increasing relative importance of a long-term perspective in assessing fiscal policy adjustments and the difficulty of designing rules that are transparent and credible while at the same time allowing sufficient flexibility.

Stabilization Policy

The perceived role that fiscal policy should play in promoting economic stabilization has undergone a considerable change in the last decade as a consequence of economic conditions and advances in economic research. We have gone from perhaps a consensus that automatic stabilizers should be the primary fiscal tool for countercyclical policy, because discretionary fiscal policy is difficult to time or relatively ineffective when implemented, to a much stronger sense of the potential value of discretionary fiscal policy to address recessions.

Part of the support for this view comes from results showing that, anecdotal evidence notwithstanding, discretionary fiscal policy actually has been reasonably well timed, at least for the United States since the early 1980s. For example, measuring discretionary policy changes either by changes in the full-employment surplus or by CBO estimates of legislated changes in revenues and spending, expansionary (contractionary) policy changes have been implemented during periods of economic weakness (strength), as measured by the gap between actual and potential GDP (Auerbach 2003).

But more central to the evolving view of discretionary fiscal policy has been a series of empirical studies that has shifted the weight of evidence, if not resulting in a complete consensus, regarding policy effectiveness. Using a variety of estimation strategies for different countries and different time periods, research has suggested that multipliers can be large for both tax and spending changes, and that the effects may be enhanced during periods of economic slack. Much of the research has been time-series based, building on the contribution by the SVAR analysis of Blanchard and Perotti (2002) by using approaches to identifying fiscal shocks that went beyond the original method of assuming no within-period discretionary policy feedbacks. Only a selection of the results from this substantial literature can be cited here, to illustrate key findings.

Relying on a narrative approach to identify tax policy changes unrelated to short-run economic factors, Romer and Romer (2010) found a peak impact multiplier of around 3 for legislated U.S. federal tax changes for the postwar period ending in 2007, just before the start of the Great Recession. Based on a regime-switching smooth-transition VAR (STVAR) approach, Auerbach and Gorodnichenko (2012) found that the

Blanchard-Perotti multiplier estimates for government spending represented an average of multipliers that were much larger in recessions than expansions, in the range of 1 to 1.5 in recessions but falling below 0.5 in expansions, and that the difference across regimes became stronger when one sharpened identification of fiscal shocks by adding real-time professional forecasts to the information set. Using as an alternative to the STVAR methodology a direct-projections approach to estimate multipliers over different horizons directly using single equations, but again controlling for professional forecasts and allowing for state dependence, Auerbach and Gorodnichenko (2013) found the same state-dependent multiplier pattern based on semiannual data for a sample of OECD countries, for GDP as well as other macroeconomic aggregates, suggesting that their original findings were not attributable to factors specific to the United States.

Finally, a large number of papers have utilized cross-state variation in spending and transfer programs within the United States to estimate multipliers, often finding very large effects (e.g., Nakamura and Steinsson 2014), including specifically for policies adopted during the Great Recession (e.g., Chodorow-Reich et al. 2012). Translating these multipliers, often in the range of 1.5 to 2 for GDP or some related output measure, into national-level multipliers is difficult because some factors (e.g., cross-state leakage) imply lower cross-section multipliers while others (e.g., little offsetting tax liability to pay for federally financed state-level spending or tax changes) imply larger ones, but under reasonable assumptions the cross-state results are consistent with large national multipliers, perhaps larger than those found by Auerbach and Gorodnichenko (2012), especially for countries facing the ZLB, for which offsetting monetary responses would not be expected (Chodorow-Reich 2018).

One final piece of evidence suggesting large multipliers during the recent Great Recession is the finding by Blanchard and Leigh (2013) that, especially early in the crisis period, output forecast errors of the IMF and other organizations were correlated with the size of fiscal consolidations undertaken by different countries, which indicates (under certain assumptions) that the multipliers used in constructing the forecasts understated the true multipliers. This is particularly noteworthy because the question of whether fiscal consolidations can make sense, even during periods of economic slack, has been debated for many years.

In theory, a fiscal consolidation can be expansionary, depending on what the alternative policy path would have been and what other reforms (e.g., of labor markets) might accompany the consolidation. Empirically, there have been conflicting results, with differences relating to sample identification and subtle methodological differences, such as how one controls for monetary policy responses, although earlier findings in favor of the expansionary effects of fiscal consolidations have given way to a range of estimates falling between mild contractionary effects (e.g., Alesina, Favero, and Giavazzi 2015) and stronger ones (Leigh et al. 2010). One fairly persistent result is that tax-based consolidations tend to have been more damaging than spending-based consolidations. The IMF (Leigh et al. 2010) traces much of this difference to tighter monetary policy responses to tax-based consolidations, although the nature of identification of consolidations makes it difficult to explain the reason for this difference in monetary policy reactions. More generally, it is hard to know whether these results would hold for a particular country choosing between the two approaches, as opposed to the choices made in the past by different countries in different circumstances.

One condition that might affect the desirability of fiscal consolidation is a country's initial fiscal position. By their nature, consolidation plans are undertaken when countries perceive the need for greater fiscal responsibility, but initial debt levels and other fiscal indicators can still vary. The literature has found mixed results regarding whether fiscal multipliers vary according to initial indebtedness, as measured by a country's debt-to-GDP ratio. Among relatively recent studies, some (e.g., Ilzetzki, Mendoza, and Végh 2013) find a lower fiscal multiplier in high-debt countries and some (e.g., Corsetti, Meier, and Müller 2012) show little difference across low- and high-debt countries.

A question that has received relatively little attention in the empirical literature is the extent to which the dependence of multipliers on levels of indebtedness interacts with their dependence on the state of the economy. For example, might having a high debt level influence the effectiveness of fiscal policy less in an expansion than in a recession, when there may be greater concern among market participants about a fiscal expansion generating a financial crisis? Or, alternatively, might the greater strength of fiscal multipliers during periods of economic slack cause markets to have a more benign response to fiscal expansion, even for high-debt countries?

The latter might hold particularly if multipliers are so large in recession that the fiscal expansion actually reduces a country's debt-GDP ratio, as a consequence of stronger output and revenue growth. The likelihood of fiscal expansions being self-financing in such circumstances has been suggested recently by DeLong and Summers (2012).

Auerbach and Gorodnichenko (2017) address this question directly by estimating the relationship between debt-to-GDP ratios and fiscal shocks, using the same OECD data set and the same direct-projections methodology as in Auerbach and Gorodnichenko (2013). Their point estimates suggest that debt-to-GDP ratios actually fall in response to fiscal expansions when economies are in recession. This result is consistent with their finding that the perceived risk of fiscal crisis, as measured using credit default swap spreads on government debt, falls at the same time.[12] These results do not hold for positive fiscal shocks adopted during economic expansions.[13]

As to the question of how these results depend on initial debt levels, Auerbach and Gorodnichenko (2017, table 5) do find some differences in the patterns of results in booms versus slumps for high- versus low-debt environments; for example, there is a significant reduction in a country's debt-to-GDP ratio when a fiscal expansion is undertaken in a slump when the debt-to-GDP ratio is low, but an insignificantly positive impact when a fiscal expansion is undertaken in a slump when the debt-to-GDP ratio is high. They also find that fiscal stimulus during a slump significantly reduces long-term interest rates only when the debt-to-GDP ratio is low. But other results, for example, with respect to GDP and the CDS spread, are not more favorable in a slump when the debt-to-GDP ratio is low rather than high, so it is hard to draw strong conclusions from the available data regarding the pattern of results in this two-way (debt-to-GDP ratio and economic strength) comparison.

Note that the findings in Auerbach and Gorodnichenko (2017) are not based just on the period surrounding the Great Recession, and therefore apply more broadly, even in periods when interest rates and debt service were not so low. On the other hand, they are based on a historical period when debt-to-GDP ratios and implicit liabilities were generally considerably lower than they are now, and so should not be seen as a prescription for countries to ignore their fiscal positions when contemplating countercyclical fiscal policies or to pursue "bridges to nowhere" when doing so.

In contrast to the resurgence of confidence in the use of discretionary fiscal policy, there has been relatively little recent attention to the role that automatic stabilizers can play as a complementary policy tool. One exception is the paper by McKay and Reis (2016), who evaluate the impact of automatic stabilizers on the U.S. economy in a calibrated DSGE model with heterogeneous agents, estimating the impact of tax and transfer systems on the smoothing of output and consumption in response to economic shocks. Their findings are largely negative, in that the existing tax and transfer system is relatively ineffective at stabilizing output or improving welfare, while emphasizing the potential importance of channels other than the one usually cited, of cushioning disposable income fluctuations. These channels include the social insurance mechanism (which, by reducing the need for precautionary saving, can lead to a lower ability to engage in consumption smoothing) and redistribution among households with different current spending propensities. Because automatic stabilizers are chosen with a longer-run focus than discretionary policy, more research on the performance of alternative types of tax and transfer programs in response to economic shocks would be quite useful for policy design, which typically proceeds without paying much attention to cyclical consequences.

Even though discretionary fiscal policy is normally undertaken with a limited horizon for its effects, it still might benefit from longer-range planning, to make discretionary policy actions more effective when they are undertaken. For example, during the process of adopting the American Recovery and Reinvestment Act of 2009 (ARRA) in the United States, there was concern that planned infrastructure spending would confront a lack of "shovel-ready" public works projects that were socially beneficial and could be undertaken rapidly and efficiently. Reflecting the likelihood of implementation delays, the ARRA legislation permitted funds provided to be spent several years afterward,[14] presumably well after any countercyclical benefit could be realized.

To shorten such delays in the future, some have proposed maintaining a bank of ready-to-go infrastructure projects that can be undertaken quickly (e.g., Transportation Research Board 2014). But the desirability of this approach is questionable, for the projects involved might be delayed for several years, depending on the timing of the next recession. This potential delay would make critically needed projects unsuitable for the program and would require continual updates to the project list to reflect changes in priorities and technology. Nevertheless, infrastructure spending remains potentially attractive as a component of fiscal stimulus packages, given the large short- and medium-run multipliers that have been estimated for it relative to other components of government spending (Leduc and Wilson 2012). More evidence on the types of government spending that might be effective tools for countercyclical policy would be useful. For the United States, an alternative channel likely to suffer from shorter lags is direct transfers to state and local governments, to lessen their need to engage in the kind of sharp tax increases and spending cuts adopted during the last recession to comply with balanced-budget rules.

Fiscal Policy in a Low-Interest-Rate Environment

How should fiscal policy change in response to low government borrowing costs? Leaving aside the circumstance of monetary policy actually being constrained by the ZLB, which would have its own implications for fiscal policy (discussed below), low borrowing costs present the prospect of a lower cost of capital for government projects and a reduction in the burden of debt service. This has led to suggestions that an appropriate response would be a more expansive undertaking of government investment and a delay in undertaking the fiscal consolidations needed to respond to high debt-to-GDP ratios (e.g., Elmendorf and Sheiner 2017). Several notes of caution apply to this conclusion.

First, as noted above, debt-to-GDP ratios provide an incomplete measure of fiscal sustainability, especially for countries undergoing population aging with large implicit liabilities associated with unfunded or underfunded old-age pension and health care commitments. Because such commitments involve future cash-flow deficits under current policy projections, lower interest rates increase their present value, in the same way that they would for an underfunded private pension plan—it will take higher contribution levels to meet the cost of such obligations. This means that a country's overall fiscal gap—measured as the permanent annual adjustment of primary surpluses relative to GDP needed to make the fiscal policy path sustainable—need not fall much, or at all, as interest rates fall.[15]

Second, a low government interest rate may reduce the expected rate of short-term government debt accumulation, but expected debt accumulation is likely not the right measure to target in an uncertain environment, given that higher debt accumulation—and the need for more fiscal consolidation—is likely to coincide with weaker economic growth and a higher value of resources to the private and public sectors; that is, government planning should reflect risk aversion of the individuals it represents by attributing a higher cost of debt service than that implied by using the safe government interest rate.[16]

This argument for using a higher interest rate in evaluating potential government investment projects grows stronger once one also takes into account that government revenues must be raised in a distortionary manner. The tax increases in future states of the world in which a stronger fiscal consolidation is needed will be especially distortionary, given the high tax rates required and the nonlinear relationship between tax rates and deadweight loss. Such future tax rates may be especially high if the sharp increase in inequality that has occurred in the United States and to some extent in most other developed countries compels increases in the use of tax policy for redistribution in addition to paying for government purchases and debt service, and the deadweight loss associated with any given tax rates also may be higher in the future as a consequence of increased international labor and capital mobility.[17]

Third, to the extent that government borrowing crowds out private investment or increases the government's own interest rate, the low rate of return on government debt may not fully reflect its opportunity cost. Finally, as concerns borrowing for the specific purpose of undertaking public investment, the irreversibility of that investment should be included as a factor in evaluating benefits. Irreversibility is a standard argument for higher required rates of return for private investment (e.g., Dixit and Pindyck 1994), but it would seem that it is a much bigger concern for many types of government investment projects—there is no secondary market for bridges and highways.

One interesting and relatively recent argument in favor of additional government borrowing based on low interest rates is the scarcity of safe assets, particularly those issued by the U.S. government and held around the world. While much of the literature on the question has focused on the positive macroeconomic effects of an increase in safe-asset supply, the U.S. government should already have its own incentive to respond; as a supplier of safe assets with considerable market power, it should be in a position to earn rents from other countries by doing so.

A need for more safe assets is certainly plausible, but the solution of supplying more government debt brings with it the question of what to do with the debt. Borrowing to cut taxes is an extremely counterintuitive policy prescription, insofar as this combination may increase the likelihood that the government will experience fiscal stress, which has led some to suggest the alternative strategy of increasing investment in public infrastructure (Caballero, Gourinchas, and Farhi 2017).

But why not use the additional government funds to finance private investment? Presumably, the choice between private and public investment should depend on where potential social returns are higher, taking into account the actual uses to which public investment funds would be put, the deadweight cost of private tax revenues forgone as a consequence of public rather than private investment, differences in the distribution of benefits, and so forth. A recent history of underinvestment in the public sector, for which a compelling case exists in the United States, would be a strong argument for focusing on public investment. But that case for public investment is different from the one made simply by ruling out private investment as a potential outlet for funds generated by additional government borrowing.

The possibility of government-funded private investment does raise additional issues, as it did in the 1990s when there was a serious policy discussion of whether the U.S. Social Security trust fund should be invested in private securities. Perhaps the most concerning, and the source of much opposition at the time, is whether this investment, particularly if undertaken on a large scale, could result in serious government interference in the private sector, going well beyond the government's current involvement through tax and regulatory policies.

Whether sufficient safeguards could be provided to make this new financial intermediation channel feasible deserves further thought, given the potential drawbacks of other uses of funds that would be raised with the purpose of making more safe assets available to investors.

Fiscal and Monetary Policies: Distinction and Coordination

The borderline between monetary and fiscal policy has never been as precise as textbooks suggest. Monetary policy as traditionally practiced (through open market operations rather than the textbook helicopter injections) generates government revenue directly through seigniorage and indirectly through inflation-induced erosion in the value of nominal government liabilities, which can be a particularly important policy tool in case of "financial repression" that keeps nominal interest rates low (Reinhart and Belen Sbrancia 2015). Fiscal policy affects inflation and the price level, the main purview of monetary policy, in a very fundamental manner if one subscribes to the fiscal theory of the price level (e.g., Woodford 1995), but also under more standard modeling assumptions.

However, recent expansions in the scope of central bank actions, spurred first by the global financial crisis and then by the constraints on traditional monetary policy imposed by the ZLB constraint, have further blurred the line. Some critics (e.g., Goodfriend 2011; Sinn 2014) have suggested that central banks have moved well beyond the acceptable division of responsibilities between monetary and fiscal authorities, especially by expanding the class of assets they have purchased to include those of lower quality and higher risk, while at the same time not making a full adjustment for such risk. In a mechanical sense, at the very least, one can view these practices as constituting fiscal policy. For example, in the United States, the Fed's purchase of nongovernmental assets instead of Treasury bills could be replicated through a fiscal policy operation by having the U.S. government issue Treasury bills in order to buy the nongovernmental assets.

As a practical matter, political limits on the implementation of effective fiscal policy broaden the scope for monetary policy, whether this occurs during a financial crisis when support for private credit markets is quickly needed, or essentially at any time when a currency union with no central fiscal authority seeks to support failing economies. On the other hand, limits on the effectiveness of monetary policy, in particular when a country faces the ZLB, invite the more active use of fiscal policy.

Theory and DSGE model simulations (e.g., Christiano, Eichenbaum, and Rebelo 2011; Eggertsson 2010; Woodford 2011) suggest that fiscal policy multipliers can be much larger when the ZLB is binding. But most of the empirical analysis finding higher fiscal multipliers in recession comes from data samples from periods when the ZLB did not apply, or applied very little, during recessionary periods.

There is some evidence from Japan, essentially the only country that has faced the ZLB for potentially a long enough period for time series analysis, that fiscal policy multipliers are much larger when the ZLB applies than when it does not, and at least some argument that this difference is not simply attributable to the ZLB applying during recessions (Miyamoto, Nguyen, and Sergeyev 2017). However, these conclusions are tentative, and without more data and empirical analysis, we cannot conclude as yet that fiscal multipliers are bigger when the ZLB applies, holding constant the state of the business cycle. At the same time, we lack a single, generally accepted theory for why fiscal multipliers are larger in recessions than expansions, when the ZLB does not apply. Coalescing around such a theory would be useful not only in understanding the existing evidence but also in determining what happens to the predicted effects of fiscal policy when the ZLB applies.

Conclusions

Recent events and research have changed our perspectives on fiscal policy. These include a largely negative experience with fiscal rules, the growing challenge of fiscal sustainability in economies with aging populations, a declining excitement based on empirical evidence about the possibility of expansionary fiscal contractions, our experience in dealing with the global financial crisis, and a prolonged period of very low government interest rates.

Our experience, along with contributions to theory and evidence, leaves us with many challenges and areas where additional research would be useful. Among them are how to develop a fiscal framework that facilitates the use of fiscal policy for stabilization, while at the same time preserving a credible commitment to fiscal sustainability, and how to make attempts at fiscal stabilization more timely and effective, to lessen some of the recent imperative to expand the scope of monetary policy.

These are challenging tasks, and governments must face them in an adverse environment in which increasing inequality within countries pushes toward greater government action through spending and redistribution, even as increasing mobility of companies and capital has led to intensified tax competition, particularly with respect to corporate taxation, and downward pressure on tax rates and revenues. Although such a discussion would go beyond the scope of this chapter, it seems evident that facing these tasks in this environment will require reform of the tax structures on which governments rely, and consideration of the extent to which the path to tax reform and more stable tax systems is through international cooperation or national initiatives.

Notes

This chapter was prepared as a paper for the conference "Rethinking Macroeconomic Policy IV," held at the Peterson Institute of International Economics, Washington, D.C., October 12–13, 2017. I am grateful to Olivier Blanchard, Bill Gale, and the conference participants for comments on an earlier draft.

1. On weaker cross-border linkages in the EU than in the United States, see the discussion in Auerbach (2011). On capital market access as a reason for adopting the fiscal rules in the United States, see Eichengreen and von Hagen (1996).

2. Auerbach (2008) considers patterns of government responses to fiscal conditions across different U.S. federal budget regimes, rather than trying to assess their overall impact on debt and deficits, and finds some differences that are consistent with the form of the budget rules. For example, there were stronger policy responses to lagged budget deficits and weaker responses to economic conditions during the Gramm-Rudman-Hollings period in the 1980s, when specific deficit targets applied.

3. Even in countries that, unlike the United States, provide public health care funding for all or most residents, health care spending is to a considerable extent an old-age program because of the much higher level of spending per capita among the elderly.

4. The unfunded liabilities for Medicare Parts B and D equal the present values of projected general revenue funding for these two programs, which, unlike Social Security and Medicare Part A, do not have dedicated funding sources.

5. Although infinite-horizon projections are not available for other countries, even calculations over a much shorter horizon (which reduces their size, given the worsening cash-flow imbalances over time) shows that health and pension liabilities, based on IMF projections through 2050, are large relative to publicly held debt for the other G-7 countries as well. See Auerbach and Gorodnichenko (2017).

6. Even with no change in the sum of explicit and implicit liabilities, one might push for such a reform to provide greater capital market access to current workers. This was an argument used during the George W. Bush administration in support of a U.S. proposal along these lines and was not without its critics. However, the reform could also be coupled with a reduction in overall liabilities, and that is presumably a motivation for the EU pension reform clause, in light of the need for countries to improve long-run fiscal sustainability.

7. In the limit, with annual contributions and benefits being reduced all the way to zero, there would be no implicit liability at all, and yet no change in the annual cash-flow balance.

8. These are that individual savers face the same tax rate when saving and withdrawing funds and may contribute the same after-tax amounts under the two systems.

9. Indeed, the U.S. government has utilized this strategy in moving from traditional (EET) IRA and 401(k) arrangements to so-called Roth (TEE) arrangements, going so far as to offer additional tax incentives for account holders to speed up tax payments by withdrawing funds from traditional accounts and depositing them in Roth accounts.

10. See Auerbach (2009).

11. See, for example, European Commission (2015), pp. 54–112.

12. The latter result is especially useful in ascertaining whether expansionary fiscal policy improves or worsens the market's perception of the government's fiscal position, to the extent that government debt fails to measure a government's fiscal stress accurately, for example, because of large looming future deficits or implicit liabilities of the kind discussed earlier.

13. The paper also provides estimates at an annual (rather than semiannual) frequency based on the IMF fiscal consolidations data set discussed earlier, with similar findings regarding the effects on debt-to-GDP ratios and CDS spreads.

14. The spending deadline—September 30, 2017, the end of the 2017 fiscal year—has only recently passed, more than eight years after the official end of the Great Recession in the United States.

15. For example, Auerbach and Gale (2009) estimated that, over the infinite horizon, the U.S. fiscal gap was actually increased by assuming that the government would face a zero interest rate for the next twenty years, rather than the interest rates being projected at the time by the CBO.

16. This is essentially the point made by Ball, Elmendorf, and Mankiw (1998) in arguing that having a safe rate of return below the rate of economic growth can still leave future generations worse off as a consequence of additional borrowing. One may also see this argument as related to the one rejecting the notion that a low safe rate of interest, below the economy's growth rate, is evidence of dynamic inefficiency (Abel et al. 1989). The point could be strengthened by the presence of implicit liabilities, which are associated with future cash-flow deficits that must be met with additional resources, if the revenues associated with entitlement programs are more sensitive to the business cycle than program costs. This would be true, for example, if, as is the case for the U.S. Social Security system, the pension benefits of those already in retirement are price-level indexed while dedicated tax revenues depend on real wages.

17. These issues are discussed further in Auerbach (2014). Note that this argument applies to some extent even if borrowing is used for capital expenditures, because most government investment projects do not yield a direct government revenue stream, although one would want to take into account any revenues generated indirectly by enhanced private productivity.

References

Abel, Andrew B., N. Gregory Mankiw, Lawrence H. Summers, and Richard J. Zeckhauser. 1989. "Assessing Dynamic Efficiency: Theory and Evidence." *Review of Economic Studies* 56 (1): 1–19.

Alesina, Alberto, Carlo Favero, and Francesco Giavazzi. 2015. "The Output Effect of Fiscal Consolidation Plans." *Journal of International Economics* 96 (S1): S19–S42.

Auerbach, Alan J. 2003. "Is There a Role for Discretionary Fiscal Policy?" In *Rethinking Stabilization Policy*, 109–150. Federal Reserve Bank of Kansas City.

Auerbach, Alan J. 2008. "Federal Budget Rules: The U.S. Experience." *Swedish Economic Policy Review* 15:57–82.

Auerbach, Alan J. 2009. "Long-Term Objectives for Government Debt." *Finanz-Archiv* 65 (4): 472–501.

Auerbach, Alan J. 2011. "Fiscal Institutions for a Currency Union." Paper presented at the conference "Fiscal and Monetary Policy Challenges in the Short and Long Run," sponsored by Deutsche Bundesbank and Banque de France, Hamburg, May 19–20.

Auerbach, Alan J. 2014. "Fiscal Uncertainty and How to Deal with It." Hutchins Center Working Paper 6. Washington, DC: Hutchins Center on Fiscal and Monetary Policy at the Brookings Institution, December 15.

Auerbach, Alan J., and William G. Gale. 2009. "The Economic Crisis and the Fiscal Crisis: 2009 and Beyond. An Update." *Tax Notes* 125 (1) (October 5): 101–130.

Auerbach, Alan J., Jagadeesh Gokhale, and Laurence J. Kotlikoff. 1991. "Generational Accounts: A Meaningful Alternative to Deficit Accounting." In *Tax Policy and the Economy*, vol. 5, ed. D. Bradford, 55–110. Cambridge, MA: National Bureau of Economic Research.

Auerbach, Alan J., and Yuriy Gorodnichenko. 2012. "Measuring the Output Responses to Fiscal Policy." *American Economic Journal: Economic Policy* 4 (2): 1–27.

Auerbach, Alan J., and Yuriy Gorodnichenko. 2013. "Fiscal Multipliers in Recession and Expansion." In *Fiscal Policy after the Financial Crisis*, ed. A. Alesina and F. Giavazzi, 63–98. Chicago: University of Chicago Press.

Auerbach, Alan J., and Yuriy Gorodnichenko. 2017. "Fiscal Stimulus and Fiscal Sustainability." In *Fostering a Dynamic Global Economy*, 217–270. Federal Reserve Bank of Kansas City.

Ball, Laurence M., Douglas W. Elmendorf, and N. Gregory Mankiw. 1998. "The Deficit Gamble." *Journal of Money, Credit and Banking* 30 (4): 699–720.

Blanchard, Olivier J., and Daniel Leigh. 2013. "Growth Forecast Errors and Fiscal Multipliers." *American Economic Review* 103 (3): 117–120.

Blanchard, Olivier J., and Roberto Perotti. 2002. "An Empirical Characterization of the Dynamic Effects of Changes in Government Spending and Taxes on Output." *Quarterly Journal of Economics* 117 (4): 1329–1368.

Board of Trustees, Federal Old-Age and Survivors Insurance and Disability Insurance Trust Funds (OASDI Trust Funds). 2017. *Annual Report*. Washington, DC.

Board of Trustees, Federal Hospital Insurance and Federal Supplementary Medical Insurance Trust Funds (HI and SMI Trust Funds). 2017. *Annual Report*. Washington, DC.

Caballero, Ricardo J., Pierre-Olivier Gourinchas, and Emmanuel Farhi. 2017. "The Safe Assets Shortage Conundrum." *Journal of Economic Perspectives* 31 (3): 29–36.

Chodorow-Reich, Gabriel. 2018. "Geographic Cross-Sectional Fiscal Spending Multipliers: What Have We Learned?" *American Economic Journal: Economic Policy*, forthcoming.

Chodorow-Reich, Gabriel, Laura Feiveson, Zachary Liscow, and William Gui Woolston. 2012. "Does State Fiscal Relief during Recessions Increase Employment? Evidence from the American Recovery and Reinvestment Act." *American Economic Journal: Economic Policy* 4 (3): 118–145.

Christiano, Lawrence, Martin Eichenbaum, and Sergio Rebelo. 2011. "When Is the Government Spending Multiplier Large?" *Journal of Political Economy* 119 (1): 78–121.

Clemens, Jeffrey, and Stephen Miran. 2012. "Fiscal Policy Multipliers on Subnational Government Spending." *American Economic Journal: Economic Policy* 4 (2): 46–68.

Corsetti, Giancarlo, Andre Meier, and Gernot J. Müller. 2012. "What Determines Government Spending Multipliers?" *Economic Policy* 27:521–565.

Debrun, Xavier, and Tidiane Kinda. 2014. "Strengthening Post-Crisis Fiscal Credibility: Fiscal Councils on the Rise—A New Dataset." IMF Working Paper WP/14/58. Washington, DC: International Monetary Fund, April.

DeLong, J. Bradford, and Lawrence H. Summers. 2012. "Fiscal Policy in a Depressed Economy." *Brookings Papers on Economic Activity* (Spring): 233–297.

Dixit, Avinash K., and Robert S. Pindyck. 1994. *Investment under Uncertainty*. Princeton, NJ: Princeton University Press.

Eggertsson, Gauti. 2010. "What Fiscal Policy Is Effective at Zero Interest Rates?" In *NBER Macroeconomics Annual*, ed. D. Acemoglu and M. Woodford, 59–112. Chicago: University of Chicago Press.

Eichengreen, Barry, and Jürgen von Hagen. 1996. "Fiscal Restrictions and Monetary Union: Rationales, Repercussions, Reforms." *Empirica* 23 (1): 3–23.

Elmendorf, Douglas W., and Louise M. Sheiner. 2017. "Federal Budget Policy with an Aging Population and Persistently Low Interest Rates." *Journal of Economic Perspectives* 31 (3): 175–194.

European Commission. 2015. *The 2015 Ageing Report: Economic and Budgetary Projections for the 28 EU Member States (2013–2060)*. Brussels: European Commission, March.

European Commission. 2017. *Vade Mecum on the Stability and Growth Pact*. Institutional Paper 052. Brussels: European Commission, March.

Goodfriend, Marvin. 2011. "Central Banking in the Credit Turmoil: An Assessment of Federal Reserve Practice." *Journal of Monetary Economics* 58 (1): 1–12.

Ilzetzki, Ethan, Enrique Mendoza, and Carlos Végh. 2013. "How Big (Small?) Are Fiscal Multipliers?" *Journal of Monetary Economics* 60 (2): 239–254.

Leduc, Sylvain, and Daniel J. Wilson. 2012. "Roads to Prosperity or Bridges to Nowhere: Theory and Evidence on the Impact of Public Infrastructure Investment." In *NBER Macroeconomic Annual 27*, ed. D. Acemoglu, J. Parker, and M. Woodford, 89–142. Cambridge, MA: National Bureau of Economic Research.

Leigh, Daniel, et al. 2010. "Will It Hurt? Macroeconomic Effects of Fiscal Consolidation." In *World Economic Outlook: Recovery, Risk, and Rebalancing*, 93–124. Washington, DC: International Monetary Fund.

McKay, Alisdair, and Ricardo Reis. 2016. "The Role of Automatic Stabilizers in the U.S. Business Cycle." *Econometrica* 84 (1): 141–194.

Miyamoto, Wataru, Thuy Lan Nguyen, and Dmitriy Sergeyev. 2017. "Government Spending Multipliers under the Zero Lower Bound: Evidence from Japan." Bank of Canada Staff Working Paper 2017-40. Ottawa, ON: Bank of Canada, September.

Nakamura, Emi, and Jón Steinsson. 2014. "Fiscal Stimulus in a Monetary Union: Evidence from U.S. Regions." *American Economic Review* 104 (3): 753–792.

Novy-Marx, Robert, and Joshua Rauh. 2011. "Public Pension Promises: How Big Are They and What Are They Worth?" *Journal of Finance* 66 (4): 1211–1249.

Poterba, James M. 1994. "State Responses to Fiscal Crises: The Effects of Budgetary Institutions and Politics." *Journal of Political Economy* 102 (4): 799–821.

Reinhart, Carmen M., and M. Belen Sbrancia. 2015. "The Liquidation of Government Debt." *Economic Policy* 30 (82): 91–333.

Romer, Christina D., and David H. Romer. 2010. "The Macroeconomic Effects of Tax Changes: Estimates Based on a New Measure of Fiscal Shocks." *American Economic Review* 100 (3): 763–801.

Sinn, Hans-Werner. 2014. *The Euro Trap*. Oxford: Oxford University Press.

Transportation Research Board. 2014. *Transportation Investments in Response to Economic Downturns*. Washington, DC: National Academies Press.

Woodford, Michael. 1995. "Price Level Determinacy without Control of a Monetary Aggregate." *Carnegie-Rochester Conference Series on Public Policy* 43 (December): 1–46.

Woodford, Michael. 2011. "Simple Analytics of the Government Expenditure Multiplier." *American Economic Journal: Macroeconomics* 3 (1): 1–35.

7

Adverse Effects of Unsound Fiscal Policies: The U.S. Example

Robert E. Rubin

I'll present my thoughts on rethinking fiscal policy in the spirit of Fischer Black, who, some years after leaving MIT for Goldman Sachs, said, though in a different context, that markets looked different from the banks of the Hudson than from the banks of the Charles.

Here I describe what I think are five potential adverse effects of America's unsound fiscal trajectory, and of any actions that worsen that trajectory, all of which effects, in turn, can have a negative impact on growth. The analysis relating to each of these five potential adverse effects is directly germane to rethinking fiscal policy.

A few preliminary comments are in order. First, I relate my analysis to the American context, but the points apply broadly. Second, I discuss the potential effects of fiscal policy decisions for a full-employment economy, but at the end, I will turn to an economy with slack labor markets. Third, the effects of fiscal policy decisions can be significantly affected by the economy's fiscal context, as captured by the debt/GDP trajectory. On that score, Alan Auerbach in chapter 6 is concerned that "implicit liabilities" are not represented on a present value basis, but I think the data are adequate because these liabilities are captured in longer-term debt/GDP trajectories. Finally, the uncertainty inherent in any conclusion about the impact of fiscal policy decisions should be included in fiscal decision making, a point made by Blanchard and Summers in the introduction to this book.

The five potential adverse effects of fiscal policy in the U.S. context are the following:

1. U.S. fiscal policy can negatively affect business confidence by creating uncertainty about future policy and by heightening concern about the political system's ability to meet U.S. challenges. Economists have difficulty measuring business confidence and tend not to include it in

their analyses, but that doesn't make it any less real. The 1993 deficit reduction program clearly significantly improved business confidence, and thus investment and growth, whereas the fiscal conditions of the preceding period had a major negative effect on business decisions, for the reasons I just mentioned.

2. America's fiscal policy reduces the resilience to deal with future economic or geopolitical emergencies.

3. It reduces the funds available for public investment by increasing interest costs as a percentage of the budget, wherever the rates may be, and by increasing the risks of deficit-funded public investment.

4. It increases sovereign and private market interest rates because of increased demand for the supply of savings and/or because of increased psychological concern about future imbalances, inflation, and interest rates. Moreover, markets sometimes have tipping points, where some relatively minor event can focus attention on, and catalyze reaction to, long-ignored risks. For example, a limited increase in the debt/GDP ratio from additional borrowing could result in a step function rather than a linear effect on sovereign debt costs when there is a risky intermediate and longer-term debt/GDP trajectory. And that, in turn, could affect private sector interest rates by increasing the safe rate and by widening spreads because of heightened concern. These market dynamics, it seems to me, are the problem with the hypothetical situation discussed by Blanchard and Summers of the government borrowing indefinitely when R is less than G, because it won't stay that way. And they do go on to suggest that their hypothetical may be an unsustainable Ponzi scheme. In any case, this is a more elaborated version of crowding out. The ability to borrow in your own currency, and to print money through the central bank, may diminish this risk. But levitation through borrowing and printing has its limits and at some unpredictable point can undermine both the currency and the debt markets. Capital inflows can also alleviate interest rate pressure, but again, unsound fiscal policies can sooner or later adversely affect confidence and thus those inflows. Extensive liquidity may modulate market pressures, but in my view, liquidity is not just a monetary phenomenon but a psychological one, and when the psychology changes, liquidity can disappear quickly as funds rush to Treasury bills to avoid risk.

5. Finally, if fiscal conditions come to be seen as sufficiently serious, the market dynamics I described earlier can lead to severe market and economic destabilization. Moreover, markets can ignore or under-weight risks, including fiscal risks, for long periods—until they don't, and then the reaction can be rapid and savage. The sovereign debt of the fiscally weaker countries in the euro zone traded at tight spreads to German Bunds for years, until suddenly and catastrophically they didn't, and spreads exploded.

It follows that the cost of funds in borrowing for a new project, such as infrastructure or a tax cut, whether in a full-employment economy or in an economy with labor market slack, is not just the interest cost on that project but the possible impacts on future borrowing costs of the federal government and the private sector and all of the other possible adverse effects I've just identified, even though many cannot be quantified. Auerbach's chapter alludes to this complexity.

Thus, analyzing any particular deficit-funded proposal involves estimating the measure's growth effect, adjusting downward for various adverse effects of the new debt net of realistic positive or, because of the debt, negative dynamic scoring, calculating a revised debt/GDP ratio, and then determining whether that would have any additional effect on growth. This as an iterative process, but it could be solved in one calculation with simultaneous equations.

In an economy that has substantial unemployment, deficit funding obviously can provide a shorter-term stimulus, while also being used in ways that boost productivity. But all of the negatives I've just discussed still apply in evaluating the effects on growth for the current period and for the longer term, including, as Auerbach observes, the effect of market concern about the risk of a fiscal crisis. However, there could also be a positive impact on business and market confidence from the additional demand and its potential effect on growth and tax revenues.

Whether any given stimulus proposal is good policy for the short term and over time depends on weighing all these factors. Auerbach states that a shorter-term stimulus should be combined with measures that address longer-term structural issues, and that's certainly right. But the political reality is that a credible commitment to longer-term fiscal sustainability is exceedingly unlikely, at least in the United States, and I would guess more broadly, for the foreseeable future.

Along the same lines, in theory, surpluses seemingly should be generated during good times to roll back any increase in the debt/GDP ratio that may have occurred from stimulus during weak economic times. But when surpluses can be achieved, that potential is generally used for tax cuts or spending increases. Thus, the debt/GDP ratio seems likely to ratchet up over successive business cycles, which should enter into decision making about the expected value over time of a stimulus proposal.

In addition, stimulus, unless it has an extraordinarily high multiplier, either ab initio or from a self-perpetuating virtuous cycle, even including the effects of hysteresis, seems to me unlikely to pay for itself. But that is a judgment to be made through weighing and balancing all the relevant variables. Also, that still leaves the critical question of how the debt/GDP ratio is affected, initially and over the longer term.

Auerbach says that support for contractionary fiscal policy in either weak or crisis economic conditions is diminishing. My view is that this is a judgment that should be made based on the facts of any given situation. Weighing and balancing the economic effects of alternative policy paths, there are conditions, again in my view, in which contractionary policy in a weak or crisis economy is either the most likely to succeed or necessary.

I have already cited the U.S. 1993 deficit reduction program implemented in the face of shaky economic conditions, which I believe contributed substantially to the recovery that followed, not simply because of interest rate effects but also because of the effect on business confidence. And in response to the Mexican financial crisis in 1995 and the Asian crises later in the decade, fiscal tightening, though contractionary, was necessary to reestablish bond market and economic stability and recovery versus the alternative of expansionary fiscal policy that would likely have fed an ever-deeper and more prolonged economic crisis.

My impression is that the same requisite for improving fiscal conditions applied in the early stages of the euro-zone crisis, though that left the question of when this should have been eased.

To conclude, advocates of deficit-funded spending or tax cuts always find reasons—whether sound or spurious—to justify the deficit funding. In some circumstances it is the optimal policy path, but it seems to me there is a strong tendency to ignore or underweight the risks and the potential adverse effects, including those that are real but cannot be quantified. That will likely create increasing costs over time and likely ultimately force even harsher remedial actions.

8

Fiscal Policy in the European Economic and Monetary Union: An Evolving View

Marco Buti

My discussion of Alan Auerbach's work focuses on the evolving view of fiscal policy in the European Economic and Monetary Union (EMU), bringing together insights from academia and politics.

Three aspects discussed by Auerbach in chapter 6 are particularly germane to the design of the EU's fiscal framework: first, the interaction between monetary policy and fiscal policy, which is at the origin of the EU fiscal rules; second, the appropriate degree to which fiscal rules can limit government policy action—an obvious issue in a supranational framework; and third, the role of fiscal rules in balancing stabilization and sustainability needs, a question with which we continue to wrestle.

The discussion in this chapter refers to these three aspects and is structured in two parts. I first review the evolution of the EMU fiscal governance framework from its start until today. I then try to identify the key missing elements to ensure a viable fiscal framework for the EMU.

Evolution of the Fiscal Governance Framework in the EMU

Rationale for the Maastricht Assignment

The Maastricht Treaty provides a clear allocation of responsibilities between fiscal and monetary policy. This allocation (known as the Maastricht assignment) can be looked at through the lenses of the economic roles attributed to governments by Musgrave (1959), namely, (1) economic efficiency, with correction of market failures and improvement of resource allocation, (2) stabilization of the economic cycle to reach a stable employment environment, and (3) income redistribution to achieve an equitable distribution of resources and sustainability to secure sound public finances.

In this respect, the Maastricht Treaty leaves the cure of inequality fully in the hands of EU member states, focuses on granting efficiency of markets with the one-market project (even if certain aspects, such as policies to support productivity and structural reforms, are fully decentralized) and sustainability with the fiscal rules, and gives a small weight to stabilization, which is based on monetary policy and automatic stabilizers.

Indeed, it delegates monetary policy to an independent European Central Bank (ECB) to tackle the time-inconsistency problem (Kydland and Prescott 1977; Barro and Gordon 1983; Rogoff 1985) and to foster credibility in fulfilling its primary mandate to keep prices stable for the euro area as a whole over the medium term. In addition, the treaty forbids the ECB from directly financing government deficits or debt to prevent a regime of fiscal dominance, which would force monetary policymakers into deficit financing (Sargent and Wallace 1981).

At the same time, fiscal policy largely remains within the purview of the EU member states, but it is constrained by the preventive and corrective arms of the Stability and Growth Pact (SGP). This setup aims at addressing the well-evidenced deficit bias (Alesina and Perotti 1996), which is reinforced by the creation of a single currency, mainly for the following two reasons.

First, a common currency gives rise to adverse incentives. In a monetary union, it remains primarily the country relaxing its budgetary policy that enjoys the short-term political benefits. But in doing so, that country taps the common pool of savings, putting upward pressure on interest rates in the whole euro area. In the absence of exchange rate risks within the monetary union, the sanctioning role of financial markets also declines. The cost of borrowing is therefore partly passed on to other member states (Beetsma and Bovenberg 1998).

Second, cross-country externalities arising from fiscal policy can lead to sizable negative spillover effects. For instance, a banking or debt crisis in one region can spill over to other regions. An extreme amplification of spillover effects can lead to "contagion" effects, as nicely explained by Allen and Gale (2000). In the case of the EMU, the implications of the contagion effect in terms of monetary policy and financial stability even put into question the viability of the euro-area project as a whole.

The underlying premise of this Maastricht assignment (Issing 2000) can be summarized as a "putting one's own house in order" approach. It puts a clear emphasis on the sustainability of public finances, reflecting the then prevailing consensus that automatic stabilizers should be the primary tool for countercyclical policy, while discretionary fiscal policy was essentially regarded with suspicion (Barro 1979). This rather strict approach also indicated the heterogeneity of the EU economies and the need to build up rapidly the stability-oriented reputation of the new policy regime (Buti, Eijffinger, and Franco 2003).

Lessons Learned from the Great Recession
The insights from the initial years of the EMU and the experiences of the Great Recession led to a reexamination of some of the assumptions underlying the Maastricht assignment. Particularly if one looks at the changes through the lenses of the Musgravian assignments, there are lessons to be learned for each assignment. Concerning efficiency, it became clear that financial markets are not always efficient but can amplify economic shocks (Rodrik 2010). In addition, the Great Recession showed that widening current account balances can indicate an imbalance hampering the smooth functioning of the EMU (Baldwin et al. 2015). These insights contributed to the launch of the Banking Union, the Capital Markets Union, and the Macroeconomic Imbalance Procedure (MIP). The view on stabilization also changed, for we realized that non-normal economic conditions can stay with us for a relatively long time, with large fiscal multipliers (Blanchard and Leigh 2013; Gros 2014; Furman 2016), which prompted the euro area to give more weight to stabilization policies and coordination. At the same time, the importance of the sustainability of public finances became evident, since high government debt can slow down economic growth (Chudik et al. 2017) and lengthen the recovery from a crisis (Jordà, Schularick, and Taylor 2016). But even relatively low levels of government debt at the beginning of a crisis were for some member states insufficient to cope with the Great Recession (Gosh, Ostry, and Qureshi 2011), since government debt can explode because of the bank-sovereign nexus (Beck 2012). This brought the EU to reinforce the fiscal rules framework and to design the Banking Union.

In particular, EU and euro-area leaders fixed gaps in the EU institutional architecture in several steps beginning in 2011.

The EU fiscal framework was improved in several dimensions.   First, the EU fiscal governance framework was strengthened. It turned out that the favorable macroeconomic conditions in the years prior to the Great Recession were not sufficiently used to build up fiscal buffers (Schuknecht et al. 2011). Some EU member states appeared to treat the deficit reference value more as a target than as an upper limit, while high debt ratios did not decline substantially. In addition, both rule design problems and governance failures have contributed to a poor enforcement of the SGP (Eyraud and Wu 2015). Therefore, the 2011 reform of the so-called "six-pack" aimed at promoting fiscal adjustment in good times (through the introduction of the "significant deviation" procedure). In addition, a debt benchmark was introduced to support the debt reduction, and the system of sanctions was made in principle more automatic. Finally, the 2013 reform of the so-called "two-pack" introduced the obligation for euro-area member states to submit their draft budgets to the European Commission and European Council before the adoption of those budgets by national parliaments.

Second, the national ownership of the fiscal framework was strengthened. The gap between national budget discussions and European surveillance was a fundamental weakness of the framework (Buti and Carnot 2012). While fiscal projections as reported by EU member states in their annual stability and convergence programs typically moved in line with prescriptions, implementation often diverged from the plans. To strengthen national ownership, national fiscal frameworks were made more powerful in 2011 by stipulating mandatory requirements at the national level in the area of accounting and statistics, forecasts, fiscal rules monitored by independent bodies, and transparency. In addition, the Treaty on Stability, Coordination and Governance (TSCG), signed in 2012, stipulates that national budgets have to be in balance or in surplus under the treaty's definition.

Third, fiscal rules were implemented with more flexibility. This reflected the greater acceptance of the role of discretionary fiscal policy in tackling large shocks as identified by Auerbach (see chapter 6). This is especially the case when monetary policy is constrained, as spillovers can be larger and multipliers higher (Blanchard, Dell'Ariccia, and Mauro 2013; Blanchard and Leigh 2013), or when economic shocks are deep, requiring complemented action from discretionary fiscal policy (Christiano,

Eichenbaum, and Rebelo 2011). As a consequence, a collective "escape clause" was introduced, effectively allowing (but not prescribing) a suspension of the rules in case of "severe economic downturn" in the EU or the euro area as a whole. The 2013 reform directed more attention to the supporting fiscal policy stance at the euro area level. Finally, in 2015 the framework was improved by better taking into account the economic cycle of individual member states.

The governance framework expanded policy surveillance to also cover macroeconomic developments. Fiscal imbalances were certainly not the only reason for the severity of the Great Recession in Europe. Instead, macroeconomic imbalances played a major role in contributing to the crisis. The massive capital flows, which ran from the center to the periphery of the euro area during the first ten years of the EMU, turned out to be unsustainable. The investment in the periphery flowed in particular to the nontradable sector, which resulted in unsustainable developments in the housing sector in such countries as Spain and Ireland (Buti and Turrini 2015). Moreover, the strong growth in the periphery led many member states to disregard the need for structural reforms. The rigidity of labor and product markets slowed down the process of restoring competitiveness. As a consequence, the European Commission developed a macroeconomic surveillance mechanism, the Macroeconomic Imbalance Procedure. The MIP aims at identifying potential macroeconomic risks early on, preventing the emergence of harmful macroeconomic imbalances and correcting the imbalances that are already in place.

A permanent crisis resolution framework was created. During the first decade of the EMU, financial markets differentiated very little among sovereign assets across the EMU, encouraged by the growing perception that the bailout clause was not credible (De Grauwe and Ji 2012). When market discipline eventually returned by the end of the decade, the "sudden stop" threatened the viability of the EMU project as a whole. Therefore, the European Stability Mechanism (ESM) was established in 2012 with the main purpose of providing stability support through a number of financial assistance instruments (in particular loans to countries) to ESM member states which are "experiencing, or are threatened by severe financing problems," subject to strict policy conditions. The framework has proved its worth in providing financial support to Greece, Ireland, Portugal, and Cyprus.

Financial supervision was strengthened. The vicious feedback cycle between banks and their governments in the EU clearly deepened and accelerated the crisis (Beck 2012; Jordà, Schularick, and Taylor 2016). This "doom loop" was further strengthened by the predominance of bank financing, which transmitted bank problems to the wider economy (Baldwin et al. 2015). To tackle the risks emerging from the sovereign-bank nexus, key elements for a proper Banking Union were launched. These consist of the Single Supervisory Mechanism (SSM), the Single Resolution Mechanism (SRM), and the Single Resolution Fund (SRF). A common deposit insurance scheme is still under construction.

What Is Still Missing in the EMU's Fiscal Framework?

Inherent Trade-offs in the Design of a Fiscal Framework
In chapter 6, Auerbach describes the EMU fiscal framework as "perhaps the most elaborate fiscal rules in existence." I know better than to take this as a compliment. However, it raises an interesting question on the unavoidable trade-offs involved in designing any fiscal framework, notably those between simplicity, adaptability, and predictability (figure 8.1).

A very simple set of rules, for instance, focused only on a headline deficit threshold, is easy to understand and predict the results of, but is also easily criticized as being insufficiently flexible to address changing economic circumstances. Conversely, introducing ever more detailed subsystems of rules to cater to every situation inevitably increases complexity and reduces transparency. This can be thought of as chasing "the complete contract."

The tension between these trade-offs is visible in the evolution of the SGP since its original conception. The SGP has gradually moved from a relatively simple, outcome-based approach to a more sophisticated, input-based approach, whereby member states are not penalized for events that are outside their control.

In addition, to limit the risk of pro-cyclical fiscal policies, increasing attention has been placed on the adequacy of requirements with respect to the economic situation, including with respect to unforeseen

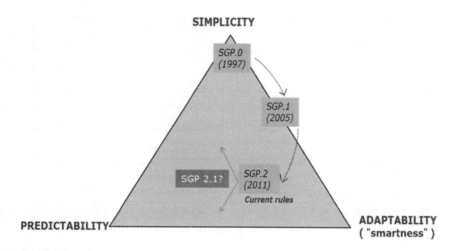

Figure 8.1

Trade-offs in the Design of an EMU Fiscal Framework.
SGP denotes Stability and Growth Pact.

developments ("adaptability of requirements"). However, this has come at the price of increased complexity, which, as Auerbach identifies, can reduce transparency, as well as raise accusations of subjectivity.

There is currently an increasing perception that predictability and (relative) simplicity should be given greater emphasis, to the detriment of adaptability. This would imply moving toward the left-hand side of the triangle in figure 8.1, as evidenced graphically by the move toward SGP 2.1.

Which Future? Searching for the Right Balance

What is necessary is a coherent synthesis of various elements that would gather sufficient political support and at the same time create a basis for a stable and functioning EMU. The EMU reflection paper of the European Commission (2017) discusses the overall fiscal architecture in the broader reflection on the future of EMU. It lays out the path to take but leaves open the balance elements of centralization and decentralization (figure 8.2).

Complete financial union: It is key to complete the Banking and Capital Markets Union to ultimately break the bank-sovereign nexus. While

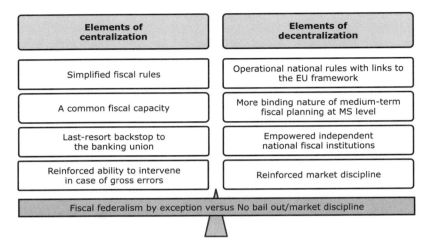

→ **Essential to conceive the different elements of the framework together**

Figure 8.2

EMU Framework: Searching for the Right Balance between Centralization and Decentralization.

substantial progress has been made, further work is needed. In particular, the Banking Union has not been completed and the exposure of national financial sectors to sovereigns remains high. Limiting and diversifying the sovereign debt on banks' balance sheets will help to break the toxic loop between banks and government. In addition, a credible fiscal backstop to the Single Resolution Fund is crucial to make the new EU framework for bank resolution effective and to avoid costs for taxpayers.

Ensure an effective implementation of the fiscal governance framework: As with any set of fiscal rules, the EU's revised governance framework will be effective only if it is implemented. Auerbach observes that there is no credible enforcement mechanism for the EU's fiscal rules, and it is true that the system has struggled with enforceability of the rules on democratically elected governments. In addition, experience to date would suggest that there are limits to the effectiveness of peer pressure. Two polar solutions appear feasible to ensure an effective implementation of the framework. One solution would be a "federalism by exception" (Trichet 2012). This means that the EU level would allow the possibility of taking over national budgetary powers in case of "gross errors" that threatened the smooth functioning of the euro area. This solution could go along with a simplification of the framework to reduce inconsistencies and facilitate communication with the public. The other solution would be to reinforce market pressure as the ultimate sanctioning mechanism for unsustainable fiscal policies. This solution would rely more on a decentralized approach and would empower the independent fiscal institutions at the national level. It would be closer with the original idea of the no-bailout clause, and it would probably require a reform of financial regulation, in particular that regarding the treatment of national sovereign exposures of the banking system and, possibly, the availability of a safe asset alternative to national debt.

Setup a fiscal capacity: The euro area lacks a capacity to withstand a further large shock. A potential vulnerability relates to the fact that the European Stability Mechanism remains dependent on national treasuries, which, in turn, can slow the decision-making process. In addition, the absence of a common stabilization capacity means there is no tool in place to help smooth asymmetric shocks and contribute to an appropriate euro-area fiscal stance in case of large symmetric shocks. As we have seen, the absence of common tools to face the recent fiscal crisis meant that a symmetric financial shock generated an asymmetric debt shock, which has been much more difficult to face. In particular, this made it very difficult to adopt a timely discretionary fiscal response to shocks, contrary to the U.S. evidence to which Auerbach refers in chapter 6.

Unburden the ECB from policy support: The coordination of the appropriate aggregate fiscal stance to support monetary policy in the euro area represents a further vulnerability in itself. What we have seen is that bottom-up coordination, through an aggregation of the individual member states' fiscal positions, may not lead to the optimal stance at the euro-area level. As a result, too much of the burden of stabilizing the euro-area economy has fallen on the shoulders of the ECB. The coordination between monetary and fiscal policy as advocated by Auerbach is thus a key missing piece in the euro area, with a possible solution being a fiscal capacity operating at the euro-area level to deliver macroeconomic and financial stability.

Conclusions

The Great Recession revealed several design flaws of the Maastricht assignment. Institutional changes since 2010 have substantially improved the EMU architecture, but more needs to be done to ensure a sustainable EMU governance framework.

A viable fiscal framework for EMU should encompass the right balance between EU and national reform abilities, and between rules/institutions and market discipline. In this regard, I noted with great interest Auerbach's suggestion that finding the optimal design of fiscal councils at the national level deserves greater attention than continuing refinement of existing fiscal rules at the supranational level.

Ultimately, as Auerbach states, a key question for any framework is how to balance the potentially competing demands for fiscal policy stabilization and a commitment to fiscal sustainability. This is something we are still working on in the euro area.

Note

I thank Philipp Mohl for his contribution in the preparation of this intervention.

References

Alesina, A., and P. Perotti. 1996. "The Political Economy of Budget Deficits." *IMF Staff Papers* 42:1–31.

Allen, F., and D. Gale. 2000. "Financial Contagion." *Journal of Political Economy* 108 (1): 1–33.

Baldwin, R., et al. 2015. "Rebooting the Eurozone: Step 1—Agreeing a Crisis Narrative." *CEPR Policy Insight* 85, November.

Barro, R. 1979. "On the Determination of the Public Debt." *Journal of Political Economy* 87 (5): 940–971.

Barro, R., and D. Gordon. 1983. "A Positive Theory of Monetary Policy in a Natural Rate Model." *Journal of Political Economy* 91:589–610.

Beck, T. 2012. *Banking Union for Europe: Risks and Challenges.* VoxEU.org.

Beetsma, R., and L. Bovenberg. 1998. "Monetary Union without Fiscal Coordination May Discipline Policymakers." *Journal of International Economics* 45 (2): 239–258.

Blanchard, O., Dell'Ariccia, G. and P. Mauro. 2013. "Rethinking Macroeconomic Policy II: Getting Granular. IMF Staff Discussion Note 13/03." Washington, DC: International Monetary Fund.

Blanchard, O., and D. Leigh. 2013. "Growth Forecast Errors and Fiscal Multipliers." NBER Working Paper 18779. Cambridge, MA: National Bureau of Economic Research, February.

Buti, M., and N. Carnot. 2012. "The EMU Debt Crisis: Early Lessons and Reforms." *Journal of Common Market Studies* 50 (6): 899–911.

Buti, M., S. Eijffinger, and D. Franco. 2003. "Revisiting the Stability and Growth Pact: Grand Design or Internal Adjustment?" CEPR Discussion Paper 3692. Washington, DC: Center for Economic and Policy Research.

Buti, M., and A. Turrini 2015. "Three Waves of Convergence: Can Eurozone Countries Start Growing Together Again?" VoxEU.org (CEPR), April 17. https://voxeu.org/article/types-ez-convergence-nominal-real-and-structural.

Christiano, L., M. Eichenbaum, and S. Rebelo. 2011. "When Is the Government Spending Multiplier Large?" *Journal of Political Economy* 119 (1): 78–121.

Chudik, A., K. Mohaddes, M. Pesaran, and M. Raissi. 2017. "Is There a Debt-Threshold Effect on Output Growth?" *Review of Economics and Statistics* 99 (1): 135–150.

De Grauwe, P., and Y. Ji. 2012. "Mispricing of Sovereign Risk and Macroeconomic Stability in the Eurozone." *Journal of Common Market Studies* 50 (6): 866–880.

European Commission. 2017. "Reflection Paper on the Deepening of the Economic and Monetary Union." Brussels: European Commission, May 31.

Eyraud, L., and T. Wu. 2015. "Playing by the Rules: Reforming Fiscal Governance in Europe." IMF Working Paper WP 15/67. Washington, DC: International Monetary Fund.

Furman, J. 2016. "The New View of Fiscal Policy and Its Application." VoxEU. org (CEPR), November 2.

Gosh, K., J. Ostry, and M. Qureshi. 2011. "Fiscal Space, Fiscal Fatigue and Debt Sustainability." NBER Working Paper 16782. Cambridge, MA: National Bureau of Economic Research, February.

Gros, D. 2014. "A Fiscal Shock Absorber for the Eurozone? Lessons from the Economics of Insurance." VoxEU.org (CEPR), March 19.

Issing, O. 2000. "How to Achieve a Durable Macro-economic Policy Mix Favourable to Growth and Employment?" Paper presented at the conference "Growth and employment in EMU," organized by the European Commission, Brussels Economic Forum, Brussels, May 4 and 5.

Jordà, Ò., M. Schularick, and A. Taylor. 2016. "Sovereigns versus Banks: Credit, Crises, and Consequences." *Journal of the European Economic Association* 14 (1): 45–79.

Kydland, F., and E. Prescott. 1977. "Rules Rather Than Discretion: The Inconsistency of Optimal Plans." *Journal of Political Economy* 85 (3): 473–492.

Musgrave, R. 1959. *The Theory of Public Finance: A Study in Public Economy.* New York: McGraw-Hill.

Rodrik, D. 2010. "The End of an Era in Finance?" Project Syndicate, June 3.

Rogoff, K. 1985. "The Optimal Degree of Commitment to an Intermediate Monetary Target." *Quarterly Journal of Economics* 100:1169–1189.

Sargent, T., and N. Wallace. 1981. "Some Unpleasant Monetarist Arithmetic." *Federal Reserve Bank of Minneapolis Quarterly Review* 5 (3): 1–17.

Schuknecht, L., P. Moutot, P. Rother, and J. Stark. 2011. "The Stability and Growth Pact: Crisis and Reform." ECB Occasional Paper 129.

Trichet, J.-C. 2012. "European Economic Governance: Towards an Economic and Fiscal Federation by Exception." Lecture, December 6.

9

Fiscal Policy: Tax and Spending Multipliers in the United States

Valerie Ramey

Alan Auerbach's chapter 6 in this volume, on fiscal policy, is a must-read for anyone contemplating the long-term fiscal challenges facing developed countries, as well as the role of fiscal policy in stabilizing the economy in the short run. The chapter sheds light on the issues involved in four major areas: (1) fiscal rules, (2) the potential for stabilization policy, (3) fiscal policy in a low-interest-rate environment, and (4) the coordination of monetary and fiscal policy. Among the many important insights is Auerbach's argument that basing fiscal rules on observable public debt while ignoring the more important unfunded liabilities accruing in entitlement programs misses the main source of potential future debt issues. Here I focus primarily on the potential for fiscal policy as a stabilization policy.

In respect to that thesis, I offer an assessment of the U.S. evidence. The following three statements summarize my views:

1. Spending stimulus multipliers are probably less than one in most instances.
2. The evidence on infrastructure multipliers is mixed.
3. The strongest, most robust evidence is that tax rate changes have the biggest multipliers.

To support these statements, I will begin by considering the evidence related to spending multipliers. Aggregate spending multipliers in the United States are typically estimated to be just below unity, both in post–World War II data and in historical data covering the twentieth century (e.g., Ramey and Zubairy 2018). In a salient paper, Auerbach and Gorodnichenko (2012) investigated whether those averages could be masking important variations in multipliers over time, and in particular during recessions versus expansions. They found much higher multipliers during recessions. Let us look at those estimates more closely.

Auerbach and Gorodnichenko (2012) reported baseline estimates of five-year multipliers that were 2.2 in recessions and −0.3 in expansions. They made two key assumptions when they constructed these estimates. First, they assumed that a recession lasts at least five years, or twenty quarters. Second, they assumed that government spending could not get the economy out of a recession. When they relaxed the second assumption, they found multipliers in recessions in the range from 1 to 1.5. However, even these multipliers were affected by their first assumption, which is that recessions last at least five years. In their sample, the median length of a recession was only three quarters, and by their definition, even the Great Recession lasted only two years. Making an assumption that is so contrary to the experience in their estimation sample turns out to have big effects on their multiplier estimates. In particular, because recessions are usually short, the estimates imply rising output growth in the future as the economy recovers from the slow growth of the recession. When one counterfactually assumes that the economy remains in recession for years, one cumulates these faster-than-current growth forecasts so that they predict that output will continue climbing indefinitely relative to trend.

An alternative method, which Auerbach and Gorodnichenko (2013) introduced in their study of multipliers in the OECD, is Jordà's (2005) local projection method, which produces estimates of the effects of government spending based on the average length of recessions and expansions over the sample. This method does not allow one to make assumptions that are counterfactual to the data analyzed. Auerbach and Gorodnichenko never applied this method to U.S. data, though. In Owyang, Ramey, and Zubairy (2013) and in Ramey and Zubairy (2018), my co-authors and I applied the Jordà local projection method to U.S. data, both historical and Auerbach and Gorodnichenko's (2012) post–World War II sample. In both cases, we found multipliers that were less than one even in recessions or when the unemployment rate was high—around 0.8 for both samples. These estimates were obtained using a military news series as shock; when we instead used Blanchard and Perotti's (2002) identification method, we found even lower multipliers in recessions (thought they were greater than the near zero multipliers estimated during expansions). Thus, applying Auerbach and Gorodnichenko's currently favored Jordà technique to the U.S. data produced multiplier estimates that are below one even in recessions. In sum, the original findings of high multipliers during recessions in the United States are fragile.

In Ramey and Zubairy (2018), we also investigated the size of multipliers during zero lower bound (ZLB) periods. When we used the entire historical sample, we found no evidence of elevated multipliers during ZLB periods. However, when we excluded the period of World War II rationing, we found some evidence of multipliers that are around 1.5 during ZLB periods. These results held when we used military news identification, but not the Blanchard and Perotti identification. In follow-up work on the Japanese economy, Miyamoto, Nguyen, and Sergeyev (forthcoming) also found evidence of multipliers around 1.5, or even higher, during Japan's ZLB decades. Thus there is some evidence of higher multipliers during ZLB periods for some samples.

To summarize, aggregate estimates suggesting multipliers above one during recessions or slack times tend to be fragile. The most robust estimates are those that yield multipliers slightly less than one. On the other hand, there is mounting evidence at this point that ZLB periods might be associated with multipliers that are greater than one.

Numerous papers have estimated multipliers using cross-state or cross-regional data or constructed multipliers using marginal propensity to consume (MPC) estimated using individual-level data. Identifying exogenous shocks at the household or state level is often easier because of handy natural experiments. Interestingly, the individual-level estimates often imply high MPCs and state-level estimates often imply high multipliers (1.5 to 2 for GDP multipliers, or around $50K per job-year for employment multipliers). However, exporting these cross-sectional estimates to the aggregate level is not straightforward, as numerous papers have argued.

To determine whether it makes sense to use cross-sectional estimates directly as aggregate estimates, it is useful to conduct simple plausibility tests. I will present two here. The first is directly from Sahm, Shapiro, Slemrod (2012) and concerns MPCs, and the second is my own, based on the cross-state estimates of the effects of the stimulus during the Great Recession.

Consider first Sahm, Shapiro, and Slemrod's (2012) plausibility test of some recent individual-level estimates of the MPC out of temporary tax rebates. In 2008, a temporary tax rebate ranging from $300 to more than $1,800, depending on household size, was enacted in February and disbursed mostly from April through July. Fortunately for economic researchers, the disbursement timing was randomized by Social Security number. Parker and co-authors (2013) worked with the Bureau of Labor Statistics to add a supplement to the Consumer Expenditure Survey to study the effects of the rebates on consumer expenditures. They looked at a variety of categories, but one striking finding, and the one focused on by Sahm and co-authors (2012), was that on average, consumers spent 40 percent of their rebate check on motor vehicle purchases. Sahm and co-authors (2012) used that estimate to conduct a simple counterfactual: ignoring any general equilibrium multipliers or price changes, what would motor vehicle expenditures have been in 2008 had there been no rebate? They show the results in table 14 at the end of their paper. I graph the results in figure 9.1 because it is easier to see the nature of the counterfactual path.[1]

Figure 9.1 shows the striking counterfactual. If one applies the marginal propensity to spend the rebate on motor vehicles estimated by Parker and colleagues (2013) to the aggregate data, it implies that *most* of the spending on motor vehicles in the summer of 2008 could be attributed to spending induced by the tax rebate. It implies that in the absence of the tax rebate, motor vehicle expenditures would have collapsed from a

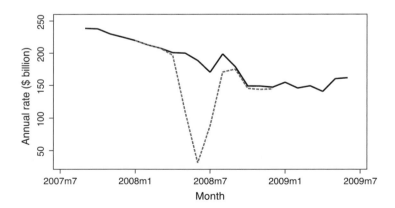

Figure 9.1

Actual and Counterfactual Expenditures on Motor Vehicles. Counterfactual estimates are from Sahm, Shapiro, and Slemrod (2012), table 14.

$208 billion annual rate in March 2008 to only a $31 billion annual rate in June 2008. Moreover, it implies that in the absence of a rebate, motor vehicle spending would have rebounded sharply when Lehman Brothers collapsed. This counterfactual is preposterous and serves as a cautionary tale about the complicated link between cross-sectional estimates and aggregate estimates.

The second plausibility test I conducted is related to the effects of the American Recovery and Reinvestment Act (ARRA) stimulus spending. A recent paper by Chodorow-Reich (forthcoming) synthesizes and standardizes the various estimates in the literature on the effect of the ARRA across states. His preferred estimate is that each $50K created one job that lasted a year (a "job-year"). Stated as a GDP multiplier, he estimates multipliers around 2. However, Chodorow-Reich (forthcoming) goes on to argue, based both on a New Keynesian model with a ZLB and on some back-of-the-envelope calculations, that the cross-state estimates of multipliers are *lower bounds* on the aggregate multiplier during ZLB times.

In the spirit of Sahm and co-authors' counterfactual exercise, I conducted a counterfactual exercise about the ARRA using Chodorow-Reich's estimates. In particular, I used his figure B.1 estimates of the impulse response of employment to the passage of the stimulus bill for the period December 2008 through December 2010. I also used his estimate that $600 billion of the ARRA had been spent by December 2010. I then calculated what his estimates imply for the lower bound of induced monthly employment at the aggregate level if we believe that the cross-state estimates are lower bounds on the aggregate. I transformed this into a counterfactual unemployment rate by adding the induced employment to the actual number unemployed. The result is shown in figure 9.2.

Figure 9.2 shows that applying Chodorow-Reich's cross-state ARRA employment estimates to the aggregate implies that the unemployment rate would have risen to 15.5 percent had the ARRA not been passed. The actual unemployment rate rose 2.7 percentage points from December 2008 to its peak of 10 percent. The counterfactual path implied by Chodorow-Reich's estimates show an unemployment rate that would have risen not 2.7 percentage points but eight percentage points, to its peak of 15.5 percent. Thus, applying his cross-state estimates to the aggregate implies that the unemployment rate would have risen by three times more in those two years than it actually did. While not as outlandish as

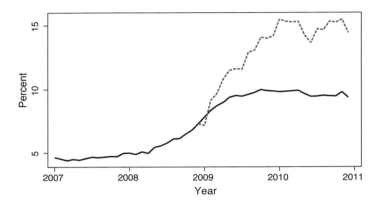

Figure 9.2

Actual and Counterfactual Unemployment Rate. Counterfactual rate is based on the author's estimates.

the counterfactual constructed by Sahm and co-authors, this counterfactual does strain plausibility.

To summarize my points for government spending multipliers for the United States, most estimates are below one, and the few estimates that are above one are typically not robust. Furthermore, estimates of multipliers at the cross-sectional level produce implausible results when directly applied to the aggregate level. This is not to say that an increase in government spending does not raise GDP, only that it raises GDP by less than the rise in government spending.

My second point is about infrastructure spending. In contrast to government spending that is not used for public capital, infrastructure spending has the potential to stimulate the economy not only through standard Keynesian multipliers but also through a supply-side effect. Recent commentators have advocated increased infrastructure spending for this reason. Little is certain, however, about the size of the infrastructure multiplier. Studies of the effects of aggregate spending projects, such as the U.S. interstate highway system, are faced with the challenge of identifying which part of aggregate output is affected by the one big wave of highway spending. Fernald's (1999) study of the differential effects of the interstate highway program on particular transportation-dependent industries suggests large effects. However, these effects are *relative* industry effects, not aggregate effects, and, as Fernald points out, a large effect of the initial

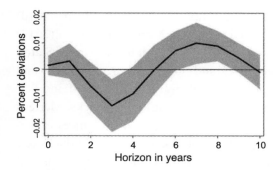

Figure 9.3

The Effects of State Highway Spending on State Employment. Shaded area is 90 percent confidence interval.
Source: Reproduced from one graph of figure 4 of Leduc and Wilson (2012).

highway program is no guarantee of such a large effect of subsequent projects, where diminishing returns might set in.

A very useful recent cross-sectional contribution is by Leduc and Wilson (2012), who analyzed the effects of highway construction across states in more recent decades. They were very careful about every detail of the nature of and timing of the announcements and spending. There are aspects of their results that raise questions about the ability of infrastructure spending to stimulate the economy in the short and medium run, however. Consider, for example, their estimates of the effects of infrastructure spending on employment in a state. I focus on employment because the results are most stark for that variable. Figure 9.3 is reproduced from the upper right graph in figure 4 of their paper. Note that the effects are essentially zero on impact in year 0, then become negative through year 5, and finally become positive in years 6 through 9 before returning to normal at year 10. Visually integrating over the graph, it appears that the cumulative effect on employment through year 10 might even be negative.

If most estimates of government spending multipliers are low, then is there no role for fiscal policy for stimulating the economy? Not necessarily. The largest, most robust multipliers appear to be for tax cuts, particularly those involving cuts in tax rates. Romer and Romer (2010) used narrative methods to identify U.S. tax changes for reasons unrelated to the current state of the economy and found multipliers as high (in magnitude) as −3 (the minus sign is because a decrease in taxes raises GDP). Cloyne (2013) found similar results for the United Kingdom. Mertens and Ravn (2014) showed the robustness of Romer and Romer's result for the United States, estimating multipliers between −2.5 and −3 using other methods, and explained the lower multiplier estimate obtained by Blanchard and Perotti (2002) by a restriction they imposed to identify tax shocks. Mertens and Ravn (2013) split the Romer and Romer series into changes in personal income tax rates and corporate tax rates. They estimate that a one percentage point cut in the average personal income tax rate leads real GDP to increase 1.4 percent on impact and up to 1.8 percent after three quarters. This implies a personal income tax multiplier of up to −2.5. A one percentage point cut in the corporate income tax rate leads real GDP to rise by 0.4 percent on impact and 0.6 percent after a year. Notably, Mertens and Ravn could not calculate the tax multiplier for a corporate income tax cut because they estimated that corporate income tax cuts *do not lower tax revenues*. That is, the stimulus effect of a corporate income tax cut on measured GDP is so large that tax revenues do not fall.

In sum, the most robust results in the literature are those for tax changes. The estimates imply a large potential role for tax cuts as a stimulus to the economy. Thus, tax policy should receive at least equal billing with government spending policy when discussing ways that fiscal policy can stimulate the economy.

Note

1. The only difference between the numbers in the graph and those in their table is that I use current vintage motor vehicle expenditure data that extend before and after 2008 to provide context.

References

Auerbach, Alan, and Yuriy Gorodnichenko. 2012. "Measuring the Output Responses to Fiscal Policy." *American Economic Journal. Economic Policy* 4 (2): 1–27.

Auerbach, Alan, and Yuriy Gorodnichenko. 2013. "Fiscal Multipliers in Recession and Expansion." In *Fiscal Policy after the Financial Crisis*, ed. Alberto Alesina and Francesco Giavazzi. Chicago: University of Chicago Press.

Blanchard, Olivier, and Roberto Perotti. 2002. "An Empirical Characterization of the Dynamic Effects of Changes in Government Spending and Taxes on Output." *Quarterly Journal of Economics* 117:1329–1368.

Chodorow-Reich, Gabriel. Forthcoming. "Geographic Cross-Sectional Fiscal Spending Multipliers: What Have We Learned?" *American Economic Journal: Economic Policy.* https://www.aeaweb.org/articles?id=10.1257/pol.20160465 &&from=f.

Cloyne, James. 2013. "Discretionary Tax Changes and the Macroeconomy: New Narrative Evidence from the United Kingdom." *American Economic Review* 103 (4): 1507–1528.

Fernald, John G. 1999. "Roads to Prosperity? Assessing the Link between Public Capital and Productivity." *American Economic Review* 89 (3): 619–638.

Jordà, Òscar. 2005. "Estimation and Inference of Impulse Responses by Local Projections." *American Economic Review* 95 (1): 161–182.

Leduc, Sylvain, and Daniel Wilson. 2012. "Roads to Prosperity or Bridges to Nowhere? Theory and Evidence on the Impact of Public Infrastructure Investment." *NBER Macroeconomics Annual* 27 (1): 89–142.

Mertens, Karel, and Morten O. Ravn. 2013. "The Dynamic Effects of Personal and Corporate Income Tax Changes in the United States." *American Economic Review* 103 (4): 1212–1247.

Mertens, Karel, and Morten O. Ravn. 2014. "A Reconciliation of SVAR and Narrative Estimates of Tax Multipliers." *Journal of Monetary Economics* 68:S1–S19.

Miyamoto, Wataru, Thuy Lan Nguyen, and Dmitriy Serfeyev. Forthcoming. "Government Spending Multipliers under the Zero Lower Bound: Evidence from Japan." *American Economic Journal: Macroeconomics.* https://www.aeaweb.org/articles?id=10.1257/mac.20170131&&from=f.

Owyang, Michael T., Valerie A. Ramey, and Sarah Zubairy. 2013. "Are Government Spending Multipliers Greater during Periods of Slack? Evidence from Twentieth-Century Historical Data." *American Economic Review* 103 (3): 129–134.

Parker, Jonathan A., Nicolas S. Souleles, David S. Johnson, and Robert McClelland. 2013. "Consumer Spending and the Economic Stimulus Payments of 2008." *American Economic Review* 103 (October): 2530–2553.

Ramey, Valerie A., and Sarah Zubairy. 2018. "Government Spending Multipliers in Good Times and in Bad: Evidence from U.S. Historical Data." *Journal of Political Economy* 126 (2): 850–901.

Romer, Christina D., and David H. Romer. 2010. "The Macroeconomic Effects of Tax Changes: Estimates Based on a New Measure of Fiscal Shocks." *American Economic Review* 100 (June): 763–801.

Sahm, Claudia R., Matthew D. Shapiro, and Joel Slemrod. 2012. "Check in the Mail or More in the Paycheck: Does the Effectiveness of Fiscal Stimulus Depend on How It Is Delivered?" *American Economic Journal. Economic Policy* 4 (August): 216–250.

10

Rethinking Fiscal Policy

Jay C. Shambaugh

The Global Financial Crisis has generated considerable discussion on how macroeconomics and macroeconomics policy should be reconsidered. It has also yielded a large amount of information on the effectiveness of fiscal policy and how countries choose to use fiscal policy.

One important lesson from the last decade is that fiscal policy at the zero lower bound (ZLB) is more effective than when not at the ZLB— that fiscal policy can be used effectively to generate additional economic activity at the ZLB. This does not mean that one should not consider the costs and benefits of fiscal policy in any given situation, and the costs of a fiscal stimulus are important, but it seems clear from the evidence that at the ZLB, fiscal multipliers are well above zero and likely well above one. This means additional fiscal spending or tax cuts can generate economic activity when the economy is depressed.

We have also learned that we may find ourselves at the ZLB far more often than we thought likely before. Here I am using "zero lower bound" as a shorthand for the effective lower bound (as in some cases central banks have pushed short-term interest rates below zero) or a point where monetary policy is limited or inhibited in some ways in its ability to have an impact on the economy. If we hit these limitations on monetary policy more often, it seems it makes a proper understanding of fiscal policy impacts and uses at the ZLB all the more important.

I think we have learned something else, something more surprising. We have seen that in some cases when the economy was quite weak, at the ZLB, and where solvency was not necessarily being debated, some countries were unwilling to use fiscal policy to generate more economic activity. I think this requires that economists take seriously the concern— whether when building fiscal rules or automatic stabilizers—that in a moment of economic crisis that calls for the active use of fiscal policy, the political system will inadequately provide fiscal stimulus or will pivot to fiscal austerity when such a move is not appropriate.

This suggests that a first-order concern is making sure fiscal stimulus happens when it *should* happen. This point takes as given all the costs discussed in Robert Rubin's contribution to this volume (see chapter 7). That is, fiscal stimulus can be costly in some situations, and in particular, deficit spending when it is not needed to stimulate the economy has costs. But it suggests that sometimes fiscal stimulus is needed, and it is important to make sure it happens.

In a podcast, Larry Summers recently said, "It does not appear that the problem of dynamically inconsistent central banks, yielding to the temptation to inflate, and lacking credibility, and therefore having excessively-high interest rates, that theoretical concern looks very remote relative to current reality" (Beckworth 2017). It seems a useful analogy to consider with respect to fiscal policy. In many papers on fiscal policy, the abstract will include something like, "We study a model in which the government is present-biased in terms of public spending." In fairness, that is a serious concern and likely more serious than the fear that the central bank will try to inflate too much because of dynamic inconsistency. We probably should worry about present-biased fiscal agents, and we see examples in history where they generate longer-term problems. But it seems the evidence from the last decade is that economics should take seriously the opposite concern as well: that in some instances the fiscal agent may be insufficiently present-biased during a downturn and may not do as much as it should to lift economic activity, in light of what we've learned about fiscal policy at the ZLB and some of the constraints monetary policy faces at the ZLB.

The contribution by Alan Auerbach in this volume is an excellent tour through many of the issues economists need to consider regarding fiscal policy—in particular, how low interest rates and fiscal policy interact. The second section of his chapter highlights the extent to which fiscal policy can be effective at generating economic activity especially at the ZLB, and that seems to suggest that if we are thinking about fiscal rules, we need to make sure those rules are not constraints on using stimulus when needed. We may need rules for a range of other reasons, but we do not want fiscal rules to stop stimulus when we think stimulus is appropriate.

Works by Chodorow-Reich and colleagues (2012), Feyrer and Sacerdote (2011), Nakamura and Steinsson (2014), and Auerbach and Gorodnichenko (2012) all demonstrate this. This work adds to our understanding of fiscal policy's effectiveness and is one reason why we should rethink fiscal policy as a tool to manage the economy. Other work goes further: results from DeLong and Summers (2012) and Auerbach and Gorodnichenko (2017) suggest that stimulus can even lower debt-to-GDP ratios. During the crisis, there were times when spreads on sovereign yields seemed to react more negatively to bad growth forecasts than to fiscal forecasts because movements in GDP can be just as important to the debt-to-GDP ratio as movements in deficits. Additional work—for example, by Blanchard and Leigh (2013)—shows us that contractionary fiscal policy can be quite contractionary to GDP, especially when monetary policy and exchange rates cannot offset the impacts.

Beyond learning that fiscal policy can be effective at the ZLB, I think we saw abundant evidence of a great deal of resistance to fiscal stimulus even in the recession and an inadequate amount of fiscal stimulus in the first few years of the crisis. Looking in the United States, one saw heavy resistance to the American Recovery and Reinvestment Act (ARRA), with opponents pushing back on the size of the package and removing effective stimulus from the bill in exchange for alternative minimum tax (AMT) relief in ways that reduced the overall effectiveness of the bill. In late 2009, an attempted infrastructure and new jobs tax credit bill failed in the Senate, and additional attempts at stimulus were often stopped (though some, like the payroll tax cuts, did go through).

In Europe, several countries either were unwilling to spend or pivoted to austerity very sharply. In some cases, there may have been pressure from markets that made spending difficult, but in a number of other cases, the choice to pivot to austerity was optional. In some ways, the G-20 needed to encourage countries to do spending and to do stimulus, and it was an important accomplishment of the G-20 in April 2009 when leaders made a commitment to stimulate their economies. But very quickly, the G-20 itself pivoted away from that position by June 2010.

Looking at a measure of fiscal impact from the Hutchins Center at Brookings, one can see that by 2011, fiscal policy was a drag on the U.S. economy. This contraction was taking place even though the Federal Reserve had interest rates at zero and would keep them there for

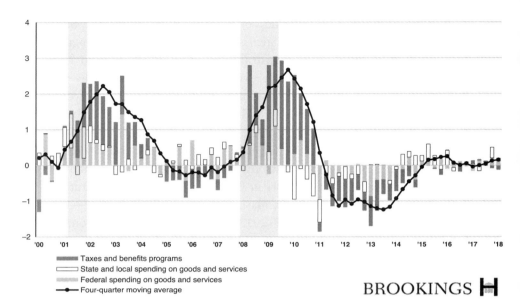

Taxes and benefits programs
State and local spending on goods and services
Federal spending on goods and services
Four-quarter moving average

BROOKINGS **H**

Figure 10.1

Hutchins Center Fiscal Impact Measure: Components. Shaded areas indicate recessions.
Source: Hutchins Center on Fiscal and Monetary Policy at the Brookings Institution, Washington, DC. Calculations from Bureau of Economic Analysis data.

years, and even though the output gap was sizable. As figure 10.1 shows, some of the problem had to do with the contractionary actions of state and local governments, but by 2011, federal policy was contractionary as well. Relative to the size of the recession and the output gap that ensued, the pivot to austerity in the United States was quick.

The IMF (2013) looked across countries to see how government spending typically evolved after a global recession. They found that in advanced economies, the initial burst of stimulus was actually slightly larger during the 2008–2009 Great Recession than in other global recessions (1975, 1982, and 1991), but after one year, the current spending patterns were sharply lower than in previous recessions. The negative influence of fiscal policy on the economy was even clearer in the euro area, where the initial spending was no different from that in other recessions, but a quick pivot to austerity meant much lower spending in the years following the recession. Euro periphery countries were spending far less four years after the

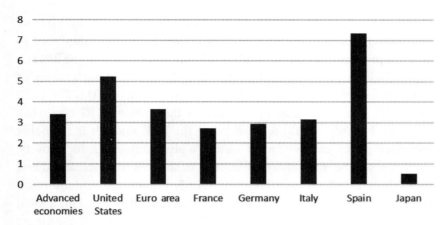

Figure 10.2

Change in Structural Surplus, 2010–2013. Author's calculations based on IMF structural fiscal data.

start of the recession than they did in other recessions, likely contributing to the negative economic outcomes.

Alternatively, one could look at the change in the structural surplus across countries (figure 10.2). Major economies were sharply cutting their structural fiscal balances from 2010 to 2013 despite still quite high unemployment rates. Spain, for example, reined in its deficit-to-GDP ratio by over seven percentage points despite unemployment rates above 20 percent. On net, these figures suggest that despite the evidence that fiscal policy can be very effective at generating economic activity at the ZLB, in general, countries were hesitant to use it. They do not seem to have been acting as present-biased fiscal agents—quite the opposite. They often seemed to be acting in a way that avoided spending when spending would have been economically beneficial.

The policy advice countries were receiving was also quite hawkish on fiscal policy. In June 2010, the IMF's background document for the G-20 summit read, "There is a pressing need, in general, for fiscal consolidation in G-20 advanced Economies" (IMF 2010). There may have been a range of opinions inside the IMF, but official pronouncements were for fiscal contraction while monetary policy was stuck at the ZLB and output gaps were large. Similar views were expressed by the Organisation for Economic Co-operation and Development (OECD) and the European

Commission. In 2011 the European Commission said, "Most Member States do not have room for a new fiscal stimulus because they need to give top priority to fiscal consolidation" (European Commission 2011).

Interestingly, policy advice had shifted by 2016, even though advanced economies were in much better shape than they were in 2011. The G-20 said, "Our fiscal strategies aim to support the economy" (G-20, 2016). Christine Lagarde, managing director of the IMF, said, "It is clear that monetary policy can no longer be the alpha and omega to recovery. Indeed, it will be much more effective with support from structural and fiscal elements" (Lagarde 2016). The OECD (2016) said, "Many countries have room for fiscal expansion to strengthen demand. This should focus on policies with strong short-run benefits and that also contribute to long-term growth." The interesting question is whether this is the same type of advice countries would be given should the economy hit another sharp downturn, and whether countries would be willing to heed that advice.

Another noteworthy section of Auerbach's contribution is the discussion of the interaction between low interest rates and fiscal policy. Beyond the normal considerations of how a change in interest costs may affect fiscal calculus, there is also the question of coordination of fiscal and monetary policy. As shown by events of the most recent decade (or two decades, if we include Japan's experience), getting out of a low-inflation recession or low-inflation slow-growth episode is quite difficult. Very creative central banks working very hard to get out of that position struggle, and that highlights the fact that fiscal policy may need to play a supportive role to get inflation back to target. The Fed's Monetary Policy Reports—statements and testimony by U.S. Federal Reserve chairs every six months to Congress, as mandated by the 1978 Humphrey-Hawkins Full Employment Act—made very clear that the central bank needed some help moving the economy forward. In Japan, the Bank of Japan established a new inflation target and was trying hard to convince the public that the central bank could move inflation to target, but then the fiscal agent raised consumption taxes in a way that helped derail that effort to shift to a higher inflation rate. The ZLB is difficult to escape; doing so would be much easier if fiscal policy were supportive.

One suggestion might be that countries establish a rule such that the interest savings that accompany quantitative easing is automatically spent. That is, if quantitative easing takes place at the ZLB and saves the Treasury a certain amount of interest costs, the Treasury would commit to spending (or perhaps distributing as a dividend to taxpayers) those savings. Regardless of the mechanism, it seems important that the fiscal agent not counteract the monetary agent when the central bank is trying to get off the ZLB.

To summarize how we may need to rethink fiscal policy:

- It is essential that fiscal rules not interfere with fiscal stimulus taking place when it is needed.
- We also need to consider different levels of government so that states within the United States or countries within Europe do not act in ways that run counter to the macroeconomic fiscal needs of the overall economic area. There is no fiscal policy taking place at the European level, leaving a decentralized running of fiscal policy. The problem is that those who can spend do not want to and those who want to cannot because of fiscal rules, with the result that there are real limitations to how productive fiscal policy can be.
- These concerns about inadequate stimulus when needed also suggest a real need for robust automatic stabilizers. In the United States automatic stabilization might have a number of facets ranging from reformed unemployment insurance that extends automatically during recessions (and does not require constant congressional action to keep going) to infrastructure funds like TIGER grants that expand during downturns to automatically push more money into the economy when needed.
- It is important that countries have systems in place that leave them *ready* to do stimulus when needed. There is a small section in Auerbach's chapter that is quite important on this topic. Making sure governments are ready to spend effectively when the need for spending arises is an important part of making sure stimulus spending is not wasteful and can happen expeditiously.

Some rethinking has been taking place. Work by Jason Furman (2016) and Alan Blinder (2016) also suggests a need to be ready to use fiscal policy to help the economy when appropriate and to learn from the experience of the last decade. In many ways, the lessons do not require massive amounts of academic work to change our views. The answers are there.

What is needed is to transform these answers into action, so the next time fiscal policy is needed for macroeconomic purposes, the policy frameworks exist to push the economies back toward health.

References

Auerbach, Alan J., and Yuriy Gorodnichenko. 2012. "Measuring the Output Responses to Fiscal Policy." *American Economic Journal: Economic Policy* 4 (2): 1–27.

Auerbach, Alan J., and Yuriy Gorodnichenko. 2017. "Fiscal Stimulus and Fiscal Sustainability." Paper presented at the symposium "Fostering a Global Dynamic Economy," sponsored by the Federal Reserve Bank of Kansas City. Jackson Hole, WY, August 24–26.

Beckworth, David. 2017. "Is Larry Summers a Fan of Nominal GDP Level Targeting?" Interview. *Macro Musings* (blog and podcast), episode 75. http://macromarketmusings.blogspot.com/2017/09/is-larry-summers-fan-of-ngdp-level.html.

Blanchard, Olivier J., and Daniel Leigh. 2013. "Growth Forecast Errors and Fiscal Multipliers." *American Economic Review* 103 (3): 117–120.

Blinder, Alan. 2016. "Fiscal Policy Reconsidered." Hamilton Project Policy Proposal 2016-05. Washington, DC: Brookings Institution.

Chodorow-Reich, Gabriel, Laura Feiveson, Zachary Liscow, and William Gui Woolston. 2012. "Does State Fiscal Relief during Recessions Increase Employment? Evidence from the American Recovery and Reinvestment Act." *American Economic Journal. Economic Policy* 4 (3): 118–145.

DeLong, J. Bradford, and Lawrence H. Summers. 2012. "Fiscal Policy in a Depressed Economy." *Brookings Papers on Economic Activity*, Spring, 233–297.

European Commission. 2011. "Communications from the Commission: A Roadmap to Stability and Growth." Brussels, October 12.

Feyrer, James, and Bruce Sacerdote. 2011. "Did the Stimulus Stimulate? Real Time Estimates of the Effects of the American Recovery and Reinvestment Act." NBER Working Paper 16759. Cambridge, MA: National Bureau of Economic Research.

Furman, Jason. 2016. "The New View of Fiscal Policy and Its Application." Speech at the conference "Global Implications of Europe's Redesign," New York, October 5.

G-20. 2016. "Communiqué: G20 Finance Ministers and Central Bank Governors Meeting." April 15. https://www.imf.org/en/News/Articles/2015/09/28/04/51/cm041616.

IMF. 2010. "G-20 Mutual Assessment Process—Alternative Policy Scenarios." Report prepared by IMF staff for the G-20 Toronto Summit, June 26–27.

IMF. 2013. *World Economic Outlook*. Washington, DC: International Monetary Fund.

Lagarde, Christine. 2016. "Decisive Action to Secure Durable Growth." Lecture at Bundesbank and Goethe University, Frankfurt, April 5.

Nakamura, Emi, and Jón Steinsson. 2014. "Fiscal Stimulus in a Monetary Union: Evidence from U.S. Regions." *American Economic Review* 104 (3): 753–792.

OECD. 2016. "OECD Economic Outlook, Interim Report." February.

III
Financial Policy

11

Rethinking Financial Stability

David Aikman, Andrew G. Haldane, Marc Hinterschweiger,
and Sujit Kapadia

The thematic title of the 2017 conference was "Rethinking Macroeconomic Policy." When it comes to financial stability, that theme could hardly be more appropriate. The global financial crisis has prompted a complete rethinking of financial stability and policies for achieving it. Over the course of the better part of a decade, a deep and wide-ranging international regulatory reform effort has been under way, as great as any since the Great Depression: wide, reflecting the multifaceted nature of the problems, market failures, and market frictions exposed within the financial system during the crisis; deep, reflecting the severity of the hit to balance sheets, risk appetite, and economic activity that the crisis has inflicted and continues to inflict.

In this chapter, we take stock of what we have learned in the years since the global financial crisis about the challenges of maintaining financial stability. The chapter is structured as follows. The next section reviews the various regulatory reforms put in place and assesses their impact through the lens of bank balance sheets and market metrics of banking risk. The following sections draw on new research and evidence to discuss, first, the calibration of regulatory standards, balancing the costs and benefits of tighter regulation, and second, the overall system of financial regulation, balancing underlaps and overlaps, simplicity and complexity, discretion and rules, and incentives to avoid regulation.

The financial system is dynamic and adaptive. So any financial regulatory regime will itself need to be adaptive if it is to contain risk within this system. In the terms used by Greenwood and co-authors (2017), resilience needs to be "dynamic." As past evidence has shown, too rigid a regulatory system will soon become otiose. And there are already calls, in some quarters and in some countries, for a rethinking and rewriting of regulatory rules on which the ink is barely dry.[1] This poses both opportunities and threats. With that in mind, we conclude the chapter with some thoughts on issues that might be fruitful for future research on regulatory policy.

International Regulatory Reform

We begin with a summarized and simplified account of the regulatory reforms undertaken by international policymakers over the past decade.[2] Our account partitions reform efforts into their microprudential and macroprudential components, recognizing that the two often overlap and are usually mutually reinforcing in their impact.[3]

Microprudential Reform

Under the umbrella of Basel III, international reform of microprudential regulation has focused on four key areas: capital, leverage, liquidity, and resolution. Taking these in turn:

Reform of risk-based capital standards has focused on increasing the quantity and quality of capital maintained by banks against their asset exposures. Minimum regulatory requirements for banks' "core" (common equity) capital have been raised from 2 percent under Basel II to 4.5 percent under Basel III, even for the smallest banks. On quality of capital, banks are now required to deduct items such as goodwill and deferred tax assets from common equity. And the types of financial instrument eligible as loss-absorbing capital (including for tier 1) have been tightened considerably. For example, certain hybrid capital instruments are no longer eligible, as they were shown during the crisis to be incapable of absorbing loss in situations of stress (Moody's 2010; Tucker 2013).

These reforms to capital standards have, encouragingly, been implemented in full by nearly all countries internationally (Financial Stability Board [FSB] 2017a). Comparing regulatory capital pre- and post-reform is not straightforward. But when changes in both the quantity and quality of capital are taken together, it has been estimated that Basel III raised risk-based capital standards for globally systemic banks by a factor of around 10 (Cecchetti 2015).

One of the new elements of the Basel III package was to supplement risk-weighted capital standards with a risk-unweighted leverage ratio.

Because this measure does not require banks or regulators to form a judgment on the riskiness of banks' assets, it is in principle simpler, more transparent, and less subject to risk-weight arbitrage (Haldane and Madouros 2012). Indeed, those were among the reasons a number of countries, including the United States and Canada, had a leverage ratio regime ahead of the crisis.[4] The Basel III leverage ratio, set at a minimum level of 3 percent of tier 1 capital, is due to be implemented internationally by 2018.

A second new element of the Basel III package was to augment solvency with liquidity-based standards. Banks' liquidity has long been a preoccupation of the Basel Committee (Goodhart 2011). But it took wholesale liquidity runs on the world's largest banks during the crisis to provide the impetus for internationally agreed-upon liquidity standards. Under Basel III, these take the form of a liquidity coverage ratio (LCR), designed to ensure banks have sufficient high-quality liquid assets to meet their 30-day liquidity needs; and a net stable funding ratio (NSFR), designed to ensure banks' funding profiles are sustainable. The LCR has been implemented in full in most countries; the NFSR is due for implementation by 2018.[5]

During the crisis, a crucial ingredient found missing from the financial regulatory architecture was the ability to wind up financial institutions in an orderly fashion—that is, while minimizing disruption to financial markets and the economy and without exposing taxpayers to risk (FSB 2014). A number of measures have been taken or are in progress to fill this gap, including the introduction of more effective national resolution regimes for financial firms and greater cross-border cooperation and coordination when dealing with international banks in situations of stress (FSB 2017c).

Another element is to ensure banks have sufficient loss-absorbing liabilities that can be "bailed in" in the event of failure, to prevent losses from being shouldered by taxpayers. The Financial Stability Board (FSB) has agreed on standards for such total loss-absorbing capacity (TLAC) for global systemically important banks (G-SIBs). These standards are to be phased in over coming years, to reach a minimum level of 16 percent beginning in 2019 and 18 percent beginning in 2022, of the resolution group's risk-weighted assets, as well as 6 percent and 6.75 percent on a leverage exposure basis, respectively.

Macroprudential Reform

These new or augmented microprudential standards have been supplemented with a set of new macroprudential measures. These measures focus on safeguarding the stability of the financial system as a whole (Tucker 2009; Bank of England 2009, 2011). The most significant of these reforms have focused on three areas: macroprudential capital buffers, stress testing, and shadow banks.

Historically, capital standards have been static requirements. As part of Basel III, a new time-varying component of banks' capital was added—the countercyclical capital buffer (CCyB). This recognizes that risks to the financial system vary over the credit cycle, typically being highest at its peak and lowest at its trough. The CCyB aims to counteract somewhat that time-varying risk profile, with additional capital required during the upswing that can be released during the downswing. There is international reciprocity in the setting of the CCyB to reduce incentives for cross-border arbitrage (Basel Committee on Banking Supervision [BCBS] 2010a). The framework has been implemented in most jurisdictions.

Similarly, one of the key lessons of the crisis was that some institutions impose greater degrees of risk on the system because of their size, complexity, or interconnectedness (FSB 2010). Basel III recognizes the need for these systemically important firms to carry a structurally higher capital requirement, currently up to 3.5 percent, to help mitigate the additional risk they bring to the system. These capital add-ons apply to the thirty designated G-SIBs and the roughly 160 domestic systemically important banks (D-SIBs), to be phased in between 2016 and 2019.

Stress tests were used by regulators before the crisis to assess whether banks had sufficient capital to withstand an adverse tail event. But these tests tended to be neither comprehensive nor transparent. In 2009, the U.S. authorities undertook a comprehensive stress test of the major U.S. banks and published the results. Banks that failed the test had regulatory restrictions imposed on their behavior. For some people, this marked the turning point for the U.S. financial system. A comprehensive annual stress-testing exercise is now undertaken in the United States.[6] More recently, the United States has been joined by the UK and the EU, among others.[7]

Finally, one of the striking features of the precrisis financial system was the emergence of the so-called shadow banking system. In the United

States, on some definitions, this grew to exceed in size the conventional banking system (Pozsar et al. 2010). Since the crisis, reform efforts have focused on two areas. First, specific reforms have been enacted to sectors that, during the crisis, were found to contain fault lines—for example, money market mutual funds (IOSCO 2012). Second, a framework has been put in place by the FSB to define and measure shadow banking entities, to publish data on them to enhance market discipline, and to help authorities identify and develop policy tools for mitigating the risks they might pose (FSB 2013a). The FSB has recently put forward a package of recommendations to address structural vulnerabilities from the asset management sector (FSB 2017d).

Balance Sheet Impact

So what has been the impact of these regulatory reform measures on banks' overall resilience? One simple set of resilience metrics focuses on bank balance sheet measures of solvency and liquidity. Comparisons of international banks' balance sheets are made difficult by changes over time in both the definitions of variables and the sample of banks. We consider a panel of international banks designated either G-SIB by the FSB in 2016 or D-SIB. This gives a panel of thirty G-SIBs and about 160 D-SIBs.[8] For each bank, we consider two solvency-based metrics (leverage and risk-weighted capital) and two liquidity-based metrics (a simple liquid asset ratio and the ratio of loans to deposits). These measures do not map precisely to Basel definitions.[9]

Figure 11.1 looks at a measure of banks' tier 1 risk-weighted capital ratios. For both the G-SIBs and the D-SIBs in our sample, these ratios have risen significantly over the past decade, almost doubling from around 8 percent to around 14–15 percent. A very similar picture emerges for leverage ratios (figure 11.2). These also have roughly doubled over the past decade, from around 3.5 percent to around 6 percent. On these metrics, there has been a material strengthening in solvency-based standards among systemically important banks over the past decade. This is also the case for measures of TLAC (see figure 11.3 for a sample of UK banks).

Liquidity metrics show a similar pattern of improvement. For example, liquid asset ratios—high-quality liquid assets as a fraction of the total balance sheet—have risen from around 7 percent in 2008 to more than 10 percent (figure 11.4). Meanwhile, the ratio of loans to deposits (LTD)

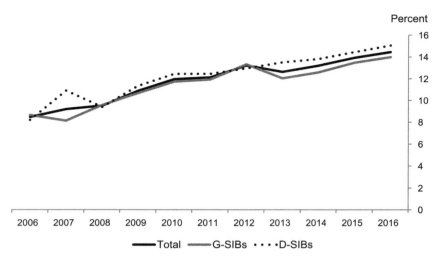

Figure 11.1

G-SIB and D-SIB Tier 1 Capital Ratios. Data from S&P Global Market Intelligence; Bank of England calculations.
Notes: Weighted average based on a sample of 189 banks that were systemically important as of 2016. Yearly is defined as the fiscal year of reporting of the individual banks. Tier 1 capital ratio = tier 1 capital/risk-weighted assets.

has also improved, with lending backed by a larger share of stable sources of funding than before the crisis (figure 11.5).

Market-Based Metrics

A second set of metrics of bank solvency and liquidity focuses on financial market perceptions of bank risk. There is a wide variety of potential such metrics, each with its own imperfections, including measures of default such as credit default swap (CDS) spreads, bond yields, and ratings; measures of volatility, such as option-implied volatilities; and measures of profitability, such as price-earnings ratios. These are summarized and evaluated in Sarin and Summers (2016).

Figure 11.6 plots a measure of default—CDS spreads—for a panel of G-SIBs. It shows a familiar pattern of precrisis underpricing of risk, a rapid repricing of default risk during the crisis, and a subsequent partial unwind. CDS spreads today sit roughly midway between their precrisis and mid-crisis averages. Bank bond spreads and ratings tell a similar

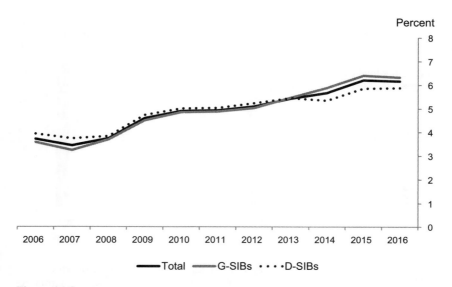

Figure 11.2

G-SIB and D-SIB leverage ratios. Data from S&P Global Market Intelligence; Bank of England calculations.
Notes: Weighted average based on a sample of 189 banks that were systemically important as of 2016. Yearly is defined as the fiscal year of reporting of the individual banks.

story. Assuming precrisis banking risk was materially underpriced, this evidence is consistent with regulatory reform having boosted the resilience of the global banking system.

At the same time, measures of bank volatility and profitability have seen fewer signs of recovery. Figure 11.7 plots a measure of the price-to-book ratio of G-SIBs and D-SIBs. This measure currently lies well below its historical average at a level little different from unity. Put differently, if we used a measure of banks' capital ratios using the market rather than the book value of their equity, the result would suggest a far smaller degree of improvement in measured bank solvency and resilience (figure 11.8), though the effect would be less pronounced for D-SIBs.

Sarin and Summers (2016) reconcile these market movements by appealing to the shifts in the franchise value of banks. Improved solvency standards have decreased the perceived default risk of banks. But coincident with lower risk are lower returns on banks' activities owing to the

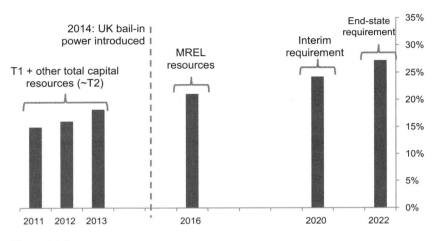

Figure 11.3

Major UK Banks' Regulatory Capital, MREL Resources and Requirements, % RWA (2011–2022). Data from Financial Services Authority (UK) regulatory returns and MREL+ returns; and Bank of England calculations.
Note: MREL, Minimum Requirement for Own Funds and Eligible Liabilities; RWA, risk-weighted assets.

combined effects of stricter regulation, misconduct fines, low levels of interest rates, and increased competition. This leaves banks a riskier proposition for equity investors than before the crisis, as the residual claimant on profits. But by and large, improved solvency standards have reduced risk among bondholders and depositors in banks.

"By and large" is used because accompanying these changes in banks' capital standards has been a move toward putting losses from default onto bondholders. This can be seen in the evolution of the implied "support ratings" given to banks by rating agencies. In 2010, holders of the major UK banks' debt enjoyed around four notches of implied ratings uplift owing to expectations of government support (figure 11.9). By 2016, that had fallen to less than one notch of support. A similar pattern is evident among other global banks.

Calibrating Regulatory Standards

Is the calibration of these new regulatory standards too tough, too lax, or just right? That has been among the most animated of the regulatory

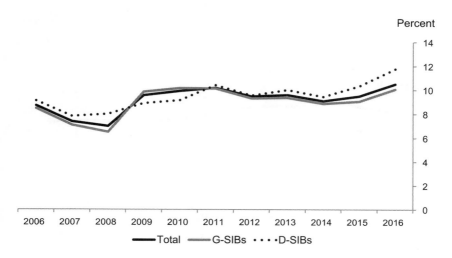

Figure 11.4

G-SIB and D-SIB High-Quality Liquid Assets (Liquid Asset Ratio). Data from S&P Global Market Intelligence; Bank of England calculations
Notes: Weighted average based on a sample of 189 banks that were systemically important as of 2016. Yearly is defined as the fiscal year of reporting of the individual banks. Liquid asset ratio = (Cash equivalents + Government securities)/ Total assets.

debates over the past decade. International regulators engaged in a detailed, quantitative exercise that sought to weigh the social costs and benefits of tighter regulation, drawing on existing empirical evidence. The Basel Committee's 2010 Long-Term Economic Impact (LEI) study is a useful starting point for discussion of the appropriate calibration of regulatory standards (BCBS 2010b).

The main conclusion from this work was that, under conservative assumptions about likely economic costs, there were positive economic benefits to society from a sizable increase in the capital banks were required to maintain. The study did not settle on an optimal level of bank capital. But the results presented were consistent with societal benefits peaking at a tier 1 risk-weighted capital ratio of between 16 and 19 percent.[10] This is north of most global banks' current capital ratios.

In this section, we revisit the assumptions underpinning the LEI study in the light of subsequent research. A little notation may be useful to organize this evidence. Suppose the aim of policy is to keep output in the

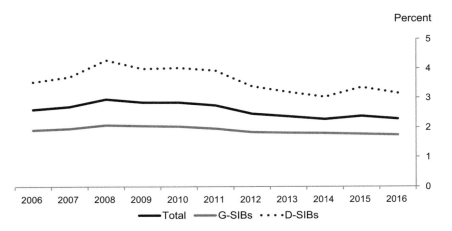

Figure 11.5

G-SIB and D-SIB Loan-to-Deposit Ratio. Data from S&P Global Market Intelligence; Bank of England calculations.
Notes: Weighted average based on a sample of 189 banks that were systemically important as of 2016. Yearly is defined as the fiscal year of reporting of the individual banks. Loan-to-deposit ratio = Loans granted by a bank/Stable deposits received. Stable deposits are assumed to be a constant share of total deposits.

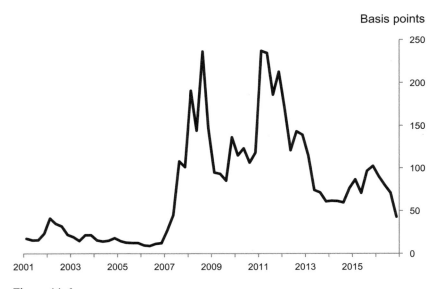

Figure 11.6

CDS Spreads for G-SIBs. Data from Bloomberg Finance L.P.; Bank of England calculations.
Note: Weighted average of twenty-two banks designated as G-SIBs as of 2016. CDS, credit default swap.

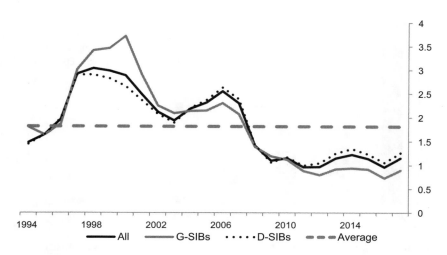

Figure 11.7

G-SIB and D-SIB Price-to-Book Ratio. Data from Bloomberg Finance L.P.; Bank of England calculations.

Note: Sample of 103 G-SIBs and D-SIBs designated as G-SIBs/D-SIBs as of 2016.

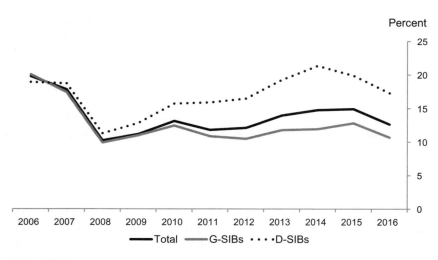

Figure 11.8

Capital Ratio Using Market Value of Equity. Data fromS&P Global Market Intelligence and Bloomberg Finance L.P.; Bank of England calculations.

Notes: Weighted average based on a sample of 189 banks that were systemically important as of 2016. Yearly is defined as the fiscal year of reporting of the individual banks. Market-based capital ratio = Market capitalization/Risk-weighted assets.

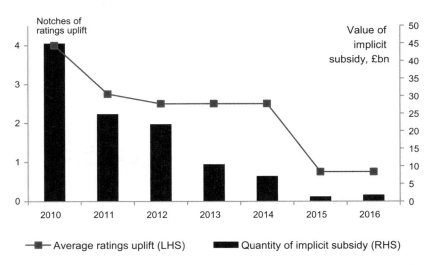

Figure 11.9

Estimates of Implicit Subsidy. Data from Moody's and Bank of America; Bank of England calculations.
Notes: Includes Barclays, HSBC, Lloyd's Banking Group, and Royal Bank of Scotland. Calculated by multiplying the spread between indicative bonds at standalone and supported credit ratings by the volume of ratings-sensitive liabilities; year-end data. Submitted as written evidence by the Bank of England to the Treasury Committee (http://data.parliament.uk/writtenevidence/committeeevidence .svc/evidencedocument/treasury-committee/capital-and-resolution/written/69208 .pdf).

economy, y, as close as possible to its trend growth path, $\overline{y}$. The objective for the authorities is then to minimize a loss function, which can be written as:

$$L = (y_t - \overline{y}_t)^2.$$

Let's simplify further and assume two factors can cause output to deviate from its trend: first, higher capital requirements, k, which act to reduce output each period by δ, and second, the occurrence of a financial crisis that, with probability γ, leads to a discrete drop in output of Δ. That is:

$$y_t = \overline{y}_t - \delta k - \gamma(k)\Delta(k).$$

This captures the view that higher bank capital could reduce credit supply, and hence economic activity, in the near term. But by making the financial system more resilient to future shocks, it may also reduce the tail risk of bad macroeconomic outcomes.

Both the probability and the severity of crises are influenced negatively by the level of bank capital, with the relationship likely to be convex $(\gamma'(k) < 0 \gamma''(k) > 0, \Delta'(k) < 0, \Delta''(k) > 0)$—that is to say, one would expect a one percentage point increase in the capital ratio to have a larger dampening impact on the probability and severity of crisis when banks are close to their regulatory minima than when capital buffers are plentiful.

In this stylized setup, the marginal condition that defines optimal bank capital is:

$$\delta = -\Delta \frac{\partial \gamma}{\partial k} - \gamma \frac{\partial \Delta}{\partial k}.$$

Optimal capital is higher the lower is δ, the economic cost of a marginal increase in capital requirements; the greater are γ and Δ, the likelihood and severity of crises; and the greater are $\frac{\partial \gamma}{\partial k}$ and $\frac{\partial \Delta}{\partial k}$, the marginal effects of capital on the likelihood and severity of crises.

What have we learned over the past decade about the likely magnitude of these parameters?

The Benefits of Higher Capital Requirements

The Basel Committee's LEI study assumed that banking crises occur, on average, once every twenty to twenty-five years; the median estimate of the cumulative discounted costs of a crisis is around 60 percent of annual precrisis GDP; each one percentage point increase in the capital ratio reduces the probability of a banking crisis by a smaller amount, ranging from 1.4 percent to 1 percent (for a capital increase from 10 percent to 11 percent) to 0.4 percent to 0.3 percent (for a capital increase from 14 percent to 15 percent); and, finally, the level of bank capital has no impact on the severity of crisis.

Since the LEI report, a rich seam of the literature has emerged addressing the determinants of crises and their severity (Δ). Some of the most illuminating parts of this research have drawn on evidence from a long historical time series and across multiple countries (e.g., Jordà, Schularick, and Taylor 2013; Taylor 2015). The key findings are as follows.

First, credit booms are probably the single most important determinant of the likelihood of crises and of economic performance in the recovery after them (Schularick and Taylor 2012; Jordà, Schularick, and Taylor 2013). A sustained one percentage point increase in the credit-to-GDP ratio raises the probability of crisis from 4 percent to around 4.3 percent per year. It also increases the severity of a crisis, with real GDP per capita almost 1 percent lower after five years.[11] Colleagues at the Bank of England have considered whether it is the level of credit or its growth prior to a crisis that matters most for subsequent economic performance (Bridges, Jackson, and McGregor 2017). They find that credit growth has historically been a significant predictor of crisis severity, whereas the level of indebtedness appears less important.

Second, not all forms of credit are equal. In the post–World War II era, mortgage credit growth has been the dominant driver of financial crisis risk. And growth in mortgages, rather than in other forms of credit, is the key determinant of the drag in the recovery phase from crisis (Jordà et al. 2017). Third, asset prices are also important, with "leveraged bubbles"— synchronized house price and mortgage credit booms—particularly dangerous (Jordà, Schularick, and Taylor 2015).

Taken together, this evidence is consistent with the probability (γ) and output costs of credit crises (Δ) being at least as large as assumed in the original LEI study, perhaps larger, in light of the still high levels of the credit-to-GDP ratio in most countries and the monetary and fiscal space available to the authorities at present relative to the average of the past. A recent paper by Romer and Romer (2017) presents evidence that this factor is a significant determinant of crisis severity.

What role does higher bank capital play in reducing the likelihood of financial crises ($\frac{\partial \gamma}{\partial k}$) or their severity ($\frac{\partial \Delta}{\partial k}$)? At least for the likelihood of crisis, subsequent evidence has tended to be rather ambiguous. Historical evidence, derived using aggregate economy-wide covariates, points to the perhaps surprising conclusion that bank capital ratios have virtually no predictive power for the occurrence of financial crises in major advanced economies (Jordà et al. 2017). That is, $\frac{\partial \gamma}{\partial k}$ is indistinguishable from zero.

Micro-econometric studies on the link between bank failure and bank capital have found a more tangible relationship, however. For example, Vazquez and Federico (2015) find that U.S. and EU banks with stronger precrisis capital and structural liquidity positions were less likely to fail. Berger and Bouwman (2013) report a similar finding using a longer-run data set of U.S. banks. And a recent study by IMF economists finds that risk-based capital ratios in the range of 15–23 percent would have been sufficient to absorb losses in the vast majority of past advanced economy banking crises (Dagher et al. 2016).[12]

At the time of the Basel Committee's study, there was little evidence of the impact of bank capital on the severity of crises ($\frac{\partial \Delta}{\partial k}$), which is why this channel was ignored in the quantitative calibration. That has since changed. Jordà and co-workers (2017) find that, while bank capital does not prevent a crisis from occurring, it matters for the pain suffered in its aftermath. They find that real GDP per head is 5 percent higher five years after the onset of a crisis-related recession if bank capital is above its historical average when the crisis hits.

The benefits of capital in reducing the severity of a crisis are also borne out by experience since the crisis. Figure 11.10 plots international banks' capital ratios prior to the crisis against their subsequent lending growth. The relationship has a statistically significant upward slope. Banks that entered the crisis with higher capital have, on average, been better able to continue their lending. On average, each extra percentage point of precrisis capital boosted banks' cumulative lending over the subsequent decade by more than 20 percent.

This finding is corroborated by micro-econometric evidence. Carlson, Shan, and Warusawitharana (2013) find that U.S. banks with higher precrisis capital ratios had stronger loan growth in the aftermath of the crisis, with the effect particularly pronounced at lower capital ratios. Cornett and co-workers (2011) and Kapan and Minoiu (2013) report that banks relying more heavily on stable sources of funding, such as core deposits and equity capital, continued to lend relative to other banks during the crisis. And Jiménez and co-workers (2014) find that, in periods of economic weakness, loan applications were less likely to be rejected by Spanish banks that were well capitalized.

A recent paper by Bank of England colleagues identifies a distinct channel through which bank capital affects crisis severity (Tracey, Schnittker, and Sowerbutts 2017). They use banks' misconduct fines as a novel instrument to identify exogenous negative bank capital shocks. They find

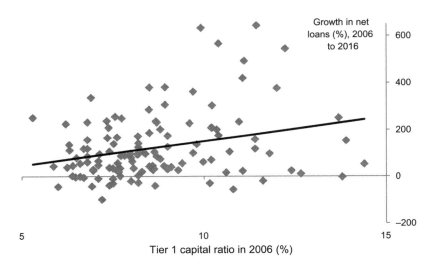

Figure 11.10

Individual Banks' 2006 Capital Positions and 2006–2016 Lending Growth. Data from S&P Global Market Intelligence; Bank of England calculations.

that banks respond to such shocks by relaxing their lending standards, as measured by the loan-to-value and loan-to-income ratios on new mortgages. This is likely to increase banks' vulnerability to future shocks, increasing crisis severity.

These results suggest that some of the benefits of higher capital requirements may have been understated in the original LEI study, with implications for the range of optimal capital requirements. For example, if we assume that every percentage point of extra capital increased the level of real GDP each period in the aftermath of a crisis by 0.1 percent, that would raise optimal capital ratios by around two percentage points, other things equal.[13]

Working in the opposite direction, however, have been developments in resolution arrangements and new standards for TLAC. No account was taken of these in the LEI study. But if TLAC can be credibly bailed in, including for systemically important institutions, this would tend to reduce both the likelihood and the severity of future crises.[14] It may also discipline banks' management, so that management does not take excessive risks in the first place. Some studies suggest this market discipline effect could be material, reducing the likelihood of a financial crisis by as much as 30 percent (Brandao Marques, Correa, and Sapriza 2013; Afonso, Santos, and Traina 2015).

Colleagues at the Bank of England (Brooke et al. 2015) have assessed that, if these estimates of the beneficial incentive effects of TLAC and credible resolution regimes are correct, and if increased resolvability in addition reduces the cost of crises by around 60 percent,[15] then optimal capital ratios for the UK banking system could be up to five percentage points lower than would otherwise be the case.[16]

The Costs of Higher Capital Requirements

The costs of higher bank capital requirements arise from potentially tighter credit supply conditions. Banks may adjust to the need to fund themselves with more equity by tightening lending rates and restricting loan volumes. The LEI study assumed that each percentage point increase in the capital ratio would raise loan spreads by around 13 basis points. That translated into a fall in GDP of around 0.1 percent relative to trend.[17]

What have we learned about these costs since the LEI study? Cecchetti (2014) shows how banks have adjusted their balance sheets and credit provision since the introduction of Basel III. He finds that banks increased their capital ratios significantly, by over four percentage points on average, across his sample. Net interest margins and profitability fell. But with the exception of European banks, banks' assets increased, their lending spreads narrowed, lending standards eased, and the ratio of bank credit-to-GDP went up.

A recent paper from the BIS (Gambacorta and Shin 2018) reaches a similar conclusion. It finds that banks with higher unweighted capital ratios have tended to have higher loan growth, with each one percentage point increase being associated with higher subsequent lending growth of 0.6 percentage points per year. This evidence is consistent with the macroeconomic costs of higher bank capital being lower than assumed in the Basel Committee's LEI study. Indeed, taken at face value, it would suggest there have been virtually no costs of achieving higher levels of capital across the global banking system, at least among most global banks.

While credit conditions have clearly improved since the crisis, it is possible that the recovery in lending might have been stronger still had capital requirements risen by less. To begin to analyze that question, figure 11.11 compares the *change* in bank capital since Basel III was introduced

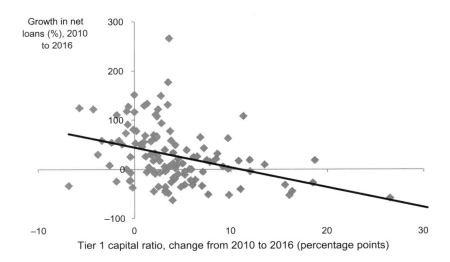

Figure 11.11

Change in Bank Capital and Lending Growth, 2010–2016. Data from S&P Global Market Intelligence; Bank of England calculations.

with subsequent lending growth among a panel of large international banks. On average, lending growth has been positive over this period, consistent with Cecchetti (2014). But credit growth has also tended to be statistically significantly lower among banks that have seen the largest increase in their capital ratios. On average, banks that have increased their capital ratios by an extra one percentage point have provided 4 percent less in cumulative credit since Basel III was introduced (3.5 percent less if we exclude European banks). This is very similar to the estimates of the Macroeconomic Assessment Group (2010), which ranged from –0.7 percent to –3.6 percent.

There are, of course, different possible interpretations of this negative relationship. Banks facing weak macroeconomic conditions may simply have seen a reduction in loan demand and responded by maintaining higher capital buffers on a voluntary basis. To parse these conflicting interpretations, we turn to recent econometric evidence.

Aiyar, Calomiris, and Wieladek (2014, 2016) find that shifts in required capital had large negative effects on UK banks' lending decisions. De-Ramon, Francis, and Harris (2016) report a similar finding. Bahaj and co-workers (2016) find that, in times of credit expansion, higher required capital has only a minimal effect on lending. But when credit growth is weak, higher required capital can result in a large reduction in lending. This echoes previous research finding that banks reduce lending in response to negative capital shocks (Peek and Rosengren 1995).

A second potential cost of higher bank capital requirements, not considered by the LEI study, is the potential for falls in market liquidity in core financial markets—for example, repo and securities financing markets. This situation could potentially raise the cost of capital for users of these markets. There are, of course, several other reasons why banks' willingness to make markets, and market liquidity more generally, might have been affected by the crisis, such as reduced risk appetite and increased counterparty risk. Moreover, it was plausibly the case that precrisis liquidity may have been *too* plentiful and *too* cheap in some financial markets so that some correction in the quantity and pricing of liquidity was to be expected, and indeed was potentially desirable, from a welfare perspective.

Research at the Bank of England has sought to identify the impact of leverage ratio requirements on the functioning of UK government bond ("gilt") and gilt repo markets, using transaction-level data (Bicu, Chen, and Elliott 2017).[18] It finds some causal impact of the leverage requirement on various metrics of liquidity, a worsening that is particularly acute at quarter-ends. Significantly, the banks most constrained by the leverage ratio reduced their activity in financial markets most. At the same time, however, dealers unaffected by the leverage ratio requirement also reduced their liquidity provision and, if anything, by more. This suggests factors other than the leverage ratio may have been at work in curtailing liquidity in these markets.

Overall Implications for Optimal Capital

How do these research findings tilt the optimal bank capital calculus relative to the LEI study? Table 11.1 summarizes the evidence. They are a mixed bag. On the benefits side, there is now stronger evidence on the costs of credit booms and the role of capital in constraining the severity of the downturn in the aftermath of these booms. It also suggests that the costs of raising extra capital are no larger, and may well be smaller, than originally anticipated. This strengthens the hand of macroprudential authorities when tightening capital requirements during a credit boom.

Table 11.1

Overall Implications of Research Findings for Optimal Capital

	Impact on optimal capital
Benefits:	
Likelihood and severity of crises	↑
Impact of capital on probability of crises	→
Impact of capital on severity of crises	↑
Impact of TLAC and resolution regimes on the probability and severity of crises	↓
Costs:	
Impact of capital on credit conditions and growth	→
Impact of capital on market liquidity (leverage ratio) in normal conditions	↓

Other things equal, it would also increase quantitative estimates of banks' optimal capital ratio.

On the other side of the ledger, the LEI study did not anticipate two factors. The first is the role of TLAC in augmenting banks' capital base in situations of stress, potentially reducing the probability and severity of crises. The second is that higher capital requirements could impose liquidity-related costs on the financial system, though their scale (and whether they are a social cost) remains open for debate. These arguments, in particular around resolution, have been used by policymakers in some countries, including the UK, when coming to the view that capital requirements should be lower than in the original LEI study. For example, having assessed all the factors and evidence within table 11.1, the Bank of England's Financial Policy Committee judged that the appropriate structural level of tier 1 equity in the system would be 13½ percent of risk-weighted assets (Bank of England 2015b).

The System of Financial Regulation

If we put together the various pieces of recent reform, we find a fundamentally different regulatory jigsaw, or system of financial regulation, than in the past. Perhaps the most important dimension of this change is the significant increase in the number of regulatory rules or constraints that now operate. To the risk-based capital standards have been added regulatory rules for liquidity, leverage, and loss-absorbing capital buffers. In this section, we explore the rationale for this move to a system of multipolar regulation (Haldane 2015); we also discuss the challenges it creates, both in terms of incentives for the regulated to arbitrage the system and in terms of the appropriate balance between rules and discretion in their operation.

The Rationale for a System of Multipolar Regulation

The key regulatory constraints on bank behavior are risk-weighted capital requirements (RWCR), the leverage ratio (LR), the liquidity coverage ratio (LCR), and the net stable funding ratio (NSFR). Some have recently contended that this multi-constraint system might be overidentified, with potentially distortionary implications for banks' business models and behavior (Cecchetti and Kashyap 2016; Greenwood et al. 2017). These are well-reasoned critiques, just the sort of academic challenge to regulatory orthodoxy that was missing in the precrisis period. Nonetheless, it is also worth reminding ourselves why and how such a framework was arrived at in the first place.

At a conceptual level, three arguments support the new multipronged approach. First, banks are subject to multiple sources of risk. Historical experience suggests they fail for a variety of different reasons. To misquote Tolstoy, while sound banks tend all to be alike, unsound banks tend to be unsound in their own way. This suggests a need for different regulatory constraints to counter different balance sheet fault lines: one instrument per market failure. This is, if you like, the Tinbergen Rule as it applies to financial regulation (Tinbergen 1952). Second, uncertainty as well as risk is pervasive in the financial system. Knightian (Knight 1921) uncertainties have multiple sources—measurement of the risks banks face, how contagion propagates across the financial system, and how regulatory actions affects behavior, to name but three. A portfolio of regulatory tools offers insurance against these uncertainties. This is, if you like, the Brainard Rule as it applies to financial regulation (Brainard 1967). Third, any individual constraint creates incentives for banks to engage in avoidance or arbitrage. Multiple regulatory constraints mitigate this risk while creating their own distortions.

We begin by discussing the conceptual case for multiple constraints before presenting some new empirical evidence. Table 11.2 summarizes some of the key arguments.

Capital and Leverage   If the true risk of an asset can be estimated accurately—a "known known"—then the RWCR is better suited than the LR to guard against solvency risk (Gordy 2003). Adopting this view, Greenwood and co-authors (2017) conclude "the social optimum can be implemented with a single requirement that each bank maintain a sufficient ratio of equity to risk-weighted assets, provided the risk weights are chosen appropriately."

The last part of this sentence is, however, an important proviso. A key question is whether risks in the financial system can be known with sufficient certainty to be estimated accurately. History suggests this assumption cannot be taken for granted. As discussed by Aikman and co-authors (2014), there are at least three reasons for this. First, assigning probabilities is particularly difficult with rare, high-impact events, such as financial crises or the failure of a large financial institution. Second, the behavior of complex, interconnected financial systems can be very sensitive to small changes in initial conditions and shocks and typically exhibit tipping points, which are difficult to predict ex ante (Anderson and May 1992; Gai and Kapadia 2010; Gai, Haldane, and Kapadia 2011). Third, because they contain human actors whose beliefs about the future shape their behavior today, financial systems are particularly prone to instabilities and sunspots (Tuckett and Taffler 2008; Tuckett 2011; Bailey et al. 2016; Shiller 2017).

In a world of such Knightian uncertainty, it may be difficult to estimate risk weights with any degree of precision. Indeed, attempts to do so may result in "overfitting," increasing the potential fragility of these model estimates out-of-sample. In uncertain settings, simpler weighting schemes have been found, in a variety of different environments, to offer a better defense against "unknown unknowns" (Gigerenzer 2014). That logic is one rationale for the use—and, in some settings, predictive superiority—of the LR in capturing solvency risks.

Liquidity and Funding   Historically, most banks failures are precipitated by insufficient liquidity. Because of maturity transformation, banks are vulnerable to a sudden withdrawal of funding as a result of a bank-specific or marketwide loss of credibility. In such circumstances, banks will be more robust if they have a buffer of high-quality liquid assets to meet outflows and other liquidity calls and, if necessary, buy time for the authorities to prepare for resolution. The Basel III LCR was designed and calibrated with these considerations in mind.

But excessive maturity transformation can also create risks over longer horizons, such as those that occurred during the crisis when wholesale funding markets closed for an extended period. This highlights the importance of funding metrics based on the overall extent to which illiquid assets are supported by unstable funding. The Basel III NSFR is designed with these risks in mind. Its architects hope it will complement the LCR by matching funding stability with asset liquidity at longer maturities, making banks less prone to fire-selling their assets, hoarding liquidity, and cutting lending when adverse shocks hit. The NSFR may also act as a brake on too rapid balance sheet expansion by requiring that it be supported by more stable funding sources.

To what extent are these conceptual benefits of a multipolar system of financial regulation borne out in the data? It is to this question we now turn.

An Empirical Assessment of Regulatory Metrics   To examine this question, we exploit a data set on the precrisis balance sheet characteristics of global banks developed by Aikman and co-workers (2014). The data set comprises almost all global banks that had more than $100 billion in assets at end-2006—116 banks in total across twenty-five countries. For each of these banks, we computed a range of balance sheet metrics at consolidated (group) level. Restricting attention to those for which data were available to compute risk-weighted capital ratios, leverage ratios, and NSFRs reduced the sample to 76 banks. When we focused on risk-weighted capital ratios, leverage ratios, and LTD ratios (as a simplified proxy for the NSFR, which captures the ratio of retail loans to retail deposits), the sample size was 96 banks.[19] We divided this sample into banks that "survived" and banks that "failed" between 2007 and the end of 2009, using the Laeven and Valencia (2010) definition and classification of failure.[20]

With this data set in hand, we considered how successful various combinations of regulatory constraints might have been in identifying failed

Table 11.2
Assessment of the Relative Suitability of Rules to Address Selected Forms of Risk

Risk	First-Best Mitigant	Second-Best Mitigant	Less Effective Mitigants
Microprudential solvency risk—"true" asset risk	**RWCR:** Requires loss-absorbing capital to cover solvency risks. If risk can be measured and risk weights can be chosen appropriately, this allows the greatest level of granularity.	**LR:** Provides loss-absorbing capacity but does not include any risk granularity by design.	**LCR and NSFR:** Neither ratio attempts to mitigate the risk of losses.
Microprudential solvency risk—"unknown" asset risk under Knightian uncertainty	**LR:** Effective when risks are unknowable and one cannot pinpoint particular asset classes of concern, especially in the face of limited historical data or fat-tailed loss distributions.	**RWCR:** Provides loss-absorbing capacity but may perform less well out-of-sample and vulnerable to model risk (IRB approach) or miscalibration of risk weights (standardized approach).	**LCR and NSFR:** Neither ratio attempts to mitigate the risk of losses.
Vulnerability to risk shifting	**RWCR:** High degree of granularity reduces the scope for risk shifting.	**LCR and NSFR:** Standardized assumptions mitigate some scope to shift risk but also allow some scope for distortion if weights are miscalibrated.	**LR:** Greatest scope for distortion through risk shifting because of lack of risk sensitivity.
Vulnerability to gaming	**LR:** Lack of granularity and degrees of freedom minimizes gaming opportunities.	**LCR and NSFR:** Small number of modeled assumptions offer some safeguard against gaming.	**RWCR:** High degree of freedom offered to banks increases incentives for gaming, especially under IRB approach.

Rapid and unsustainable balance sheet expansion	**LR:** Requires banks to raise capital to support credit creation, regardless of asset composition.	**NSFR:** Limits reliance on short- and medium-term wholesale funding to support balance sheet expansion.	**RWCR:** Susceptible to expansion into assets with low measured risk. Places no constraint on debt funding. **LCR:** 30-day time horizon only limits the expansion funded by very short-term liabilities.
Sudden withdrawal of funding due to firm-specific or short-lived marketwide loss of credibility	**LCR:** Ensures available buffer of liquid assets to meet immediate outflows, enabling survival of first stages of run and preparation for resolution if appropriate. **NSFR:** Matches liquidity of assets against stability of liabilities to ensure bank is broadly resilient to a medium-term funding run.	**NSFR:** Reduces runnable fraction of liabilities, thus decreasing ex ante the risk of being exposed to a run, but does not directly ensure bank has a buffer of usable short-term liquidity.	**RWCR and LR:** Higher capital should in principle help banks retain funding but does not provide a cushion if a run occurs.
Sustained loss of funding due to marketwide liquidity stress leading to slow-burn insolvency	**NSFR:** Reduces banks' vulnerability to medium-term liquidity risks and hence the probability of being required to deleverage rapidly in periods of stress to shore up their liquidity position.	**LCR:** Ensures available buffer of liquid assets to meet immediate outflows but not that maturity transformation is sustainable beyond 30-day horizon.	**RWCR and LR:** Require small fraction of liabilities to be non-runnable equity but a small amount relative to illiquid assets.
Crystallization of systemic liquidity risk leading to fire sales, liquidity hoarding, and/or a contraction in lending		**LCR:** Reduces reliance on the most unstable short-dated liabilities. Risk that banks liquidating buffers to meet outflows in a stress could exacerbate a fire sale.	**RWCR and LR:** Do not directly mitigate the likelihood of deleveraging due to liquidity problems.

Note: RWCR, risk-weighted capital requirements; LR, leverage ratio; LCR, liquidity coverage ratio; NSFR, net stable funding ratio.

and surviving banks.[21] To fix ideas, consider a prediction threshold based on a leverage ratio of 3 percent. Banks with leverage ratios below this threshold in 2006 were predicted to fail, whereas those with leverage ratios above were predicted to survive. The "hit rate" is the number of banks for which the prediction of failure subsequently proved correct, relative to the total number of banks that failed. The "false alarm rate" is the number of banks for which the prediction proved incorrect, relative to the total number of banks that survived. If a 3 percent leverage ratio could perfectly discriminate failed from surviving banks, the hit rate would be 100 percent and the false alarm rate would be 0 percent.

Table 11.3 reports the thresholds required to achieve target hit rates for the leverage ratio and other metrics, alongside the corresponding false alarm rate. Figure 11.12 presents this information a different way by plotting the locus of hit rates and false alarm rates achieved by varying the threshold for each metric—this is referred to in the literature as the receiver operating characteristic (ROC) curve. Metrics that are better discriminators of failed and surviving banks have ROC curves that lie in the top-left section of this chart. A metric with no information value for distinguishing failed from surviving banks would trace out the 45-degree line on this chart.

It is notable that hit rates of up to 70 percent are achievable with a leverage ratio threshold of around 4 percent. This means that a 4 percent leverage ratio requirement before the crisis would not have been

Table 11.3
Calibration of Individual Metrics to Achieve Target Hit Rates

Target Hit Rate (%)	LR Calibration	False Alarm Rate for LR Calibration (%)	RWCR Calibration	False Alarm Rate for RWCR Calibration (%)	NSFR Calibration	False Alarm Rate for NSFR Calibration (%)
70	3.82	29.3	8.61	58.5	0.99	70.7
75	4.14	39.0	8.66	58.5	1.05	82.9
80	4.15	39.0	8.71	61.0	1.06	82.9
85	5.00	75.6	9.04	68.3	1.12	87.8
90	5.66	82.9	9.83	73.2	1.17	87.8

Note: LR, leverage ratio; RWCR, risk-weighted capital requirements; NSFR, net stable funding ratio.

Hit rate

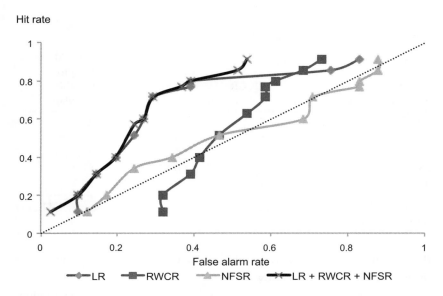

Figure 11.12

Receiver Operating Characteristic (ROC) Curves for Individual and Combined Regulatory Tools (76 bank sample with NSFR). Calculations by Bank of England and Max Planck Institute for Human Development.

met by around 70 percent of banks that subsequently ended up failing. Moreover, the relatively low false alarm rate of around 30 percent at this threshold indicates that most surviving banks had a leverage ratio above 4 percent prior to the crisis. Taken together, these observations suggest that such a leverage ratio constraint may have helped to curtail banks' risk taking, reducing their likelihood of failure.

However, the balance of marginal benefits to costs deteriorates sharply when we attempt to increase the hit rate above this level. For example, the leverage ratio threshold required to achieve a 90 percent hit rate is around 5.7 percent, while the false alarm rate at this threshold jumps to over 80 percent. This matters if the costs of higher capital requirements increase nonlinearly (Greenwood et al. 2017).

These points are also evident if we assess individually the performance of the RWCR and NSFR. Figure 11.12 and table 11.3 show that hit rates of 80 or 90 percent can only be achieved with high false alarm rates and stringent calibrations of these metrics. Overall, the performance of each metric individually in balancing hit and false alarm rates is inferior to

Table 11.4
Combinations of Metrics Required to Achieve Target Hit Rates

Target Hit Rate (%)	LR Calibration	RWCR Calibration	NSFR Calibration	False Alarm Rate for Combined Regulation (%)
70	3.82	5.52	0.63	29.3
75	3.80	5.52	0.72	36.6
80	4.15	5.52	0.63	39.0
85	3.71	5.52	0.83	51.2
90	4.07	5.53	0.83	53.7

Note: LR, leverage ratio; RWCR, risk-weighted capital requirements; NSFR, net stable funding ratio.

the leverage ratio. Similar results hold when the LTD ratio is considered instead of the NSFR (not shown).

Now suppose that the regulator can deploy a range of metrics to identify failing banks. Figure 11.12 and table 11.4 show the results from these multi-constraint simulations. At a target hit rate of 70 percent, a portfolio of regulatory measures does no better than the leverage ratio on its own in signaling bank stress. But at target hit rates of over 80 percent, that picture changes. The ROC curve for the portfolio of metrics lies to the left of all those corresponding to individual metrics. In other words, it is possible to achieve lower false alarm rates for the same hit rate when multiple regulatory metrics are used. The calibration of each metric in the portfolio is also less stringent than when applied individually. This suggests that imposing a small number of regulatory constraints can achieve the same hit rate as any singular constraint but at a materially lower societal and regulatory cost, as measured by levels of capital and liquidity and/or regulatory false alarms.

To understand where the benefits of combining metrics stems from, it is instructive to consider two banks that failed during the global financial crisis: the American bank Countrywide and the Belgian bank KBC Group. At the end of 2006, Countrywide had a leverage ratio of 7.7 percent and a risk-weighted capital ratio of 11.6 percent. Even if capital regulation had been much more stringent in 2006, Countrywide may not have been required to raise capital. But its NSFR was just 0.76, indicative of the structural liquidity risk it was undertaking. By including the NSFR in the suite of regulatory metrics, it may have been possible to capture the risks that Countrywide was undertaking without resorting to materially more stringent capital regulation. By contrast, KBC Group had an NSFR of 1.12, well above the current indicative regulatory standard. It also had a reasonable risk-weighted capital ratio of 8.7 percent, well above the median capital ratio in the sample. But its leverage ratio was 3.5 percent. A system of regulation that excluded the leverage ratio would have been unable to capture risks of the type KBC Group was undertaking prior to the crisis.

The conclusion we draw from this simple counterfactual exercise is that multiple regulatory metrics may have helped in capturing the multiple dimensions of fragility exhibited by banks before the crisis. With the benefit of hindsight, a combination of limits on risk-based capital, leverage, and net stable funding would have identified most failing banks, avoiding high false alarm rates or punitive calibrations of regulatory standards.

Challenges Associated with the System of Multipolar Regulation
The empirical exercise in the previous section looked at how a set of regulatory standards, applied counterfactually, might have done in spotting stress among a set of banks. Any such counterfactual exercise is subject to significant caveats. The most important of these is that it cannot take into account how changes in the regulatory regime might themselves have reshaped risk-taking incentives at the time.[22] The Lucas Critique plainly looms large. A multiple-constraint framework also raises the question of how these constraints should be set and adjusted through time, whether by rules or at regulators' discretion. We briefly discuss both issues in turn.

Incentives and Arbitrage   Financial regulation, like any tax, is very likely to change the behavior of the party subject to it. The history of financial regulation can be seen as an ongoing evolutionary race to adjust regulatory rules to limit avoidance incentives (Haldane 2013). This race has been characterized as "bloodhounds in pursuit of greyhounds" (Eichengreen 2009). Regulators need both to learn from past experience and to anticipate future opportunities for avoidance (Woods 2017).

The arbitrage problems faced by the bloodhounds were well exemplified in the run-up to the global financial crisis. These included the migration of activity and risk to unregulated "shadow banks" (Adrian and Ashcraft 2012), the hard-wiring of rating agency risk assessments into the regulatory engine (Edmonds 2016), the payment of bank CEOs in common equity, encouraging "gambling for resurrection" (IMF 2014), and the implicit subsidies conferred on "too-big-to-fail" institutions, encouraging them to become larger and more complex and connected still (FSB 2013b).

Another example of these incentive effects came in the area of capital regulation. Whichever risk-weighting scheme is in place, it is likely to give rise to incentives to adjust asset positions to maximize profits. For example, if the regulatory constraint takes the form of a leverage ratio, there are incentives to alter the composition of assets toward those with higher risk weights—though the evidence on such "risk shifting" is mixed (Sheldon 1996; Furlong 1988). Contrarily, if assets are risk-weighted and determined by banks' internal models, there are incentives to lower modeled risk weights over time (Mariathasan and Merrouche 2014). In short, when setting capital standards for banks, there is a *two-sided* incentive problem.

Before the crisis, both incentives were at play, though to differing degrees in different parts of the global financial system. In the United States, where a leverage ratio was in operation and often the binding constraint, there were incentives for banks to seek higher-risk assets rather than expand balance sheets (figure 11.13). In Europe, without a leverage ratio but with risk-based capital standards, there were incentives for banks to expand balance sheets and shade downward risk weights. Canadian banks' incentives sat somewhere in between.

Recent research has considered how the leverage ratio has affected behavior among a panel of over 650 European banks (Acosta-Smith, Grill, and Lang 2017). It finds a significant increase in risk taking among those banks for which the new regime was a binding constraint. This risk taking was greater the further these banks were from meeting the new 3 percent threshold: banks with leverage ratios of 1.5 percent, 2 percent, and 2.5 percent were found to increase their risk taking by 3.4, 2.3, and 1.1 percentage points of risk-weighted assets, respectively. This is clear empirical evidence of the risk-shifting channel at work.

This is only, however, one side of the risk equation. There were two mitigating factors on the other side. First, a rise in the leverage ratio also

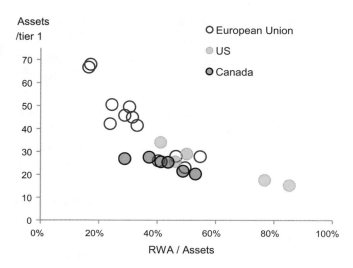

Figure 11.13

Average 2007 Risk Weights, Leverage Ratios, and Capital Ratios of Major EU, U.S., and Canadian Banks. Data from Bloomberg Finance L.P. and FDIC annual reports.
Notes: Data as of end-2007. Sample includes Bank of America, Barclays, BMO, BNP Paribas, Bank of New York, Canadian Imperial Bank of Commerce, Citigroup, Crédit Agricole, Credit Suisse, Deutsche Bank, HBOS, HSBC, J.P. Morgan, Lloyd's, National Bank of Commerce, Royal Bank of Canada, Royal Bank of Scotland, Santander, Scotiabank, Société Générale, State Street, Toronto-Dominion, UBS, UniCredit, Wachovia, and Wells Fargo. The balance sheet size of Canadian and U.S. banks is adjusted for IFRS.

boosts these banks' capital. Once translated into default probabilities, Acosta-Smith, Grill, and Lang (2017) find that the second effect swamps the first: a one percentage point rise in the leverage ratio raises the odds ratio (on banks being in distress versus safe) through risk shifting by 1–3.5 percent. But the reduction in the odds ratio from lower leverage is close to 40–50 percent. Second, the leverage regime is not a replacement for the risk-weighted capital regime but an addition to it. The capital regime places an automatic upper bound on the extent to which banks can increase their risk-weighted assets. In other words, the capital ratio regime places constraints on incentives to risk shift. Conversely, the leverage ratio can serve as an effective constraint on incentives to game or shade risk weights. Risk-taking incentives are, in effect, book-ended by the leverage and capital constraints.

There are other means of constraining adverse incentives. Incentives to game risk weights can be constrained by imposing floors or by using standardized approaches for certain categories of assets.[23] Some countries already make use of such approaches, including the United States, the UK, Germany, France, and Spain. The stress-testing regimes operating in a number of countries are also a way of cross-checking, and backstopping, the models used by banks. In a world of uncertainty as well as risk, having this portfolio of approaches for dealing with avoidance incentives—some discretionary, others rule-like—makes sense.

Discretion and Rules   The new architecture has introduced measures that are likely to make for a greater degree of supervisory or policymaker discretion in the setting of regulatory standards. This arises most obviously, in the application of supervisory judgment, to the stress-testing regime, and to macroprudential policy. As in the monetary policy sphere, there is a question about whether this new regulatory regime strikes the right balance between regulatory rules and the degree of discretion with which they are operated.

The time-inconsistency problem that pervades the debate over the balance between rules and discretion in monetary policy (Kydland and Prescott 1977; Barro and Gordon 1983) is arguably even more acute for prudential policy. This is partly because adverse crisis outcomes are highly nonlinear and costly, making it more difficult to precommit to avoiding forbearance and bailout. The low probability of crises may also mean that policymakers are insufficiently tough in tackling financial sector risks when times are good and memories of previous crises distant (Reinhart and Rogoff 2009; Malmendier and Nagel 2011; Gennaioli, Shleifer, and Vishny 2015). This can create political pressures to relax regulations to support shorter-term goals. Public choice theory (Olson 1965) would also suggest that lobbying pressure is likely to be more acute for regulatory policy than for monetary policy. The private costs of regulation are borne strongly by narrow but powerful interest groups in the financial industry. And while higher-than-target inflation is quickly observable, it may be very difficult to judge in real time that regulation is insufficiently stringent, owing to the difficulties of quantifying the probability of future financial crises.

These arguments point to the need for strong institutional frameworks, supported by clear objectives and instruments, to deliver financial stability policy. This is particularly so for the macroprudential policies, where there is further to go in clarifying the motivation behind interventions and the circumstances that might justify different instruments—in short, in defining and refining the macroprudential policy reaction function. The UK's Financial Policy Committee has made some progress in this area, most notably in setting out its strategy for using the countercyclical capital buffer (Bank of England 2016).

The benefits of pursuing this path are clear from monetary policy experience. Increasing the predictability of policy can enhance the ex ante signaling and expectations channels of regulatory policy, as has been achieved in relation to monetary policy (Bernanke and Mishkin 1997). It enhances ex post accountability to stakeholders, political and societal. And it reduces the potential behavioral biases otherwise associated with discretionary decision making and that have been found in the past to affect discretionary regulatory policy, including regulatory capture (Dal Bó 2006) and defensive decision making (Gigerenzer 2014). At the same time, there is clearly a balance to be struck. As Greenwood and co-workers (2017) argue, strict rules-based systems are likely to be arbitraged and exploited by banks. For example, recent theoretical work and experimental evidence suggest remuneration contracts can be restructured to recreate the excessive risk-taking incentives that new rules seek to reduce (Thanassoulis and Tanaka 2018; Harris et al. forthcoming).

These arguments make it difficult to specify strict regulatory rules for all seasons. They point to the need for a forward-looking, horizon-scanning approach with scope for supervisory judgment and macroprudential discretion (BCBS 2017). This does not, however, obviate the potential benefits from seeking, over time, to specify clearer mandates and regulatory reaction functions, especially on the macroprudential front.

Future Research and Policy

Financial regulation has undergone a fundamental rethink and reform since the global financial crisis. By most accounts and on most evidence, that has resulted in a financial system that is more resilient than in the past, better equipped to head off market frictions and failures of various kinds, better attuned to various adverse incentive effects, and better able to safeguard against risks that imperil the financial system as a whole. It is a regime of "constrained discretion," comprising a portfolio of regulatory measures calibrated, if roughly, to equate societal costs and benefits. That's the easy bit.

The hard bit is what happens next. Not least because of the scale of regulatory change over the past decade, this new regulatory framework will plainly need to adapt in the period ahead in the light of the new evidence, experience, and incentives associated with operating it. This chapter has discussed some of those issues. From a potentially very long list, we conclude by highlighting some of the areas where we think further research and practical exploration might be useful in the future debate on regulatory reform.[24]

a. *Optimal Levels of Capital*: One of the most animated, ongoing areas of regulatory debate is whether capital standards have been appropriately calibrated. Relative to the precrisis LEI study, current levels of capital requirements in most countries are below that calibration. The single most important reason for that is the LEI study did not take into account the potential impact of nonequity sources of capital, specifically TLAC, in reducing the impact and probability of crisis. The key question, then, is whether these instruments prove to be as loss-absorbing in future situations of stress where bail-in becomes necessary. This issue is particularly relevant when it involves systemically important institutions or sets of institution, when the costs of bailing-in (and bailing-out) are large and lumpy. At this early stage, the jury must still be out. On the one hand, historical evidence on bailing-in different types of notionally loss-absorbing bank liabilities in situations of systemic stress has not been encouraging, reflecting the acuteness of the time-consistency problem facing the authorities in these cases. On the other, new statutory resolution arrangements are much stronger than ever previously, and statutory TLAC requirements are now prescribed in advance. This means next time could plausibly be different. Because of its importance to the overall capital calibration, this issue deserves further empirical and theoretical consideration.

b. *Multipolar Regulation*: The new regulatory framework is a different beast from its predecessors with respect to the number, complexity, and discretionary nature of the constraints it imposes. There are good conceptual and empirical grounds for such a portfolio approach in insuring against future risks and, in particular, uncertainties. And from a risk- and uncertainty-averse social welfare perspective, even a marginally overidentified system might, in general, be preferable to a marginally underidentified one, if recent crisis experience is any guide. Indeed, that is the essence of robust control. Ultimately, however, the past is another country. There are legitimate questions to answer about whether multiple regulatory constraints could lead to excessive homogeneity and inefficiency in the financial system. And arbitrage is an ever-present threat, even with multiple regulatory metrics. This is an area where further research and practical experience with operating the new regime will be essential in gauging whether there is scope for streamlining, provided the resulting regulatory regime remains robust to the radical uncertainty that necessarily affects any complex, adaptive system such as finance.[25]

c. *Models of Financial Stability*: In a world of monetary, macroprudential, and microprudential policy, all having an impact on the economy and on the financial system, there is an increased emphasis on developing quantitative frameworks that enable us to understand those impacts, individually and collectively, and their interactions (Bank of England 2015a). That calls for models able to capture quantitatively monetary, financial, and regulatory channels of transmission and the feedback mechanisms between them. Progress has been made, in particular since the crisis, in developing macro models with an explicit financial sector that can capture rich, two-way feedbacks between the economy and financial system (e.g., Brunnermeier, Eisenbach, and Sannikov 2012; Brunnermeier and Sannikov 2014). There has been progress, too, in developing models of systemic risk that assign prominent roles to macroeconomic factors and within-system feedbacks (Greenwood, Landier, and Thesmar, 2014; Cont and Schaanning 2017). Yet we are still probably in the foothills when developing a unified framework for bringing these factors together in one place, a framework that could capture the rich feedback and amplification mechanisms that operate in practice and a model that could then serve as a test bed for each of the three arms of policy. Indeed, it could be that a single, holy grail framework is infeasible or indeed undesirable.

d. *Future of Stress Testing*: Bank stress testing has evolved considerably since the financial crisis and is now a cornerstone of the regulatory regime in many jurisdictions. The direction of travel necessary to enrich these tests and to make them truly macroprudential is to incorporate feedback effects that can amplify the actions of individual institutions at the systemwide level (Brazier 2015; Demekas 2015; Tarullo 2016)—feedbacks, for instance, that result from fire-selling assets, hoarding liquidity, and counterparty risk.[26] A natural consequence is that we might need to extend the field of vision for such simulations to include nonbank parts of the financial system. Nonbank sources of systemic risk proved to be potent during the crisis, in particular among shadow banks. As regulation has squeezed the banking system, there has been further migration of financial activity into the shadows, particularly within Europe. What was once credit and funding risk on the balance sheets of banking firms is metamorphosing into market and liquidity risk on the balance sheets of funds and investment vehicles of various types (Stein 2013). Understanding these risks calls for new and enhanced surveillance tools. Systematic, marketwide stress simulations might be needed to capture new market and liquidity risks and their propagation across different financial institutions and markets (Brazier 2017). The same considerations apply to key pieces of the financial infrastructure, in particular, central counterparties (Coeuré 2017; Duffie 2017). As a potentially new "too-big-to-fail" entity, they too need to be stress-tested and their resolution plans agreed to and implemented. This is a whole new risk-management agenda, one where work has only just begun in earnest.

e. *Market-Based Finance*: The emergence of a large and diverse shadow banking system, both prior to the crisis in the United States and subsequent to it elsewhere around the world, plainly poses both considerable opportunities and potential threats to financial stability. So-called market-based finance provides the financial system with a second, nonbank engine on which to fly, which could be beneficial in a diversity sense. Nonetheless, it also gives rise to potentially new sources of systemic risk and contagion, as risks change shape and location. The FSB has made significant progress in advancing the regulatory debate on such matters (FSB 2017e). Certainly, these trends carry implications for both the conduct of regulation and for central bank procedures. A world of greater market and liquidity risk may call for different sets of regulatory instrument than the bank-based solvency and liquidity metrics of Basel III. Market-based instruments, such as margin requirements, may have a greater role to play (see, e.g., European Systemic Risk Board 2017). It may also call for different types of market intervention by central banks—different markets, different instruments, different counterparties. The crisis has already seen a mini-revolution in the design of liquidity facilities by central banks. As the financial system changes shape, it seems plausible to think that further change could be necessary. If so, that change would benefit from further research on the costs and benefits of the extended regulatory and central bank safety net.

f. *The Macroprudential Policy Framework:* As a still fledgling framework, the macroprudential framework still faces a wide range of questions. There is no settled, practical approach to defining the breadth of objectives of a macroprudential regime. Should the potential for aggregate demand externalities associated with a debt overhang in the household sector, for instance, fall under the purview of a macroprudential authority? Nor, in the main, is there any settled approach to defining the appropriate set of macroprudential instruments, whether for banks or, especially, for nonbanks, or the optimal strategy for using them to address emerging vulnerabilities. If household debt externalities are within scope, is it better to deal with this risk by restricting mortgage lending directly through loan to income or loan to value limits or by adding a macroprudential overlay to risk weights on mortgages (Turner 2017)? This lack of a settled approach has some benefits, in that it results in diverse cross-country experiences. This is equivalent to "learning by doing" among regulators. It does, however, come at some cost. A regime without especially well-defined objectives is likely to suffer greater problems of time-inconsistency. It may also increase uncertainty among outside participants about the likely regulatory policy reaction function. The direction of travel, over time, probably needs to be toward somewhat clearer constraints, and somewhat more circumscribed discretion, if macroprudential regimes are to be effective, robust, and transparent.

g. *Political Economy of Financial Regulation*: The scope and range of regulatory responsibilities assigned to central banks and regulators have expanded materially during the course of the crisis. Accompanying that, some of the new regulatory requirements and practices put in place are quite discretionary in nature, including stress testing and some other macroprudential measures. A number involve regulators making overtly distributional choices, for example, around access to credit. This takes central banks and regulators more explicitly into the realm of political economy than at any time in their recent (and perhaps distant) history. It has probably also contributed to some people questioning the appropriate scope of central banking, its degree of independence from the political process and from wider society, and appropriate accountability mechanisms (Balls, Howat, and Stansbury 2016). There is a debate to be had, an analytical debate, about the appropriate degree of discretion to confer on regulators, to ensure they retain the flexibility they need to respond to events while ensuring their decisions are clear, transparent, and unpolluted by behavioral biases and time-inconsistency problems. There are also interesting issues to explore about how regulators explain and account for their decisions to wider society, particularly when those actions have strongly distributional consequences. This is clearly unfinished business.

h. *The Contribution of the Financial System to the Economy and to Society*: One of the striking features of the past several decades has been the rising share of financial services in measures of economy-wide value added and, in tandem, rising financial sector balance sheets as a fraction of GDP in a number of economies. Sometimes this goes by the name "financialization." There are good reasons to think increasing financial depth is a natural feature of economies as they grow and develop. Indeed, there is a fairly well-established literature quantifying the boost to growth and productivity that arises from financial depth, especially for developing countries (Levine, Loayza, and Beck 2000). Lately, however, the question has been asked whether it is possible to have too much of a good thing. Some have asked why the cost of financial intermediation continues to rise and what this might signal about the efficiency of financial services as an industry (Friedman 2009; Philippon 2015). Others have pointed to a possible U-shaped relationship between measures of financial depth and productivity and growth (Cecchetti and Kharroubi 2012; Heil 2017). These questions have an important bearing on the contribution the financial system makes to the economy and to society. They are also meta-questions for regulatory policy. They warrant further research.

i. *Financial Stability Implications of Fintech*: Technologically enabled innovation in financial services, or fintech, has grown rapidly in recent years. The FSB's recent report contains a useful taxonomy of such innovations (FSB 2017f). With this development comes the promise of greater consumer choice, improved access to credit for some borrowers, and greater efficiency and productivity in the traditional intermediary sector. There are also potential resilience benefits from increasing diversity in the provision of financial services (Carney 2017a). While the sector is probably too small at present to pose a threat to financial stability, there is ample historical experience of risks emerging rapidly in fast-growing sectors if risks are left unchecked. Such future risks might include conventional vulnerabilities associated with excessive use of leverage and maturity, liquidity, and credit transformation; the emergence of new, highly interconnected entities; and cyber and other operational risks. There is also the potential for these developments to make traditional universal banks less resilient, if they are forced to rely on less stable funding sources, for example. A challenge for policymakers is to ensure that the regulatory regime, and the wider policy framework—including the scope of central banks' liquidity facilities—adapt to keep pace with these developments (Lagarde 2017).

Notes

This chapter is an abridged version of a paper presented at the "Rethinking Macroeconomic Policy IV" conference, organized by the Peterson Institute for International Economics, Washington, D.C. The views expressed herein are those of the authors, and not necessarily those of the Bank of England or its committees or those of the European Central Bank. We are grateful to Andrew Bell, Olivier Blanchard, Alex Brazier, Paul Brione, Markus Brunnermeier, Marcus Buckmann, Oliver Bush, Patrick Calver, Shiv Chowla, Benoît Coeuré, Sebastian de-Ramon, Stephen Dickinson, Nic Garbarino, Andrew Gracie, Amit Kothiyal, Antoine

Lallour, Nellie Liang, Katie Low, Damien Lynch, Clare Macallan, Alex Michie, Ali Moussavi, Casey Murphy, Tobi Neumann, Simon Pittaway, Adam Posen, Amar Radia, Ani Rajan, Katie Rismanchi, Fiona Shaikh, Tamarah Shakir, Jeremy Stein, and Larry Summers for comments and contributions. Philip Massoud and Karam Shergill provided excellent research assistance.

1. See, for example, Calomiris (2017), Greenwood and co-authors (2017), and Duffie (2017).

2. For more detailed accounts of these reforms, see Sarin and Summers (2016), Carney (2017b), Duffie (2017), FSB (2017a), Greenwood et al. (2017), and Yellen (2017).

3. We focus here squarely on international banking regulation. We do not cover insurance regulation or international accounting standards, or regulatory reforms undertaken nationally, such as the Volcker Rule in the United States (Financial Stability Oversight Council 2011) and the "Vickers proposals" in the UK (Independent Commission on Banking 2011). Nor do we discuss international reforms of market infrastructure—for example, clearing—and financial market instruments (FSB 2017b). Finally, we do not cover changes to banks' large exposures regime and a range of pay and governance reforms.

4. A number of countries, including the UK, introduced leverage ratio capital requirements in the aftermath of the crisis.

5. For LCR, see BCBS (2013a); for NSFR, see BCBS (2014).

6. The Comprehensive Capital Analysis and Review, or CCAR.

7. Dent, Westwood, and Segoviano (2016) includes a comparison of international concurrent stress-testing practices.

8. These banks have been identified based on publicly available lists of systemically important firms, including (1) the FSB's list of G-SIBs as of November 21, 2016; (2) O-SIIs notified to the European Banking Authority as of April 23, 2016; (3) U.S. bank holding companies subject to the Federal Reserve's annual Comprehensive Capital Analysis and Review as of March 2014; (4) banks designated as systemically important financial groups by the Swiss National Bank; (5) the four major banks in Australia; and (7) the five largest banks in Canada. These include bank holding companies, as well as their primary operating companies, where applicable, and foreign subsidiaries that are explicitly designated as systemically important for a particular country.

9. The data are from the S&P Global Market Intelligence database.

10. These figures are expressed in terms of current definitions of capital and risk-weighted assets. The mapping from the estimates reported in the LEI report and those above are due to Brooke and co-authors (2015). A contemporaneous study by Miles and co-workers (2013) concluded that optimal capital requirements were likely to be higher—perhaps around 20 percent—if the offsetting risk and cost of capital effects of higher solvency standards were taken into account (the Modigliani-Miller offset [Modigliani and Miller 1958]).

11. This echoes and extends findings from earlier research by Borio and Lowe (2002, 2004) and Drehmann, Borio, and Tsatsaronis (2011), which found credit gap measures to be key determinants of crisis risk.

12. Relatedly, Demirgüç-Kunt, Detragiache, and Merrouche (2010) and Beltratti and Stulz (2012) find that poorly capitalized banks had lower stock returns during the financial crisis. And Boyson, Helwege, and Jindraà (2014) find that banks that entered the recent financial crisis with higher capital were less likely to see their funding dry up during the crisis.

13. This calculation is based on the marginal condition for optimal capital reported earlier. We parameterize the crisis probability and severity functions as follows: $\gamma = \exp(\beta_0 + \beta_1 k) / (1 + \exp(\beta_0 + \beta_1 k))$; $\Delta = \theta_0 + \theta_1 k$. The model is calibrated to deliver an optimal capital ratio of around 18 percent when $\theta_1 = 0$, that is, the LEI case. We achieve this by setting $\delta = 0.1, \beta_0 = 0.5, \beta_1 = -0.2$, and $\theta_0 = 10$; that is to say, a crisis reduces the level of GDP by 10 percent relative to baseline. If instead we set $\theta_1 = -0.1$, such that each percentage point increase in capital reduced the GDP hit in a crisis by 0.1 percent, the optimal capital ratio would increase to more than 20 percent.

14. See Cunliffe (2017) and Bank of England (2017) for a discussion of resolution.

15. This estimate is based on the difference in the estimated cost of crises across their sample depending on whether they occurred under more or less credible resolution regimes.

16. A recent study by economists at the Federal Reserve Board (Firestone, Lorenc, and Ranish 2017) also considers the impact of improved resolution arrangements. They use estimates from Homar and van Wijnbergen (2017) to model a reduction in the expected duration of crises from such arrangements. Overall, they find that optimal capital levels for the U.S. banking system can range from 13 percent to 25 percent.

17. Admati and Hellwig (2013) have forcefully questioned the basis for assuming such costs, given that standard finance theory would predict that the cost of debt and equity funding for a bank will decline in response to an increase in its capital position.

18. See the Financial Policy Committee's June 2016 Financial Stability Report (pp. 27–33) for an assessment of market liquidity in UK markets more broadly. The Securities and Exchange Commission's Report to Congress contains a detailed assessment of the impact of Basel III and the Volcker Rule on liquidity in U.S. Treasury and corporate debt markets (Securities and Exchange Commission 2017).

19. The data set also includes a liquid asset ratio, but this is a relatively poor proxy for the liquidity coverage ratio (LCR), so we exclude consideration of the LCR from this analysis.

20. Because very few banks technically defaulted during the crisis but many would have without significant government intervention, the definition of failure is necessarily somewhat judgmental. Beyond clear-cut cases of default or nationalization, Laeven and Valencia (2010) define banks to have failed if at least three of the following six conditions were present: (1) extensive liquidity support (5 percent of deposits and liabilities to nonresidents), (2) bank restructuring costs (at least 3 percent of GDP), (3) partial bank nationalization (e.g., government

recapitalization), (4) significant guarantees put in place, (5) significant asset purchases (at least percent of GDP), and (6) deposit freezes and bank holidays. See Aikman and co-authors (2014) for a description of where the classification of failure departs from Laeven and Valencia (2010).

21. For related analyses of the performance of regulatory metrics in identifying failed and surviving banks during the crisis, see Huang and Ratnovski (2009), Demirgüç-Kunt, Detragiache, and Merrouche (2010), Bologna (2011), Arjani and Paulin (2013), Vazquez and Federico (2015), and Lallour and Mio (2016).

22. Multiple regulatory constraints may also reduce diversity in the financial system (Greenwood et al. 2017). Excessive homogeneity of the financial system can create systemic risks (Haldane 2009; Wagner 2010). How much it does so is, however, a matter of degree. If regulatory constraints act as control bounds on structurally defective business models, that strengthens the financial system, even if (indeed, precisely because) it constrains diversity.

23. See BCSBS (2016) and BCBS (2013b).

24. See also Calomiris (2017), Duffie (2017), and Greenwood and co-authors (2017).

25. The FSB (2017e), for example, describes a policy evaluation framework to achieve efficient resilience.

26. For example, the results of the Bank of England's 2014 stress test showed that risk-weight pro-cyclicality was a significant contributor to the change in capital ratios in the stress test scenario (Bank of England 2014).

References

Acosta-Smith, Jonathan, Michael Grill, and Jan Hannes Lang. 2017. "The Leverage Ratio, Risk-taking and Bank Stability." ECB Working Paper 2079.

Admati, Anat, and Martin Hellwig. 2013. *The Bankers' New Clothes: What's Wrong with Banking and What to Do about It*. Princeton, NJ: Princeton University Press.

Adrian, Tobias, and Adam B. Ashcraft. 2012. "Shadow Banking Regulation." *Annual Review of Financial Economics* 4 (1): 99–140.

Afonso, Gara, João A. Santos, and James Traina. 2015. "Do 'Too-Big-to-Fail' Banks Take on More Risk?" *Journal of Financial Perspectives* 3 (2): 129–143.

Aikman, David, Mirta Galesic, Gerd Gigerenzer, Sujit Kapadia, Konstantinos Katsikopoulos, Amit Kothiyal, Emma Murphy, and Tobias Neumann. 2014. "Taking Uncertainty Seriously: Simplicity versus Complexity in Financial Regulation." Bank of England Financial Stability Paper 28. London: Bank of England.

Aiyar, Shekhar, Charles W. Calomiris, and Tomasz Wieladek. 2014. "Does Macro-Prudential Regulation Leak? Evidence from a UK Policy Experiment." *Journal of Money, Credit and Banking* 46 (suppl. 1): 181–214.

Aiyar, Shekhar, Charles W. Calomiris, and Tomasz Wieladek. 2016. "How Does Credit Supply Respond to Monetary Policy and Bank Minimum Capital Requirements?" *European Economic Review* 82:142–165.

Anderson, Roy M., and Robert M. May. 1992. *Infectious Diseases of Humans: Dynamics and Control*, rev. ed. Oxford: Oxford University Press.

Arjani, Neville, and Graydon Paulin. 2013. "Lessons from the Financial Crisis: Bank Performance and Regulatory Reform." Bank of Canada Discussion Paper 2013-4. Ottawa: Bank of Canada.

Bahaj, Saleem, Jonathan Bridges, Frederic Malherbe, and Cian O'Neill. 2016. "What Determines How Banks Respond to Changes in Capital Requirements?" Bank of England Staff Working Paper 593. London: Bank of England.

Bailey, Michael, Ruiqing Cao, Theresa Kuchler, and Johannes Stroebel. 2016. *Social Networks and Housing Markets*. Cambridge, MA: National Bureau of Economic Research.

Balls, Ed, James Howat, and Anna Stansbury. 2016. "Central Bank Independence Revisited: After the Financial Crisis, What Should a Model Central Bank Look Like?" M-RCBG Associate Working Paper Series 67. Cambridge, MA: Mossavar-Rahmani Center of the Harvard Kennedy School.

Bank of England. 2009. "The Role of Macroprudential Policy." Discussion Paper. London: Bank of England, November 2009.

Bank of England. 2011. "Instruments of Macroprudential Policy." Discussion Paper. London: Bank of England, December 2011.

Bank of England. 2014. "Stress Testing the UK Banking System: 2014 Results." London: Bank of England, December.

Bank of England. 2015a. "One Bank Research Agenda." Discussion Paper. London: Bank of England.

Bank of England. 2015b. "Supplement to the December 2015 Financial Stability Report: The Framework of Capital Requirements for UK Banks." London: Bank of England.

Bank of England. 2016. "The Financial Policy Committee's Approach to Setting the Countercyclical Capital Buffer." Policy Statement. London: Bank of England, April.

Bank of England. 2017. "The Bank of England's Approach to Resolution." London: Bank of England.

Barro, Robert J., and David B. Gordon. 1983. "Rules, Discretion and Reputation in a Model of Monetary Policy." *Journal of Monetary Economics* 12:101–121.

Basel Committee on Banking Supervision. 2010a. "Guidance for National Authorities Operating the Countercyclical Capital Buffer." Basel: Bank for International Settlements.

Basel Committee on Banking Supervision. 2010b. "An Assessment of the Long-Term Economic Impact of Stronger Capital and Liquidity Requirements." Basel: Bank for International Settlements, August.

Basel Committee on Banking Supervision. 2013a. "Basel III: The Liquidity Coverage Ratio and Liquidity Risk Monitoring Tools." Basel: Bank for International Settlements, January.

Basel Committee on Banking Supervision. 2013b. "The Regulatory Framework: Balancing Risk Sensitivity, Simplicity and Comparability." Discussion Paper. Basel: Bank for International Settlements.

Basel Committee on Banking Supervision. 2014. "Basel III: The Net Stable Funding Ratio." Basel: Bank for International Settlements.

Basel Committee on Banking Supervision. 2016. "Reducing Variation in Credit Risk–Weighted Assets: Constraints on the Use of Internal Model Approaches." Consultative Document. Basel: Bank for International Settlements.

Basel Committee on Banking Supervision. 2017. "The Basel Committee's Work Programme," updated April 25. Basel: Bank for International Settlements. www.bis.org/bcbs/bcbs_work.htm.

Beltratti, Andrea, and René M. Stulz. 2012. "The Credit Crisis around the Globe: Why Did Some Banks Perform Better?" *Journal of Financial Economics* 105 (1): 1–17.

Berger, Allen N., and Christa H. Bouwman. 2013. "How Does Capital Affect Bank Performance during Financial Crises?" *Journal of Financial Economics* 109 (1): 146–176.

Bernanke, Ben S., and Frederic S. Mishkin. 1997. "Inflation Targeting: A New Framework for Monetary Policy?" *Journal of Economic Perspectives* 11 (2): 97–116.

Bicu, Andreea, Louisa Chen, and David Elliott. 2017. "The Leverage Ratio and Liquidity in the Gilt and Repo Markets." Bank of England Working Paper 690. London: Bank of England.

Bologna, Pierluigi. 2011. "Is There a Role for Funding in Explaining Recent US Banks' Failures?" IMF Working Paper 11/180. Washington, DC: International Monetary Fund.

Borio, Claudio, and Philip William Lowe. 2002. "Asset Prices, Financial and Monetary Stability: Exploring the Nexus." BIS Working Paper 114. Basel: Bank for International Settlements, July.

Borio, Claudio, and Philip William Lowe. 2004. "Securing Sustainable Price Stability: Should Credit Come Back from the Wilderness?" BIS Working Paper 157. Basel: Bank for International Settlements.

Boyson, Nicole, Jean Helwege, and Jan Jindra. 2014. "Crises, Liquidity Shocks, and Fire Sales at Commercial Banks." *Financial Management* 43 (4): 857–884.

Brainard, William C. 1967. "Uncertainty and the Effectiveness of Policy." *American Economic Review* 57 (2): 411–425.

Brandao Marques, Luis, Ricardo Correa, and Horacio Sapriza. 2013. "International Evidence on Government Support and Risk Taking in the Banking Sector." IMF Working Paper WP/13/94. Washington, DC: International Monetary Fund.

Brazier, Alex. 2015. "The Bank of England's Approach to Stress Testing the UK Banking System." Speech given at London School of Economics Systemic Risk Centre, October 30.

Brazier, Alex. 2017. "Simulating Stress across the Financial System: The Resilience of Corporate Bond Markets and the Role of Investment Funds." Bank of England Financial Stability Paper 42. London: Bank of England, July.

Bridges, Jonathan, Christopher Jackson, and Daisy McGregor. 2017. "Down in the Slumps: The Role of Credit in Five Decades of Recessions." Bank of England Staff Working Paper 659. London: Bank of England.

Brooke, Martin, Oliver Bush, Robert Edwards, Jas Ellis, Bill Francis, Rashmi Harimohan, Katharine Neiss, and Caspar Siegert. 2015. "Measuring the Macroeconomic Costs and Benefits of Higher UK Bank Capital Requirements." Bank of England Financial Stability Paper 35. London: Bank of England.

Brunnermeier, Markus K., Thomas M. Eisenbach, and Yuliy Sannikov. 2012. "Macroeconomics with Financial Frictions: A Survey." NBER Working Paper 18102. Cambridge, MA: National Bureau of Economic Research.

Brunnermeier, Markus K., and Yuliy Sannikov. 2014. "A Macroeconomic Model with a Financial Sector." *American Economic Review* 104 (2): 379–421.

Calomiris, Charles W. 2017. *Reforming Financial Regulation after Dodd-Frank*. New York: Manhattan Institute for Policy Research.

Carlson, Mark, Hui Shan, and Missaka Warusawitharana. 2013. "Capital Ratios and Bank Lending: A Matched Bank Approach." *Journal of Financial Intermediation* 22 (4): 663–687.

Carney, Mark. 2017a. "The Promise of FinTech: Something New under the Sun?" Speech at the Deutsche Bundesbank G-20 conference, "Digitizing Finance, Financial Inclusion and Financial Literacy," Wiesbaden, September.

Carney, Mark. 2017b. "What a Difference a Decade Makes." Speech at the Institute of International Finance's Washington Policy Summit, Washington, DC, April 20.

Cecchetti, Stephen. 2014. "The Jury Is In." In *The New International Financial System: Analyzing the Cumulative Impact of Regulatory Reform*. World Scientific Studies in Economics, vol. 48, ed. Douglas D. Evanoff, Andrew G. Haldane, and George G. Kaufman, 407–424. Hackensack, NJ: World Scientific.

Cecchetti, Stephen. 2015. "The Road to Financial Stability: Capital Regulation, Liquidity Regulation, and Resolution." *International Journal of Central Banking* 11 (3): 127–139.

Cecchetti, Stephen, and Anil K. Kashyap. 2016. "What Binds? Interactions between Bank Capital and Liquidity Regulations." Working paper, University of Chicago Booth School of Business. http://faculty.chicagobooth.edu/anil.kashyap/research/papers/What_Binds_Interactions-between-bank-capital-and-liquidity-regulations_2016.pdf.

Cecchetti, Stephen, and Enisse Kharroubi. 2012. "Reassessing the Impact of Finance on Growth." BIS Working Paper 381. Basel: Bank for International Settlements.

Coeuré, Benoît. 2017. "Central Clearing: Reaping the Benefits, Controlling the Risks." In "The Impact of Financial Reforms 97." *Banque de France Financial Stability Review* 21, April.

Cont, Rama, and Eric Finn Schaanning. 2017. "Fire Sales, Indirect Contagion and Systemic Stress-Testing." https://papers.ssrn.com/sol3/papers.cfm?abstract_id =2541114.

Cornett, Marcia Millon, Jamie John McNutt, Philip E. Strahan, and Hassan Tehranian. 2011. "Liquidity Risk Management and Credit Supply in the Financial Crisis." *Journal of Financial Economics* 101 (2): 297–312.

Cunliffe, John. 2017. "Ten Years On: Lessons from Northern Rock." Speech at the Single Resolution Board Annual Conference, Brussels.

Dagher, Jihad C., Giovanni Dell'Ariccia, Luc Laeven, Lev Ratnovski, and Hui Tong. 2016. "Benefits and Costs of Bank Capital." https://www.imf.org/external/ pubs/ft/sdn/2016/sdn1604.pdf.

Dal Bó, Ernesto. 2006. "Regulatory Capture: A Review." *Oxford Review of Economic Policy* 22 (2): 203–225.

Demekas, Dimitri G. 2015. "Designing Effective Macroprudential Stress Tests: Progress So Far and the Way Forward." IMF Working Paper WP/15/146. Washington, DC: International Monetary Fund, June.

Demirgüç-Kunt, Asli, Enrica Detragiache, and Ouarda Merrouche. 2010. "Bank Capital: Lessons from the Financial Crisis." World Bank Policy Research Working Paper 5473. Washington, DC: World Bank.

Dent, Kieran, Ben Westwood, and Miguel Segoviano. 2016. "Stress Testing of Banks: An Introduction." *Bank of England Quarterly Bulletin* (2016 Q3).

De-Ramon, Sebastian, William Francis, and Qun Harris. 2016. "Bank Capital Requirements and Balance Sheet Management Practices: Has the Relationship Changed after the Crisis?" Bank of England Staff Working Paper 635. London: Bank of England.

Drehmann, Mathias, Claudio Borio, and Kostas Tsatsaronis. 2011. "Anchoring Countercyclical Capital Buffers: The Role of Credit Aggregates." *International Journal of Central Banking* 7 (4): 189–240.

Duffie, Darrell. 2017. "Financial Regulatory Reform after the Crisis: An Assessment." *Management Science*.

Edmonds, Timothy. 2016. "Credit Ratings Agencies Regulation." House of Commons Library Briefing Paper SN05603, London, January 7.

Eichengreen, Barry. 2009. "The Financial Crisis and Global Policy Reforms." Paper presented at the Federal Reserve Bank of San Francisco Asia Economic Policy Conference.

European Systemic Risk Board. 2017. "The Macroprudential Use of Margins and Haircuts." Frankfurt: European Systemic Risk Board, European Central Bank, February.

Financial Stability Board. 2010. "Reducing the Moral Hazard Posed by Systemically Important Financial Institutions." FSB Recommendations and Time Lines. Basel, October 20.

Financial Stability Board. 2013a. "Strengthening Oversight and Regulation of Shadow Banking." Policy Framework for Strengthening Oversight and Regulation of Shadow Banking Entities. Basel, August 29.

Financial Stability Board. 2013b. "Progress and Next Steps towards Ending 'Too-Big-to-Fail' (TBTF)." Report of the Financial Stability Board to the G-20. Basel, September 2.

Financial Stability Board. 2014. "Key Attributes of Effective Resolution Regimes for Financial Institutions." Basel, October 15.

Financial Stability Board. 2017a. "Implementation and Effects of the G-20 Financial Regulatory Reforms. 3rd Annual Report." Basel, July 3.

Financial Stability Board. 2017b. "Review of OTC Derivatives Market Reforms: Effectiveness and Broader Effects of the Reforms." Basel, June 29.

Financial Stability Board. 2017c. "Ten Years On: Taking Stock of Post-crisis Resolution Reforms." *Sixth Report on the Implementation of Resolution Reforms.* Basel: FSB, July 6.

Financial Stability Board. 2017d. "Policy Recommendations to Address Structural Vulnerabilities from Asset Management Activities." Basel, January 12.

Financial Stability Board. 2017e. "FSB Chair's Letter to G-20 Leaders: Building a Safer, Simpler and Fairer Financial System." Basel, July.

Financial Stability Board. 2017f. "Financial Stability Implications from FinTech: Supervisory and Regulatory Issues That Merit Authorities' Attention." Basel, June 27.

Firestone, Simon, Amy G. Lorenc, and Benjamin Ranish. 2017. "An Empirical Economic Assessment of the Costs and Benefits of Bank Capital in the US." Finance and Economics Discussion Series 2017-034. New York: Board of Governors of the Federal Reserve System.

Friedman, Benjamin. 2009. "Overmighty Finance Levies a Tithe on Growth." *Financial Times*, August 26.

Furlong, Frederick. 1988. "Changes in Bank Risk-Taking." *Federal Reserve Bank of San Francisco Economic Review* 2:45–56.

Gai, Prasanna, Andrew Haldane, and Sujit Kapadia. 2011. "Complexity, Concentration and Contagion." *Journal of Monetary Economics* 58 (5): 453–470.

Gai, Prasanna, and Sujit Kapadia. 2010. "Contagion in Financial Networks." *Proceedings of the Royal Society of London A: Mathematical, Physical and Engineering Sciences* 466 (2120): 2401–2423.

Gambacorta, Leonardo, and Hyun Song Shin. 2018. "Why Bank Capital Matters for Monetary Policy." *Journal of Financial Intermediation* 35 (PB): 17–29.

Gennaioli, Nicola, Andrei Shleifer, and Robert Vishny. 2015. "Neglected Risks: The Psychology of Financial Crises." *American Economic Review* 105 (5): 310–314.

Gigerenzer, Gerd. 2014. *Risk Savvy: How to Make Good Decisions.* London: Penguin.

Goodhart, Charles. 2011. *The Basel Committee on Banking Supervision: A History of the Early Years 1974–1997.* Cambridge: Cambridge University Press.

Gordy, Michael B. 2003. "A Risk-Factor Model Foundation for Ratings-Based Bank Capital Rules." *Journal of Financial Intermediation* 12 (3): 199–232.

Greenwood, Robin, Steen G. Hanson, Jeremy C. Stein, and Adi Sunderam. 2017. "Strengthening and Streamlining Bank Capital Regulation." *Brookings Papers on Economic Activity,* BPEA Conference Drafts, September 7–8.

Greenwood, Robin, Augustin Landier, and David Thesmar. 2014. "Vulnerable Banks." *Journal of Financial Economics* 115 (3): 471–485.

Haldane, Andrew G. 2009. "Rethinking the Financial Network." Speech delivered at the Financial Student Association, Amsterdam, April 28.

Haldane, Andrew G. 2013. "Constraining Discretion in Bank Regulation." Speech delivered at the Federal Reserve Bank of Atlanta conference, "Maintaining Financial Stability: Holding a Tiger by the Tail(s)," Federal Reserve Bank of Atlanta, April 9.

Haldane, Andrew G. 2015. "Multi-polar Regulation." *International Journal of Central Banking* 11 (3): 385–401.

Haldane, Andrew G., and Vasileious Madouros. 2012. "The Dog and the Frisbee." Speech by Andrew G. Haldane at the Federal Reserve Bank of Kansas City's 366th Economic Policy Symposium, "The Changing Policy Landscape," Jackson Hole, WY, August 31.

Harris, Qun, Analise Mercieca, Emma Soane, and Misa Tanaka. Forthcoming. "How Do Bonus Cap and Clawback Affect Risk and Effort Choice? Insight from a Lab Experiment." Bank of England Staff Working Paper. London: Bank of England.

Heil, M. 2017. "Finance and Productivity: A Literature Review." OECD Economics Department Working Paper 1374. Paris: OECD Publishing.

Homar, Timotej, and Sweder J. G. van Wijnbergen. 2017. "Bank Recapitalization and Economic Recovery after Financial Crises." *Journal of Financial Intermediation* 32 (C): 16–28.

Huang, R., and L. Ratnovski. 2009. "Why Are Canadian Banks More Resilient?" IMF Working Paper WP/09/152. Washington, DC: International Monetary Fund.

IMF. 2014. "Global Financial Stability Report. Risk Taking, Liquidity, and Shadow Banking: Curbing Excess While Promoting Growth." Washington, DC: International Monetary Fund, October.

Independent Commission on Banking. 2011. "Final Report—Recommendations." London: Independent Commission on Banking, September 12. http://bankingcommission.independent.gov.uk.

International Organization of Securities Commissions. 2012. "Policy Recommendations for Money Market Funds: Final Report." IOSCO/MR/27/2012. Madrid, October 9.

Jiménez, G., S. Ongena, J. L. Peydró, and J. Saurina. 2014. "Hazardous Times for Monetary Policy: What Do Twenty-Three Million Bank Loans Say about the Effects of Monetary Policy on Credit Risk-Taking?" *Econometrica* 82 (2): 463–505.

Jordà, Òscar, Björn Richter, Moritz Schularick, and Alan M. Taylor. 2017. "Bank Capital Redux: Solvency, Liquidity, and Crisis." NBER Working Paper 23287. Cambridge, MA: National Bureau of Economic Research.

Jordà, Òscar, Moritz Schularick, and Alan M. Taylor. 2013. "When Credit Bites Back." *Journal of Money, Credit and Banking* 45 (no. s2): 3–28.

Jordà, Òscar, Moritz Schularick, and Alan M. Taylor. 2015. "Leveraged Bubbles." *Journal of Monetary Economics* 76:1–20.

Kapan, Tümer, and Camelia Minoiu. 2013. "Balance Sheet Strength and Bank Lending during the Global Financial Crisis." IMF Working Paper WP/13/102. Washington, DC: International Monetary Fund.

Knight, Frank H. 1921. *Risk, Uncertainty, and Profit.* Boston: Hart, Schaffner & Marx / Houghton Mifflin.

Kydland, Finn E., and Edward C. Prescott. 1977. "Rules Rather Than Discretion: The Inconsistency of Optimal Plans." *Journal of Political Economy* 85 (3): 473–491.

Laeven, Luc, and Fabian Valencia. 2010. "Resolution of Banking Crises: The Good, the Bad, and the Ugly." IMF Working Paper WP/10/146. Washington, DC: International Monetary Fund.

Lagarde, Christine. 2017. "Central Banking and Fintech: A Brave New World?" Speech given at Bank of England conference, London, September 29.

Lallour, Antoine, and Hitoshi Mio. 2016. "Do We Need a Stable Funding Ratio? Banks' Funding in the Global Financial Crisis." Bank of England Staff Working Paper 602. London: Bank of England, May 20.

Levine, Ross, Norman Loayza, and Thorsten Beck. 2000. "Financial Intermediation and Growth: Causality and Causes." *Journal of Monetary Economics* 46 (1): 31–77.

Macroeconomic Assessment Group. 2010. "Assessing the Macroeconomic Impact of the Transition to Stronger Capital and Liquidity Requirements." Basel: Bank for International Settlements, December.

Malmendier, Ulrike, and Stefan Nagel. 2011. "Depression Babies: Do Macroeconomic Experiences Affect Risk Taking?" *Quarterly Journal of Economics* 126 (1): 373–416.

Mariathasan, Mike, and Ouarda Merrouche. 2014. "The Manipulation of Basel Risk-Weights." *Journal of Financial Intermediation* 23 (3): 300–321.

Miles, David, Jing Yang, and Gilberto Marcheggiano. 2013. "Optimal Bank Capital." *Economic Journal (Oxford)* 123 (567): 1–37.

Modigliani, Franco, and Merton H. Miller. 1958. "The Cost of Capital, Corporation Finance and the Theory of Investment." *American Economic Review* 48 (3): 261–297.

Moody's. 2010. "Revisions to Moody's Hybrid Tool Kit." July 1.

Olson, Mancur. 1965. *The Logic of Collective Action: Public Goods and the Theory of Groups.* Cambridge, MA: Harvard University Press.

Peek, Joe, and Eric Rosengren. 1995. "Bank Regulation and the Credit Crunch." *Journal of Banking & Finance* 19 (3): 679–692.

Philippon, Thomas. 2015. "Has the US Finance Industry Become Less Efficient? On the Theory and Measurement of Financial Intermediation." *American Economic Review* 105 (4): 1408–1438.

Pozsar, Zoltan, Tobias Adrian, Adam B. Ashcraft, and Haley Boesky. 2010. "Shadow Banking." Federal Reserve Bank of New York Staff Report 458.

Reinhart, Carmen M., and Kenneth S. Rogoff. 2009. *This Time Is Different: Eight Centuries of Financial Folly.* Princeton, NJ: Princeton University Press.

Romer, Christina D., and David H. Romer. 2017. "Why Some Times Are Different: Macroeconomic Policy and the Aftermath of Financial Crises." NBER Working Paper 23931. Cambridge, MA: National Bureau of Economic Research.

Sarin, Natasha, and Lawrence H. Summers. 2016. "Understanding Bank Risk through Market Measures." *Brookings Papers on Economic Activity* 2016 (2): 57–127.

Schularick, Moritz, and Alan M. Taylor. 2012. "Credit Booms Gone Bust: Monetary Policy, Leverage Cycles, and Financial Crises, 1870–2008." *American Economic Review* 102 (2): 1029–1061.

Securities and Exchange Commission. 2017. "Report to Congress. Access to Capital and Market Liquidity." Washington, DC, August 2017.

Sheldon, George. 1996. "Capital Adequacy Rules and the Risk-seeking Behavior of Banks: A Firm-Level Analysis." *Schweizerische Zeitschrift für Volkswirtschaft und Statistik* 132 (4): 709–734.

Shiller, Robert. 2017. "Narrative Economics." Cowles Foundation Discussion Paper 2069. New Haven, CT: Yale University, Cowles Foundation for Research in Economics.

Stein, Jeremy C. 2013. "Overheating in Credit Markets: Origins, Measurement, and Policy Responses." Speech at Research Symposium sponsored by the Federal Reserve Bank of St. Louis, February 7.

Tarullo, Daniel K. 2016. "Next Steps in the Evolution of Stress Testing." Speech at the Yale University School of Management Leaders Forum, New Haven, CT, September 26.

Taylor, Alan M. 2015. "Credit, Financial Stability, and the Macroeconomy." *Annual Review of Economics* 7 (1): 309–339.

Thanassoulis, John, and Misa Tanaka. 2018. "Optimal Pay Regulation for Too-Big-to-Fail Banks." *Journal of Financial Intermediation* 33: 83–97.

Tinbergen, J. 1952. *On the Theory of Economic Policy.* Amsterdam: North Holland.

Tracey, Belinda, Christian Schnittker, and Rhiannon Sowerbutts. 2017. "Bank Capital and Risk-taking: Evidence from Misconduct Provisions." Bank of England Staff Working Paper 671. London: Bank of England, August.

Tucker, Paul. 2009. "The Debate on Financial System Resilience: Macroprudential Instruments." Barclays Annual Lecture, London, October 22.

Tucker, Paul. 2013. "The Reform of International Banking: Some Remaining Challenges." Speech at the Oliver Wyman Institute Conference, London, October 1.

Tuckett, David. 2011. *Minding the Markets: An Emotional Finance View of Financial Instability*. Basingstoke, UK: Palgrave Macmillan.

Tuckett, David, and Richard Taffler. 2008. "Phantastic Objects and the Financial Market's Sense of Reality: A Psychoanalytic Contribution to the Understanding of Stock Market Instability." *International Journal of Psycho-Analysis* 89 (2): 389–412.

Turner, Adair. 2017. "Does the Model Remain Fit for Purpose? Financial Stability Considerations." https://www.bankofengland.co.uk/events/2017/september/20-years-on.

Vazquez, Francisco, and Pablo Federico. 2015. "Bank Funding Structures and Risk: Evidence from the Global Financial Crisis." *Journal of Banking & Finance* 61:1–14.

Wagner, Wolf. 2010. "Diversification at Financial Institutions and Systemic Crises." *Journal of Financial Intermediation* 19 (3): 373–386.

Woods, Sam. 2017. "Looking Both Ways." Remarks prepared for the May 2017 Building Society Association (BSA) Annual Conference.

Yellen, Janet L. 2017. "Financial Stability a Decade after the Onset of the Crisis." Paper presented at the Federal Reserve Bank of Kansas City Economic Policy Forum "Fostering a Dynamic Global Recovery," Jackson Hole, WY, August 25.

12

The Role of Monetary Policy in Guaranteeing Financial Stability

Markus K. Brunnermeier

The financial crisis of 2007–2009 revealed the fragility of the global financial system. It is thus not surprising that the past few years have seen a concerted reform effort to improve the resiliency of the financial architecture. In chapter 11, David Aikman, Andrew Haldane, Marc Hinterschweiger, and Sujit Kapadia provided a comprehensive overview of these reform efforts, sketched the rationale underlying the redesign of the global financial system, and tried to gauge the likely eventual impact of the reforms on the performance of the financial system as a whole. I would like to take their important work as a starting point to probe deeper into the evolution of economic thinking triggered by the global financial crisis. In particular, I will argue that there has been a shift in thinking about interlinkages between financial stability and macroeconomic management, manifested notably in the role of monetary policy in guaranteeing both real and financial stability. The key to these insights lies in replacing the usual representative agent model approach with a setting in which heterogeneous agents face financial frictions. My argument is organized around six key pillars corresponding to respective shifts in economic thinking, and throughout I try to link each of these pillars to the reform efforts we have seen in practice.

1   From Impulse Response Curves in Levels to Endogenous Volatility Dynamics and Time-Varying Risk Premia

The first shift is about the role of disturbances buffeting the macroeconomy—a view evolving from exogenous shocks to endogenous volatility dynamics. In conventional models of business cycle dynamics, time-invariant exogenous level shock processes perturb the economy.

Amplification effects and their persistence are typically illustrated with impulse response curves.[1] Many standard macro models are routinely solved using log-linearization, so agents respond to these shocks under certainty equivalence. It is thus not surprising that extant research in this class of models focuses on the responses of real quantities and aggregate prices to structural shocks and has neglected (1) stochastic volatility dynamics (higher-moment dynamics) and (2) time-varying risk premia—which of course are front and center in recent finance research. Examples of this neglect are the expectations hypothesis and uncovered interest rate parity, which are typically assumed to hold, despite ample evidence of their violation in practice. In response to the crisis, however, a greater emphasis has been put on risk determination and risk dynamics. In modern macro finance models, risk and risk premia in the economy are (partially) endogenous and time-varying. In a sense, the macro literature has joined the finance literature in viewing risk premia as significantly more important than cash flow variations. Recent macro models do not simply study amplification in levels and flows but also incorporate the endogenous dynamics in volatility and their interaction with macro flow and stock variables.

Of note, as risk or risk allocation and hence aggregate risk-bearing capacity vary over time, so does the natural rate of interest r^*, and with it the non-accelerating inflation rate of unemployment (NAIRU). For example, an increase in uninsurable idiosyncratic risk or a reduction in intermediaries' ability to diversify idiosyncratic risks away heightens precautionary savings and temporarily depresses the important theoretical benchmark rate r^*.[2]

2   From Paradox of Thrift to Paradox of Prudence

Conventional risk models effectively treat individual financial entities in isolation. The emphasis is put on the risk faced by individual institutions, and little attention is devoted to spillover risks. In practice, financial institutions are linked, most obviously through direct contractual linkages: individual bank defaults lead to knock-on effects for other institutions. They may subsequently also default, triggering second- and higher-order effects that ultimately spread through the system. Position data can be used to gauge the potential dangers of these ripple-through losses due to bankruptcies or defaults. At the same time, there are also important *indirect* spillover effects: financial distress leads to adverse price movements, which in turn affect other institutions with the same or similar exposures. That is, a shock can ripple through the system even when various market participants do not have direct exposure to each other and are not contractually linked. Liquidity spirals are a particularly important example of these amplification effects. Whether risk spreads depends crucially on whether other market participants behave as *shock absorbers* or *shock amplifiers*; that is, the consequences depend on their response function. In a world with strategic complementarities, a single entity's shock is amplified by the reaction of the rest of the market. A new fallacy of composition can emerge. While Keynes's paradox of thrift concerned the household's consumption-versus-saving decision—each household's decision to increase its propensity to save leads to less saving overall—a similar paradox in the risk space can arise, dubbed the "paradox of prudence" by Brunnermeier and Sannikov (2017). Individual banks' microprudent behavior is macro-imprudent when it exacerbates endogenous systemic macro risks and results in fat-tail return distributions. Overall, it is paramount for regulators to focus on market participants' response functions in order to distinguish between shock amplifiers—those exhibiting the strategic complementarities noted above—and shock absorbers—those that do not. One response indicator is the liquidity mismatch. Market participants with low liquidity mismatch are likely to view a price drop as a cheap buying opportunity, while market participants with high liquidity mismatch will contribute to fire sales and amplify the initial shock.

3   From Contemporaneously Measured Risks to Hidden Buildup of Risk and Procyclicality

The third change concerns the shift from the focus on contemporaneous risk measures to the hidden buildup of risk. In conventional models, a disturbance simply materializes and then propagates through the system, with internal propagation usually rather weak. As a result of the financial crisis, however, there has been a realization that the buildup that makes an economy vulnerable to risk realization can actually be endogenous and happen gradually over time, against the background of a seemingly well-functioning economy. Underlying this buildup is a hidden shift from strategic substitutability to strategic complementarity. To give a concrete example, if most market participants are not levered or VaR-constrained, then a price drop (e.g., due to the sales by certain market participants) means a cheap buying opportunity for the rest of the market. In contrast, when strategic substitutability through a buildup of leverage morphs into strategic complementarity, then a sale by others (which depresses prices) tightens leverage and VaR constraints, which in turn forces most of the remaining market participants to also sell. The end result of these forces is the volatility paradox: low measured VaR indicates that everything is fine, but this leads to financial institutions adopting higher leverage (as risk weights can be low, with the financial system seemingly very stable), thus making the financial system even more vulnerable to an eventual shock. Formally, even with exogenous risk vanishingly small, amplification rises correspondingly to bound endogenous risk away from zero, and so any given exogenous shock can get substantially amplified. These forces paint a more nuanced picture of the desirability of higher debt levels. One the one hand, empirical evidence suggests that more advanced economies exhibit a higher debt-to-GDP ratio—a force labeled "financial deepening." On the other hand, higher debt due to a buildup of leverage that occurs when contemporaneously measured volatility is low can be a harbinger of future financial crisis.

4   From Risk-Free Asset Benchmark to Bubbly Safe Assets

The fourth shift in thinking acknowledges the increased importance of safe assets. The widely observed "flight to safety" contributed to this shift. In traditional macro models, the most important benchmark is the risk-free rate. Risk-free assets are risk-free at a particular predetermined horizon, say, one month, one year, or thirty years. In contrast, according to Brunnermeier and Haddad (2014), safe assets are liquid and valuable during crises that occur at random horizons. Safe assets are like a good friend. They are around when one needs them. They are good stores of value and instruments to save in for precautionary reasons. A second feature is the "safe asset tautology." Safe assets are safe because they are perceived to be safe. Formally, this points to multiple equilibria. Safe assets can assume the form of bubbles, like government debt in Samuelson's (1958) overlapping generations model or in the incomplete markets settings of Bewley

(1980) and Brunnermeier and Sannikov (2016a, 2016b). For example, gold is considered a safe store of value though not risk-free, since it tends to appreciate in times of crisis. Safe assets are also generally information-ally insensitive and are typically held by agents to have a precautionary buffer counterbalancing the risk they hold otherwise.

Safe assets also have an international dimension. The most detrimental flight-to-safety episodes involve international cross-border capital flows. The underlying cause of this phenomenon is that safe assets are not sup-plied symmetrically across countries. Foreign reserve holdings, IMF credit facilities, and central banks' swap line arrangements provide some protec-tion against potential cross-border flight-to-safety episodes. The creation of safe assets via securitization in the form of sovereign bond–backed securities (SBBS) allows one to rechannel the flight-to-safety flows from cross-border flows to flows across different asset classes. Brunnermeier, Langfield, and co-authors (2017) describe the stabilizing properties of SBBS/ESBies for the euro area, and Brunnermeier and Huang (2018) do the same for SBBS in emerging market economies.

5   From Separation Principles to Interlinkages between Macroprudential and Monetary Policy

The fifth pillar concerns the linkages between macroprudential and mon-etary policy. Precrisis thinking called for a separation, while now these linkages are explicitly acknowledged. The common belief, as reflected in precrisis macro modeling, was that monetary policy and prudential policy should be kept separate, with monetary policy ensuring price and output stability through the divine coincidence and macroprudential pol-icy stabilizing the financial system. Underlying this perspective was also the standard philosophy that clearly assigned accountability is the best institutional arrangement across different government agencies. Indeed, central banks had historically been charged with maintaining financial stability, but in the decades leading up to the crisis these tasks were rel-egated to newly created special agencies. In recent years, in contrast, it has been realized that monetary policy has redistributive effects, with important implications for financial stability (see, e.g., Brunnermeier and Sannikov 2013). Conventional interest rate cuts boost long-term bond prices and unconventional asset purchases boost asset prices, so monetary policy overall redistributes toward the original holders of these assets. This stealth recapitalization leads to lower risk premia and mitigates the deflationary and liquidity spirals reviewed above, thus stabilizing the economy. In particular, this stealth recapitalization works even when direct (fiscal) recapitalization is not feasible, usually because of political economy constraints. Emerging economies provide a further illustration of the entanglement of macroprudential and monetary policy. In fact, in those economies, the distinction between these tools is not even clear. For example, in India, a liquidity requirement for banks to hold government debt was considered as a monetary policy tool and not only a macroprudential tool.

6 From a Risk Perspective to a Resilience Perspective

The final pillar concerns longer-term considerations—the effect of downturns, in particular those related to financial stability, on long-term economic performance. It is a debate of stability versus resilience. In conventional models, the economy fluctuates around a stable (exogenous) long-term growth path, with exogenous shocks leading to temporary, but never permanent, losses in the productive capacity of the economy.[3] Risk is thus only of second-order importance, and the costs of business cycles are dwarfed by considerations of long-term economic growth. Lucas (1987) concludes that macroeconomists should focus on growth rather than studying business cycles. The fallout from the financial crisis, however, has made it clear (again) to economists that, in fact, recessions can have permanent scarring effects.[4] Financial crises in particular have the potential to leave long-lasting scars and permanently lower the long-term growth rate of the economy. Risk thus matters. The key trade-off for policymakers, then, is that additional regulation may make the economy more resilient (so preventing the large and permanent crisis-induced output losses), but at the cost of reducing average efficiency. Overall, instead of trying to reduce volatility—the traditional focus of business cycle theory—the emphasis of research should lie on mean reversion and a return to the previous trend line. Figuratively speaking, instead of trying to build a "concrete support wall" that prevents the economy from dropping beyond a certain level, one should design a "trampoline" that allows the economy to potentially deviate further but then bounce back to its long-run trend.

To varying extents, all of the different aspects highlighted above feature in a new class of macro models that explicitly integrate a nontrivial financial sector and consider global dynamics, with special emphasis on the endogenous emergence of crisis zones. Financial stability and macro stability are intertwined; these models allow us to understand the sources of this entanglement and the relevant policy implications. More work, however, is needed, in particular on quantification on these models. A more quantitatively realistic generation of models then holds the promise to inform optimal policymaking and gauge the reform efforts implemented in the past years.

Notes

I am grateful for feedback on this chapter from Olivier Blanchard, Thomas Pellet, and Christian Wolf.

1. In settings with sufficiently pronounced strategic complementarities, amplification can turn into multiplicity. In the latter case (nonfundamental), sunspot shocks alone are sufficient to generate fluctuations in endogenous macro quantities.

2. In "The I Theory of Money" (Brunnermeier and Sannikov 2016a), intermediaries' willingness to diversify risk depends on their capitalization.

3. Macroeconomists disagree whether the long-run trend should be measured from peak to peak, with recessions as deviations from normal capturing output gaps, as in the famous Friedman plucking model, or whether to consider a (HP filtered) trend from which the economy deviates in both directions, that is, output gaps are positive and negative.

4. Blanchard and Summers (1987) document that long-term recessions lead to further hysteresis as human capital deteriorates with the unemployment spell.

References

Bewley, Truman. 1980. "The Optimum Quantity of Money." In *Models of Monetary Economies: Proceedings and Contributions from Participants of a December 1978 Conference Sponsored by the Federal Reserve Bank of Minneapolis*, ed. John H. Kareken and Neil Wallace. Federal Reserve Bank of Minneapolis.

Blanchard, Olivier, and Lawrence H. Summers. 1987. "Hysteresis in Unemployment." *European Economic Review* 31:288–295.

Brunnermeier, M. K., and V. Haddad. 2014. "Safe Assets." https://www.newyorkfed.org/medialibrary/media/aboutthefed/pdf/FAR_Oct2014.pdf.

Brunnermeier, Markus K., and Lunyang Huang. 2018. "GloSSBS: A Global Safe Asset from and for Emerging Market Economies." Paper presented at the 21st

Annual Conference of the Central Bank of Chile, "Monetary Policy and Financial Stability: Transmission Mechanisms and Policy Implications," Santiago, November.

Brunnermeier, Markus K., Sam Langfield, Marco Pagano, Ricardo Reis, Stijn van Nieuwerburgh, and Dimitri Vayanos. 2017. "ESBies: Safety in the Tranches." *Economic Policy* 32 (90): 175–219.

Brunnermeier, Markus K., and Yuliy Sannikov. 2013. "Redistributive Monetary Policy." In *The Changing Policy Landscape: Proceedings of the 2012 Jackson Hole Economic Policy Symposium*, 331–384. Federal Reserve Bank of Kansas City.

Brunnermeier, Markus K., and Yuliy Sannikov. 2016a. "The I Theory of Money." NBER Working Paper 22533. Cambridge, MA: National Bureau of Economic Research.

Brunnermeier, Markus K., and Yuliy Sannikov. 2016b. "On the Optimal Inflation Rate." *American Economic Review* 106 (5): 484–489.

Brunnermeier, Markus K., and Yuliy Sannikov. 2017. "Macro, Money and Finance: A Continuous-Time Approach." In *Handbook of Macroeconomics*, vol. 2, 1497–1546. Amsterdam: North-Holland.

Lucas, R. E. 1987. *Models of Business Cycles*. New York: Basil Blackwell.

Samuelson, Paul. 1958. "An Exact Consumption-Loan Model of Interest with or without the Social Contrivance of Money." *Journal of Political Economy* 66 (6): 467–482.

13

The Known Unknowns of Financial Regulation

Benoît Coeuré

Financial intermediation is at a crossroad. Arguably, never before in history have banks faced as many significant challenges as they do today. Exceptionally low interest rates and more rigorous post-crisis regulation are weighing on banks' earnings and limiting, at times, their ability to make full use of their balance sheets. Technological change too is threatening incumbents in many ways. Although technological progress has often probed the adaptability and flexibility of financial intermediaries in the past, the speed and scope of current innovations have the potential to change more radically the way financial services are provided to households and firms.

These circumstances naturally also create challenges for regulators, central banks, and other policymakers. Ten years after the start of the crisis, it is time to take stock of the impact of the wealth of rules and regulations that have been adopted since then. The Financial Stability Board (FSB) has initiated important work in this direction and is expected to conduct a thorough evaluation of the effects of the G-20 financial regulatory reforms.

The work presented by David Aikman, Andrew Haldane, Marc Hinterschweiger, and Sujit Kapadia in chapter 11 is a powerful guide to these evaluations. They conclude, correctly in my view, that the loudly voiced concerns about higher capital requirements leading to lower lending do not seem to have materialized, giving some credence to the claims that capital requirements could have been calibrated at a higher level, even though the combined impact of the total loss absorption capacity and capital requirements remains to be fully understood (see Admati and Hellwig 2014; Kashkari 2016). Moreover, Aikman and colleagues emphasize the complementary nature of the existing rules and provide empirical evidence in defense of the current "multipolar"—that is, silo-based—regulatory regime. Their work further strengthens the case for any review of the new regulatory framework to err on the side of conservatism, and to withstand pressure from vested interest groups.

Though I cannot do justice to all the dimensions of Aikman and colleagues' ideas, I plan to do two things. First, I will expand on one of their chapter's key aspects, namely, the potential trade-offs involved in multipolar regulation. And, second, I will touch on one issue that has arguably received less attention so far—the effects of financial regulation on financial structures, in particular during times of fast technological change.

A Holistic View on Regulatory Trade-offs

Over the past ten years, the financial market landscape has changed significantly, both in terms of how risk is being transformed and in terms of how it is being pooled and managed. On the intermediation side, the non-bank financial sector has substantially increased its share of the market, from 43 percent in 2008 to 55 percent in early 2017. On the risk management side, central clearing houses have emerged following the introduction of mandatory central clearing for standardized over-the-counter (OTC) derivatives—as agreed on by the G-20 at its Pittsburgh summit in 2009.

These changes have also had an impact on the nature and scope of financial regulation. For example, the FSB has progressed toward tighter regulation of market-based finance, while the Committee on Payments and Market Infrastructures, the International Organization of Securities Commissions, and other international bodies have worked tirelessly since 2012 to establish a regulatory framework that makes central clearing counterparties (CCPs) more resilient and easier to resolve (see Coeuré 2017).[1]

A more diverse financial sector, however, also means that regulatory spillovers have become both more likely and more difficult to identify. I will use the example of CCPs and their interactions with the Basel III leverage ratio. Because clearing services require clients to post collateral, the non-recognition of such collateral in the leverage ratio framework may cause banks to scale back their clearing services, potentially leading to an unhealthy concentration of clearing services.

In other words, there is a risk that the leverage ratio could potentially make our markets more, not less, risky. Some have publicly concluded on this issue, asking the Basel Committee to consider how it could be amended. Others are still reviewing these dynamics, including an FSB-led review of incentives to centrally clear, the Derivatives Assessment Team.

So, different from regulation for one category of financial players, such as banks, where overlapping rules may be desirable for the reasons explained by Aikman and colleagues (the "Tinbergen" and "Brainard" rules applied to financial regulation[2]), regulatory spillovers across financial players may be more a source of concern.

Ideally, quantitative models would support policymakers in characterizing and overcoming such trade-offs. This approach, however, faces two high hurdles. The first is that policymakers would need to specify better their loss function, giving clear weights to different, and potentially conflicting, objectives. This is a highly delicate endeavor, however. And second, even if we could spell out our objective function, the way our quantitative models depict the financial sector lacks the granularity needed to quantify trade-offs in a sufficiently precise manner. So, in the end, I generally agree with Aikman and colleagues' conclusion that we will likely keep shooting in the dark, which means shooting many arrows at the same target.

Ultimately, however, potential adverse spillovers cannot be an excuse to undo what has been achieved since 2009. But when adverse spillovers are obvious, such as in the case of the leverage ratio and central clearing, then we should not hesitate to correct them. This also relates to the undesired consequences of a lack of international cooperation in some pockets of the regulatory domain. Consider again CCP oversight and supervision. Some CCPs are clearly global in nature because of the range of clearing members they serve or the markets and currencies they clear.

It would therefore be important for all jurisdictions to recognize the need for non-domestic supervisors and central banks to be involved in the oversight of such global CCPs and in establishing cooperative oversight arrangements where relevant. A supervisory approach that recognizes the legitimate interests of non-domestic authorities is vital for tackling the global repercussions of a potential CCP failure, including its recovery and resolution.

The European Commission proposal to amend the EMIR regulation is a case in point. After the UK's decision to leave the EU, and with UK CCPs clearing approximately 90 percent of the euro-denominated interest rate swaps of euro-area banks, there would be clear risks in allowing the current EU arrangements for the supervision of third-country CCPs to continue as they are. The proposal provides EU supervisors and the relevant central banks of issue with the tools they need to monitor and address risks to the EU's financial system.[3]

So more, not less, international cooperation is crucial to safeguard financial stability. This is a point worth emphasizing, particularly when a retreat from internationally agreed standards is being discussed openly. In an integrated global economy, financial regulation *has* to rely on internationally agreed-on standards. Turning back the clock on international financial regulation would revive distrust, create financial fragmentation, and risk regulatory arbitrage and a race to the bottom.

Effects of Financial Regulation on Financial Structures

Let me now turn to another challenge the regulatory community faces, namely, the impact—whether desired or not—of regulation on the financial structure of our economies.[4] There are two broad ways in which the regulatory framework is likely to affect the funding mix of firms and households. The first one works through some forms of financing receiving preferential treatment. The second works through protecting incumbents from new competitors. Both channels can be intended or unintended by regulators, and both can ultimately steer an economy toward adopting a financial structure that may look different from the one it would have adopted were market forces left to their own devices.

Despite these allocative effects, regulation is rarely based on first principles. In fact, regulators are caught between a rock and a hard place. Ignoring the effects of regulation on our economies' financial structures is likely to be naïve and delusional—we may not know the speed and scope of the impact, but we can be relatively certain that the effect will not be neutral. At the same time, internalizing the effects would make it increasingly difficult to distinguish between prudential and industry objectives. This could create misplaced incentives and could run the risk of failing to fulfill the financial stability mandate.

The good news is that academic research has long been suggesting that even if financial rules were to distort the first-best allocation, the impact on growth and society in general would likely be immaterial.[5] The assertion is that both bank and market-based finance tends to support economic development and living standards in similar ways.[6]

More recent research, however, challenges these findings. Evidence is growing that large banking systems are associated with more systemic risk and lower economic growth, especially as countries grow richer (see Demirgüç-Kunt, Feyen, and Levine 2013; Langfield and Papagano 2016). Other research suggests that deeper equity markets are more effective in bringing economies closer to the technological frontier (see Hsu, Tian, and Xu 2014).

On balance, therefore, empirical research is increasingly probing the role and importance of banks in developed economies, both in terms of their marginal contribution to growth and as shock absorbers. This is also reflected in the political discussion. The European push toward a capital markets union reflects not only the need for increased cross-border risk sharing in a currency union but also the understanding that a more balanced funding mix is better at helping to absorb economic shocks, much in line with Alan Greenspan's "spare tire" hypothesis (see Greenspan 1999). There is also the hope that deeper and better-integrated equity markets will support innovation and productivity growth in the EU.

In addition, we can see that banks are increasingly challenged by technological shifts. New competitors are emerging rapidly and threaten to conquer banks' market shares in some of their core income-generating areas. Crowd funding or peer-to-peer lending, for example, has the potential to affect bank lending services. E-trading or robo-advising, meanwhile, may crowd banks out of typical investment management or advisory functions. Other areas of competition involve the provision of payment services.

Of course, this does not mean that banks have become redundant or a drag on society. Banks play a key social role of pooling savings and engaging in maturity and risk transformation, and they should continue doing so. But it does raise two important questions. First, are we at a tipping point at which the future of banks is challenged? And second, should regulators care? That is, should we protect banks from recent technological shifts and the emergence of new competitors? Should regulators have a preconceived idea of which financial structure is best for society, bearing in mind the trade-off I mentioned earlier?

So far, the regulatory approach has generally been built on the assumption that opening up market access to new fintech companies will increase social surplus and spur innovation, similar to what we have seen in other network industries. At the same time, rules are still in place that protect incumbents. For example, fintech firms lack access to the customer transaction data they would need to provide a broader range of financial services—data that banks can use to cross-sell financial services at a price that might be higher than if information sharing was less restricted.

As an example, the revision of Europe's Payment Services Directive (PSD2), due to be implemented by EU member states in January 2018, is designed to introduce more competition by requiring banks to share account information. With access to such data, fintech companies could increasingly shake up the banking sector.

In this regulatory landscape, I see two broad scenarios for the future. In the first one, incumbents rise to the challenge. They join forces with startups, embrace new technologies, cut costs, and gain new sources of revenue. Some of these partnerships are happening as we speak. The outcome under this scenario is generally benign as, first, new technologies are likely to spread more rapidly through banks' existing networks, fostering productivity and growth, and second, current prudential regulation is already geared toward banks, thereby preserving financial stability.

However, I can already see one challenge for regulators, which is to let banks reap the economies of scale inherent in digital technologies while not recreating risks of "too big to fail." This scenario also crucially assumes that banks are profitable enough to carry out the necessary investments, which in Europe involves reducing costs and addressing forcefully nonperforming loans.

In the second scenario banks remain more defensive or, as they would probably like to argue, stifled by regulation and the low-interest-rate environment. As a result, they increasingly risk failing to meet the changing demands of customers, who, in a digitalized world, expect financial services to be available in real time, anywhere and at any time. This scenario could be a real threat to incumbents, in particular if digital giants, who already have access to large amounts of customer data, were to start targeting parts of the banking value chain, which would limit banks' ability to cross-sell and ultimately crowd banks out of a large swath of financial services.

For society as a whole, would this scenario be worse? Firms and households could benefit from a growing number of financial products and services, lower prices, and faster provision. The problem, however, would be that banking services would likely migrate toward the less regulated parts of the financial system where many fintechs—as non–deposit takers—still operate.[7] This is what Charles Goodhart (2008) has called the "boundary problem" of financial regulation. In this case, to avoid regulators once again being "bloodhounds in pursuit of greyhounds" (Eichengreen 2009), current regulatory loopholes would need to be closed to ensure that financial intermediation outside the banking sector remained safe and sound.

Here is where normative questions might arise, however. The reason is that financial regulation may affect the direction and rate of change at which financial structures evolve. On the one hand, preemptively drawing in the reins in the name of financial stability could stifle innovation and prevent fintechs from growing important economies of scale. So it could also put small businesses and households at a disadvantage as they would potentially benefit from faster technological progress, provided it remained safe. On the other hand, allowing risks to accumulate in the unregulated sector could lead to over-exuberance, re-create risks to financial stability, and forgo the benefits of past regulatory efforts.

Finding the right balance and identifying the risks in real time is an inherently difficult task, of course. I have no quick or easy solutions to offer. But what we should do, in my view, is to more systematically encourage more research on these important matters.

Central banks are not innocent bystanders in this process. We have to be mindful about the impact of our own decisions on the future of financial structures. Digital currencies, for example, could undermine commercial banks' monopoly on creating inside money (see He et al. 2017). Negative interest rates, meanwhile, can have adverse consequences for banks' profitability over time despite being extremely effective in complementing other non-conventional monetary policy instruments and helping central banks overcome the zero lower bound constraint. So far, the general equilibrium effects of negative rates have clearly dominated. More generally, it is hard to believe that central banks keeping very large balance sheets for a considerable amount of time will not have an impact on financial intermediation.

Looking forward, low productivity and aging societies may mean that our economies have gravitated toward a low-growth, low-interest-rate environment that may weigh more permanently on banks' profits and hence financial stability. Monetary policy, in turn, may have to resort more often to nonstandard measures to meet its price stability mandate. In these circumstances, we need to be mindful of risks to financial stability. A too protracted period of asset purchases, for example, may cause financial imbalances to build up, with potentially adverse consequences for price stability.

Conclusion

Preserving financial stability has become a much more complex and intertwined endeavor than it was ten or twenty years ago. These interconnections can profoundly change the balance of regulatory trade-offs across major financial market participants. What is more, the financial system is evolving quickly. Intra-temporal trade-offs are made worse by appreciable inter-temporal trade-offs, where policymakers need to keep a watchful eye on the allocative repercussions of their regulatory decisions.

In this environment, there are no quick fixes or easy solutions. But there are two principles on which we should continue to build. The first is cooperation among regulators, both within and across borders. Only by joining forces will we be able to break up remaining silos and identify common solutions to the challenging trade-offs we face. The second is cooperation across policymakers. Conferences like this one bring together policymakers from different fora—monetary policy, fiscal policy, and financial stability. They force us to think beyond our usual boundaries and have the potential to raise awareness and sensitivities.

I would therefore like to thank Olivier Blanchard and the Peterson Institute for International Economics wholeheartedly.

Notes

1. On market-based finance, see, for example, the Financial Stability Board's 2017 policy recommendations to address structural vulnerabilities from asset management activities.

2. The Tinbergen Rule states that different policy objectives call for different policy instruments, while the Brainard Rule states that the choice of instruments depends on the type of uncertainty surrounding their effects (see chapter 11).

3. See the October 4, 2017, ECB Opinion on a proposal for a regulation of the European Parliament and of the Council amending Regulation (EU) No. 1095/2010 and Regulation (EU) No. 648/2012 with regard to the procedures and authorities involved for the authorization of central counterparties (https:// www.ecb.europa.eu/ecb/legal/pdf/en_con_2017_39_eu_f_sign.pdf). In June 2017 the ECB Governing Council unanimously adopted a recommendation to amend Article 22 of the Statute of the European System of Central Banks (ESCB) and of the ECB to provide the ECB with a regulatory competence in the area of central clearing.

4. On financial structures, see Claessens (2016).

5. For an excellent review of this topic, see Popov (2017).

6. This conclusion is supported by both micro- and macroeconomic evidence and is robust across a wide set of economies and sectors. See, for example, Arestis, Demetriades, and Luintel (2001), Beck and Levine (2002), and Beck and Levine (2004).

7. Depending on the type of activity they carry out, many fintech companies are already subject to one or more pieces of EU sectoral financial services legislation.

References

Admati, A., and M. Hellwig. 2014. *The Bankers' New Clothes: What's Wrong with Banking and What to Do about It*, with a new preface by the authors. Princeton, NJ: Princeton University Press.

Arestis, P., P. Demetriades, and K. B. Luintel. 2001. "Financial Development and Economic Growth: The Role of Stock Markets." *Journal of Money, Credit, and Banking* 33:16–41.

Beck, T., and R. Levine. 2002. "Industry Growth and Capital Allocation: Does Having a Market- or Bank-Based System Matter?" *Journal of Financial Economics* 64:147–180.

Beck, T., and R. Levine. 2004. "Stock Markets, Banks, and Growth: Panel Evidence." *Journal of Banking and Finance* 28:423–442.

Claessens, S. 2016. "Regulation and Structural Change in Financial Systems." ECB Forum on Central Banking, June.

Cœuré, B. 2017. "Central Clearing: Reaping the Benefits, Controlling the Risks." *Financial Stability Review (Banque de France)* 21 (April).

Demirgüç-Kunt, A., E. Feyen, and R. Levine. 2013. "The Evolving Importance of Banks and Securities Markets." *World Bank Economic Review* 27 (3): 476–490.

Eichengreen, B. 2009. "The Financial Crisis and Global Policy Reforms." In *Proceedings of the Federal Reserve Bank of San Francisco Asia Economic Policy Conference*, 18–20.

Goodhart, C. 2008. "The Boundary Problem in Financial Regulation." *National Institute Economic Review* 206:48–55.

Greenspan, A. 1999. "Do Efficient Financial Markets Mitigate Financial Crises?" Speech at the 1999 Financial Markets Conference of the Federal Reserve Bank of Atlanta, Sea Island, GA, October 19.

He, Dong, Ross B. Leckow, Vikram Haksar, Tommaso Mancini Griffoli, et al. 2017. "Fintech and Financial Services: Initial Considerations." IMF Staff Discussion Note 17/05. Washington, DC: International Monetary Fund.

Hsu, P., X. Tian, and Y. Xu. 2014. "Financial Development and Innovation: Cross-Country Evidence." *Journal of Financial Economics* 112 (1): 116–135.

Kashkari, N. 2016. "The Minneapolis Plan to End Too Big to Fail." Speech at the event, "Too Big to Fail at the Economic Club of New York," Economic Club of New York, November 16.

Langfield, S., and M. Pagano. 2016. "Bank Bias in Europe: Effects on Systemic Risk and Growth." *Economic Policy* 31 (85): 51–106.

Popov, A. 2018. "Evidence on Finance and Economic Growth." In *Handbook on Finance and Development*, ed. T. Beck and R. Levine. London: Edward Elgar, forthcoming.

14

Financial Stability and Macroprudential Policies

Nellie Liang

David Aikman, Andrew Haldane, Marc Hinterschweiger, and Sujit Kapadia in chapter 11 present a comprehensive review of current research on financial stability policy issues and raise some important questions for future work to promote financial stability. I will expand on two research areas related to implementing macroprudential policies. The first area concerns empirical estimates of the effects of financial conditions on economic growth, and specifically on downside risks to growth. This line of research translates financial stability risks into risks to output growth, and thus allows policymakers to use a common language for macroprudential policies and monetary policy or other macro policies. The second area has to do with the governance structure for macroprudential policies, which is critical for actually taking action. In particular, can monetary policymakers assume there are effective macroprudential authorities in place to implement policies promoting financial stability? Can monetary policymakers safely ignore financial stability considerations in their own policy deliberations?

For this discussion, I will define macroprudential policies as financial regulatory policies with time-varying parameters. There are important arguments for using dynamic policies in addition to structural time-invariant policies. In particular, risk-taking behavior is pro-cyclical, many regulations and models are pro-cyclical as well, and static regulations can be arbitraged, especially in countries with sophisticated non-bank sectors. These three reasons are not just abstract concepts, and they suggest important limitations to static structural policies on their own to promote financial stability.

In addition, the objectives for macroprudential policy can be broad. The authors of chapter 11 point out that the Bank of England as early as

2009 raised the question of whether it should target only the resilience of financial firms and markets or whether it should also aim more boldly for smoothing credit cycles of households and businesses. In my view, there are strong theoretical and empirical arguments for macroprudential policies to aim for both, to target both lenders and borrowers, since there are negative externalities when either is stressed. Clearly, undercapitalized financial firms make economic growth highly vulnerable, and borrowers with high debt loads who are forced to deleverage can lead to a collapse in aggregate demand, and thus to a liquidity trap.

Estimating Growth at Risk from the Financial Sector

While there are strong arguments for wanting to implement macroprudential policies with dynamic parameters, there are challenges. A critical question is, when are risks sufficiently large to take preemptive action? This question is more difficult to answer than responding to a crisis when it is obvious that there is a problem to be addressed. But such issues of timing are common to monetary policy as well, wherein central banks aim to raise rates before inflation gets too high, rather than wait and risk letting inflation expectations become unbounded. In this vein, there is recent, early-stage work to develop surveillance measures that express financial stability risks in terms of risks to future economic growth. I will mention three empirical exercises.

One exercise evaluates the effects of financial conditions on economic growth and whether they vary with macrofinancial imbalances, such as private nonfinancial credit. Excess private nonfinancial credit relative to its long-run trend has been found to predict recessions and crises and now is reviewed regularly by many countries for setting the countercyclical capital buffer. For the U.S. economy, we test the significance of excess credit for economic growth (Aikman et al. 2017). In particular, we use a threshold VAR specification to test whether the effects of financial conditions vary depending on whether the credit gap is high or low. In our model, financial conditions reflect risk premiums for asset prices and lending standards. We find that looser financial conditions will boost GDP in near-term quarters in both low and high credit gap periods but that growth is less sustainable in high credit gap periods than in low ones. That is, while the effects of financial conditions are positive in near-term quarters, they lead to negative growth in the medium term when the credit gap is high. These results suggest important nonlinearities, consistent with models of occasionally binding collateral constraints that can lead to sharp discontinuities. The results are robust to tests that high credit is not approximating for other factors, such as a recession.

A second exercise is presented in chapter 3 of the IMF's October 2017 *Global Financial Stability Report*. The authors present a measure of growth-at-risk from financial conditions, which provides a measure of financial stability expressed in terms of economic growth. They evaluate whether financial sector conditions can help predict the probability distribution of future GDP growth (building on Adrian, Boyarchenko, and Giannone 2016 for the United States). Using quantile regressions, they show the fifth, median, and ninety-fifth percentile of predicted year-ahead GDP growth based on financial conditions, estimated for twenty-one countries. They show that tighter financial conditions have stronger effects on downside risks to growth relative to upside risks at one year ahead. These results suggest that looking only at median growth may ignore some key downside risks.

In particular, looser financial conditions predict lower downside risks in the near term, roughly a horizon of one year ahead. In contrast, higher borrower leverage (looser financial conditions) can signal greater downside risks in the medium term, at two to three years ahead. That is, looser conditions reduce growth volatility in the near term but increase it in the medium term, suggesting an intertemporal trade-off from looser financial conditions.

This growth-at-risk measure, which captures the expected path, volatility, and skewness of GDP growth, puts financial stability risks into the same language used for assessing other macro policies. Countries could track this growth-at-risk measure over different horizons over time. It has the potential to gauge the need for macroprudential policies at any time, and to evaluate the success of those policies.

A third empirical exercise reflects a combination of these two and extends the growth-at-risk exercise by conditioning the growth effects of financial conditions on excess credit and testing for nonlinear dynamics. In preliminary work for eleven advanced economies, we find the combination of high credit and loose financial conditions—an exuberant period— leads to a greater increase in the volatility of growth in the medium term, indicating less sustainable growth and reinforcing the result of an intertemporal trade-off.

These three examples test and find results consistent with a framework that looks at financial stability as the ability of the system to absorb rather than amplify any negative shocks (see Adrian, Covitz, and Liang 2015). Vulnerabilities can build in a predictable way and result in greater downside risks because of occasionally binding collateral constraints that lead to sharp discontinuous adjustments through aggregate demand externalities, fire sales, and investor runs.

Governance Structures for Macroprudential Policies

An important part of effectively setting macroprudential policies is having appropriate governance structures in place for evaluating risks and taking policy actions. This issue is especially interesting in the current environment, as many advanced economies are concerned that inflation remains below target, while asset valuations are rising rapidly. At the same time, global credit is rising, as reported by the IMF in its October 2017 *Global Financial Stability Report*. A current question is, what entities are monitoring systemic risks that could arise from the combination of high asset prices and rising credit and taking preemptive actions to prevent a possibly costly fallout if asset prices were to drop sharply?

In a paper with Rochelle Edge (Edge and Liang 2017), we evaluate new macroprudential authorities to answer the question of who makes decisions about dynamic macroprudential policies. We constructed a new data set of macroprudential authorities for a sample of fifty-eight countries. Macroprudential policies likely require a good deal of coordination across regulators and a greater focus on time-varying risks or on nonregulated institutions, and thus may warrant new governance arrangements. The database reflects information through 2016 from public official documents, and we are making it available to others (Correa, Edge, and Liang 2017).

Many countries (forty-one) have established interagency financial stability committees (FSCs), formal or de facto, and fifteen countries have designated a single entity to be the macroprudential authority. The single entity is almost always the central bank, which for these countries is also a prudential regulator. Weighting the arrangements by GDP shows that

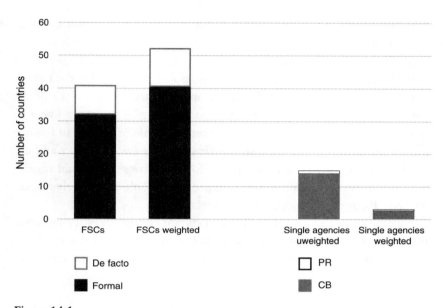

Figure 14.1

Types of Macroprudential Authorities. Number of countries weighted by GDP. *Source:* Edge and Liang (2017).

larger countries set up FSCs, while smaller countries rely on the central bank to be the single authority (figure 14.1). No country in our sample created a new agency to independently set dynamic policies; instead, they built on microprudential regulatory structures already in place. It appears that since microprudential regulators were not set up to implement macroprudential policies, countries chose to establish committees by including the central bank and often the Ministry of Finance. In terms of what governs global activity, committees clearly are the arrangement to focus on.

To evaluate the committees, we first looked at membership and leadership. We found that FSCs in the forty-one countries typically have between three and five agencies as members. Membership is important because the different agencies have different skills and objectives, which will affect macroprudential policy choices. Many international bodies have recommended that central banks have a prominent role in macroprudential policies because of their analytical expertise for time-varying risks and operational independence in the conduct of monetary policy.

However, because some macroprudential policies may involve distributional choices, finance ministries as representing elected officials may be needed to provide legitimacy to the FSCs, though they may be less willing than the central bank to implement unpopular policies. Our data show that central banks are on all FSCs but one, and are the sole chair of the FSC in twelve countries. However, finance ministries are more likely to be the *sole* chair of the FSC than is the central bank: ministries of finance (or the government) claim the sole chair in twenty-one countries and are co-chairs or rotate as chairs in another four countries. Prudential regulators are always on the committees but are never a sole chair, likely reflecting their focus on microprudential issues.

Judging the effectiveness of financial stability committees is somewhat subjective. But we can use three criteria that the IMF (2014) has set out as important: can they coordinate, do they enable taking actions, and are they willing to act?

Coordination. All the FSCs state they work to promote information sharing. The FSCs appear to have the right set of members. We tested the hypothesis that FSCs are set up to facilitate coordination against taking advantage of the skills of the central banks, and found evidence of setups reflecting a greater need for coordination. In this way, FSCs are a step forward.

Ability to act. We looked at whether FSCs themselves had any specific tools, such as the authority to direct actions of its members, countercyclical capital buffer, stress tests, or loan-to-value ratios. Only two FSCs—in the United Kingdom and France—have hard tools, which means they can direct an action of their members. Another nine have "comply or explain" powers, which means the FSC can publicly express a view that an agency should take an action, but the agency has a choice and can choose to explain why it does not. That indicates that most FSCs (thirty) meet just to share information.

Of course, the separate regulators often have the authority to set policies, and the central bank can provide the time-varying analysis to assess risks. But the regulators may not, on their own, have financial stability mandates, and so there may be a disconnect between the authority over tools and responsibility for financial stability.

Willingness to act. This criterion is the hardest to assess, and it is too early to draw conclusions since most of the FSCs were not established until after 2010. But most FSCs do not have tools, and macroprudential actions might be unpopular ("taking away the punch bowl"); in the absence of clear mandates, it is hard to see how new committees will want to take forceful actions to deter financial stability risks from rising, especially if there is a cost to current growth. But willingness to act is an area to track over time as conditions warrant more actions.[1]

In the meantime, monetary policymakers should not assume that new committees will take actions to offset pro-cyclicality in the financial sector to reduce dynamic financial stability risks. While new FSCs are formal arrangements to meet regularly and exchange views on financial stability, the lack of tools and political independence will limit the ability of new FSCs to act.

Conclusion

Substantial progress to increase the resilience of the financial system has been made since the financial crisis. Policymakers now should evaluate the net effects of the substantial set of new regulations on growth, although financial systems are still adjusting, and it may be too soon to make major changes.

More work is needed to develop frameworks for implementing dynamic macroprudential policies, as there are potential large benefits to be realized from developing these policies. Macroprudential policies can be an important complement to monetary policy, and countries that use both have the potential to achieve greater macroeconomic stability than if they relied only on monetary policy. With respect to the framework, I am optimistic about models that define a target based on risks to future economic growth but less optimistic that the new governance structures that have been set up are able and willing to take actions. For most large countries, monetary policy may be the only time-varying macro-stabilization tool, and monetary policymakers should be aware of the limitations of macroprudential policies.

Note

1. Lim and co-authors (2013) look at whether a more important role for the central bank leads to more timely macroprudential policy actions, based on a sample of thirty-one countries through 2010. While they find evidence of somewhat more rapid responses, they do not distinguish whether the benefits might arise from less need to coordinate when the central bank is a single authority or whether it has better skills for implementing time-varying policies.

References

Adrian, Tobias, Nina Boyarchenko, and Domenico Giannone. 2016. "Vulnerable Growth." Federal Reserve Bank of New York Staff Report 794.

Adrian, Tobias, Daniel Covitz, and Nellie Liang. 2015. "Financial Stability Monitoring." *Annual Review of Financial Economics* 7:357–395.

Aikman, David, Andreas Lehnert, Nellie Liang, and Michele Modugno. 2017. "Credit, Financial Conditions, and Monetary Policy Transmission." Hutchins Center Working Paper 39. Washington, DC: Hutchins Center on Fiscal and Monetary Policy at the Brookings Institution (revised draft of "Financial Vulnerabilities, Macroeconomic Dynamics, and Monetary Policy," Finance and Economics Discussion Series 2016–055).

Correa, Ricardo, Rochelle M. Edge, and Nellie Liang. 2017. "A New Dataset of Macroprudential Policy Governance Structures." *IFDP Notes*. Washington, DC: Board of Governors of the Federal Reserve System, November.

Edge, Rochelle M., and Nellie Liang. 2017. "New Financial Stability Governance Structures and Central Banks." Hutchins Center Working Paper 32. Washington, DC: Hutchins Center on Fiscal and Monetary Policy at the Brookings Institution.

IMF. 2014. "Staff Guidance Note on Macroprudential Policy." Washington, DC: International Monetary Fund.

IMF. 2017. *Global Financial Stability Report October 2017: Is Growth at Risk?* Washington, DC: International Monetary Fund.

Lim, C., I. Krznar, F. Lipinsky, A. Otani, and X. Wu. 2013. "The Macroprudential Framework: Policy Responsiveness and Institutional Arrangements." IMF Working Paper 13/166. Washington, DC: International Monetary Fund.

15

Some Thoughts on the Merits of Multipolar Regulation

Jeremy C. Stein

I agree with much of what David Aikman, Andrew G. Haldane, Marc Hinterschweiger, and Sujit Kapadia have to say about rethinking financial stability in chapter 11, in particular the suggestions that even now, after all of the reforms of the past several years, we are probably at the low end of the ideal range on overall bank capital levels, and that some of the more dramatic claims that were made about the adverse impact of higher capital on credit supply have not been borne out. Instead of belaboring this agreement, here I will focus on the one area where I have a somewhat different view than Aiken and colleagues, namely, the merits of what they call "multipolar" regulation. Much of what I have to say in what follows draws directly on recent work with Robin Greenwood, Sam Hanson, and Adi Sunderam (Greenwood et al. 2017).

By "multipolar" regulation, Aikman and colleagues mean a belt-and-suspenders regime in which there are multiple potentially binding constraints on the same item, namely, bank equity capital. The leading example here is the coexistence of a conventional risk-based capital requirement, which specifies that equity must exceed some fraction of risk-weighted assets, alongside a relatively aggressively calibrated version of the leverage ratio, which specifies that equity must also exceed some (lower) fraction of total unweighted balance sheet assets.

Proponents of a belt-and-suspenders approach such as Aiken and colleagues typically point to a couple of problems with the standard risk-based capital requirements. First, they are both complicated and vulnerable to gaming—especially when the risk weights are determined using banks' own internal models. In support of this point, their work shows that risk-based metrics were generally not very useful in predicting which banks failed during the crisis and that adding a simple leverage ratio to the failure-prediction equation significantly enhanced its predictive power. This empirical pattern likely reflects the extent to which the risk-based rules were being arbitraged in the precrisis period. Second, in a world of Knightian (1921) uncertainty, it is impossible for any single risk model to be "right." Therefore, the argument goes, a system that relies on multiple different rules, each with its own implicit risk model, is likely to be more robust.

While both of these observations are surely correct, and of crucial relevance in the design of a regulatory regime, it is less obvious that they point specifically to the need for a regime with multiple potentially binding constraints. With respect to gaming, *any* rule that has to be codified ex ante is going to be vulnerable to regulatory arbitrage; the overarching problem is not any particular risk-weighting scheme or set of risk models but rather timing. If the regulator moves first, and sets the rules in stone, and then the banks get to optimize against these rigid rules, they will inevitably find weaknesses in them, no matter how many different sets of rules there are. Seen in this light, the poor predictive power of the risk-based metrics for bank failure in the precrisis period likely reflects the fact that these were precisely the metrics that banks were most aggressively trying to exploit, insofar as the risk-based capital standards were the binding regulatory constraint during this period. As Goodhart's (1975) law cautions, once the leverage ratio starts being the test that more banks have to study for, it is likely to lose some of its predictive power for bank failure, for exactly the same gaming-related reasons. So it is somewhat dicey to rely on historical evidence of this sort to make a case for changing the nature of the rules.

With respect to Knightian uncertainty, there is no doubt that any given risk model is likely to be wrong. While this argues for entertaining multiple models, it need not argue for multiple competing constraints. Rather, one can imagine still having a single risk-based constraint, but one where the risk weights for any given asset are derived by, loosely speaking, averaging across a variety of plausible models or scenarios. This approach would tend to have the effect of increasing the risk weights on those assets for which there is the most Knightian uncertainty, and would probably make it very hard to defend near-zero risk weights for almost any asset. But, it is important to note, it need not be implemented with a system of multiple competing constraints.

Moreover, as Greenwood and co-authors (2017) demonstrate, there is a clear downside to having multiple potentially binding constraints. This is because when banks have heterogeneous business models, different constraints can bind in equilibrium for different banks. As a result, two banks can face divergent risk weights when performing the same activities, which distorts their behavior, just as would happen if different nonfinancial firms faced different relative marginal tax rates for the same two activities.

To illustrate, consider a situation in which we have only two constraints, a conventional risk-based ratio and an unweighted leverage ratio; two banks; and two categories of activity, consumer lending and intermediating Treasury securities. Under the risk-based regime, consumer lending has a risk weight of 100 percent, while holding Treasury securities has a risk weight of 0 percent. In contrast, under the leverage, both activities face a risk weight of 100 percent. Now suppose that bank A (for concreteness, think of Wells Fargo) has a strong consumer lending franchise but has no particular reason to be involved in holding much in the way of Treasury securities. Meanwhile, bank B (think of Goldman Sachs) has a broker-dealer business that requires it to hold many Treasuries but has no natural competitive strength in consumer lending. In this configuration, bank A, whose portfolio has a high concentration of consumer loans and a low concentration of Treasuries, will tend to be more tightly bound by the risk-based regime, and bank B will be more constrained by the leverage ratio.

As a result, Treasuries will look relatively more attractive at the margin to bank A than to bank B. From bank A's perspective, Treasuries require no incremental capital under its more binding constraint (the risk-based regime). In contrast, from bank B's perspective, both consumer loans and Treasuries require the same incremental equity under its more binding constraint (the leverage ratio). Thus bank A will have an incentive to take away some of bank B's broker-dealer business because bank A faces a zero marginal cost of inventorying Treasuries. Conversely, bank B will have an incentive to move into consumer lending, even though it is not any good at it. The result is a long-run "universal banking" equilibrium that tends in the direction of all banks doing the same thing, as opposed to specializing in those areas where they have a natural competitive advantage. To the extent that such a convergence in business models makes the financial system less resilient to certain kinds of systemic shocks, it is not something that should be artificially encouraged by the regulatory regime. And indeed, Greenwood and co-authors (2017) present some preliminary evidence that suggests that some convergence along these lines is already taking place.

However, even if a multipolar system of belt and suspenders is not the right way to deal with the problem of regulatory arbitrage, such arbitrage is nevertheless a first-order challenge that has to be addressed. So what can be done besides adding to the set of rules? Again, it is helpful to conceptualize the problem as being fundamentally one of timing, and of contingencies that are impossible to write into the rules as of the initial ex ante date. Consider, for example, a situation where, ex post, the regulator notices that banks are loading up to an unexpected degree on a particular type of loan that has a low risk weight in the rule that was written down ex ante. Moreover, the regulator suspects that this is in part because the loan is exposed to a type of risk that was not well captured in the ex ante risk-weighting scheme, that is, to a risk that was not contractible ex ante but that has now been revealed to be important by the banks' actions.

Greenwood and co-authors (2017) argue that a better response is not to impose another rigid ex ante rule as a patch on the first but instead to use the annual bank stress-testing process to fill in this ex post observable contingency after the fact. For example, the stress test in any given year could be designed to make particularly pessimistic assumptions about loan losses on any loan type that has grown unusually rapidly in the past year or two. Admittedly, this approach raises legitimate concerns about regulatory discretion and lack of transparency, but if the goal is to combat regulatory arbitrage, it may be more effective than proliferating more ex ante constraints.

As a matter of practical reality, the leverage ratio is not going to be abolished, and there are sensible arguments for keeping it in the background, as a less binding constraint that comes into play only in unusual circumstances. But the above discussion suggests that it would be desirable to calibrate it less aggressively, so that it has less effect on bank behavior in normal times. At the same time, the concerns about regulatory arbitrage highlighted by proponents of the leverage ratio like Aiken and his co-authors remain absolutely crucial, and one of the leading challenges for regulators to deal with going forward.

References

Goodhart, Charles A. E. 1975. "Problems of Monetary Management: The UK Experience." In *Monetary Theory and Practice: The UK Experience*. London: Macmillan.

Greenwood, Robin, Steen G. Hanson, Jeremy C. Stein, and Adi Sunderam. 2017. "Strengthening and Streamlining Bank Capital Regulation." *Brookings Papers on Economic Activity*. BPEA Conference Drafts, September 7–8.

Knight, Frank H. 1921. *Risk, Uncertainty, and Profit*. Boston: Hart, Schaffner & Marx / Houghton Mifflin.

IV

Inequality and Political Economy

16

Should Policymakers Care Whether Inequality Is Helpful or Harmful for Growth?

Jason Furman

The view that inequality is harmful for growth is increasingly fashionable among policymakers around the world. In the strongest form of this argument, high levels of inequality can make sustained growth impossible or even cause recessions. In a weaker form, lower levels of inequality are good for growth. Among policymakers, this view has almost entirely supplanted the traditional economic view that there was a trade-off between inequality and growth, and that greater inequality might be the cost of higher levels of growth.

This chapter is not a fresh attempt to assess the empirical evidence on inequality and growth or a survey of the existing literature. Instead the discussion addresses the question of whether policymakers should even be interested in this question in its traditional form and answers with a resounding no, for three reasons.

First, although more recent papers have reached the conclusion that exogenously higher levels of inequality result in lower longer-run growth rates, a number of studies have found more nuanced and complicated results: the magnitude and importance of inequality are not so high that inequality deserves a special place as an explanatory variable, and in general, cross-country growth regressions are inherently limited in their ability to make definitive and robust causal claims. Moreover, inequality can itself be endogenous, and different sources of inequality can have different consequences for growth. As a result, it is unlikely that any general statement about the relationship between inequality and growth would even be true—and even if one were true, it is unlikely that we could definitively document it.

Second, and more important, the cross-country literature has mostly focused on the impact of inequality on growth, not on the impact of policies to reduce inequality on growth. The former is of interest to social scientists and historians but it is the latter that is relevant for policymakers.

Third, and fundamentally, the question itself is misspecified, at least from the perspective of policymakers. From a normative perspective most policymakers do not care about the average of incomes in the economy—the left-hand-side variable posed in most of this literature—which accords equal weight to $1 added to the income of a poor person or a billionaire. Most social welfare functions would give that additional $1 more weight on the bottom than on the top. Certainly, politicians generally like to talk about the impact of their policies on "the middle class" or the poor or some other group, not simply the arithmetic average across the population. So even if inequality was bad for average growth, it still might be good for welfare, depending on the social welfare function used.

The aggregate question posed in much of the literature is not convincingly answerable, policy focused, or normatively relevant. Instead more research should focus on developing and analyzing left-hand-side variables that are normatively relevant, from simple ones such as median income, the income of the bottom quintile, or the mean of log income to more complicated aggregates such as the Organisation for Economic Co-operation and Development's (OECD)'s Multi-dimensional Living Standards (Boarini et al. 2016). Moreover, the right-hand-side variable of interest is not inequality in the aggregate but specific policies that might increase or reduce inequality.

Policies that reduce inequality while increasing growth—and there are many—are clearly worth prioritizing. But in many cases, there are trade-offs that need to be evaluated based on the magnitude of the trade-off and a social welfare function. The answer will vary area by area, but I provide some examples and evidence that suggest that in advanced economies, a lexicographic framework that focuses exclusively on distributional analysis, and considers growth only when the distribution of different policies is the same is generally likely to be appropriate under a broad range of social welfare functions. This is because the distributional effects of many policies are at least an order of magnitude larger than the growth effects. This is not to say that policies to promote growth are not important—they are. It is just that in the range of plausible policies, they are unlikely to have such large growth effects as to reverse the conclusions of a more naïve analysis that examined distribution alone.

In developing economies, the scope for policy- and institutionally induced variations in growth rates is much larger, and thus the lexicographic approach is unlikely to be as widely appropriate.

The first part of this chapter addresses the question in the title, namely, why many of the existing approaches to evaluating the impact of inequality on growth are misguided. In the second part of the chapter, I discuss some policy areas where reducing inequality and growth are complementary and how to evaluate trade-offs (if any), and assess how approaches might differ between developing and advanced economies.

Aggregate Analysis of the Impact of Inequality on Growth

Many surveys have considered the ways in which inequality could foster or impede growth; this is not the place to repeat them at length. Traditionally, more of an emphasis was placed on ways that inequality could support growth. From a macroeconomic perspective, Nicholas Kaldor (1955) argued that because higher-income households saved more, more skewed incomes would increase national savings, capital accumulation, and thus the level of output. The traditional microeconomic argument is that inequality provides an incentive for greater investments in human capital, risk taking, and entrepreneurship, all of which are critical for growth (Mirrlees 1971; Lazear and Rosen 1981).

On the other side, a number of arguments have been put forward about ways in which inequality is harmful for growth, including by cutting off segments of the population from the education they would need to be maximally innovative (Bell et al. 2017), by reducing trust and thus requiring more inefficient contracts (Stiglitz 1974; Bowles 2012), by making it harder to take risks because the consequences of failure can be even larger, and by leading to political instability and economically harmful policies (Alesina and Perotti 1996; Keefer and Knack 2002).

A steady stream of papers has attempted to empirically estimate the answer to this question. The aggregate literature starts with Alesina and Rodrik (1994), runs through a spate of papers in the late 1990s and early 2000s, and has recently been revived with notable contributions by the IMF and OECD. On balance, this literature, much of which has been summarized elsewhere (e.g., Cingano 2014; Boushey and Price 2014), has more often found that inequality is harmful to growth than helpful to growth, although the conclusion has varied a lot from paper to paper. Findings from a number of papers also suggest differential effects by a country's level of development, with inequality having a negative impact on growth for poorer countries and an insignificant or even positive effect for richer countries (e.g., Deininger and Squire 1998; Barro 2000; Forbes 2000; Knowles 2005; Castelló-Climent 2010), though some more recent research finds the opposite conclusion (Brueckner and Lederman 2015).

This literature, like all cross-country growth literature, is in some ways the best we can do in answering aggregate, general equilibrium questions. But like all cross-country growth regressions, it struggles with untangling causation from correlation, the noisiness and comparability of data, and the degrees of freedom problem when there are fewer countries than there are explanations of inequality. Although instrumental variables are used to find plausibly exogenous variations in inequality, the weakness of the instruments has raised doubts about the results (Kraay 2015).

Moreover, the literature may also suffer from the problem that there is not one true answer. For example, if inequality was caused by an increase in innovation that rewarded the innovators, it might be associated with stronger growth. But if inequality was caused by an expansion of rent seeking that limits competition, then it might be associated with lower growth. In reality, inequality may be the result of a mixture of such competitive and noncompetitive factors, depending on countries and periods, making it impossible to have a universal answer to the question of the impact of inequality on growth.

As a social scientist, if forced to answer the question of the effect of inequality on growth—recognizing the inevitably limited evidence and absence of anything resembling convincing causal identification—I would wager that inequality was harmful to growth if offered the opportunity at even odds but would not take the bet at anything worse than those odds. As a policymaker, however, I would not find that conclusion particularly useful for any specific decision or broader prioritization. In part, this is because of the lack of certainty about the evidence and the magnitude of those effects. In these results, reducing inequality is not necessarily the most important factor for boosting growth, and reasonable reductions in inequality do not result in large increases in growth. This is not to say that reducing inequality is not good, just that these empirical estimates give little reason to argue that the motivation for such reductions should be to achieve higher growth.

More important, however, the interpretation of the cross-country research suffers from two other issues: the interpretation of the right-hand-side variable of inequality and the meaningfulness of the left-hand-side variable of growth.

The Right-Hand-Side Variable: Inequality

The right-hand-side variable in almost all of this empirical work is inequality itself, not redistribution—with the notable exceptions of Ostry, Berg, and Tsangarides (2014) and OECD (2015), which examine the impact of both inequality and redistribution as measured by the difference between the Gini index for market income and the Gini index for post-tax and transfer income. In part, this focus has been the result of data limitations: until recently there were not comprehensive data sets that included measures of redistribution—and even now there are serious questions about the noisiness of those measures (Wittenberg 2015). However, it also reflects researchers' focus on a social science question—why do some countries grow more than others?—rather than on a policy-relevant question.

To illustrate the difference, imagine a literature that tried to determine whether it was better for a country to have an asset-to-GDP ratio of 75 or a debt-to-GDP ratio of 75. Undoubtedly, it would find that the former is better than the latter. Everything else being equal, what country would not prefer to have a sizable asset to a meaningful debt? It would not follow, however, that the right policy for a country with a 75 percent debt-to-GDP ratio would be to run large surpluses until it ended up with a 75 percent asset-to-GDP ratio.

Most of the literature and speculation on the aggregate impact of inequality is similar. One example is Alesina and Rodrik (1994), the paper that started the modern literature on the impact of growth on inequality. That paper found a statistically significant, economically meaningful, and robust negative impact of inequality on growth—the relevant conclusion for social scientists seeking to understand growth. But the model underlying the paper provided exactly the opposite lesson for policymakers. Specifically, the Alesina-Rodrik model has two features. The first feature of the model is that redistribution is economically inefficient, reducing growth (in their model, this is because the instrument of redistribution is capital taxation). The second feature of the model is that the greater the degree of inequality, the more a government will engage in redistribution (in their model, the median voter is decisive and her difference from the mean voter determines the magnitude of redistribution).

In the Alesina-Rodrik model, inequality is bad for growth only because it leads policymakers to undertake policies that are bad for growth. The same types of features persist in models up through today; for example, Halter, Oechslin, and Zweimüller (2014) have a model in which greater inequality leads the median voter to want more transfers at the expense of less investment in long-term public goods and thus less long-run growth. They too find that in the long run, inequality is detrimental to growth.

If these models are taken seriously, they suggest two lessons for policymakers. The first is that you are better off being born in a country that is endowed with a low level of inequality, which is about as useful as the advice that it is better to start with a large public asset than a large public debt. The second lesson, however, is that if your goal is to maximize growth, then you should *not* try to reduce inequality—either through the tax system (Alesina and Rodrik) or the transfer system (Halter, Oechslin, and Zweimüller)—because that would be bad for growth. That is precisely the opposite of the naïve interpretation of the headline empirical finding that inequality is bad for growth. Moreover, these particular models do not admit an "efficient" way to redistribute, and if they did, they would no longer explain their empirical finding that inequality is bad for growth. Effectively, these models are subject to the Lucas critique that if you try to exploit the reduced-form relationships they find in the data, the relationship will go away.

Consider an alternative model that has two features: policies to engage in upward redistribution through rent seeking and foreclosure of creative destruction are harmful to economic growth, and the greater the magnitude of inequality, the more powerful elites will be (this is not too far from the work of Daron Acemoglu, Simon Johnson, and James Robinson; see, e.g., Acemoglu, Johnson, and Robinson 2001). Such a model would be observationally equivalent to the Alesina-Rodrik or Halter-Oechslin-Zweimüller models in the cross-country growth literature. But it would have exactly the opposite conclusions, both about political economy (it would imply that to maximize growth, elites' power should be limited) and about policy (inequality-increasing policies themselves are bad for growth).

The purpose of this overview is not to take a stand on which of these interpretations is correct, just to suggest some of the limits of the policy relevance of the aggregate research and encourage more research on the specific links in the argument—or at least promote more clarity about what results are relevant to social scientists and what results are relevant to policymakers.

Some of the policy questions are discussed in the next section, but first I want to discuss the left-hand-side variable, economic growth.

The Left-Hand-Side Variable: Economic Growth

An even more fundamental issue about the question of whether inequality is good or bad for growth is that growth itself has limited normative usefulness as a guide to public policy. In part this is for the broadly accepted and conceptually straightforward reason that growth is not the same as welfare. A policy that raises GDP by one percentage point through everyone working harder will not increase everyone's welfare by one percentage point after the cost of the lost leisure is taken into account. For this reason, optimal policies in areas such as public finance and regulatory policies are generally based on welfare analysis or cost-benefit analysis and not on a simple GDP maximization exercise. As discussed below, this can be particularly relevant in assessing tax policies—especially when they present trade-offs between growth and inequality—because the welfare benefits can be only about one quarter of the headline growth effects.

More important is the fact that growth rates record the growth of the arithmetic average of individual or household incomes. This reflects one particular social welfare function in which $1 of income is equally good whether it goes to a billionaire or to a poor person. Similarly, under this metric a policy that raised a billionaire's income by $1,000 while lowering everyone else's by a combined $500 would be preferred to one that provided $400 evenly divided across the income distribution. This, of course, does not reflect the social welfare function that most policymakers would defend, as policies are more often advocated based on their purported benefits for the middle class. The view that $1 is equal at every income level is also inconsistent with the way individuals treat risk and marginal additions to their income.

Unfortunately, however, there is no unambiguously accepted social welfare function. One simple summary statistic would be to use median income instead of mean income, which has the virtue of being understandable to policymakers and may capture more of the normatively relevant changes in well-being than mean income. Of course, such a measure also throws out a tremendous amount of information about how incomes are changing for everyone who is not at the median.

An economist's first instinct might be to reach for the mean of log income. This metric reflects a particular way to combine growth and inequality, with a mean-preserving spread of incomes (i.e., greater inequality) lowering the indicator. In particular, it corresponds to the normative assumption that a 10 percent increase in income for a lower-income household is equivalent to a 10 percent increase in income for a higher-income household. There is some evidence from household-level and cross-country data that this is a reasonable description of the way people view their own satisfaction (Stevenson and Wolfers 2008). The evidence, however, does not rule out other possibilities for the curvature of the utility function.

A large literature on how people respond to risk finds the coefficient of relative risk aversion somewhere in the range of 1 to 4, with 2 being a general consensus value. This suggests that someone would be willing to give up somewhat more than 10 percent of his or her income in a high-income state to protect against a 10 percent loss of income in a low-income state. To the degree this intrapersonal experience is used as a basis of social welfare comparisons, it would suggest that the change in log income would understate the costs of inequality. Moreover, long-standing ethical arguments have advanced the proposition that the interpersonal comparison should be based on a greater degree of risk aversion than is empirically associated with individuals. In the extreme, infinite risk aversion would lead to the Rawlsian view that changes in welfare should be judged by the change for the worst-off person (Rawls 1971). In practical terms, such a welfare metric might correspond to looking at the change in income for the bottom quintile, a measure that, like the median income, has the benefit of being comprehensible to policymakers.

The Atkinson (1970) generalized mean provides a flexible framework that encompasses all of these alternative metrics. Most important, it allows policymakers to choose a normative parameter that reflects the weight that they put on changes in different parts of the income distribution, which can range from zero (which corresponds to mean incomes) to infinity (which corresponds to the Rawlsian case), with values of 1.5 (roughly corresponding to median income) and 50 (roughly corresponding to the bottom quintile) often employed (Boarini et al. 2016). Such measures, however, have the disadvantage that they are not readily understandable by policymakers and are not readily available.

Recent efforts by the OECD build on the Atkinson index to also incorporate the ways in which people value longevity and are averse to a greater risk of becoming unemployed, combining these measures together into Multi-dimensional Living Standards (Boarini et al. 2016). This measure moves even closer to a welfare-relevant metric, but at the cost of being even less intuitively meaningful to policymakers. Moreover, it places a lot of weight on mortality—which may correctly reflect individual preferences but has the downside of varying a lot based on factors beyond the traditional considerations.

If all of these measures generally moved together, then these considerations would be purely theoretical. Dollar and Kraay (2002) found that the level and growth of GDP are highly correlated with the level and growth of the bottom quintile in a large sample of countries. If you are only interested in the relative well-being of the bottom 20 percent across the Central African Republic, Brazil, and the United States, comparing GDP per capita will give you a reasonable approximation. But the differences among the Central African Republic, Brazil, and the United States are much greater in magnitude than what could be driven by policy choices, especially in rich countries with relatively mature economic institutions over any relevant time horizon. In the case of the advanced economies, in particular, aggregate growth rates are a poor proxy for alternative normative metrics.

An illustration of these differences is provided by table 16.1, which shows growth rates for the G-7 countries from 1995 to 2015 or the closest available dates. The United States is tied with the United Kingdom for the highest growth rate in GDP per capita over this period but is near the bottom of the group in the growth of the incomes of the bottom 20 percent, the median household, and the OECD's two measures of Multi-dimensional Living Standards. The measure of the change in log income—measured indirectly using the change in income and the change in the Gini coefficient under the assumptions that incomes are

Table 16.1

Annualized Growth Rates of Alternative Measures of Economic Growth in G-7 Countries, 1995–2015

| | GDP per Capita | Bottom Quintile Average Household Income | Median Household Income | OECD Multi-dimensional Living Standards | | Mean Log GDP per Capita |
				Poorest 10% of Households	Median Household	
Canada	1.4	0.4	0.7	3.0	3.4	1.3
France	1.0	0.7	0.6	2.4	2.7	0.9
Germany	1.3	−0.2	−0.2	2.4	2.6	0.6
Italy	0.2	1.1	0.3	0.9	1.3	−0.1
Japan	0.8			1.1	1.4	0.5
United Kingdom	1.5	2.0	1.8	2.8	3.4	1.7
United States	1.5	0.0	0.3	1.5	2.4	1.2

Note: Bottom quintile and median household income are from 1994–2010 for Canada, France, and Germany; from 1995–2010 for Italy; and from 1994–2014 for the United Kingdom and United States. Mean log GDP per capita is from 1995–2014 for France, Germany, Italy, and Japan.
Sources: Organisation for Economic Co-operation and Development, Gornick and others (2016), Solt (2016), and author's calculations.

log-normally distributed (Stevenson and Wolfers 2016)—shows a different trend as well.

Moreover, the relevant question for policymakers is not whether the level or growth of incomes is correlated with the level or growth of these welfare-based measures. This is still the example of the Central African Republic versus the United States. Instead, the relevant question is this: What is the impact of a *policy-induced change* on the change in average incomes and these other welfare measures? To the degree that one is considering policies that create trade-offs between growth and distribution—which is the only question that requires thinking through these issues—then the correlation in the policy-driven deltas on these different metrics might be even lower than in the aggregate data.

Evaluating Particular Policies That Affect Inequality and Growth

There is no unambiguously correct metric for assessing policies. But ultimately, policymakers are concerned with the question of how a given policy intervention affects the well-being of the bottom quintile, the typical citizen, the bulk of the middle class, or possibly, in some rare cases (the exceedingly rational policymakers in Singapore?), mean log income.

This question shifts the focus from broader macroeconomic considerations to the more microeconomic analysis of specific policies. Posed this way, it is clear that there is no one answer to the question. Clearly, there are policies that support both growth and inequality reduction, education being one widely accepted example. There are also inequality-reducing policies that dramatically reduce growth, likely making everyone worse off—with Venezuela being just the most vivid recent case. And there are policies that might result in a small reduction in growth rates (measured in the conventional manner) but, by reducing inequality, would actually increase the growth in living standards for the bulk of citizens. The fact that policies in the real world reflect a mixture of all of the above is another reason to believe that there is no single and true answer to the question of whether inequality is good or bad for growth.

All-Good-Things-Go-Together Policies

The easiest case is policies where all good things go together, increasing growth rates (or creating a one-time increase in the level of output) and reducing inequality. Such policies are worth adopting on any of the metrics for adopting them. There appears to be a wide range of such policies, perhaps wider than policymakers had traditionally considered.

One of the strongest cases for an all-good-things-go-together policy is in education. This is clearly the case for reforms that do not cost money, for example, reforms to improve the quality of K–12 education or shifting to a more Australian-like system of income-based repayments for higher education. Many reforms that do cost money, for example, expanded preschool in the United States, would also likely generate economic benefits that exceed the deadweight loss associated with the taxes to fund them (Council of Economic Advisers [CEA] 2015).

A second area may be support for low-income households with children. Traditionally, economists viewed public programs like Medicaid and nutrition assistance through the lens of moral hazard, treating them as providing consumption-smoothing insurance or redistribution but at the cost of work incentives. A newer literature that uses long-term administrative data to focus on the children in households receiving these benefits is finding substantial long-term increases in college graduation rates, improved labor earnings, and decreased mortality associated with benefits received in childhood (e.g., Heckman et al. 2010 and Ludwig and Miller 2007 for preschool; Brown, Kowalski, and Lurie 2015 for Medicaid; Hoynes, Schanzenbach, and Almond 2016 for Medicaid; and Chetty, Hendren, and Katz 2016 for housing vouchers).

A third potential area for all-good-things-go-together policies is competition policy. Specifically, recent research has identified a number of ways in which imperfect competition in labor or product markets is leading to increased inequality—the so-called "rise of rents" (Stiglitz 2012; Furman and Orszag 2015; Barkai 2016). Moreover, the same lack of competition that gave rise to these rents may also be inhibiting investment and innovation (Aghion et al. 2005; Gilbert 2006; Gutiérrez and Philippon 2017). To the degree that greater competition can reduce these rents, both the distribution of income and efficiency would improve.

This could be relevant in product markets, for example, through more vigorous antitrust policy, less strict intellectual property policies, or increased ownership by consumers of their data. It also could be relevant in labor markets, where efforts to combat collusion, reduce noncompete agreements, or increase the minimum wage or unionization have the prospect not only of reducing inequality but also of reducing or redistributing rents in a manner that is efficiency-neutral or even efficiency-improving.

Policies that improve either growth (conventionally measured) without affecting the distribution of income or, conversely, the distribution of income without affecting growth would also fall into this category. Revenue-neutral business tax reform, for example, has the prospect of raising the level of output with no meaningful impact on the distribution of income. Other growth-enhancing measures, such as infrastructure spending or expanded research funding, might affect the distribution of income but in ways that have been little studied and could reasonably be considered second order for this purpose.

Evaluating Trade-offs: The Example of Tax Reform

While one might debate whether specific policies truly belong in the all-good-things-go-together category, there is no debate that policies in this category are worth pursuing. The trickier question arises when policies cause a trade-off. To understand how to evaluate trade-offs in theory and how they actually work out in practice, I will examine a toy example from tax policy that reflects the canonical trade-off between output and distribution generally assumed in the public finance literature (although not necessarily universal; see, e.g., Zidar 2017 on evidence that tax cuts for lower-income households might have larger effects on employment than tax cuts for higher-income households).

Specifically, consider a 10 percent reduction in labor taxes paid for by a lump-sum tax in the Ramsey framework put forward by N. Gregory Mankiw and Matthew Weinzierl (2006). Under these parameters, this policy would increase output by 1 percent and raise welfare by an amount equivalent to a 0.5 percent increase in consumption in the long run for the representative agent (the welfare increase is lower because of the cost of forgone leisure).[1]

The representative agent case, of course, is not particularly relevant for assessing the distributional impacts of public policy. To do that I drop the representative agent assumption and apply this tax policy to the actual distribution of U.S. incomes in 2010. In this case essentially all households see an increase in their before-tax labor incomes—just as in the representative agent case, as shown in table 16.2. But two-thirds of households see an increase in their taxes, as the $900 lump-sum tax needed to finance the rate reduction (net of the dynamic feedback effect of 12 percent) is larger than the 10 percent rate reduction. For example, consider households in the second quintile. On average they would see a $570 net increase in their taxes from the shift to lump sum taxation—which would not be offset by the additional $180 they earned by working more hours.

Overall, when both of these are taken into account, only 46 percent of households see an increase in their after-tax incomes. This is not the only consideration for welfare. In the case of the middle quintile, for example, the increased earnings and the increased taxes roughly offset each other, but with work hours up 1 percent, the overall impact on utility would be equivalent to a 0.6 percent reduction in consumption. Families in the top two quintiles, however, would be better off on average.

Table 16.2

Economic Effects of Shifting from a Hypothetical 25% Proportional Income Tax to a 22.5% Labor Income Tax, 25% Capital Income Tax, and $900 Lump-Sum Tax

	Percent of Households
Before-tax income increase	96
Tax increase	67
After-tax income increase	46
Welfare increase	41

Note: Aggregate economic impacts were computed using the macroeconomic model of Mankiw and Weinzierl (2006). Values for individual families are assumed to change by the same percentage as the aggregate values. The distribution of income is derived from the 2010 IRS Statistics of Income Public Use File. See Furman (2016) for additional details. Utility is computed as log(after-tax income) $- n^{(1 + 1/\sigma)}$, where n is the value of labor supply generated by the Mankiw-Weinzierl model (assuming an isoelastic specification of labor disutility).
Source: Furman (2016).

To map this back into the framework discussed above, while mean after-tax income rises by 1 percent, the log of after-tax income falls by 1 percent, as shown in table 16.3. Using the utility function assumed in the model and assuming these utilities are interpersonally, additively comparable, then welfare also declines. The same is also true of a social welfare function that uses the log of utility to effectively place less weight on the utility of higher-income households than lower-income households.

These results do not provide an answer to the question of whether this tax policy is a good idea. But I suspect that most of the policymakers who might otherwise have been attracted to the promise of the higher growth associated with this particular reform would overall object to the policy if they understood that this growth was achieved by higher taxes on two-thirds of households, a policy that would leave the median household working harder to earn about the same after-tax income.

Importantly, these results generalize to a large class of tax policies. Oversimplifying somewhat, greater growth can be achieved only by making the tax system less progressive in most models. The traditional revenue-neutral, distribution-neutral tax reform will leave the effective tax rate on labor income unchanged.[2] Moreover, the growth effects of tax changes are about an order of magnitude smaller than the distributional

Table 16.3

Economic Effects of Shifting from a Hypothetical 25% Proportional Income Tax to a 22.5% Labor Income Tax, 25% Capital Income Tax, and $900 Lump-Sum Tax

	Baseline (25% Flat Tax)	Alternative (22.5% Labor Tax + $900 Lump Sum)	Percent Change
Income			
Mean after-tax income	50,221	50,788	**1.1**
Log after-tax income	10.2	10.1	**−1.0**
Welfare			
Mean utility	10.00	9.89	
Mean log of (Utility + 1)	2.39	2.36	

Note: Aggregate economic impacts were computed using the macroeconomic model of Mankiw and Weinzierl (2006). Values for individual families are assumed to change by the same percentage as the aggregate values. The distribution of income is derived from the 2010 IRS Statistics of Income Public Use File. Utility is computed as log(after-tax income) − $n^{(1 + 1/\sigma)}$, where n is the value of labor supply generated by the Mankiw-Weinzierl model (assuming an isoelastic specification of labor disutility). See Furman (2016) for additional details.
Source: Furman (2016).

effects of tax changes—and the disparity between the welfare and distribution effects is even larger. For example, the U.S. Department of the Treasury's (2006b) analysis of the 2005 Bush Tax Reform Panel's Simplified Income Tax plan found it would increase national income by 0.2 to 0.9 percent in the long run, and Altig and others (2001) found that a flat tax with transition relief would increase national income by 2 percent in the long run. These are similar in magnitudes to a wide range of estimates from official organizations of recent tax proposals, as shown in table 16.4.

Moreover, the estimates in table 16.4 are for growth, not welfare. To the extent growth was generated by reduced leisure (i.e., more work) or reduced consumption (i.e., greater savings), the welfare increases could be considerably smaller than the growth numbers would suggest. Also, policies that boost GDP growth by increasing foreign borrowing would result in a larger fraction of future GDP being used to repay foreigners—and thus a smaller increase in GNP or National Income, which are closer to the welfare-relevant measures.

Table 16.4

Select Estimates of the Effect of Tax Reform on the Level of Output

Source	Policy Change	Short Run	Long Run
Gravelle (2014)	Stylized reform: 20% reduction in income tax rates	NR	0.7–4.0
JCT (2014)	Camp Plan	0.1–1.6	NR
U.S. Department of the Treasury (2006b)	President's Advisory Panel on Tax Reform		
	Simplified income tax	0.0–0.4	0.2–0.9
	Growth and investment tax	0.1–1.9	1.4–4.8
	Progressive consumption tax	0.2–2.3	1.9–6.0
U.S. Department of the Treasury (2006a)	Permanent extension of the 2001/2003 tax cuts		
	Financed with future spending cuts	0.5	0.7
	Financed with future tax increases	0.8	(0.9)
JCT (2005)	Cut in federal individual income tax rates (4.0% in first decade, 2.9% thereafter)		
	Not financed	0.0–0.5	(0.2)–(0.6)
	Financed with future spending cuts	0.1–0.3	0.3–0.4
	20% cut in federal corporate tax rate		
	Not financed	0.2–0.4	0.0–0.3
	Financed with future spending cuts	0.2–0.4	0.5–0.9
Dennis et al. (2004)	10% cut in federal individual income tax rates		
	Financed with future spending cuts	0.2	(0.4)
	Financed with future tax increases	0.3	(2.1)
Altig et al. (2001)	Stylized revenue-neutral tax reforms		
	Flat tax with transition relief	0.5	1.9

Notes: Output measure is (in order of preference if multiple measures are reported) national income, real gross national product, and real gross domestic product. Time period for short-run effects varies across studies, but (in most cases) is an average over several years in the first decade. Long-run effects typically reflect estimates of the change in the steady state level of output. NR = Not reported. Italics indicate negative values. JCT refers to U.S. Congress, Joint Committee on Taxation, for the relevant years.

Source: Furman (2016)

Table 16.5
Change in After-Tax Income Due to Changes in Average Tax Rates by Income Percentile, 1986 to 2013

Income Percentile	Percent Change
0–20	6.6
20–40	7.1
40–60	6.5
60–80	4.5
80–90	2.7
90–95	0.7
95–99	−3.4
99–100	−12.4

Note: Net of tax rate is 100 minus the average tax rate. Change in after-tax income due to changes in average tax rate is the percent change in the net of tax rate.
Source: Furman (2016).

In contrast, table 16.5 shows the impact on after-tax incomes of the cumulative tax and spending changes from 1986 to 2013, showing that these can easily raise or lower incomes by 6 or even 12 percent. The expanded tax credits and health insurance subsidies enacted in 2009 and 2010, for example, raised the after-tax income of the bottom two quintiles by 18 percent and 6 percent, respectively (CEA 2016). No mainstream modeling of a tax plan has an effect close to as large, let alone one that would take effect immediately.

The implications of this are that a welfarist analyzing tax policies that entail trade-offs between efficiency and equity would not be far off in just looking at static distribution tables and ignoring any dynamic effects altogether. This is true for just about any social welfare function that places a greater weight on absolute gains for households at the bottom than at the top. Under such an approach, policymaking could still be done under a lexicographic process—so two tax plans with the same distribution would be evaluated on the basis of whichever had higher growth rates (e.g., a reformed business tax system versus the status quo). But in this case growth would be the last consideration, not the first.

Does the Tax Reform Example Generalize to Other Policies?
Analyzing tax policies has the advantage of drawing on a broad set of theoretical and empirical models that integrate output, distribution, and

welfare. In most other policy domains we do not have anything close to this. Nevertheless, I would speculate that the lexicographic approach of considering distribution first and then growth is broadly applicable to the types of policy decisions facing the advanced economies, not to the types of policy decisions facing the emerging economies.

The basis for the speculation that policymakers in advanced economies should effectively prioritize distribution while policymakers in emerging markets should balance the two comes from the fact that mature economies have relatively small variations in their growth rates while less mature ones have much wider variations. As shown in figure 16.1, which plots annual growth rates for 1980 to 2014 against per capita income levels in 1980 for all the non-oil economies for which data are available, lower-income countries have exhibited substantial variations in per capita annual growth rates that are largely not explained by convergence (Pritchett 1997). In contrast, higher-income countries have all had much more similar growth rates, with even the smaller differences explained largely by convergence as the initially lower-income countries caught up with the higher-income ones.

Overall, the interquartile range of growth rates for the countries that met the World Bank's classification for low- or middle-income countries

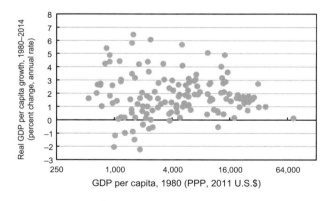

Figure 16.1

Absolute Convergence across the World.
Note: PPP denotes purchasing power parity. Excludes oil economies.
Source: Penn World table, version 9.0 (https://www.rug.nl/ggdc/productivity/pwt); author's calculations.

at the beginning of the period was 2.1 percent, while for high-income countries it was 0.5 percent. Looking at the residuals from a regression of per capita growth rates on log per capita initial incomes, the respective interquartile ranges are also 2.1 percent and 0.5 percent.

These numbers provide an indicative sense of the upper bound on policy shifts. For an advanced economy, moving the tax, regulatory, legal, educational, trade, and other policies from the 25th percentile of peer countries to the 75th percentile of peer countries would be a herculean effort. And the fact that the growth rates between these percentiles vary by a few tenths annually suggests the difficulty of achieving much larger growth effects from such a policy.

This exercise does not establish bounds on the impact of policies. On the one hand, these ranges could overstate the plausible impact of policy changes if luck or endowments had a substantial impact on growth rates. On the other hand, if countries have offsetting collections of good and bad policies, then just shifting all policies in a good direction could have a larger impact on growth than is found in actual sample of countries. Nevertheless, it appears consistent with a much wider scope for policies to have an impact on growth rates in developing countries than in advanced economies.

Overall, that the United States and France have nearly identical levels of productivity even though France fares considerably worse on most measures of regulation is just a vivid example of the fact that for mature economies with mature institutions, the difference in growth rates that results from different policies is considerably lower than one might suspect. This is true based both on bottom-up estimates of the growth impacts of individual policies and the top-down analysis presented here of the difference in growth rates across the advanced economies.

Conclusion

The question of whether inequality is good or bad for growth is an interesting and important one that deserves time and attention from social scientists, though I am skeptical it lends itself to a clear answer because the many different sources of inequality may have many different impacts on growth.

The interests of policymakers are different from the interests of social scientists. Policymakers are concerned not with inequality per se—which they cannot choose—but with policies that affect inequality. And they are, or at least profess to be, not concerned with growth but with how the policies they pursue affect their population, understood variously as the median income, the bottom quintile, the average income for the bottom 90 percent, or the many other metrics that draw on information from across the distribution.

Policies exist in all quadrants of the two-by-two matrix: good for both growth and distribution, good for one but not the other, or bad for both. Two of those quadrants are straightforward: policymakers should be working to identify all-good-things-go-together policies and avoid the opposite. In the case of trade-offs, the answer is less obvious, but as an empirical matter it is plausible that a number of policies in advanced economies have first-order distributional impacts but only second-order effects on growth, which suggests that policymakers focused on just about anything except mean incomes would be better off evaluating their merits solely on the basis of the static impact on distribution.

It is plausible that a flat tax, for example, might have boosted U.S. growth—but by only a tenth or two annually, which would not be enough to materially change the results from just looking at the direct effect of the tax change on incomes. In contrast, just about anyone would take China's deal of higher growth rates plus higher inequality—including the more than 800 million people lifted out of extreme poverty in China since 1980.

Going forward, as we continue to rethink macroeconomics, better incorporating welfare and distributional considerations into models and understanding how they relate to specific policy instruments will be important. The fact that we cannot agree on the appropriate social welfare function is not an argument for choosing one particular social welfare function—the average of incomes—that is inconsistent with the way most policymakers describe their ultimate goals.

Notes

1. See Furman (2016) for details underlying these calculations.

2. Such a reform lowers the statutory tax rate but also raises the after-tax price of items the person would like to buy, such as mortgages, charity, or health care. As a result, the effective rate is essentially unchanged—although the details depend on the income elasticity of specific base broadeners and on how behavior works in practice.

References

Acemoglu, Daron, Simon Johnson, and James A. Robinson. 2001. "The Colonial Origins of Comparative Development: An Empirical Investigation." *American Economic Review* 91 (5): 1369–1401.

Aghion, Philippe, Nick Bloom, Richard Blundell, Rachel Griffith, and Peter Howitt. 2005. "Competition and Innovation: An Inverted-U Relationship." *Quarterly Journal of Economics* 120 (2): 701–728.

Alesina, Alberto, and Roberto Perotti. 1996. "Income Distribution, Political Instability, and Investment." *European Economic Review* 40 (6): 1203–1228.

Alesina, Alberto, and Dani Rodrik. 1994. "Distributive Politics and Economic Growth." *Quarterly Journal of Economics* 109 (2): 465–490.

Altig, David, Alan J. Auerbach, Laurence J. Kotlikoff, Kent A. Smetters, and Jan Walliser. 2001. "Simulating Fundamental Tax Reform in the United States." *American Economic Review* 91 (3): 574–595.

Atkinson, Anthony B. 1970. "On the Measurement of Inequality." *Journal of Economic Theory* 2 (3): 244–263.

Barkai, Simcha. 2016. "Declining Labor and Capital Shares." Stigler Center New Working Paper Series 2. Chicago: University of Chicago, Booth School of Business.

Barro, Robert J. 2000. "Inequality and Growth in a Panel of Countries." *Journal of Economic Growth* 5 (1): 5–32.

Bell, Alexander M., Raj Chetty, Xavier Jaravel, Neviana Petkova, and John Van Reenan. 2017. "Who Becomes an Inventor in America? The Importance of Exposure to Innovation." NBER Working Paper 24062. Cambridge, MA: National Bureau of Economic Research.

Boarini, Romina, Fabrice Murtin, Paul Schreyer, and Marc Fleurbaey. 2016. "Multi-dimensional Living Standards: A Welfare Measure Based on Preferences." OECD Statistics Working Paper 2016/05. Paris: OECD Publishing.

Boushey, Heather, and Carter C. Price. 2014. *How Are Economic Inequality and Growth Connected? A Review of Recent Research*. Washington, DC: Washington Center for Equitable Growth.

Bowles, Samuel. 2012. *The New Economics of Inequality and Redistribution*. Cambridge: Cambridge University Press.

Brown, David W., Amanda E. Kowalski, and Ithai Z. Lurie. 2015. "Medicaid as an Investment in Children: What Is the Long-term Impact on Tax Receipts?" NBER Working Paper 20835. Cambridge, MA: National Bureau of Economic Research.

Brueckner, Markus, and Daniel Lederman. 2015. "Effects of Income Inequality on Aggregate Output." Policy Research Working Paper 7317. Washington, DC: World Bank.

Castelló-Climent, Amparo. 2010. "Inequality and Growth in Advanced Economies: An Empirical Investigation." *Journal of Economic Inequality* 8 (3): 293–321.

Chetty, Raj, Nathaniel Hendren, and Lawrence F. Katz. 2016. "The Effects of Exposure to Better Neighborhoods on Children: New Evidence from the Moving to Opportunity Experiment." *American Economic Review* 106 (4): 855–902.

Cingano, Frederico. 2014. "Trends in Income Inequality and Its Impact on Economic Growth." OECD Social, Employment and Migration Working Papers 163. Paris: OECD Publishing.

Council of Economic Advisers. 2015. "The Economics of Early Childhood Investments." Report. The White House, January. https://obamawhitehouse.archives.gov/sites/default/files/docs/early_childhood_report_update_final_non-embargo.pdf.

Council of Economic Advisers. 2016. "The Economic Record of the Obama Administration: Progress Reducing Inequality." Report. The White House, September. https://obamawhitehouse.archives.gov/sites/default/files/page/files/20160923_record_inequality_cea.pdf.

Deininger, Klaus, and Lyn Squire. 1998. "New Ways of Looking at Old Issues: Inequality and Growth." *Journal of Development Economics* 57 (2): 259–287.

Dennis, Robert, et al. 2004. "Macroeconomic Analysis of a 10 Percent Cut in Income Tax Rates." CBO Technical Paper Series 2004–07. Washington, DC: Congressional Budget Office.

Dollar, David, and Aart Kraay. 2002. "Growth Is Good for the Poor." *Journal of Economic Growth* 7 (3): 195–225.

Forbes, Kristin J. 2000. "A Reassessment of the Relationship between Inequality and Growth." *American Economic Review* 90 (4): 869–887.

Furman, Jason. 2016 "Dynamic Analysis, Welfare, and Implications for Tax Reform." Remarks at the National Bureau of Economic Research Conference "Tax Policy and the Economy," Washington, DC, September 22.

Furman, Jason, and Peter Orszag. 2015. "A Firm-Level Perspective on the Role of Rents in the Rise in Inequality." Paper presented at "A Just Society" Centennial Event in Honor of Joseph Stiglitz, New York, October 16.

Gilbert, Robert. 2006. "Looking for Mr. Schumpeter: Where Are We in the Competition-Innovation Debate?" *Innovation Policy and the Economy* 6:159–215.

Gornick, Janet, Thierry Kruten, Branko Milanovic, David Leonhardt, and Kevin Quealy. 2016. LIS/*New York Times* Income Distribution Database (2016). April.

Gravelle, Jane G. 2014. *Dynamic Scoring for Tax Legislation: A Review of Models*. Washington, DC: Congressional Research Service.

Gutiérrez, Germán, and Thomas Philippon. 2017. "Declining Competition and Investment in the U.S." NBER Working Paper 23583. Cambridge, MA: National Bureau of Economic Research.

Halter, Daniel, Manuel Oechslin, and Josef Zweimüller. 2014. "Inequality and Growth: The Neglected Time Dimension." *Journal of Economic Growth* 19 (1): 81–104.

Heckman, James J., Seong Hyeok Moona, Rodrigo Pintoa, Peter A. Savelyeva, and Adam Yavitz. 2010. "The Rate of Return to the High/Scope Perry Preschool Program." *Journal of Public Economics* 94 (1): 114–128.

Hoynes, Hilary, Diane Whitmore Schanzenbach, and Douglas Almond. 2016. "Long-Run Impacts of Childhood Access to the Safety Net." *American Economic Review* 106 (4): 903–934.

Kaldor, Nicholas. 1955. "Alternative Theories of Distribution." *Review of Economic Studies* 23 (2): 83–100.

Keefer, Philip, and Stephen Knack. 2002. "Polarization, Politics and Property Rights: Links between Inequality and Growth." *Public Choice* 111 (1): 127–154.

Knowles, Stephen. 2005. "Inequality and Economic Growth: The Empirical Relationship Reconsidered in the Light of Comparable Data." *Journal of Development Studies* 41 (1): 135–159.

Kraay, Aart. 2015. "Weak Instruments in Growth Regressions: Implications for Recent Cross-Country Evidence on Inequality and Growth." World Bank Policy Research Working Paper 7494. Washington, DC: World Bank.

Lazear, Edward P., and Sherwin Rosen. 1981. "Rank-Order Tournaments as Optimum Labor Contracts." *Journal of Political Economy* 89 (5): 841–864.

Ludwig, Jens, and Douglas Miller. 2007. "Does Head Start Improve Children's Life Chances? Evidence from a Regression Discontinuity Design." *Quarterly Journal of Economics* 122 (1): 159–208.

Mankiw, N. Gregory, and Matthew Weinzierl. 2006. "Dynamic Scoring: A Back-of-the-Envelope Guide." *Journal of Public Economics* 90 (8): 1415–1433.

Mirrlees, James A. 1971. "An Exploration in the Theory of Optimum Income Taxation." *Review of Economic Studies* 38 (2): 175–208.

Organisation for Economic Co-operation and Development. 2015. "The Impact of Income Inequality on Economic Growth." In *In It Together: Why Less Inequality Benefits All*. Paris: OECD Publishing.

Ostry, Jonathan D, Andrew Berg, and Charalambos G. Tsangarides. 2014. "Redistribution, Inequality, and Growth." IMF Staff Discussion Note 14/02. Washington, DC: International Monetary Fund.

Pritchett, Lant. 1997. "Divergence, Big Time." *Journal of Economic Perspectives* 11 (3): 3–17.

Rawls, John. 1971. *A Theory of Justice*. Cambridge, MA: Belknap Press of Harvard University Press.

Solt, Frederick. 2016. "The Standardized World Income Inequality Database." *Social Science Quarterly* 97 (5): 1267–1281. SWIID Version 6.0, July 2017.

Stevenson, Betsey, and Justin Wolfers. 2008. "Economic Growth and Subjective Well-Being: Reassessing the Easterlin Paradox." *Brookings Papers on Economic Activity* (1): 1–87.

Stevenson, Betsey, and Justin Wolfers. 2016. *Inequality and Subjective Well-Being.* Slides.

Stiglitz, Joseph E. 1974. "Incentives and Risk Sharing in Sharecropping." *Review of Economic Studies* 41 (2): 219–255.

Stiglitz, Joseph E. 2012. *The Price of Inequality: How Today's Divided Society Endangers Our Future.* New York: W. W. Norton.

U.S. Congress, Joint Committee on Taxation. 2005. "Macroeconomic Analysis of Various Proposals to Provide $500 Billion in Tax Relief." Report JCX-4-05. http://www.jct.gov/x-4-05.pdf.

U.S. Congress, Joint Committee on Taxation. 2014. "Macroeconomic Analysis of the 'Tax Reform Act of 2014.'" Report JCX-22-14. https://www.jct.gov/publications.html?func=startdown&id=4564.

U.S. Department of the Treasury, Office of Tax Analysis. 2006a. "A Dynamic Analysis of Permanent Extension of the President's Tax Relief." July 25. https://www.treasury.gov/resource-center/tax-policy/Documents/Report-Dynamic-Analysis-2006.pdf.

U.S. Department of the Treasury, Office of Tax Analysis. 2006b. "A Summary of the Dynamic Analysis of the Tax Reform Options Prepared for the President's Advisory Panel on Federal Tax Reform."

Wittenberg, Martin. 2015. "Problems with SWIID: The Case of South Africa." *Journal of Economic Inequality* 13 (4): 673–677.

Zidar, Owen M. 2017. "Tax Cuts for Whom? Heterogeneous Effects of Income Tax Changes on Growth and Employment." NBER Working Paper 21035. Cambridge, MA: National Bureau of Economic Research.

17
Policy, Inequality, and Growth

Dani Rodrik

Jason Furman in chapter 16 has written an important and insightful piece that should be read by all policymakers and applied economists. It stands as a nice example of how economic theory and evidence can be combined with policy judgment to produce meaningful input to public policy. I have organized my responses to his chapter under the headings of the three claims that I take to be central to his argument.

The first claim is that cross-country inequality-growth regressions are not very helpful for policy. I agree, as one of the early authors who contributed to that literature. There are several key issues here. One is that it is not always clear in these regressions what the actual policy is that affects inequality. Furman nicely illustrates the point by using my old paper with Alesina, where we find inequality is negatively correlated with growth, but the argument is that inequality-reducing policy (a tax on capital) is actually detrimental to growth. A deeper, related point is that the econometrics that one uses here tends to be immune to policy implications. Social scientists want to explain and look for clear identification, which usually comes through exogenous variation due to history or geography. Paradoxically, the more successful they are (in the sense of high explanatory power), the less room there is for agency for policymakers.

We could, of course, relate inequality outcomes directly to policy choices. But this runs into another problem that Furman does not discuss. Policy choices are not random but respond to various objectives— economic and political, desirable or undesirable. In these circumstances, the partial correlation between policy and outcomes does not reveal the true underlying relationship. Consider the simplest case where policymakers choose policy to maximize its impact on growth. The partial correlation in the data will be zero (since that is what the first-order condition of the policymaker's optimization problem requires). But that certainly does not mean that the policy in question has no effect on growth. For a generalization of this point to diverse policy settings and policy objectives, including political ones, see Rodrik (2012).

I would, however, say that the cross-country empirical literature has not been entirely useless. It has countered a widely held view that inequality is desirable for—or a necessary concomitant of—growth. We know now that this is not the case. There is no necessary trade-off.

Furman's second claim in chapter 16 is that the "growth" effects of actual policies (such as tax changes) are much smaller than the redistributive effects. I put "growth" in quotation marks because the effects that Furman discusses (at least in the original version of the work) are not long-run growth effects but steady-state level effects. This is a valid point for the kind of tax rates we normally discuss, and one that is not often noticed. Heuristically, it follows from the fact that distributive effects are rectangles ($\approx qX\Delta p$) while efficiency gains are triangles ($\approx \frac{1}{2}\,\Delta qX\Delta p$).

In discussing why trade policy is politically so contentious, I have often made a similar argument in the context of tariffs—which are, after all, another kind of tax, on imports. Specifically, let's define the ratio of the redistribution to the efficiency/output gains of a policy change as the "political cost-benefit ratio" (PCBR) of the change. In Rodrik (1994, 2018), I discuss how this ratio can be calculated in stylized economic settings. Two conclusions come across.

First, as Furman suggests, the amount of redistribution that is required to generate $1 of efficiency gain is typically very large, of the order of $5 or more. But there is a second conclusion that is also important: redistribution increases relative to efficiency gains as the taxes that are removed or reduced get smaller. In other words, the PCBR is falling in the tax wedge that is eliminated. This result is general and follows from a central insight of public finance: the efficiency loss due to a tax rises not linearly but with the square of the tax. The redistributive effects, meanwhile, are linear. Put these two together, and you get the result on PCBR just stated.

Are these just theoretical points, with little empirical import? Not really. Peterson Institute claims notwithstanding, the tariff reductions associated with NAFTA have produced sharp distributional consequences and very small real output gains for the U.S. economy as a whole. On this, see in particular Hakobyan and McLaren (2016), who estimate that wage growth in the industries most affected by NAFTA was reduced by seventeen percentage points (relative to other industries), and see Caliendo and Parro (2015) on the minute output gains.

In the face of such results, a typical response is that these models underestimate the true, dynamic effects of trade liberalization. Similarly, Furman's numbers can be criticized because they are level effects. The problem here is that standard economic theory has little room for these alleged dynamic effects. A reduction in the tax from t_0 to t_1 produces an increase in real GDP (in the long-run steady state) of x percent—not an increase in the growth rate of the economy by y percentage points. And since an increase in the long-run growth rate could swamp any distributional effects, the critics may have a point.

The right way to evaluate this counterclaim would be in the context of endogenous growth models, which do have the feature that changes in policies produce permanent growth effects. The wrinkle here is that the details of the models would matter enormously. Endogenous growth models typically run off scale economies and/or technological externalities, both of which are hard to reconcile with competitive markets. Therefore, they inevitably live in the world of second-best economics. A tax cut can produce enlarged economic benefits and a long-run growth boost. But it may also produce fewer economic benefits than in the benchmark model and reduced economic growth. Endogenous growth effects do not necessarily magnify the gains from tax reductions; they expand the range of possible outcomes on *either side* of the benchmark result.

Moreover, it is important not to confuse growth effects with welfare (in the limited sense of efficiency). A permanently higher investment rate that produces higher growth of output need not necessarily be more "welfare enhancing" since higher investment comes at the cost of greater saving and lower consumption today. There is a bigger welfare boost only if there was a wedge between the social and private marginal product of capital to begin with.

In other words, it is hard to say anything in general about these long-run growth effects. When people make strong unconditional assertions of the form "longer-run dynamic effects are much larger," they are typically acting as advocates rather than as analysts.

A third claim in chapter 16 is that *developing economies should place comparatively more weight on growth because growth rate differentials there are much larger.* Now, it is true that growth rates vary much more in the developing world—from 7–8 percent in per capita terms to the occasionally negative. But what matters for Furman's argument is the portion of the variation that is exploitable by policy. Just because growth rates vary a lot does not mean that we have a predictable way of moving growth rates around. We know remarkably little about the relationship between actual policy and long-run growth, even in developing countries. We are surely on stronger ground with the extremes of bad policy: we can be pretty certain that hyperinflation or a constant threat of expropriation is pretty damaging. But we would be hard-pressed to conclude that there is a determinate relationship between tax or tariff rates and economic growth for the vast majority of developing nations.

I would make Furman's point somewhat differently here. Remember the argument above about PCBR. To the extent that taxes and tariffs are higher in developing countries compared to advanced economies, there is a levels-based argument for placing somewhat lower emphasis on distributional outcomes in the former.

To conclude, I broadly agree with Furman and sympathize with the aims of his analysis in chapter 16. The redistributive effects of tax and trade policies tend to be large and, perhaps more important, are more predictable ex ante. This is particularly important when tax or trade distortions are "small." Recognizing these points should make us economists pay more attention to the distributional consequences of policy reforms than we typically do. But I would add that we need to distinguish between level and steady-state effects, on the one hand, and long-run growth effects on the other. The latter can be quantitatively much more significant, though we understand them a lot less well, and they could as easily go in the wrong direction. Finally, I would make the obvious point that none of this implies we should give up trying to get a grip on how policy affects long-run growth.

References

Caliendo, Lorenzo, and Fernando Parro. 2015. "Estimates of the Trade and Welfare Effects of NAFTA." *Review of Economic Studies* 82:1–44.

Hakobyan, Shushanik, and John McLaren. 2016. "Looking for Local Labor Market Effects of NAFTA." *Review of Economics and Statistics* 98 (4): 728–741.

Rodrik, Dani. 1994. "The Rush to Free Trade in the Developing World: Why So Late? Why Now? Will It Last?" In *Voting for Reform: Democracy, Political Liberalization, and Economic Adjustment*, ed. S. Haggard and S. Webb. New York: Oxford University Press.

Rodrik, Dani. 2012. "Why We Learn Nothing from Regressing Economic Growth on Policies." *Seoul Journal of Economics* 25 (2): 137–151.

Rodrik, Dani. 2018. "Populism and the Economics of Globalization." *Journal of International Business Policy* 1:12–33.

18

Absolute Mobility Matters, Too: Regenerating People and Cities

Tharman Shanmugaratnam

Jason Furman's discussion in chapter 16 brings clarity to a field in which the headlines have run well ahead of the evidence. He explains why the recently growing empirical literature on whether inequality helps or harms growth has limited policy relevance. I will comment briefly on Furman's argument before going on to a few issues that lack easy policy remedy but that deserve a lot more attention if we are to achieve a more inclusive pattern of growth. There are some lessons we are learning from around the world.

I agree with Furman's main points: the cross-country empirical literature does not allow us to claim a robust causal relationship between inequality and growth, and the literature is in any event not directed at the questions that policymakers should be concerned about.

My take on the findings of the cross-country literature is that they are too fragile to support the recently prominent view that inequality is bad for growth. Neither do they support the traditional view that inequality is good for growth at certain stages of development. But, like Furman, I think the important questions for policy do not lie in the average relationship between inequality and growth. Behind that weak average relationship is a more illuminating picture of how the relationship has varied across countries. For any given level of inequality, we have seen a wide variation in growth outcomes. And some broadly similar growth stories have been accompanied by very different trajectories of inequality.

We need only look broadly at the East Asian development experience to see such differences. The story of how the first group of East Asian newly industrializing economies achieved rapid growth with little increase in inequality over the three decades from the 1960s—the so-called "East Asian miracle," in World Bank parlance—contrasts with that of China, whose equally dramatic growth and reduction of poverty after it opened up to global markets have been accompanied by a sharp increase in overall inequality. Indonesia's pick-up in growth in the 2000s has also been accompanied by a significant increase in inequality compared to the 1990s.

What these variations also suggest is the need to look behind simple Gini coefficients to the sources of inequality. As Furman and others highlight, different sources of inequality surely have different implications for growth. A boom in innovation should increase economic dynamism, though it often means that incomes at the top get pulled up faster than the rest. I would add that the successful growth of a middle class in some developing economies, pulling away from the poor, also increases inequality as assessed by some simple measures. But there is a range of other sources of inequality that don't help growth—such as the widened economic rents we see in both advanced and developing economies, or high-speed financial market trading. The policy trade-offs, and the political economy implications, clearly differ depending on what causes inequality. Regulations aimed at tackling elite capture, for example, should pose little trade-off in growth.

Furman also makes the useful point about the left-hand side of the equation being misspecified in the empirical literature. Policymakers do not—and if we do, we shouldn't—aim at growth of the simple average of incomes or of GDP per capita. The normatively relevant measure of growth always aims to capture something about how widely shared it is. In Singapore, for example, we focus regularly on the growth of median incomes and those in the bottom quintile, as key targets of economic policy. But I don't envy anyone estimating relationships across any large set of countries. Data on median incomes is not consistently published, and few among even the OECD countries publish incomes by decile or quintile. That's a call for more data to be published.

But let me leave aside the challenges of cross-country regressions and make a few broader points about what matters normatively. First, people attach significance to absolute mobility of incomes, not just to how they fare relative to others in their generation. So should we, as policymakers, and the reason why we should has to do with more than just economics.

Most people know whether their lives are improving over time, and whether daughters and sons are doing better than their mothers and fathers. They know whether they have opportunities to do better in life or whether they are blocked. But when the absolute growth of incomes is diminished or when incomes are stagnant over a long period, the relativities between people, and between different social classes, gain importance. I take that as a stylized sociological fact.

And in that regard, it is not just the relativities that are normally talked about that become important. It is not simply about the middle class wanting to reduce the gap between them and those at the top. People quite enjoy the spectacle of someone at the top of the ladder taking a tumble. But most in the middle class don't enjoy seeing someone who had been below them moving up and displacing them. That's a second stylized sociological fact that's relevant.

It's uncomfortable enough to move down in relative terms in normal times but even more so when absolute income growth is down as well. And that's one of the challenges of policy—that we want as much social mobility as possible in our societies but that fluidity is best accepted, embraced, and celebrated when there are absolute improvements for everyone, or for most people.

So when we think about the "all-good-things-go-together" quadrant in Furman's chapter, it's first and foremost about achieving a broad-based, absolute growth of incomes. We are not doing well on that score in much of the advanced world nor in a significant part of the emerging and developing world.

We know the basic story of how median household incomes have stalled in recent decades across a range of advanced societies. What's even more troubling is the longer-run, longitudinal data on how children are doing relative to their parents. The work of Raj Chetty and his collaborators shows how mobility from one generation to the next has stalled. If you look at the generation of men in their thirties today, those born in the early 1980s, only half of them are earning as much as or more than what their fathers earned at the same age (in real terms). In the Rust Belt, it is well below 50 percent—in other words, less than half of today's sons there are earning as much as their fathers did. That's a remarkable change. It is perceived, it is felt, and it becomes a new narrative. The data has been compiled for the United States, but the result is not at odds with what we see more impressionistically in some other countries.

Combine that with a third stylized sociological fact, or I should say a stylized fact of social psychology, which is that most people tend to form expectations of how well they should be doing in life based on extrapolations from the past—so if your parents made it into the middle class and saw their lives steadily improve, you would expect and certainly hope that incomes keep that path of improvement in your life too. So when those expectations are not realized, it leads to great disappointment. And if that happens when, at the same time, those who were below you are gradually moving up or catching up with you, you get a more complex brew—with the political economy implications that we have begun to see.

A second worrying story is the persistent lack of convergence among a large number of developing countries toward the income levels of the advanced world or the more developed emerging countries. The simple logic of convergence in economic development was that if you started far from the frontier of productivity, you could borrow technologies and best practices, and grow more quickly than countries at the frontier did. It has worked out that way for some countries, in particular in East Asia, but it hasn't worked out for much of Africa and Latin America, and parts of South Asia, for several decades now.

I was just looking at the IMF's October 2017 *World Economic Outlook*, which has a chapter on recent trends in convergence. Projecting into the next five years, the authors of the report see a continuation of past trends—countries that were converging will continue to converge and countries that weren't converging will remain that way.

With the same technology sets and best practices being available in the markets, some countries are converging and others aren't. That's in fact true of both their overall economic growth trajectories and broad-based income growth. Part of the difference no doubt reflects some old legacies of industrial structure, which lead to countries plugging differently into the global economy. But the growth divergences have persisted over decades, suggesting that domestic policies and institutions explain a great deal of what happens in life.

I'd like to mention three contemporary policy issues that matter if we are to achieve inclusive growth. They are all domestic policy challenges, and they apply variously to all of us, in both advanced and developing countries.

First, how do we *speed up learning between firms?* We know of the puzzling divergence in productivity growth between firms that are close to the frontier and those that are not anywhere close. Again, the catch-up by firms that start with lower levels of productivity hasn't been happening. For reasons that we do not fully understand, there has been a slowdown in the pace of technological diffusion, in industry after industry, between firms on the frontier of innovation and the rest of industry. Whether through transmission up and down the supply chain, or takeovers, or other market mechanisms, technological diffusion has slowed.

It is of interest not just from the point of view of productivity growth and hence average income growth, but for wage inequalities. Studies by Furman and others have found that a good part of wage inequality in the United States, Germany, and some other places is really inequality between workers with the same job profiles in different firms rather than inequality across different jobs.

What can we do to speed up learning within each industry and the economy as a whole? That has to be a key focus of public policy aimed at inclusive growth. There are lessons from around the world. Some countries are doing it better than others. It is not just about history and culture. It is also about mechanisms and institutions. Germany, for instance, has institutions that help smaller firms adopt the latest technologies, and they do it in a way that helps the firms customize the technologies to their needs. The role of the Fraunhofer institutes is well known: they translate R&D in universities and research institutions into solutions on the production floor in smaller and medium-sized firms. There's also the less-well-known story of the Steinbeis Foundation, a fascinating institution with several thousand experts and specialists who are deployed to firms to assist in technological upgrading. It is a market-driven system, actually quite a chaotic system, quite un-German, that matches experts to small enterprises in exchange for a commission and remuneration for the expert. The general lesson here is that we need intermediaries to help markets learn faster, to help spread new and existing technologies more quickly.

The second policy challenge that deserves more attention has to do with *place, or the geographic locale, of economic gains and losses.* It shouldn't have taken electoral results to tell us how important this is, but it's been a striking picture—whether it's Brexit or the latest U.S. elections or the recent French and Turkish elections—voting patterns have exhibited marked divergences among cities, suburbs, small towns, and rural areas. These patterns also match the way in which some places have been left behind while others have moved ahead.

The emerging narrative of "compensating the losers" is, I think, both inadequate and misplaced. It's a defeatist approach. It takes market outcomes as given and looks to redistribution as the solution. I'm not saying we don't need redistribution. We do. But it is in a fundamental and profound sense secondary to the idea of helping people regenerate themselves and helping places regenerate themselves. The real challenge, before we think about new redistributive strategies, has to be about regeneration.

The natural workings of the market don't assure us of this. We need a new ambition in government, one that can enable globalization, new technologies, and agglomeration economies to work well for more places.

And we know it can be done because some places have done it, and done it better. The Danes and Swedes do it better than many other advanced countries. Singapore too tries hard to do it. Even in the United States, there are in reality two stories of the Rust Belt. Some towns and cities have reemerged with a positive spiral—Milwaukee or Minneapolis or Pittsburgh—while others are caught in a negative spiral. It is the same story in a whole range of countries. In Germany the vibrant towns in Baden-Württemberg, not far from Stuttgart, contrast with the depressed towns in the Ruhr Valley, and the same can be seen in France, Italy, and the United Kingdom. Some places get back into a positive spiral, others stay in a negative loop and develop what appears to be a social form of hysteresis.

Why do these divergences between cities and regions within the same country persist, sometimes over decades? We know that economic losses and gains have always been concentrated geographically. It's in the nature of economic specialization. Agglomeration economies have accentuated the impact of globalization and technological change. And while some places can bounce back after their core industries and jobs have been lost to new technologies or global competition, not every place can do so. Not every town and city can develop new agglomeration economies.

But there is more to these divergences than just the workings of the market. The regeneration of towns and cities owes itself very often to local leadership, partnerships, and activism, aimed in particular at creating communities of learning. I say communities because there's something in a local social compact that creates a sense of mutual obligation, that binds business leaders, college deans and teachers, local mayors and officials, unions, and ordinary people together, and that ultimately motivates people. We can build it in a town or in a city-scale nation like Singapore, but it is not so easy to build that sense of community on a larger normal national scale. People must know each other and form social bonds, not just have economic obligations to each other.

A central theme in public policy must therefore be to help people to adjust to the vicissitudes of globalization and technology, and to regenerate themselves. It's not just about providing the needed fiscal resources but about the activism and partnerships that develop communities of learning. That's also what gives people confidence in themselves and a sense of optimism.

All that takes me to my third set of issues. *We have to rethink higher education.* It has become greatly inefficient in economic terms in a wide range of countries, and in many respects it is socially inequitable too. The data speaks for itself in the United States. One out of two college students in the United States doesn't graduate within five years. The ratio is higher in the case of public universities, but even at private universities some 40 percent don't graduate within five years. The typical cost of a college education, by the way, is not what it costs over four years, but more. It is expensive and produces weak job outcomes. Of those who do graduate, 40 percent are not working in jobs that require a college degree. And the bottom quartile of college graduates earn little premium in wages compared to high school graduates—a fact that the measured wage premiums based on averages obscure.

Much the same scenario is playing out in India, China, Korea, and Taiwan, which are experiencing significant underemployment of college grads. In several European countries, large numbers enroll in university before dropping out later. It's a huge inefficiency not only in economic terms but in being able to develop people to their best and to spur social mobility.

This is not an argument against people going on to higher education. A good-quality higher education program is now a prerequisite for doing well in a technology-enriched world. But it is an argument for rethinking the form and content of a college education. We've trundled into an overacademicized form of higher education that doesn't develop the mix of intellectual and applied abilities needed in the real world, doesn't match the diverse learning styles that we see in any population, and doesn't develop a large segment of young people very well for the future. We need a better mix of academic and applied models of higher education in any future-oriented higher education system.

The stock defense of the regular four-year college, whether it provides a liberal arts education or some other academically oriented education, is that it does a better job at developing the generic skills that young people will need over their lives—the soft skills, learning skills, and creative and critical thinking skills. I think there's a certain elitism that goes into that proposition. We should not assume that the applied model of education, the model of education that involves both doing and thinking, is bereft of means for developing generic skills. There are different types of generic skills that we need for life, and there is little evidence that the learning skills, team skills, and cross-cultural skills, as well as the creative skills that an applied or dual education system cultivates, are inferior to those acquired in a regular academic program. This is in addition to such institutions preparing students well for the world of jobs—which remains the main reason why people say they want to go to college.

It's not too late to change. There's discussion now in the United Kingdom, which in an earlier era converted all its polytechnics to universities, about rediscovering the applied or dual form of education. There are good examples in Northern Europe to learn from. In Singapore, we have moved in the same direction, as have other countries. There are also some extremely good examples of this form of education in the United States. Not far from the global institutions in Washington, D.C., for example, is the Northern Virginia Community College, a good example of a college working with local government and businesses to identify and develop skills people need to have confidence in their future, whether they are poised to enter the working world or are mid-career.

A related shift involves reinvesting in learning at every stage of life. The old model of front-loading education during the first twenty or twenty-two years of a person's life is depreciating. The new game is lifelong learning, with bouts of education across the life span. Again, it is both an economic strategy—essential in a world that requires continuous reskilling and adaptation in the face of disruptive technologies—and a social strategy, a way to keep finding ways to equalize opportunities through life. It happens to be our most important strategy in Singapore. We call it SkillsFuture.

I'd like to end there. Jason Furman's work stimulates thinking. We need to think especially about strategies for reinvesting in people and cities, and for speeding up learning in industry to lift productivity and reduce wage dispersion. And it helps for us all to borrow lessons from places where things are working, including some places in the United States itself.

V

International Economy Issues

19
Rethinking International Macroeconomic Policy

Gita Gopinath

The global financial crisis and its aftermath have inspired many new ideas on international macroeconomic policy, though to survey them all is nearly impossible. Some of these ideas, such as arguments in favor of capital controls, have been discussed at length over the years, and I touch on them only briefly. Instead I focus on a subset of issues about which I believe the "rethinking" is relatively new in terms of both empirical evidence and theory and that are not as well absorbed. Perhaps not surprisingly, I have paid more attention to them in my own work.

I have organized the chapter as a set of ten remarks on exchange rate policy, capital flow management, protectionism, and global cooperation:

1. The gains to exchange rate flexibility are worse than you think.
2. The "trilemma" lives on.
3. The U.S. dollar exchange rate drives global trade prices and volumes.
4. Gross capital flows matter as much as net flows, and global banks have internationalized U.S. monetary policy.
5. Emerging markets' tilt away from foreign currency to local currency debt reduces their exposure to global risk factors.
6. Low-interest-rate environments can lead to misallocation of resources and lower productivity.
7. The relationship among global imbalances, reserve accumulation, and currency manipulation is not well identified.
8. Uniform border taxes are not neutral.
9. Trade is not the main driver of earnings inequality, but at the same time, policy has failed to address its redistributive consequences.
10. Global coordination of financial regulation is essential, along with country-level macroprudential polices. Reserve accumulation and

currency swap lines do not substitute for the lender-of-last-resort role of the IMF.

On exchange rate policy, discussed in section 1, I highlight new thinking on the virtues and vices of exchange rate flexibility for emerging markets and on the "trilemma," and discuss a new finding on the relationship between the U.S. dollar and global trade. On the topic of capital flow management, I make three remarks in section 2. I first flag the new focus on gross capital flows and its components, as opposed to the traditional focus on the current account, and the sharp rise in global banking flows that transmit conventional and unconventional monetary policies in the advanced economies to the rest of the world. Second, I describe the decline of "original sin" in emerging markets with the shift in the currency composition of emerging market sovereign external borrowing away from foreign and toward local currency and how that lowers the sensitivity of sovereign borrowing cost to global shocks. Third, I highlight a perverse cost of low interest rates when financial markets are underdeveloped that is related to the misallocation of resources.

The disenchantment with globalization in the developed world has triggered an appetite for protectionism unlike anything seen since the world wars. There is yet to be a real reversal of globalization, but the threat is high, and in this context, in section 3 I examine the issues of currency manipulation, uniform border taxes, the challenges to globalization, and the evidence on trade protectionism and growth.

Finally, section 4 addresses issues of global coordination of policies, safety nets, and multilateralism, likely the final frontier of international macroeconomic policy.

1   Exchange Rate Policy

The vast majority of countries in the world have de facto embraced "limited flexibility" as their exchange rate policy. Ilzetzki, Reinhart, and Rogoff (2017) estimate that limited flexibility exchange rate arrangements now describe 80 percent of all countries and half of the world GDP. Following the collapse of the Bretton Woods system, countries have indeed moved away from explicit de jure pegs, but then have settled into managed floats away from the corner of freely floating exchange rates. There is every reason to believe that for most countries, especially in the developing world, this will continue to be the constrained optimal policy. This leads me to my first remark.

Remark 1 *The gains to exchange rate flexibility are worse than you think.*

The classic argument for the optimality of floating exchange rates, dating back to Milton Friedman, goes along the following lines: When prices are sticky, shocks to the economy generate deviations of output from its potential, and consequently inefficient recessions and booms. For example, a positive productivity shock at home should with flexible prices lower the price of home goods relative to that of foreign goods. When prices are sticky in the producer's currency, however, this relative price adjustment does not happen automatically. In such a case a depreciation of the exchange rate can bring about the right relative price adjustment. A depreciation raises the price of imports relative to that of exports, generating a depreciation of the terms of trade and therefore a shift in demand toward domestically produced goods and away from foreign goods. This exchange rate flexibility closes the output gap and leaves the economy at its first-best level. On the other hand, if the exchange rate is fixed, then the economy suffers from a negative output gap (output below its potential).

A core piece of this argument that favors flexible exchange rates is the strong comovement of the nominal exchange rate and the terms of trade: a depreciation of the nominal exchange rate should be associated with an almost one-to-one depreciation of the terms of trade (of goods with sticky prices). That is, a 1 percent depreciation of the bilateral exchange rate should be associated with a close to 1 percent depreciation of the terms of trade.

Boz, Gopinath, and Plagborg-Møller (2017) find no evidence of this in the data. Using a newly constructed data set of harmonized (noncommodity) annual bilateral import and export unit value and volume indices for fifty-five countries covering 91 percent of world trade for the period 1989–2015, they estimate that a 1 percent depreciation of the bilateral exchange rate is associated with only a 0.1 percent depreciation of the bilateral terms of trade (in the year of the depreciation), a coefficient that is not significantly different from zero, as reported in table 19.1.

This finding, while strongly counter to the implications of the Mundell-Fleming producer currency pricing assumptions that drive the

Table 19.1
Disconnect between Exchange Rate and Terms of Trade

Variables	(1) $\Delta tot_{ij,t}$
$\Delta e_{ij,t}$	0.0121
	(0.0127)
$\Delta e_{ij,t-1}$	−0.0126
	(0.0169)
$\Delta e_{ij,t-2}$	−0.00807
	(0.0105)
PPI controls	Yes

Source: Boz, Gopinath, and Plagborg-Møller (2017).

case for flexible exchange rates, is consistent with the fact that prices in international trade are not sticky in the producer's currency but are sticky in a dominant currency, which is overwhelmingly the dollar. It is important to note that the dollar's share in trade invoicing is far out of proportion to the U.S. economy's role as an exporter or importer of traded goods. In a sample of forty-three countries, Gopinath (2015) finds that the dollar's share as an invoicing currency is approximately 4.7 times the share of U.S. goods in world imports and 3.1 times its share in world exports. In comparison, the euro invoicing share is more closely aligned with its share in world trade as the corresponding multiple is 1.2 only (figure 19.1). For the vast majority of countries, the share of their own currency in their own trade with the world is close to zero.

Casas and co-authors (2017) incorporate this dollar-dominance fact into a Keynesian framework and develop a "dominant-currency paradigm" in which trade prices are sticky in dollars, and demonstrate that this predicts stable terms of trade even at annual frequencies. Quite simply, when imports and exports are all priced and sticky in dollars, in the short run the terms of trade, which are the ratio of the two, should be insensitive to the exchange rate. While invoicing alone does not guarantee that prices are also sticky in the invoicing currency, the evidence in Casas and co-authors (2017) and Boz, Gopinath, and Plagborg-Møller (2017) strongly supports the sticky price assumption.

An important implication of the dominant-currency paradigm is that even in the best-case scenario, there is no "divine coincidence"; that is, inflation targeting does not suffice to close the output gap, a result that is

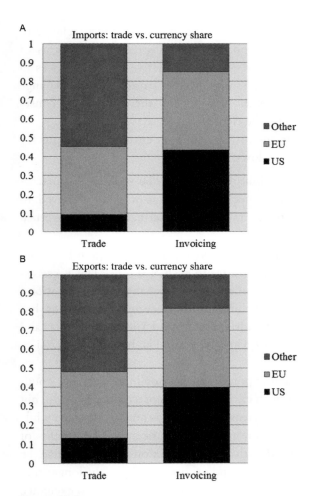

Figure 19.1
Dollar Dominance in World Trade.
Source: Gopinath (2015).

obtained under Mundell-Fleming assumptions. As derived in Casas and co-authors (2017), inflation targeting (domestic producer price inflation) continues to be optimal monetary policy from a small open economy's perspective, except that now the output gap fluctuates with shocks, and this gap is greater the more open the economy is.

The reason the output gap does not close can be understood as follows. Under Mundell-Fleming assumptions an exchange rate depreciation accomplishes two things. First, it raises the prices of imports relative to domestically produced goods, and second, it depreciates the terms of trade, that is, it lowers the price of exports relative to world prices in world currency. Under the dominant-currency paradigm the exchange rate depreciation accomplishes the first but not the second, and consequently the output gap cannot be closed.

The additional implications of the dominant-currency paradigm for exchange rate policy are as follows:

1. While exchange rate flexibility continues to be valuable for macroeconomic stabilization, it is not as powerful as originally believed, to the degree that international trade is best described as being governed by dominant-currency pricing.

2. The exports of non-dominant-currency countries (non-U.S. and non-euro) will not be very sensitive to exchange rates. This is consistent with the weak response of exports to exchange rate fluctuations, including during large devaluations in emerging markets, as has been documented by Alessandria, Pratap, and Yue (2013), Casas and co-authors (2017), and Boz, Gopinath, and Plagborg-Møller (2017), among others.

3. This does not imply that exporters in non-dominant-currency countries do not benefit from an exchange rate depreciation. They do, but it mainly works through increases in markups and profits even while the quantity exported does not change significantly. The benefits of higher profits in a world with financial frictions can, of course, be large, and can raise production and export capacity in the longer run.

4. Tourism is the one export that should be most sensitive to exchange rate changes insofar as its prices are sticky in the producer's currency. The dramatic growth in tourism in Iceland following the large exchange rate depreciation is testimony to this (Benediktsdottir, Eggertsson, and Prarinsson 2017).

5. Once all the other arguments for the disruptive effects of exchange rate flexibility in emerging markets are included, the rationale for "fear of floating" is strengthened. These disruptions include the "balance sheet channel," according to which exchange rate depreciations worsen the balance sheets of firms that mainly earn in local currency but borrow in dollars. This in turn has real consequences, such as

lower investment. For developing countries, imperfect credibility of monetary policy remains a challenge, and large swings in exchange rates can lead to sharp exits of risk-averse international lenders, a movement that in turn amplifies exchange rate fluctuations.

6. At the other extreme, the arguments against hard pegs—namely, loss of monetary independence and an increased risk of speculative currency attacks—support the shift away from hard pegs. The commodity price collapse of 2014 also highlights the virtues of having some exchange rate flexibility over none, as commodity exporters with flexible exchange rates appear to have had greater resilience to the shock.

This last comment presumes that flexible exchange rates allow greater independence of monetary policy. This presumption has, however, been questioned in recent years, triggered by Rey (2013). In my next remark I summarize the state of our knowledge on this all-important question of whether or not exchange rate flexibility allows for greater monetary policy independence.

Remark 2 *The "trilemma" lives on.*

Rey (2013), in highly influential work, argues that flexible exchange rates alone do not suffice to maintain monetary policy independence as long as capital mobility is unrestricted. This goes counter to the "trilemma," namely, that countries can choose two of the following three— stable exchange rates, monetary policy independence, and free capital mobility—but not all three. According to the "dilemma, not trilemma" version, once you allow capital mobility, then you give up monetary policy independence, regardless of your exchange rate regime. This dilemma follows from the astute observation of Rey (2013) that there is a global financial cycle in capital flows, asset prices, and credit growth and that this cycle is influenced by U.S. monetary policy. This claim finds strong support from the evidence on spillovers of U.S. monetary policy onto long-term interest rates in the rest of the world via global banks.

However, just to ensure that the pendulum does not swing to the other extreme such that flexible exchange rates provide no greater monetary independence and ability to control credit growth (something I suspect Rey would not argue for), it is important to recognize the following findings. First, Shambaugh (2004) demonstrates that the short-term rates of

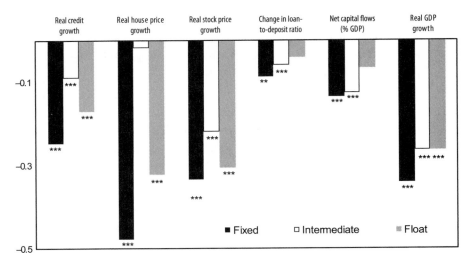

Figure 19.2
Trilemma. Figure plots the correlation of financial and macroeconomic variables in emerging market economies with global investor risk aversion.
Source: Obstfeld, Ostry, and Qureshi (2017).

countries with pegged exchange rates track the short-term rates of the country whose currency they are pegged to much more closely as compared to floaters, even conditional on capital mobility, in direct support of the trilemma. Second, Obstfeld, Ostry, and Qureshi (2017) document that while increases in global risk measures like the VIX negatively affect capital flows into emerging markets, their domestic credit growth, and their asset prices, this negative effect is greater for emerging markets that are on a fixed exchange rate than for those using pure floats or managed floats (figure 19.2). They conclude that consistent with the trilemma, fixed exchange rate regimes are more sensitive to global risk shocks and therefore more prone to economic boom-bust cycles because of the greater loss of monetary independence. So the takeaway from this research is that while the trilemma is weakened for reasons Rey (2013) highlights, it continues to have bite.

Both remark 1 and remark 2 are related to the dollar's dominance in world trade and in asset markets. While it has long been known that the dollar has a special status in international markets, the implications of this have been fleshed out only recently. I highlight here in remark 3 one consequence of dollar dominance that has not been fully recognized.

Remark 3 *The U.S. dollar exchange rate drives global trade prices and volumes.*

Countries (and researchers more generally) assess the impact of exchange rate fluctuations on their economy by estimating the pass-through of *bilateral* or *trade-weighted* exchange rates into export and import prices and volumes. This practice follows naturally from the classic Mundell-Fleming paradigm of sticky prices and producer currency pricing wherein exporting firms infrequently change prices denominated in their own home currency. Casas and co-authors (2017) and Boz, Gopinath, and Plagborg-Møller (2017) demonstrate that in fact, it is not the bilateral exchange rate but the dollar exchange rate that drives trade between country pairs. That is, the dollar exchange rate quantitatively dominates the bilateral exchange rate in price pass-through and trade elasticity regressions for country pairs where the U.S. is on neither side of the trade transaction.

Boz, Gopinath, and Plagborg-Møller (2017) estimate that a 1 percent depreciation of an importing country's currency relative to the dollar raises the import prices of goods in home currency by 0.78 percent, even when its bilateral exchange rate with its trading partner is controlled for. On the other hand, a 1 percent depreciation relative to its trading partner's currency raises import prices by only 0.16 percent when the importing country's exchange rate relative to the dollar is controlled for. The strength of the U.S. dollar is therefore shown to be a key predictor of rest-of-world aggregate trade volume and consumer/producer price inflation. Specifically, they establish that a persistent 1 percent U.S. dollar appreciation against all other currencies in the world predicts a 0.6–0.8 percent decline within a year in the volume of total trade between countries in the rest of the world, with various proxies for the global business cycle held constant. The dollar's role as an invoicing currency is also special as it handily beats the explanatory power of the euro in predicting trade prices and volumes.

To summarize, the consequences of exchange rate variability and the determination of exchange rate policy should be viewed through the lens of the dominant-currency paradigm because of the dollar's dominance in world trade. Flexible exchange rates provide greater monetary policy independence, but its benefits in an open economy environment may not be as large as you think.

2   Capital Flow Management

In this section I address issues related to capital flows and its management. This is an area where there has been a major rethinking of policy over the last many years, even before the financial crisis. There is now a new consensus that capital account liberalization is a mixed blessing: it is associated with excess volatility tied to abrupt surges and reversals in capital flows, and consequently there can be prudent limits to capital account liberalization.

The recent financial crisis and its aftermath made these trade-offs with capital flows even more stark with the collapse in capital flows in the immediate aftermath of the financial crisis and the surge in capital inflows into emerging markets during the period of exceptionally loose monetary policy and quantitative easing in advanced economies. In my next remark I address two important lessons from the last two decades of capital flows.

Remark 4   *Gross capital flows matter as much as net flows, and global banks have internationalized U.S. monetary policy.*

As argued by Obstfeld (2012) and Gourinchas and Rey (2014), the crisis made a compelling case for the importance of expanding surveillance beyond the traditional focus on current accounts that is the difference between net savings and investment decisions to include gross flows. In the run-up to the crisis there were large increases in gross flows (figure 19.3), especially between advanced economies, that did not necessarily show up as large net imbalances but were a major source of financial instability.

A separate but equally important gross flow that does not show up in measures of cross-border flows but played an important role in the transmission of the crisis has been highlighted by Shin (2012) and Bruno and Shin (2015). This was the phenomenon of European banks raising dollar funds in the United States and reinvesting them in U.S. subprime mortgages (figure 19.4). These flows do not show up in the current account or as cross-border gross flows because the transactions take place within the boundaries of the United States. Avdjiev, McCauley, and Shin (2016) argue that such flows played a central role in the transmission of the financial crisis and should therefore be monitored.

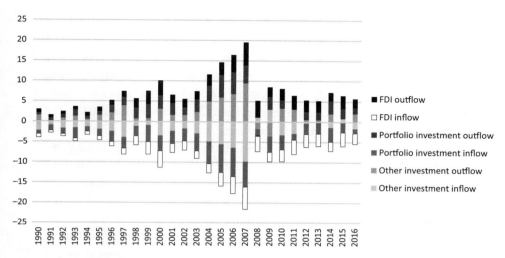

Figure 19.3

Cross-Border Gross Flows Matter: Global Gross Financial Flows, 1990–2106 (% of GDP).
Source: Obstfeld (2017).

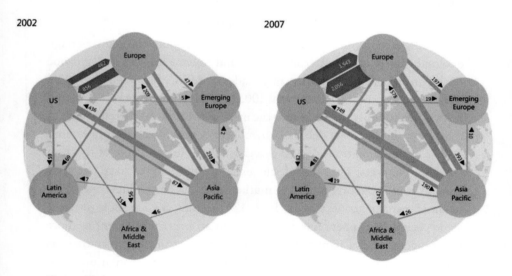

Figure 19.4

Within-Country Gross Flows Matter.
Source: Avdjiev, McCauley, and Shin (2016).

Post-crisis, there is a renewed focus on the so-called global financial cycle, which captures the comovement of global capital flows triggered mainly by monetary policy and risk appetite in advanced economies (Rey 2013; Blanchard et al. 2016). In the case of emerging markets, these flows have been primarily intermediated through global banks and large domestic banks, and, as highlighted in Bräuning and Ivashina (2017), the claims of global banks nearly doubled since the onset of the global financial crisis, reaching about \$7 trillion in 2016. According to Bräuning and Ivashina (2017), over a typical U.S. monetary easing cycle there is a 32 percent loan volume increase for emerging market economies, with a similarly large effect on reversal of the U.S. monetary stance (demand factors controlled for). Baskaya and co-authors (2017) estimate that increases in global risk appetite (VIX) enabled large domestic banks in Turkey to lower credit rates and that this channel explains 43 percent of the observed credit growth in Turkey.

While global banking has raised sensitivity to global factors, there is one phenomenon that has reduced it:

Remark 5 *Emerging markets' tilt away from foreign currency to local currency debt reduces their exposure to global risk factors.*

The shift in the currency composition of emerging market sovereign external borrowing away from foreign and toward local currency is one of the prominent trends of recent decades, a decline in so-called original sin (Eichengreen and Hausmann 2005) for emerging markets. Du and Schregger (2016b) document that the mean share of local currency debt in total external sovereign debt held by nonresidents increased from around 10 percent in 2000 to nearly 60 percent in 2013 for a sample of fourteen emerging markets. They also document that the share of local currency debt in total offshore emerging market debt trading volume increased from 35 percent to 66 percent in 2013, reaching \$3.5 trillion over the same period. This phenomenon was due to an important extent to more independent central banks and inflation targeting in these countries, as foreign investors worried less about losing real value through unanticipated devaluations. The IMF (2016) attributes some of the greater resilience of emerging markets to the postfinancial crisis slowdown in net capital inflows to the decline in the reliance of emerging markets on foreign currency debt (figures 19.5, 19.6, and 19.7).

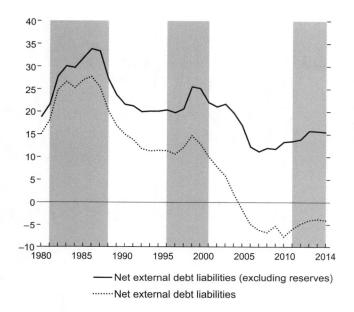

Figure 19.5

Net External Debt Liabilities of Emerging Market Economies (% of GDP), 1980–2014.
Source: IMF (2016).

While the balance sheet gains of matching the currency of assets and liabilities are well understood, Du and Schregger (2016a) point to other, less-recognized benefits of local currency debt. In particular, they show that local currency credit spreads are much less correlated across countries and with global risk factors than foreign currency credit spreads. They estimate that the average pairwise correlation of local currency credit spreads between countries is only 43 percent, in contrast to 73 percent for foreign currency credit spreads. Also, global factors explain less than 54 percent of the variation in local currency credit spreads but more than 77 percent of the variation in foreign currency credit spreads.

These findings highlight the additional virtues of local currency borrowing: it both reduces the exposure of emerging markets to external shocks and improves their resilience. As Du and Schregger (2016b) point out, the decline in original sin is, however, limited to sovereign borrowing because emerging market corporates continue to borrow in foreign

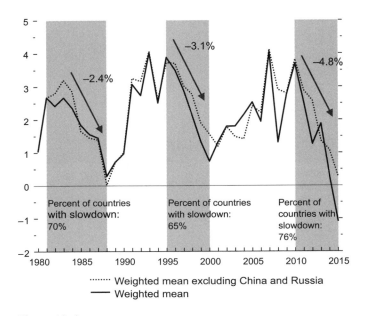

Figure 19.6

Episodes of Net Capital Inflows Slowdown (% of GDP).
Source: IMF (2016).

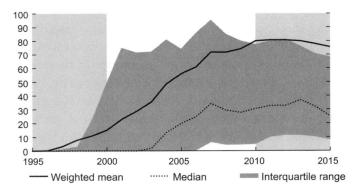

Figure 19.7

Local Currency Financing of Government Debt (% of total).
Source: IMF (2016).

currency. Policies that encourage a switch away from foreign currency debt (along with maintaining sustainable overall debt levels) should therefore continue to be a part of the toolkit of capital flow management.

Remark 6 *Low-interest-rate environments can lead to misallocation of resources and lower productivity.*

Interest rates are predicted to remain at low levels in advanced economies (Summers 2014; Gourinchas and Rey 2016), and therefore it is helpful to keep in mind the potential risks they pose, especially when unaccompanied by financial sector reforms. Besides the risks associated with disruptive capital flows to emerging markets in the search for yield and the temptation for the finance industry to load up on risk, another lesson of the financial crisis is the potential for low interest rates to cause a misallocation of resources and therefore lower aggregate productivity.

One striking feature of the run-up to the euro crisis was the divergence in the current accounts of Germany and Spain, along with a divergence in productivity (figure 19.8). From 1999 to 2007, Germany ran large current account surpluses and was a net lender while experiencing strong productivity growth. During the same period, Spain ran large current account deficits financed by large capital inflows while experiencing a decline productivity. This is an allocation puzzle if ever there was one as standard forces would predict that capital would flow into the country with higher productivity growth.

Gopinath and colleagues (2017) provide an explanation that reverses the direction of causation. They argue that the lower borrowing costs for Spain that arose from the euro convergence caused a decline in productivity through greater misallocation of resources. The mechanism is as follows: Lower borrowing costs disproportionately benefit larger (high-net-worth) firms because they are less constrained in their borrowing in financial markets than small firms. Because larger firms are not necessarily the most productive firms, this leads to resources being misallocated away from more productive to less productive firms, thus generating a decline in aggregate productivity. In support of this argument, they show that for manufacturing firms in Spain between 1999 and 2007, capital was increasingly misallocated as the dispersion of the return on capital (marginal revenue product of capital) across firms increased significantly without an increase in dispersion of the return on labor

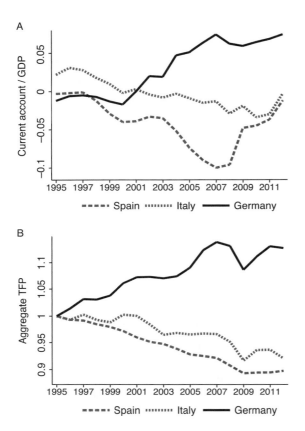

Figure 19.8
Misallocation of Capital.
Source: Gopinath et al. (2017).

(marginal revenue product of labor), as shown in figure 19.9. Further, this rise in dispersion was not evident within the group of large firms but was driven by the difference in returns on capital across large and small firms. They estimate that the increasing misallocation of resources led to a significant decline in productivity.

A lesson of this period, therefore, is that low-interest-rate environments, when combined with less-developed financial markets, can have perverse effects on productivity. As in the case of Spain, low interest rates can lead to rapid capital accumulation but weaken productivity through inefficient resource allocation.

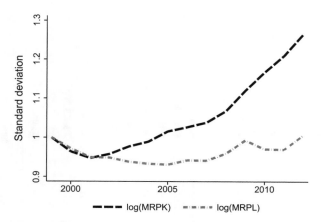

Figure 19.9

Misallocation of Capital in Spain's Manufacturing.
Source: Gopinath et al. (2017).

To summarize, international finance, like domestic finance, turns out to be far less benign than previously thought, and all its complexity deserves attention, including the strong spillovers across countries in a world of globalized finance. There are sound arguments for intervening in capital markets, including the use of capital controls and macroprudential regulation, based on market failures such as pecuniary externalities and aggregate demand externalities. At the same time, one certainly should not throw the baby out with the bathwater, as not all capital flows have negative consequences for recipient countries. Foreign direct investment continues to get top billing among capital flows, but some portfolio flows and loan flows are shown to have a positive impact on growth and consequently have benefits for the recipient country (Blanchard et al. 2016; Varela 2018).

3 Protectionism and Currency Wars

Globalization faces serious threats, and though to date there have been no major reversals in trade policy, the odds that it will happen have risen significantly over the past year. Surveys by the Pew Research Center on attitudes toward international trade point to a divergence between developed and developing economies, with the former viewing trade far more

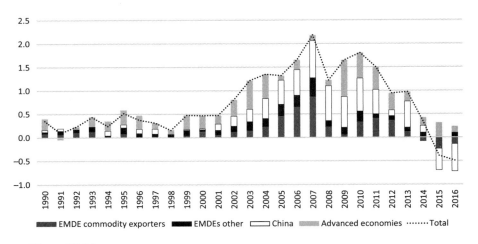

Figure 19.10

Global Imbalances and Reserve Accumulation. Figure shows purchases by region, 1990–2016 (% of world GSP).
Source Obstfeld (2017).

unfavorably in recent years than the latter. There is a sense in the developed world that it has lost its prosperity to developing countries because of trade.

This perception triggers concerns of unfair trade practices in developing countries with large surpluses. One prominent accusation is that China has engaged in currency manipulation. The dramatic accumulation of dollar reserves by China is believed by some to be directly causing its large surpluses (figure 19.10). Such arguments have led to proposals to include currency manipulation clauses in trade agreements (Bergsten and Gagnon 2017).

Large imbalances certainly raise concerns of sustainable global growth and require monitoring and redressal; however, it is important to note that the state of knowledge on what *causally* drives global imbalances is quite limited. This is because imbalances are equilibrium phenomena and are driven by the decisions of private agents, the government, and domestic and foreign shocks, all of which interact in nonlinear ways. Moreover, there exist several explanations for global imbalances that have nothing to do with manipulation, such as differential (across countries) demand for precautionary savings, differing ability to produce financial assets, differing demographics, and so on (Gourinchas and Rey 2014). For these reasons:

Remark 7 *The empirical relationship among global imbalances, reserve accumulation, and currency manipulation is not well identified.*

Bayoumi, Gagnon, and Sabarowski (2015), Gagnon and co-authors (2017), and Chinn (2017) explore the empirical relation between reserve accumulation and current account balances. While this research provides valuable insights, the estimated relation is sensitive to the sample period covered and the variables controlled for (see also the discussion by Obstfeld 2017). Germany's large current account surpluses clearly have no relation to reserve accumulation. While more research is required, the bottom line is that caution needs to be exercised in arriving at conclusions of currency manipulation and its ability to cause trade surpluses.

A policy that recently grabbed headlines is the border adjustment tax (BAT) proposed as part of the House Republican plan for U.S. business tax reform (Auerbach et al. 2017). The BAT disallows deductions of imported input costs from corporate revenue when computing taxable corporate profits and excludes export revenue from taxation. This sparked a debate on whether this amounted to protectionism and what the implications were for trade. Some argued that the U.S. dollar would appreciate to offset the tax advantage fully and therefore trade would be unaffected. More strongly, the BAT itself would be *neutral*, that is, it would have no effect on real allocations, consumption, GDP, investment, saving, and so forth, as flexible exchange rates would adjust to undo any real effect of the border tax. There were others who questioned both the prediction about the exchange rate and the claims of neutrality.

It now seems unlikely that the BAT will be implemented, but I doubt this is the last time countries consider tax interventions of this kind. Moreover, there are other tax interventions that are in the same economic equivalence class as BAT, such as uniform changes to the value-added tax (VAT) and the payroll tax. These are all forms of "uniform border taxes (UBT)." It is therefore useful to be clear what the economic consequences are to inform current and future policy. Here I summarize the state of knowledge on UBTs and the reasons that such taxes are unlikely to be neutral.

Remark 8 *Uniform border taxes are not neutral.*

The prediction that UBTs are neutral has its origins in a classic result in the field of international trade called the Lerner (1936) symmetry, and in its applications in Grossman (1980) and Feldstein and Krugman (1990). According to this result, when prices and wages are *fully flexible* and *trade is balanced*, a combination of a uniform import tariff and an export subsidy of the same magnitude must be neutral, having no effect on imports, exports, and other economic outcomes. This is because the tax leads to an increase in domestic wages relative to foreign wages (in a common currency), which in turn leaves unchanged the post-tax relative price of imported to domestically produced goods in all countries. That is, despite the higher tax on imports relative to the tax on domestically produced goods, the lower relative wage of foreign products leaves the relative price of imported to domestic goods unchanged. Similarly, on the export side, despite the export subsidy, the higher relative domestic wage leaves unchanged the relative price of domestic goods in foreign markets. This result follows through if instead the tax combination was a uniform VAT increase and a cut in payroll taxes, or the BAT. If, in addition, monetary policy targets the price level, then the nominal exchange rate does all the adjusting, and we obtain the prediction that the nominal exchange rate appreciates by the amount of the tax and there are no real effects.

It is, of course, unrealistic to assume that prices are flexible and trade is balanced. Based on the work of Farhi, Gopinath, and Itskhoki (2014) and Barbiero and co-authors (2017), I summarize the five conditions that all must hold to maintain neutrality when we depart from these assumptions (see Gopinath 2017 for a lengthier discussion).

1.   When prices/wages are sticky, if there is *symmetry* in the pass-through of exchange rates and taxes into prices faced by buyers in each market, then neutrality is preserved. This symmetry is satisfied when prices are sticky in the producer's currency or in the local currency. In the former case, with fully preset prices, the pass-through of either is 100 percent, and consequently the exchange rate appreciation offsets taxes, and there are no real effects. In the latter case the pass-through is zero in either case, and there are no real effects.

In reality, though, prices of traded goods are sticky in dollars regardless of origin and destination, which leads to a breakdown of neutrality. In this case, with fully preset prices, the exchange rate appreciation has no pass-through into import prices faced by domestic households and firms while taxes have 100 percent pass-through. On the flip side, the tax has no pass-through into export prices (in foreign currency) while the exchange rate has 100 percent pass-through. In this case, the exchange rate appreciation leads to a decline in imports and exports and therefore a decline in overall trade in the short run. These results hold more generally with staggered or state-contingent pricing.

2. Monetary policy should respond only to the output gap and CPI inflation, and should not respond to the exchange rate, to maintain neutrality. If exchange rates are targeted, then these same taxes serve the purpose of stimulating the economy. Famously, Keynes in 1931 proposed in the Macmillan Report to the British Parliament that a combination of an import tariff and an export subsidy be used to mimic the effects of an exchange rate devaluation while maintaining the gold pound parity. Farhi, Gopinath, and Itskhoki (2014) demonstrate the equivalence of the VAT-payroll tax swap policy to replicate the effects of a nominal exchange rate devaluation in economies with a fixed exchange rate. Relatedly, if foreign monetary authorities attempt to mitigate the depreciation of their currencies, a reasonable assumption, it will also lead to a breakdown in neutrality.

3. When trade is not balanced, neutrality continues to hold as long as all international assets and liabilities are in *foreign currency*. If, however, some international holdings are in domestic currency, then neutrality is no longer preserved. Because this assumption breaks down for the United States with its large dollar liabilities, the BAT would lead to wealth transfers from the United States to the rest of the world.

4. The implementation of the BAT must take the form of a *one-time permanent* and *unanticipated* policy shift for it to be neutral. Otherwise, expectations of a border tax in the future will cause immediate exchange rate appreciations that have an impact on the portfolio choices of private agents and therefore will have real consequences. Similarly, neutrality fails to hold if the policy is expected to be reversed and therefore transitory, or if the other countries are expected to retaliate with their own policies in the future.

5. Neutrality requires that the border taxes be *uniform* and cover all goods and services. Service sectors such as tourism whose sales to

foreigners take place within borders are not treated the same as exports that cross borders, which in turn affects neutrality.

Because all these conditions need to be satisfied simultaneously, the UBTs are unlikely to be neutral and will have significant consequences for international trade.

Remark 9 *Trade is not the main driver of earnings inequality, but at the same time, policy has failed to address its redistributive consequences.*

In terms of the bigger picture, the main policy challenge to globalization is to ensure that the gains are more fairly shared. While it is well understood that trade, despite raising aggregate welfare, creates winners and losers, the expectation was that losers would be compensated and would migrate to better-performing sectors and geographic locations. The evidence, however, points to limited interregional mobility and trade assistant programs not coming close to compensating losers (Pavcnik 2017). Consequently, the adverse effects of trade on labor markets have persisted for long periods in some countries. Dix-Carneiro and Kovak (2016) note that in the case of Brazil, the negative effects of import liberalization lasted twenty years. Autor and co-authors (2014) similarly point to the longlasting negative effects of China's import competition on U.S. labor markets in some geographic areas.

While the academic literature has concluded that trade is not the main driver of earnings inequality within countries and that factors such as automation and skill-biased technical change play a bigger role (Helpman 2016), the bottom line is that trade will continue to be a scapegoat for labor market woes. It is therefore imperative to correct the failures in addressing the redistributive effects arising not just from trade but also from technology, to avoid a costly reversal in globalization.

Because some advanced country administrations are trigger-happy with protectionism, it is useful to remind ourselves of the empirical evidence on protectionism and growth. Despite the contentious nature of the evidence, I believe a fair summary is that there is no evidence that tariffs are good for growth in *high-income* countries in the post–world war period. DeJong and Ripoll (2006) examine the relationship between ad valorem tariffs and growth, using a panel data set comprising sixty countries and spanning 1975–2000. They find that while there is no significant relation between tariffs and growth in low-income countries, higher tariffs

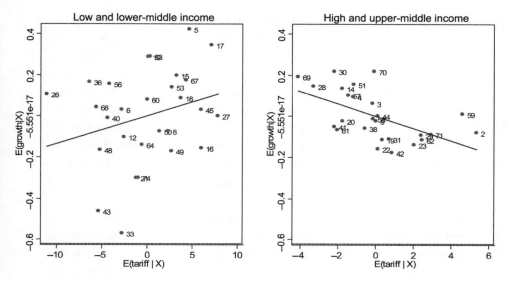

Figure 19.11

Protectionism and Growth.
Source: DeJong and Ripoll (2006).

are associated with significantly lower growth in high-income countries (figure 19.11). Specifically, a 10 percentage point increase in tariff rates corresponds to a 1.6 percentage point decline in per capita growth rate for the country.

4   Global Cooperation

Issues related to cross-border cooperation on financial regulation, on global safety nets, and maybe even on monetary policy will continue to take center stage in discussions on the next generation of the international financial and monetary system. Despite the United States threatening to withdraw from multilateralism, the arguments for cooperation have only strengthened over time. This leads me to my last remark:

Remark 10   *Global coordination of financial regulation is required alongside individual countries' macroprudential polices. Reserve accumulation and currency swap lines do not substitute for the lender-of-last-resort role of the International Monetary Fund.*

The arguments in favor of international cooperation in financial regulation are clearly articulated in Cecchetti and Tucker (2016). Quite simply, when financial institutions are global, individual countries that maximize their own welfare do not internalize all the costs and benefits of their regulatory policies, and consequently such policies are suboptimal. Countries can engage in a race to the bottom with lax regulations to win the favor of the financial services industry while imposing large costs on the rest of the world. The lessons of the financial crisis should, if anything, highlight the costs of weak financial regulation and the virtues of international coordination of regulatory standards.

Safety Nets   The many financial crises of the 1980s and 1990s in emerging markets have led them to accumulate large amounts of international reserves as a rainy-day fund for future crisis. These reserves certainly help countries weather crises, as evidenced by experience during the recent financial crisis, and therefore should continue to be a part of the arsenal of macroprudential policies. That said, countries appear to display a "fear of losing international reserves," as articulated by Aizenman and Sun (2009), with the majority of the emerging markets not willing to deplete their reserves by more than 25 percent. This suggests there are hard-to-explain limits to how reserves can be used in the event of a crisis, which then should be weighed against the costs of accumulating these reserves.

One very successful act of global cooperation that emerged during the financial crisis was the creation of the central bank swap lines, which were created to deal with the dollar shortage in financial markets following the Lehman Brothers collapse. Since then there has been a proliferation of bilateral and regional swap lines with the potential to ameliorate panic-driven currency shortages (Denbee, Jung, and Paternó 2016). The virtue of these swap lines is that they appear limitless, and consequently they are a useful deterrence tool for self-fulfilling panics. The downside is that they can be used only if they are consistent with the mandate of the country providing the liquidity, and the loans tend to be of very short duration—up to three months, which may in turn reduce their deterrence potential.

As a result of these limitations to reserve accumulation and swap lines, it is apparent that they are not substitutes for the IMF's role as the international lender of last resort. As highlighted in Denbee, Jung, and Paternó

(2016), IMF financing has the following virtues. First, it shares risks across the largest group of countries (all of its 188 members). Second, it serves a broader purpose than just dealing with currency shortages by targeting all the manifestations of a balance-of-payments crisis. Third, the lending is of longer, three- to five-year maturities. The main critique of the IMF's role is the stigma attached to borrowing from the IMF, which leads countries to not use their facilities. That has changed somewhat over the past few years with the creation of facilities that provide funding without conditionalities, such as the Flexible Credit Line for countries with sound fundamentals.

The structure of the international monetary system, in which the dollar dominates in international trade, finance, and central bank reserves, poses its own challenges. One such challenge is the new-age Triffin dilemma arising from a potential conflict between demand for U.S. safe assets and the fiscal capacity of the United States to produce these safe assets. In addition, there are the spillover effects of U.S. monetary policy onto global trade that I previously described. Further, the dollar's role as a funding currency in international markets raises the sensitivity of non-U.S. balance sheets to dollar exchange rate fluctuations (Avdjiev, McCauler, and Shin 2016). While these spillovers raise demands for greater cooperation in monetary policy, the answers as to how to get this done will probably remain elusive. It is thus all the more important for countries to cooperate on financial regulation, to strengthen the global safety net, and to reduce the stigma attached to the IMF's role as lender of last resort.

The creation of regional monetary funds such as the European Stability Mechanism (ESB), set up in 2012; the Chiang Mai Initiative Multilateralization (CMIM), set up in 2012; the BRICS Contingent Reserve Arrangement (CRA), set up in 2014, and other smaller regional arrangements that, taken together, have committed resources of U.S. \$1.3 trillion, similar to the amount committed by the IMF (Denbee, Jung, and Paternó 2016), is a welcome development. These funds complement the IMF in supporting a well-functioning international monetary and financial system.

Note

This chapter was prepared for the conference "Rethinking Macroeconomic Policy IV," organized by the Peterson Institute for International Economics, Washington,

D.C. I acknowledge that the content is based on work supported by the NSF under Grant No. 1628874. Any opinions, findings, conclusions, or recommendations expressed in this material are those of the author and do not necessarily reflect the views of the NSF. All remaining errors are my own.

References

Aizenman, J., and Y. Sun. 2009. "The Financial Crisis and Sizable International Reserves Depletion: From 'Fear of Floating' to the 'Fear of Losing International Reserves'?" NBER Working Paper 15308. Cambridge, MA: National Bureau of Economic Research.

Alessandria, G., S. Pratap, and V. Z. Yue. 2013. "Export Dynamics in Large Devaluations." International Finance Discussion Paper 1087. New York: Board of Governors of the Federal Reserve System.

Auerbach, A. J., Devereux, M. P., Keen, M., and Vella, J. 2017. "Destination-Based Cash Flow Taxation." Oxford University Centre for Business Taxation Working Paper WP 17/01. Oxford, January 27.

Autor, D. H., D. Dorn, G. H. Hanson, and J. Song. 2014. "Trade Adjustment: Worker-Level Evidence." *Quarterly Journal of Economics* 129 (4): 1799–1860.

Avdjiev, S., R. N. McCauley, and H. S. Shin. 2016. "Breaking Free of the Triple Coincidence in International Finance." *Economic Policy* 31 (87): 409–451.

Barbiero, O., E. Farhi, G. Gopinath, and O. Itskhoki. 2017. "The Economics of Border Adjustment Tax." Working paper, Harvard University.

Baskaya, Y. S., J. di Giovanni, S. Kalemli-Ozcan, and M. F. Ulu. 2017. "International Spillovers and Local Credit Cycles." Working paper.

Bayoumi, T., J. Gagnon, and C. Saborowski. 2015. "Official Financial Flows, Capital Mobility, and Global Imbalances." *Journal of International Money and Finance* 52:146–174.

Benediktsdottir, S., G. Eggertsson, and E. Prarinsson. 2017. "The Rise, the Fall, and the Resurrection of Iceland." Working paper.

Bergsten, C. F., and J. E. Gagnon. 2017. *Currency Conflict and Trade Policy: A New Strategy for the United States*. Washington, DC: Peterson Institute for International Economics.

Blanchard, O., J. D. Ostry, A. R. Ghosh, and M. Chamon. 2016. "Capital Flows: Expansionary or Contractionary?" *American Economic Review* 106 (5): 565–569.

Boz, E., G. Gopinath, and M. Plagborg-Møller. 2017. "Global Trade and the Dollar." IMF Working Paper 17/239. Washington, DC: International Monetary Fund, November 13.

Bräuning, F., and V. Ivashina. 2017. "Monetary Policy and Global Banking." NBER Working Paper 23316. Cambridge, MA: National Bureau of Economic Research.

Bruno, V., and H. Shin. 2015. "Cross-Border Banking and Global Liquidity." *Review of Economic Studies* 82 (2): 1–30.

Casas, C., F. J. Díez, G. Gopinath, and P.-O. Gourinchas. 2017. "Dominant Currency Paradigm: A New Model for Small Open Economies." IMF Working Paper 17/264. Washington, DC: International Monetary Fund.

Cecchetti, S. G., and P. M. W. Tucker. 2016. "Is There Macroprudential Policy without International Cooperation?" CEPR Discussion Paper 11042. Washington, DC: Center for Economic and Policy Research.

Chinn, M. D. 2017. "The Once and Future Global Imbalances? Interpreting the Post-Crisis Record." Paper presented at the 2017 Federal Reserve Bank of Kansas City Economic Policy Symposium at Jackson Hole, WY.

DeJong, D. N., and M. Ripoll. 2006. "Tariffs and Growth: An Empirical Exploration of Contingent Relationships." *Review of Economics and Statistics* 88 (4): 625–640.

Denbee, E., Jung, C., and Paternó, F. 2016. "Stitching Together the Global Financial Safety Net." Bank of England Financial Stability Paper 36. London: Bank of England.

Dix-Carneiro, R., and B. K. Kovak. 2016. " Trade Reform and Regional Dynamics: Evidence from 25 Years of Brazilian Matched Employer-Employee Data. *American Economic Review* 107 (10): 2908–2946.

Du, W., and J. Schregger. 2016a. "Local Currency Sovereign Risk." *Journal of Finance* 71 (3): 1027–1070.

Du, W., and J. Schregger. 2016b. "Sovereign Risk, Currency Risk, and Corporate Balance Sheets." Working paper, Harvard Business School.

Eichengreen, B., and R. Hausmann. 2005. *Other People's Money: Debt Denomination and Financial Instability in Emerging Market Economies.* Chicago: University of Chicago Press.

Farhi, E., G. Gopinath, and O. Itskhoki. 2014. "Fiscal Devaluations." *Review of Economic Studies* 81 (2): 725–760.

Feldstein, M. S., and P. R. Krugman. 1990. "International Trade Effects of Value-Added Taxation." In *Taxation in the Global Economy*, ed. Assaf Rezin and Joel Slemrod, 263–282. Cambridge, MA: National Bureau of Economic Research.

Gagnon, J. E., T. Bayoumi, J. M. Londono, C. Saborowski, and H. Sapriza. 2017. "Direct and Spillover Effects of Unconventional Monetary and Exchange Rate Policies." IMF Working Paper WP/17/56. Washington, DC: International Monetary Fund.

Gopinath, G. 2015. "The International Price System." In *Inflation Dynamics and Monetary Policy: Proceedings of the 2015 Federal Reserve Bank of Kansas City Economic Policy Symposium at Jackson Hole*, 71–150.

Gopinath, G. 2017. "A Macroeconomic Perspective on Border Taxes." *Brookings Papers on Economic Activity*, BPEA Conference drafts, September 7–8.

Gopinath, G., S. Kalemli-Ozcan, L. Karabarbounis, and C. Villegas-Sanchez. 2017. "Capital Allocation and Productivity in South Europe." *Quarterly Journal of Economics* 132 (4): 1915–1967.

Gourinchas, P.-O., and H. Rey. 2014. "External Adjustment, Global Imbalances, Valuation Effects." In *Handbook of International Economics*, vol. 4, ed. Gita Gopinath, Elhanan Helpman, and Kenneth Rogoff, 585–645. New York: Elsevier.

Gourinchas, P.-O., and H. Rey. 2016. "Real Interest Rates, Imbalances and the Curse of Regional Safe Asset Providers at the Zero Lower Bound." Presented at the ECB Forum on Central Banking, "The Future of the International Financial and Monetary Architecture," Sintra, Portugal, June 27–29.

Grossman, G. M. 1980. "Border Tax Adjustments: Do They Distort Trade?" *Journal of International Economics* 10 (1): 117–128.

Helpman, E. 2016. "Globalization and Wage Inequality." NBER Working Paper 22944. Cambridge, MA: National Bureau of Economic Research.

Ilzetzki, E., C. M. Reinhart, and K. S. Rogoff. 2017. "Exchange Arrangements Entering the 21st Century: Which Anchor Will Hold?" NBER Working Paper 23134. Cambridge, MA: National Bureau of Economic Research, February.

IMF. 2016. "Understanding the Slowdown in Capital Flows to Emerging Markets." In *World Economic Outlook*, chap. 2. Washington, DC: International Monetary Fund.

Lerner, A. P. 1936. "The Symmetry between Import and Export Taxes." *Economica* 3:306–313.

Obstfeld, M. 2012. "Does the Current Account Still Matter?" *American Economic Review* 102 (3): 1–23.

Obstfeld, M. 2017. "Comments on 'The Once and Future Global Imbalances? Interpreting the Post-crisis Record,' by Menzie D. Chinn." https://azdoc.site/comments-on-the-once-and-future-global-imbalances-interpreti.html.

Obstfeld, M., J. D. Ostry, and M. S. Qureshi. 2017. "A Tie That Binds: Revisiting the Trilemma in Emerging Market Economies." IMF Working Paper 17/130. Washington, DC: International Monetary Fund, August.

Pavcnik, N. 2017. "The Impact of Trade on Inequality in Developing Countries." NBER Working Paper 23878. Cambridge, MA: National Bureau of Economic Research, September.

Rey, H. 2013. "Dilemma Not Trilemma: The Global Financial Cycle and Monetary Policy Independence." In *Proceedings of the 2013 Federal Reserve Bank of Kansas City Economic Policy Symposium at Jackson Hole*, 285–333.

Shambaugh, J. C. 2004. "The Effect of Fixed Exchange Rates on Monetary Policy." *Quarterly Journal of Economics* 119 (1): 301–352.

Shin, H. S. 2012. "Global Banking Glut and Loan Risk Premium." *IMF Economic Review* 60:155–192.

Summers, L. H. 2014. "U.S. Economic Prospects: Secular Stagnation, Hysteresis, and the Zero Lower Bound." *Business Economics* 49 (2): 65–73.

Varela, L. 2018. "Reallocation, Competition and Productivity: Evidence from a Financial Liberalization Episode." *Review of Economic Studies* 85 (2): 1279–1313.

20

The Difficulty of Separation

Raghuram Rajan

I will take up Gita Gopinath's excellent work from the perspective of a (former) emerging market central banker. Her contribution correctly recognizes that the world is messy and that there are no clean policy answers.

The precrisis consensus was grounded on the assumption of a clean separation between policy spheres. Monetary policy was about interest rates, financial stability was about capital requirements, and each country could optimize policy for its environment because its flexible exchange rate bought it policy independence. The postcrisis consensus is that everything is linked. The banking sector is linked to the nonbanking financial sector, the macroeconomy is linked to the financial sector, and countries across the world are linked. This does not mean policy irrelevance, of course, but it does mean substantial spillovers from policies across sectors and countries.

There are far more linkages than we thought existed earlier. One source of linkage is liquidity, by which I mean very accommodative financial conditions, including low interest rates, low spreads, high availability of finance, and an expectation this state of affairs will continue. The expectation of an accommodative monetary policy delivered by central banks leads to ample liquidity, followed by a buildup of leverage in the corporate and financial system, which leads to yet more liquidity as the central bank understands the consequences of tightening liquidity abruptly.[1] I will return to this point shortly.

We all have received the advice that we should let the exchange rate adjust when faced with capital inflows or outflows. Gopinath is correct that this is easier said than done. Consider four reasons why this is not so easy. First, there is positive feedback trading: when investors who have put money into your country see higher returns as the exchange rate appreciates, they experience fund inflows and put more money back to work in your country. Also, domestic firms look less levered, especially if they have borrowed in foreign currency. So exchange rate appreciation not only doesn't decrease the flow of money, it may actually increase it, something Hyun Shin has pointed out quite carefully in a number of papers. Moreover, because our markets are relatively illiquid, the capital flowing in can have large effects on the exchange rate, and thus on foreign investor returns, increasing the feedback further.

The second problem is that borrowing is augmented by moral hazard. Bankruptcy for large firms in emerging markets, if it exists, can be very long-drawn-out and very creditor-unfriendly. So corporate borrowers believe that if they borrow in dollars at low interest rates, and if the domestic currency depreciates significantly, they will go to a very owner-friendly bankruptcy court. If, however, the currency does not depreciate, the borrower gets a tremendous benefit from the low dollar interest rate. Essentially, heads I win, tails the creditor loses. Clearly, the question then is why creditors take these one-way losing bets. Here too there is the possibility of moral hazard. Many foreign loan contracts are written with London or New York as the jurisdiction in which the creditor can enforce its claims. So if the borrower looks as though it will default, the foreign creditor threatens to take the borrower to a London court and strip it of its foreign assets. Fearing the borrower's business will be severely damaged and the borrower's large outstanding loans will become unserviceable, domestic banks lend the borrower money to pay off the foreign creditor. Essentially, the foreign creditor has super-seniority, no matter when it lends and what its actual priority is, because domestic banks have weak enforcement rights. Ultimately, the source of the moral hazard is poorly governed domestic banks that do not pay sufficient heed to what the borrower does or do not write in contractual provisions to prevent the borrower from taking these loans. However, if we had strong governance, we would not be an emerging market!

A third reason to not let the exchange rate adjust is that the fiscal budget is not insensitive to the exchange rate, and budgetary room is used asymmetrically. In India, oil was heavily subsidized. So when the rupee appreciated against the dollar, suddenly there was more fiscal room because subsidies in rupee terms went down. Obviously, the government took advantage of this situation and spent the money. However, when the converse happened and fiscal room diminished, deficits simply exploded. So by allowing the exchange rate to appreciate with inflows, we also induce fiscal expansion, without commensurate fiscal contraction in the future. This is clearly a source of macroeconomic instability.

Finally, emerging market central banks have limited independence and limited monetary credibility. So if the exchange rate appreciation reduces inflation, emerging market central banks face tremendous public pressure to cut rates, which may be unwarranted if we think the exchange rate will reverse as the pressure of inflows eases. At the same time, if the exchange rate starts depreciating with outflows, and inflation picks up, it is much harder for emerging market central banks to prevent the inflationary spiral because they have less credibility.

In general, these asymmetries mean it is harder for emerging market central bankers to use the exchange rate as a buffer. Emerging markets live in a world between the dilemma that Hélène Rey emphasizes and the more traditional trilemma. Exchange rate policy is one of muddling through; hence emerging market central bankers never allow a perfect float, nor do we keep it absolutely fixed.

Let me turn to foreign capital. We love foreign capital, we want foreign capital to come in, but we want it to come in at the long end, and we want it to be risk-absorbing capital to finance the major infrastructure projects and other long-term activities that we need financed. Instead, a lot of what we get is short-term capital, essentially sitting on overnight positions, waiting to leave at a moment's notice. We don't mind guests, but we would love their departure to be based on local conditions, if not actually predictable. Unfortunately, these are guests who depart our countries when the call comes from elsewhere. If you are an innkeeper and you never know when your guests are going to leave and they don't leave one at a time, they leave together, you cannot use their advance payment because they may demand it back. Instead, you keep their money in a safe, that is, build foreign exchange buffers as a form of macroprudential policy. Somewhat paradoxically, you end up paying them high rates, as well as offering them liquidity (for which you, the central bank, have to maintain foreign reserves with low returns), even though you cannot use their money. Unfortunately, we rarely have capital flow management measures that can clearly keep such investors out.

One last thing about reserves: Could emerging market central bankers build up sufficient reserves to insulate the country's economy from external concerns and thus achieve some measure of separation? Unfortunately not. When you look at reserves from the perspective of a central banker, you know that both the level and the change matters. The level matters for standard Krugman-style run reasons—it sends a message to speculators that you have enough ammunition to pay them off. The change also matters because it carries information about the potential problems you have, and the size of the speculative interest. Therefore, you have to be careful about spending reserves too rapidly for fear of setting off a run. If you have $4 trillion in reserves when most people believe $1.5 trillion is a sufficient level, you are still not comfortable when you go down to $3 trillion. You may say that you have twice the level that people said you needed, but speculators can also take comfort from the fact that you lost $1 trillion rapidly. The broader point is that it is hard to feel comfortable with any level of reserves, so it is better to make sure that your macroeconomic fundamentals are reasonable and you don't have to depend on the reserves for protection. Nevertheless, you have to accumulate some.

More broadly, we have to recognize there are policy spillovers, which are significant across sectors and across countries, and there are no policy interventions that will lead back to separation easily. What you have to do as a policymaker is muddle through.

Let me end with a pet beef. An acute form of separation is the belief that monetary policy had nothing to do with the crisis, that the crisis happened because bankers had strange incentives. A less acute form, which is more widely held, is that even if accommodative monetary policy was mildly responsible for the precrisis leveraging and the deterioration in lending standards, those effects can be eliminated using macroprudential regulation to achieve separation once more. I think the problem with this view is that it ignores the effect of easy liquidity on leverage. Macroprudential policies may work on the banking system, but monetary policy works on the entire financial system, as Jeremy Stein has often argued. So in the boom, monetary policy is too easy, and once leverage builds up outside the regulator's macroprudential reach, the central bank has to fear the consequences of tightening. In the inevitable bust, the central bank floods the market with liquidity so as to push for a recovery, even as the private sector deleverages. Overall, monetary policy is doomed to be too easy if you ignore the spillovers from liquidity to leverage and assume you can control leverage through macroprudential policy.

Finally, the temptation to stay easy is accentuated in the bust if the central bank is fixated on achieving its inflation mandate. Unfortunately, as we have seen in Japan in the 1990s and the rest of the world since the financial crisis, it is not easy to get inflation above the lower band of the inflation target after a severe bust. The problem then is that the central bank tries more and more aggressive unconventional policies, assuming that these policies are, at worst, benign since macroprudential policies will eliminate the risk to the financial system. If, as I argue, the macroprudential policies are ineffective against some kinds of leverage buildup, then the pressure to achieve the inflation target sets up the fragilities of the future. We get locked into a cycle of monetary policy–induced financial excess. This is why I support normalizing monetary policy as activity picks up, even if we are not comfortable that we have achieved our inflation target. If and when central bankers get the time for reflection, it might be useful for them to take a fresh look at their inflation mandates, in light of the impossibility of separation.

Finally, a comment on what puzzles me about the dollar-pricing part of Gopinath's contribution. I am surprised that firms do not adjust over time even if they price in dollars. So what horizon do you think prices are fixed at in dollars, and do firms adjust eventually based on movements in the bilateral exchange rate against the dollar?

Note

1. See Douglas Diamond, Yunzhi Hu, and Raghuram Rajan, "Pledgeability, Industry Liquidity, and Financing Cycles," Working Paper, University of Chicago Booth School of Business, 2017; and Douglas W. Diamond and Raghuram G. Rajan, "Illiquid Banks, Financial Stability, and Interest Rate Policy," *Journal of Political Economy* 120, no. 3 (2012): 552–591.

21

Some Factors Shaping the International Financial Landscape of the Future

Pierre-Olivier Gourinchas

In chapter 19, Gita Gopinath presents a masterful overview of some of the key outstanding research and policy questions in international macroeconomics. Not surprisingly, I very much agree with her assessment.

Rather than review the issues she raises, my comments will pick up and expand on a few themes, offering along the way slightly different perspectives. I have organized my remarks around three themes: the dilemma versus trilemma debate, the role of the dollar and the link to the modern Triffin paradox, and the safe asset scarcity hypothesis.

Dilemma versus Trilemma

I will start with the dilemma versus trilemma debate that followed Hélène Rey's (2013) influential work. While the debate centers on the gains from exchange rate flexibility, there is a more fundamental question:

How does monetary policy transmit from the center to the periphery and within the periphery?

Transmission from the center to the periphery matters since we need to understand through what channels a tightening of monetary policy in the United States ripples through the global economy. Transmission within the periphery matters, too, since it helps monetary authorities formulate the appropriate local response to a U.S. tightening. Only by putting the answers to these two questions together can we say something about the overall benefits of exchange rate flexibility.

In her remark 1, Gopinath emphasizes that "the gains to exchange rate flexibility are worse than you think" since internationally traded goods are often invoiced in a common currency such as the dollar. This dominant-currency pricing mutes the effect of exchange rates on the terms of trade, and therefore on relative demands for imported versus exported goods. But the story does not end there: with (dollar) destination prices unchanged and (dollar) production costs varying with the exchange rate, exporters must absorb currency movements in their profit margins. The key point is that these changes in the exporter's profit margins do not, in general, restore productive efficiency in the way that a flexible exchange rate would when prices are sticky in the producer's currency. This is why the gains from flexible exchange rate are not as high as previously thought.

It does not follow from the preceding discussion that exchange rate flexibility becomes undesirable. It is simply not a cure-all medicine anymore! In fact, in the model of Casas and co-authors (2017), Gopinath and her co-authors (including myself) find that, although it does not fully stabilize the output gap any longer, domestic inflation targeting remains optimal for small open economies in a model with dominant-currency pricing. It follows that a flexible exchange rate—which allows for domestic inflation targeting—is preferable to a fixed exchange rate, which does not.

Besides dominant-currency pricing with sticky prices, other distortions can lead us to rethink the stabilizing role of exchange rates. For instance, Rey (2013) argues that U.S. monetary policy could have disproportionate effects on peripheral economies because of financial spillovers, regardless of the latter's exchange rate regime. For instance, currency mismatches between assets and liabilities could amplify the contractionary effects of a depreciation of the local currency, which would increase the real value of foreign currency debts. Similarly, an appreciation against the dollar could increase the dollar value of local assets, relaxing borrowing constraints and stimulating the local economy. More broadly, monetary policy in the center may influence global risk appetite, amplifying capital flows to or from emerging market economies and driving a global financial cycle.

With a muted effect of exchange rates on terms of trade as a result of dollar invoicing, and with sufficiently strong financial spillovers, it becomes more likely that a monetary policy tightening in the United States is contractionary abroad, despite (or because of) a depreciation of the local currency against the dollar. Yet even in such an environment,

Gourinchas (2017) argues that flexible exchange rates may become more, not less, desirable.

To see why this might be the case, suppose that it is indeed the case that a U.S. monetary policy tightening is contractionary locally (i.e., in the periphery). How local monetary authorities should respond depends in turn on how *local* monetary policy transmits to its own economy. It is a simple matter of logic to observe that, if a local monetary policy easing is expansionary (as is usually assumed), then the optimal response to the contractionary impulse originating from the center remains a local monetary easing. It follows immediately that the local currency must be allowed to depreciate against the dollar. Financial frictions, in other words, may well make flexible exchange rates more, not less, desirable.

A fixed exchange rate would be desirable if local monetary policy tightenings were *"perversely" expansionary* locally instead of contractionary. In that case, the contractionary impulse from the center would be countered by tightening domestic monetary conditions, leaving the exchange rate more or less unchanged. Such a perverse case can occur if financial spillovers are sufficiently strong. In that case, the direct expansionary effects of an appreciation become so large that they overwhelm the other and more usual channels of transmission of monetary policy. If this is the world we live in, very little would indeed be gained from exchange rate flexibility: output stability would go hand in hand with real exchange rate stability.

Ultimately, then, this is an empirical question: What do we know about the transmission of monetary policy from the center to the periphery and within the periphery? While this is a first-order question, and one that is presumably at the forefront of policymakers' concerns around the world, it is also one about which we can say with some degree of confidence that we don't know much!

The reasons are varied but boil down to the simple fact that there just are not enough data or powerful instruments with current empirical techniques to tease out the separate effects of U.S. and local monetary policy. The results reported in the extant empirical literature, often based on structural vector autoregressions (VARs), typically are not robust to the sample of countries, the time period, the choice of variables and lags, or identification assumptions of the VAR. Ramey (2016), in her handbook chapter review, makes a similar observation about the estimated effects of U.S. monetary policy on U.S. output and prices. While that question has attracted a tremendous amount of attention from many very talented scholars, the results also appear distinctly nonrobust.[1]

In my view, few research questions in international macroeconomics remain as important and as unsettled as this one. If indeed we want to design and implement appropriate monetary (and exchange rate) policies, we need to renew our efforts to properly identify how monetary policy transmits from the center to the periphery and within the periphery itself. Only then will we be able to make progress on these questions.

We Live in a Dollar World. For How Long?

A second critical observation that emerges from Gopinath's first set of remarks is the global importance of the dollar. This is true both on the real side, where dollar invoicing is dominant, and on the financial side, where dollar funding is essential to global banks and nonfinancial corporations, and dollar reserves are the dominant form of official reserve accumulation. Ilzetzki, Reinhart, and Rogoff (2017), for instance, carefully document how the role of the dollar has increased significantly since the demise of the Bretton Woods system of fixed but adjustable rates. In short, we live in a dollar world, even more so than when the dollar was formally at the center of the international monetary system. As Gopinath notes in her closing remarks, this creates a challenge since continued rapid growth of emerging market economies mechanically implies that the share of the U.S. economy in the global economy is expected to shrink significantly in coming decades. Figure 21.1 illustrates this point by reporting admittedly heroic projections of output shares far into the future from the Centre d'Études Prospectives et d'Informations Internationales EconMap database. According to these estimates, the share of U.S. output in global output is expected to decline from roughly 25 percent in 2015 to less than 12 percent in 2100. Over the same period, India and China see their corresponding output share rise from 10 percent to 30 percent and from 2.5 percent to 9 percent, respectively. While anyone could take issue with these forecasts, the trend is clear, and the associated economic transformation under way is unlike anything we have seen since the emergence of the United States as a global economic power in the early twentieth century. The potential for dramatic economic dislocations is very significant.

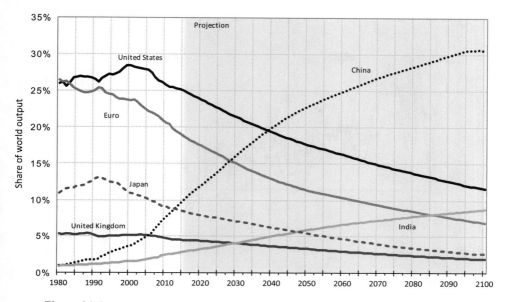

Figure 21.1

Share of World Output, 1980–2100
Source: Centre d'Études Prospectives et d'Informations Internationales EconMap.
Fouré et al. (2012).

One such dislocation is already upon us. The rise of emerging markets, combined with population aging in advanced economies, has significantly increased global desired savings relative to global desired investments and increasingly tilted the former toward "safe" assets. The result has been both a decline in global risk-free rates (figure 21.2) and a shift in the external balance sheet of emerging economies toward safe assets (figure 21.3).

In that context, a danger, first discussed in Farhi, Gourinchas, and Rey (2011) and Obstfeld (2013) and formally analyzed by Farhi and Maggiori (2018), is that the supplier of safe assets could suffer from a modern version of the Triffin dilemma. Specifically, a growing demand for U.S. "safe" assets in a world where the fiscal backing for these assets is shrinking (in relation to world output) could eventually make the U.S. vulnerable to a run.

As discussed in Caballero, Farhi, and Gourinchas (2017), solutions to the Triffin dilemma exist either on the supply side (through a trend

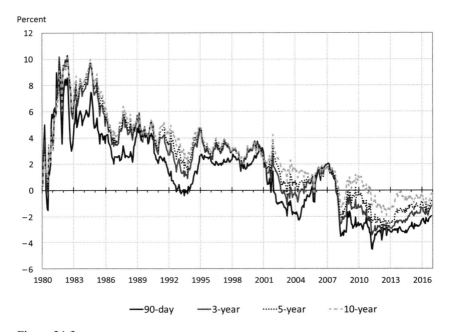

Figure 21.2

Safe Real Interest Rates, 1980–2016. The figure shows ex ante real yields on U.S. Treasury securities constructed using median expected price changes from the University of Michigan's Survey of Consumers.
Source: Federal Reserve Economic Data (https://fred.stlouisfed.org).

appreciation of the issuer's currency, the shift to a multipolar world, or private substitutes) or on the demand side (through local financial development, improvements in the global safety net, or adjustments in regulatory frameworks). Any of these developments will have profound implications for the future international financial landscape.

Safe Asset Scarcity and Stagnation

While Gopinath discusses the potential for allocative inefficiencies in low-interest-rate environments (remark 6), I want to emphasize here another and complementary aspect arising from the interaction between low global risk-free interest rates and bounds on conventional monetary policy. As long as natural real rates remain safely above the effective

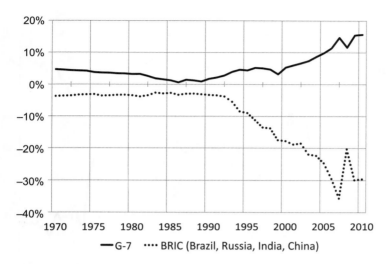

Figure 21.3

Net Risky Position (% of GDP), G-7 Countries Compared to BRIC Countries. Net risky position is defined as gross equity and direct investment assets, minus gross equity and direct investment liabilities. BRIC countries are long safe and short risky.

Source: Lane and Milesi-Ferretti (2007), updated to 2011.

lower bound on real rates achievable through monetary policy, the growing demand for savings (especially of the safe assets variety) can be accommodated naturally by a decline in real risk-free rates and the corresponding pattern of current account surpluses and deficits (e.g., "global imbalances") are mostly benign, reflecting the geographic origin of excess desired savings over desired investments. As Caballero, Farhi, and Gourinchas (2016) have argued, the effective lower bound constitutes a tipping point for the global economy, beyond which output is pushed below its potential and economies become increasingly interdependent. In such a "safety trap," current account surpluses spread recessions, and the exchange rate becomes a powerful beggar-thy-neighbor tool to reallocate demand toward the domestic economy.

The declining trend in the supply of safe assets (relative to world output and desired demand for these assets) and the concomitant decline in the real risk-free rate suggest that we could now be caught in a cycle of recurrent safety traps.

Percent

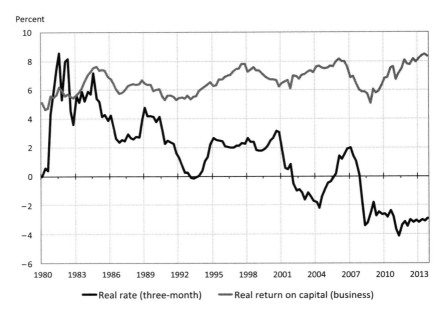

Figure 21.4

Safe Rates vs. Return to Capital, 1980–2013. U.S. real (ex ante) three-month real rate and U.S. real after-tax return on all capital, adjusted for intangibles.
Source: Gomme, Ravikumar, and Rupert (2011).

Safety traps are similar to liquidity traps in that real rates are unable to fall sufficiently, causing a recession. However, because they originate from an excess demand for safe assets (relative to other types of assets), they are also associated with an increase in risk premia. Figure 21.4 suggests that this may have indeed been the case, at least since 2001. The figure reports the real risk-free rate (in this case the real ex ante yield on three-month Treasuries) against the real after-tax return on U.S. business capital, estimated as in Gomme, Ravikumar, and Rupert (2011) between 1980 and 2013. The figure documents a first-order macroeconomic fact: despite the dramatic decline in risk-free rates, the expected return on capital has increased over time, and the spread between the two returns now exceeds 10 percent. Two broad factors can account for an increase in this spread: an increase in economic risk premia or an increase in product price markup (or in factor prices markdown). In Caballero, Farhi, and Gourinchas (2017), we propose a simple macroeconomic decomposition that allows for risk-premia, rents, and robots (i.e., increased automation or capital augmenting technical progress). The macro evidence is tentative but suggests that risk premia may indeed have increased substantially.

The implications for the research agenda in international economics of the patterns described above are profound. I will conclude by mentioning three areas in need of more research:

1. The financial and macroeconomic stability consequences of a world with persistently low real interest rates in which countries cycle in and out of safety traps;
2. The allocative and redistributive consequences of a world with high risk premiums, increasing rents, and automation; and
3. The roles of gross and net capital flows, exchange rates, and reserve accumulation in insulating local economies from global developments.

Note

1. My point here is not to claim that U.S. monetary policy is also "perverse," simply that the almost forty years of empirical literature on this topic since Sims's introduction of VARs have failed to deliver a resounding answer to the question. One might also argue that identification is easier in the case of the impact of U.S. monetary policy shocks on the rest of the world. After all, U.S. monetary policy is rarely adjusted in response to economic conditions in other countries, so endogeneity is less of an issue. This, unfortunately, does not solve all problems since local central banks rarely remain passive when the Fed adjusts its monetary policy stance. What ends up being estimated is the joint response of the local economy to a U.S. monetary impulse and the response to it by the local central bank.

References

Caballero, R., E. Farhi, and P.-O. Gourinchas. 2016. "Global Imbalances and Currency Wars at the ZLB." NBER Working Paper 21670. Cambridge, MA: National Bureau of Economic Research.

Caballero R., E. Farhi, and P.-O. Gourinchas. 2017. "The Safe Assets Shortage Conundrum." *Journal of Economic Perspectives* 31 (3): 29–46.

Casas, C., F. J. Díez, G. Gopinath, and P.-O. Gourinchas. 2017. "Dominant Currency Paradigm: A New Model for Small Open Economies." IMF Working Paper 17/264. Washington, DC: International Monetary Fund.

Farhi, E., P.-O. Gourinchas, and H. Rey. 2011. *Reforming the International Monetary System*. London: Centre for Economic Policy Research.

Farhi, E., and M. Maggiori. 2018. "A Model of the International Monetary System." *Quarterly Journal of Economics* 131 (1): 295–355.

Fouré, J., A. Bénassy-Quéré, and L. Fontagné. 2012. "The Great Shift: Macroeconomic Projections for the World Economy at the 2050 Horizon." CEPII Working Paper 2012–03. Paris: Centre d'Études Prospectives et d'Informations Internationales.

Gomme, P., B. Ravikumar, and P. Rupert. 2011. "The Return to Capital and the Business Cycle." *Review of Economic Dynamics* 14 (2): 262–278.

Gourinchas, P.-O. 2017. "Monetary Policy Transmission in Emerging Markets: An Application to Chile." Prepared for the 20th Annual Research Conference of the Banco Central de Chile.

Ilzetzki, E., C. M. Reinhart, and K. S. Rogoff. 2017. "Exchange Arrangements Entering the 21st Century: Which Anchor Will Hold?" Working paper.

Lane, P. R., and G. M. Milesi-Ferretti. 2007. "The External Wealth of Nations Mark II: Revised and Extended Estimates of Foreign Assets and Liabilities, 1970–2004." *Journal of International Economics* 73 (2): 223–250.

Obstfeld, M. 2013. "The International Monetary System: Living with Asymmetry." In *Globalization in an Age of Crisis: Multilateral Economic Cooperation in the Twenty First Century*, ed. Robert C. Feenstra and Alan M. Taylor. Chicago: University of Chicago Press.

Ramey, V. A. 2016. "Macroeconomic Shocks and Their Propagation." In *Handbook of Macroeconomics*, ed. John B. Taylor and Harald Uhlig, vol. 2, 71–162. New York: Elsevier.

Rey, H. 2013. "Dilemma Not Trilemma: The Global Financial Cycle and Monetary Policy Independence." In *Jackson Hole Symposium*. Federal Reserve Bank at Kansas City.

22

Dollar Pricing in International Trade and Finance

Barry Eichengreen

Gita Gopinath has made a useful and important contribution in chapter 19. She reminds us that there is a large body of new research on key topics in international economics: exchange rates and international adjustment, capital flows and their management, trade flows and global imbalances, and international liquidity and reserves. Like a traditional French chef, Gopinath is guided by the classics.

Gopinath's first two points may be restated as "exchange rate changes provide less than full insulation from foreign disturbances and may not completely offset shocks to the trade balance." So restated, these are familiar observations. We've long known that exchange rates provide less than full insulation in a world of capital mobility and that the response of the trade balance to devaluation is subject to long and variable lags. Revealingly, Gopinath has to go back to Milton Friedman in 1953 for an unqualified assertion of the proposition that flexible exchange rates provide complete insulation and immediate balance-of-payments adjustment.

The research she cites, and to which she herself has made substantial contributions, shows that these anomalies and their implications are easier to understand once we recognize the pervasiveness of dollar pricing. Dollar invoicing and sticky dollar prices can explain why the terms of trade move by less than the exchange rate. They help can explain why the exports of other countries are not more responsive to the exchange rate. They help to explain why emerging markets are not more enthusiastic about floating rates.

But her findings also raise questions. It seems clear that exporters to the United States are reluctant to change their dollar prices in response to changes in the dollar exchange rate, but is it plausible that they *never* change those prices, regardless of the size and permanence of the exchange-rate change? These are menu costs with a vengeance. Moreover, I do not see an evaluation of the importance of dollar invoicing relative to other factors that can equally well explain Gopinath's observations. A long list of other explanations has been offered for the fear-of-floating phenomenon, for example, independent of the prevalence of dollar invoicing in international trade.

Nor do I see an explanation for dollar pricing itself. One traditional explanation is network effects: that it pays to price your exports in the same unit as other producers, since this makes it easier for customers to compare prices and for aspiring exporters to break into international markets. But though this argument may have made sense once upon a time, when you had to call your broker to obtain an exchange rate quotation, it makes little sense in a high-tech financial world where everyone carries an electronic currency converter in his or her pocket. Alternatively, it is sometimes argued that because producers in emerging markets borrow in dollars, they are inclined to price their exports in dollars as a natural hedge. But Gopinath shows that dollar borrowing is in decline as well. Elsewhere, she argues that global value chains make foreign currency invoicing attractive (if a firm's imported inputs are invoiced in dollars, it makes sense for that firm to invoice its final-goods exports in dollars). But this observation is hard to square with the existence of financial hedging instruments with the same duration as the production cycle.

In addition, we see considerable variation across countries in the extent of foreign currency invoicing. Ito and Chinn (2014) and Goldberg and Tille (2008) show that the propensity to invoice in dollars is associated with trade openness, the commodity composition of exports, the stability of monetary and fiscal policies, and financial development, among other factors. If I'm shown a correlation between dollar invoicing, on the one hand, and the elasticity of exports with respect to the exchange rate on the other, I will wonder whether that correlation in fact reflects the effects of these other variables.

Inevitably, I feel obliged to say a few words in defense of the concept of "original sin." I think Du and Schregger (2016) may overstate the extent of the shift toward domestic-currency issuance because they focus on a handful of mostly large emerging markets that have more scope for issuing domestic-currency-denominated debt that the typical developing country.

Gopinath could also have emphasized more strongly that the shift away from foreign currency debt documented by these authors affects sovereign debt but not corporate debt, a fact that again raises questions. Why sovereigns have made progress in placing local currency debt in local markets but emerging market corporates have not, and why the latter continue to fund themselves in foreign currency, are not well understood. Charles Engel and JungJae Park (2017) conjecture that improved monetary discipline (less danger that the authorities will choose to inflate away the value of domestic debt) has enhanced the ability of governments to borrow in domestic currency, but why corporates should not also benefit from this shift is far from obvious. Galina Hale, Peter Jones, and Mark Spiegel (2016) suggest that technological advances in financial markets have reduced the minimum efficient scale needed to issue in domestic currency, but why even large emerging market corporations have been slow to move in this direction remains something of a mystery. There's also a peculiar tension between the observation that these countries have moved toward borrowing in local currency while continuing to price their exports in dollars. Where's the hedge, in other words?

Finally, on international reserves and the global safety net, Gopinath reminds us that much remains to be done. Central bank swaps, regional financial arrangements, and IMF facilities remain small relative to own-country reserves, and relying on reserve accumulation for balance-of-payments insurance is expensive. I would add two observations. First, foreign reserves may provide even less insurance than meets the eye. Although countries accumulate reserves, they are reluctant to use them, since doing so may sent a negative signal. It would be useful to have more work on why and what might be done about this.

Second, the alternative of contingent insurance through the IMF is problematic insofar as there is a lingering problem of IMF stigma. While Mexico, Colombia, and Poland applied for Flexible Credit Lines, no Asian country has done so. Whenever I go to Asia, I ask my colleagues, what would be enough to eliminate the problem of the IMF stigma and for you—Indonesia, Malaysia, South Korea—to apply for a Flexible Credit Line? I rarely get an encouraging answer. More research on the nature of the IMF stigma and what can be done about it is clearly called for.

References

Du, Wenxin, and Jesse Schregger. 2016. "Local Currency Sovereign Risk." *Journal of Finance* 71:1027–1070.

Engel, Charles, and JungJae Park. 2017. "Debauchery and Original Sin: Currency Composition of Foreign Debt." Working paper, University of Wisconsin, Madison, February.

Goldberg, Linda, and Cedric Tille. 2008. "Vehicle Currency Use in International Trade." *Journal of International Economics* 76:177–192.

Hale, Galina, Peter Jones, and Mark Spiegel. 2016. "The Rise in Home Currency Issuance." Working paper, Federal Reserve Bank of San Francisco, May.

Ito, Hiro, and Menzie Chinn. 2014. "The Rise of the 'Redback' and China's Capital Account Liberalization: An Empirical Analysis of the Determinants of Invoicing Currencies." Paper presented at the ADBI Conference on Currency Internationalization, August.

23

The Triffin Dilemma, Chinese Opacity, and Capital Mobility: Concluding Remarks on International Macroeconomic Policy

Carmen Reinhart

In this concluding chapter, I will try to add important nuances regarding, and a few differences with, the many interesting contributions made earlier in the book. Some of my comments are about areas for further research. On other points, I will challenge what has been said. I will conclude by adding an eleventh element to the ten-item list that Gita Gopinath proposed, in part following Pierre-Olivier Gourinchas's observations in chapter 21.

Gopinath presented a very forceful statement making us think about the big agenda in international macroeconomic policy. On exchange rate flexibility, she mentioned that in some of my recent work with Ethan Ilzetzki and Ken Rogoff, we point out that limited exchange rate flexibility is a dominant exchange rate arrangement (figure 23.1). As a result of some of the shifts that have taken place in the last decade, there is comparatively little flexibility vis-à-vis textbook floating exchange rate.

But there is a lot more de jure flexibility, meaning that countries are not preannouncing. This reflects a shift toward more discretion. That is, some floats are managed with unknown parameters as to when exactly the central banks are going to intervene and when they are going to abstain.

Many crawling pegs are not preannounced. This has the advantage of setting the rate of crawl and tolerating deviations. In other words, I would characterize it as "Yes, there are a lot of very limited flexibility cases, but ones in which a lot of the corner textbook cases of fix/fix versus flex/flex are avoided." I think that is for a good reason.

Let me also highlight that some of the reasons why the world has shifted toward less exchange rate flexibility are not all connected to emerging markets but also have to do with Europe. The IMF, for reasons

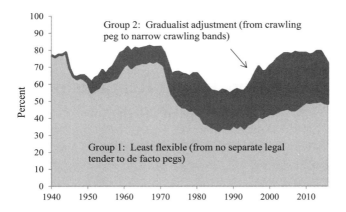

Figure 23.1

De Facto Exchange Rate Arrangements, Coarse Classification, 1946–2016: Share of (Independent) Countries in Each Group. Less flexible arrangements indicate primarily nominal exchange rate anchors.
Source: Ilzetzki, Reinhart, and Rogoff (2017).

I do not understand, classifies every euro-zone country as having a floating exchange rate.

Now, we are not debating that the euro floats, but that Portugal does not have a floating exchange rate. Few of us would argue Portugal has an independent monetary policy. At the beginning, when the euro was introduced in 1999, the IMF classified the euro-zone countries as having no independent currencies of their own.

Sometime along the way that classification shifted, and they're now all magically floating. In our own classification, we do not append the floating label to currencies of euro-zone countries. As a result, those countries contribute to the count that suggests that limited flexibility is a dominant exchange rate arrangement.

Let me move on to some comments on the dilemma versus trilemma raised in chapter 19 and discussed in the follow-up chapters. Think of the triangle: you have independent monetary policy, perfect capital mobility, and a fixed exchange rate. Those are the three endpoints of the triangle.

I would suggest that perhaps it is time to recast perfect capital mobility as something much more general. What do I mean? Most discussions of capital mobility limit themselves to whether there are capital controls or not. I think the scope for independent, or some independent, monetary policy in a lot of emerging market economies comes not just from the existence of capital controls but also from the fact that assets are imperfect substitutes, and many foreign exchange and sovereign bond markets are illiquid.

In effect, for an emerging market that has very limited liquidity in its foreign exchange market, that acts like a capital control, because entrants don't go into in the first place. Which are the markets that are the natural hedges? The liquid markets in the emerging markets space are Hong Kong, Brazil, Mexico, and Israel. I would like to recast some of the questions raised by Gopinath. Perhaps we should rethink the trilemma in terms not just of capital mobility but of capital mobility/asset substitutability/market liquidity.

I do lean toward very much Raghu Rajan's interpretation of the dilemma versus trilemma (see chapter 20). I think it is still a trilemma over certain time horizons. Not every central banker can be wrong in believing that sterilized intervention works, at least over certain time horizons. This observation again argues that, over the short run, there is some monetary policy independence. The recent literature on the effectiveness of sterilized intervention in emerging markets broadly supports that statement.

Let me move on to another item. As perhaps my single biggest criticism of the remarks presented by Gopinath, I heard something of a victorious tone with respect to emerging markets having conquered their "original sin."

Barry Eichengreen in chapter 22 has already listed a number of reasons why that statement perhaps overstates reality. In the old days, domestic debt was domestic debt and foreign debt was foreign debt. And domestic debt was issued under domestic law, denominated in domestic currency, and held by residents. Foreign debt, conversely, was issued under foreign law, linked to a foreign currency, and held by nonresidents.

Those lines are blurring. There is a lot of participation by foreign entrants into domestic debt markets. In effect, much of the domestic debt that's being issued by (especially) corporations is linked to a foreign currency. But none of that shows up in the official numbers.

So the official numbers that segment public sector debt, external debt, and domestic debt do not reflect the fact that much of the domestic debt that is being issued, even some of the domestic debt of the public sector, is linked to a foreign currency. Remember that Mexican *tesobonos*, famous in 1994 and 1995, were technically classified as domestic debt by the World Bank because they were issued under domestic law. In reality, they were clearly foreign currency debt held by nonresidents.

So I agree with Barry that it's too early to call victory over original sin.

On the low-interest-rate environment, since 2011 I have been publishing papers saying that low rates are likely to remain low for an extended period of time. What were my arguments back in 2011? Apart from secular stagnation and the saving glut, we have low rates because policymakers in the major central banks and regulators in the world's largest economies have decided we need low rates.

A large footprint of the official sector—that is, the portfolio holdings of central banks, combined with heavier regulation by supervisors, which I have placed under the broad umbrella of financial repression—is an outgrowth of the fact that advanced economies also are highly leveraged and highly indebted, and not just the public sector but the private sector as well.

And when both public and private sectors are highly leveraged, what can be more threatening to the financial system than interest rate spikes?

My last observation on Gopinath's contribution concerns the global imbalances and the interrelation between global imbalances and current account and reserve accumulations.

First, as a modest proposal, let us recast discussion of global imbalances in the recognition that the United States has a big current account deficit. Over the years, that big current account deficit has been with various trading partners, but that is the bottom line of global imbalances, for the reasons Pierre-Olivier Gourinchas alluded to in chapter 21.

We may not know a lot about the link between global imbalances and reserve accumulation, but we know more than Gopinath's reflections reveal. Yes, China and Korea have accumulated large reserves, but Germany has major trade surpluses with no reserve accumulation.

That is not the case. The IMF's International Financial Statistics database does not report the Target2 balances, which reflect within-Europe capital flows, as international reserves. Table 23.1 highlights how significant these balances are for "peripheral" euro-zone countries. And that is the big story for Germany. They are inflows from the rest of Europe, not inflows from outside Europe, and should count as reserve accumulation.

Table 23.1
Target2 Balance as a Percent of GDP (Selected Countries, as of June 2017)

Country	Balance
Germany	23
Greece	−40
Italy	−21
Portugal	−38
Spain	−28

Source: European Central Bank.

Finally, the eleventh item I'd like to add to Gopinath's list of ten takes its starting point in Gourinchas's discussion of the modern-day Triffin dilemma in chapter 21. China's role in the global economy has expanded. It is currently second in terms of the share of its GDP in the world's economy and quickly moving to first place.

We know very little about China's global financial linkages with its trading partners, however. Those linkages have grown enormously, while the documentation has lagged considerably. And how is this connected to the Triffin dilemma?

Go back to the end of the nineteenth century and the beginning of the twentieth century, when the dollar began to overtake the British pound as the reference currency. One could monitor the gains that the United States was making in the global economy. Data on bonds were transparent in those days, and increasingly, bond issuance was denominated in dollars rather than in British pounds. That was measurable. That was visible. And in general, it showed that New York was overtaking London.

We are seeing a similar switch today, but we're not really able to measure it. Specifically, a lot of China's lending to developing countries is not in the form of BIS bank loans and does not show up in BIS data. It is also not that countries are issuing bonds. It's not bond debt. It's not commercial loan bank debt. It is lending, often from official or semi-official development institutions, to a range of countries. And those flows are opaque.

With respect to opaqueness, consider central bank credit lines. Argentina and Brazil have had major credit lines, but the quantities are unknown. What share of those loans is now in arrears or in default? We don't know.

So China's big imprint in global finance is poorly documented. This is a good item for any research agenda.

Reference

Ilzetzki, Ethan, Carmen M. Reinhart, and Kenneth S. Rogoff. 2017. "Exchange Arrangements Entering the 21st Century: Which Anchor Will Hold?" NBER Working Paper 23134. Cambridge, MA: National Bureau of Economic Research, February.

Contributors

David Aikman is Technical Head of Division in the Macroprudential Strategy and Support Division within the Bank of England's Financial Stability and Strategy Directorate. From 2013 to 2015, he worked as an adviser to the Board of Governors of the Federal Reserve System in Washington, D.C. He has also been a visiting scholar at the Bank of Japan's Institute for Monetary and Economic Studies.

Alan J. Auerbach is Robert D. Burch Professor of Economics and Law and Director of the Burch Center for Tax Policy and Public Finance at the University of California, Berkeley. He has served as Deputy Chief of Staff of the U.S. Joint Committee on Taxation (1992) and has chaired the Department of Economics on two occasions.

Ben S. Bernanke served as Chairman of the Federal Reserve's Board of Governors (2006 to 2014), after serving as Board member from 2002 to 2005. Bernanke also served as Chairman of the President's Council of Economic Advisers from June 2005 to January 2006. He also held a number of academic positions, including Professor in Princeton University's Department of Economics from 1985 to 2002. He is currently a Distinguished Fellow in Residence at the Brookings Institution.

Olivier Blanchard is the first C. Fred Bergsten Senior Fellow at the Peterson Institute for International Economics. He is also the Robert M. Solow Professor Emeritus at MIT and served as Economic Counselor and Director of the Research Department of the IMF from 2008 to 2014.

Lael Brainard has been a member of the Board of Governors of the Federal Reserve System since June 2014. She served as Undersecretary of the Treasury from 2010 to 2013 and Counselor to the Secretary of the Treasury in 2009. During this time, she was the U.S. Representative to the G-20 Finance Deputies and G-7 Deputies and was a member of the Financial Stability Board.

Markus K. Brunnermeier is the Edwards S. Sanford Professor at Princeton University. He is a faculty member of the Department of Economics and director of Princeton's Bendheim Center for Finance. He is also a research associate at NBER, CEPR, and CESifo and has been a member of several advisory groups, including to the International Monetary Fund, the Federal Reserve of New York, the European Systemic Risk Board, the Bundesbank, and the U.S. Congressional Budget Office.

Marco Buti has been the Director-General for Economic and Financial Affairs of the European Commission since November 2008.

Benoît Coeuré is Member of the Executive Board of the European Central Bank since January 2012.

Mario Draghi has been the President of the European Central Bank and Chair of the European Systemic Risk Board since November 2011. He also has been the Chair of the Group of Governors and Heads of Supervision (GHOS) at the Bank for International Settlements since June 2013.

Barry Eichengreen is the George C. Pardee and Helen N. Pardee Professor of Economics and Political Science at the University of California, Berkeley.

Jason Furman is Professor of the Practice of Economic Policy at the Harvard Kennedy School of Government. He is also a nonresident senior fellow at the Peterson Institute for International Economics. This followed eight years as a top economic adviser to President Barack Obama, including serving as the twenty-eighth Chairman of the Council of Economic Advisers from August 2013 to January 2017, acting as President Obama's chief economist and a member of the cabinet.

Gita Gopinath is the John Zwaanstra Professor of International Studies and of Economics at Harvard University. She is also co-director of the International Finance and Macroeconomics Program at the National Bureau of Economic Research, a visiting scholar at the Federal Reserve Bank of Boston, and a member of the economic advisory panel of the Federal Reserve Bank of New York.

Pierre-Olivier Gourinchas is Professor of Economics at the University of California, Berkeley and S. K. and Angela Chan Professor of Global Management at the Haas School of Business. He is also Director of the Clausen Center for International Business and Policy.

Andrew G. Haldane is the Chief Economist at the Bank of England. He is also Executive Director for Monetary Analysis, Research, and Statistics. Haldane is a member of the Bank's Monetary Policy Committee.

Philipp Hildebrand is Vice Chairman of BlackRock. Until January 2012, he served as Chairman of the Governing Board of the Swiss National Bank and Vice-Chairman of the Financial Stability Board.

Marc Hinterschweiger is an economist in the Bank of England's Prudential Policy Directorate.

Sujit Kapadia is Head of the Market-Based Finance Division at the European Central Bank. Prior to joining the ECB in December 2017, he spent twelve years at the Bank of England, most recently as Head of Research from 2014 until 2017.

Nellie Liang is the Miriam K. Carliner Senior Fellow in Economic Studies at the Brookings Institution. Liang is also a Visiting Scholar in the International Monetary Fund's Monetary and Capital Markets Department and is a member of the Congressional Budget Office's Panel of Economic Advisors. Before joining Brookings in 2017, Liang was the director of the Division of Financial Stability at the Board of Governors of the Federal Reserve System.

Adam S. Posen has been president of the Peterson Institute for International Economics since January 2013, after first joining in July 1997. In September 2009, Posen was appointed by the UK Chancellor of the Exchequer to serve a three-year term as an external voting member of the Bank of England's rate-setting Monetary Policy Committee.

Raghuram Rajan is the Katherine Dusak Miller Distinguished Service Professor of Finance at Chicago Booth. He was the twenty-third Governor of the Reserve Bank of India between September 2013 and September 2016. Between 2003 and 2006, he was the Chief Economist and Director of Research at the International Monetary Fund.

Valerie Ramey is currently a Professor of Economics at the University of California, San Diego and a Research Associate of the National Bureau of Economic Research. She has served as co-editor of the American Economic Review and Chair of the Economics Department at UCSD. She is currently a member of the Panel of Economic Advisers for the Congressional Budget Office.

Carmen Reinhart is the Minos A. Zombanakis Professor of the International Financial System at Harvard Kennedy School. Previously, she was the Dennis Weatherstone Senior Fellow at the Peterson Institute for International Economics and Professor of Economics and Director of the Center for International Economics at the University of Maryland.

Dani Rodrik is the Ford Foundation Professor of International Political Economy at Harvard's John F. Kennedy School of Government. He was previously the Albert O. Hirschman Professor in the School of Social Science at the Institute for Advanced Study in Princeton (2013–2015).

Robert E. Rubin is currently Co-Chairman Emeritus of the Council on Foreign Relations and senior counselor to Centerview Partners. He served as the seventieth U.S. Secretary of the Treasury, from 1995 until 1999, and was the first Director of the National Economic Council from 1993 to 1994. He was Co-Chairman at Goldman Sachs and senior adviser to Citigroup.

Jay C. Shambaugh is the Director of the Hamilton Project and a Senior Fellow in Economic Studies at the Brookings Institution. He is also a Professor of Economics and International Affairs at the Elliott School of International Affairs at the George Washington University. He also served on the White House Council of Economic Advisers as First Senior Economist for International Economics, Chief Economist (2009–2011), and Member (2015–2017).

Tharman Shanmugaratnam is Deputy Prime Minister and Coordinating Minister for Economic and Social Policies in Singapore. He also chairs the Group of Thirty. In addition, he chaired the G-20 Eminent Persons Group on Global Financial Governance, which concluded its work in October 2018. Tharman led the International Monetary and Financial Committee, the key policy forum of the IMF, from 2011 to 2014; he was its first Asian chair.

Jeremy C. Stein is the Moise Y. Safra Professor of Economics at Harvard University and serves on the board of directors of the Harvard Management Company. From May 2012 to May 2014, he was a member of the Board of Governors of the Federal Reserve System.

Lawrence H. Summers is the Charles W. Eliot University Professor and President Emeritus at Harvard University. During the past two decades, he has served in a series of senior positions, including as the seventy-first Secretary of the Treasury for President Bill Clinton, Director of the National Economic Council for President Barack Obama, and Vice President of Development Economics and Chief Economist of the World Bank.

Index